W9-AAT-796

The Merger

OTHER BOOKS BY JEFFREY ROBINSON

Fiction

A True and Perfect Knight
The Monk's Disciples
The Margin of the Bulls
The Ginger Jar
Pietrov and Other Games

Non-Fiction

The Manipulators
The Hotel
The Laundrymen
Bardot – Two Lives
The End of the American Century
The Risk Takers – Five Years On
Rainier and Grace
Yamani – The Inside Story
Minus Millionaires
The Risk Takers
Teamwork
Bette Davis

The Merger

HOW ORGANIZED CRIME IS TAKING OVER CANADA AND THE WORLD

JEFFREY ROBINSON

Canadian Cataloguing in Publication Data

Robinson, Jeffrey, 1945–
The merger: how organized crime is taking over Canada and the world

Includes index.
ISBN 0-7710-7565-0

1. Transnational crime. 2. Organized crime. I. Title.

HV6252.R62 1999 364.1'06 C99-931655-9

We acknowledge the financial support of the Government of Canada through the Book Publishing Industry Development Program for our publishing activities. Canadä

We further acknowledge the support of the Canada Council for the Arts and the Ontario Arts Council for our publishing program.

Typesetting by Laura Brady
Printed and bound in Canada

McClelland & Stewart Inc.
The Canadian Publishers
481 University Avenue
Toronto, Ontario
M5G 2E9

1 2 3 4 5 03 02 01 00 99

For Barbara Silverwise
of Baltimore, Toronto, Washington, and Boston
1945–1981
with Love

CONTENTS

PROLOGUE

On the outskirts of Vienna, about six miles from the centre of town, past the Ferris wheel where *The Third Man*'s Harry Lime plied his trade, is the City Club. It is a massive hotel and leisure complex, the heart of which is the huge climate-controlled glass pyramid hothouse where a swimming pool sits in a tropical jungle. It is artificial global warming at its most luxurious.

It is also where, over Easter 1990, some twenty men with disparate backgrounds met for the first time, to get to know each other and to explore the feasibility of forming strategic alliances.

There were Italians, including Sicilian Mafiosi, members of the Camorra from Naples, members of the 'Ndrangheta from Calabria, and representatives of the Christian Democratic political party. There were Russians, mostly from Moscow but also a few living in Hungary and Czechoslovakia. There were some Poles. And there were some Colombians.

They knew each other on a one-to-one basis but there had never been a meeting of all these men together.

Their cover was a forum sponsored by "The Italian Association." The City Club management was told, somewhat ironically, that the topic of the meeting was how European countries could help South American countries develop their economies in Europe. For security reasons, the group insisted on renting the entire complex for the weekend.

They'd originally tried to book a Club Med, but the management there wanted them to pay in advance, and when the money wasn't paid, Club Med refused to hold their reservations. So they wound up at the City Club, sitting around long tables in conference rooms, exactly like the life insurance salesmen and bankers and heart surgeons who have met there since. Except that, every now and then, according to staff working there at the time, the men who appeared to be the leaders of each faction would get up and walk out, to speak quietly among themselves in the hallway, where there was no possibility of conversations being overheard.

Any worry about being bugged was misplaced. The only person who realized the significance of this secret meeting was a French Foreign Intelligence Service agent assigned to the nearby United Nations. He did what little he could to find out who was there and what they were talking about. He even dispatched a report to Paris, suggesting that these men were meeting to talk about joint ventures and strategic alliances. Italians. Russians. Colombians. Politicians. The report was filed away, never to be seen again.

Except for him, there were no other witnesses to the birth of modern transnational crime.

I

SPREADING THE VIRUS

As legitimate business understood and adjusted to the complexities of this new global marketplace, so did international criminal organizations.

– Arnaud de Borchgrave, Center for Strategic and International Studies

The anus of the earth is cut into the jungle on the Paraguay side of the Paraná River. It's a home away from home for the South American drug cartels, Chinese Triads, Japanese yakuza, Italian gangsters, Russian gangsters, Nigerian gangsters, and Hezbollah terrorists. It's called Ciudad del Este.

A city of two hundred thousand hustlers, whores, hoodlums, revolutionaries, thugs, drug traffickers, drug addicts, murderers, racketeers, pirates, mobsters, extortionists, smugglers, hitmen, pimps, and criminal wannabes, it was the creation of Paraguay's former dictator, Alfredo Stroessner, the same man who welcomed fugitive Nazis like Josef Mengele. He originally named the place after himself, and it remained Ciudad de Stroessner until he was deposed in 1989.

Its very remoteness is the major factor in its appeal. Because you have to want to get there in order to get there – no one ever just stumbles across it – Ciudad has always been an ideal spot for secret meetings. High government officials mingled there with agents of Taiwanese and South Korean counterfeiters, filling their own coffers with kickbacks as the counterfeiters filled the town with phony goods. Military dictators gathered there to cement friendships while they ruled the Southern Cone of South America.

The world's organized criminals still break bread there, in harmony, with each other.

Hezbollah guerrillas based themselves in Ciudad while planning and carrying out the 1992 bombing of the Israeli embassy in Argentina, which killed twenty-nine people, and the 1994 bombing of a Buenos Aires Jewish community centre, which killed eighty-six people.

In January 1999, the Uruguayans arrested Egyptian terrorist El Said Hassan Ali Mohamed Mukhlis when he crawled out of his hiding place – he'd been living in Ciudad like a Cold War mole for five years – on his way to plant a bomb in Britain. A suspect in the 1997 killings of fifty-eight foreign tourists and four nationals at Luxor, he is also believed to have knowledge of the bombings of the U.S. embassies in Kenya and Tanzania.

More than one hundred landing strips are scattered around the Tri-Border, as the region is known, none of them regulated by any authority, all of them in constant use by small planes. Convoys of trucks and vans and private cars nightly leave Rio de Janeiro – and other cities in Brazil and cities in Argentina, too – arriving in Ciudad del Este early the next morning, creating a massive, noisy, and fume-riddled daily traffic jam. The two-lane bridge they inch across from the Brazilian border town of Foz do Iguaçu brings in thirty thousand people a day. Beneath the bridge, young boys shift boxes and crates from the Paraguayan side to the Brazilian side, often in plain sight of the police.

They come to Ciudad because it's a market town where they can buy absolutely anything, *caveat emptor* being the only law of the land, as just about everything on sale in the five thousand shops that fill the twenty-block centre of this cesspool is fake.

Except the drugs. Three tons of cocaine moves through Ciudad every month on its way to Europe, North America, and South Africa. Colombian heroin comes through as well. Marijuana, grown in Paraguay, gets smuggled from there into Brazil and Argentina, while the chemicals needed to refine cocaine are smuggled in from Argentina. Although "smuggled" might not be the right word, because fifteen hundred to two thousand TIR-sized trucks drive across the bridge in each direction every month, and rarely are any of them ever stopped. Much of the money that the Colombians earn there is washed through an illegal betting racket in Rio de Janeiro, set up as a money-laundering sink-for-hire, under the ultimate direction of the American La Cosa Nostra (LCN).

The weapons that are bought, sold, and negotiated there are also real. It was in Ciudad that the Italian P-2 Lodge facilitated the sale of Exocet missiles and spare parts to the Argentinians for use against the British during the Falklands War.

The lives sold there are real, as well. You can buy cheap sex, cheap slaves, wholesale body parts for medical transplants, or just have someone killed. Murder in Ciudad costs as little as a thousand dollars for a non-white victim, only slightly more for a Caucasian.

You can even buy a new identity. A Chinese Triad gang has cornered the market on counterfeit Argentinian identity papers. Most are sold in batches to other organized crime groups with interests in alien smuggling. But anybody looking for a set of papers can find one. The particular appeal of Argentinian papers lies in the fact that Argentina is currently the only Latin American nation whose citizens do not need to apply in advance for visas to enter the United States.

Today, Ciudad is not only the continent's most important black market, it is the city with the third-largest volume of cash transactions, behind Hong Kong and Miami.

Counterfeit designer goods, counterfeit currency, counterfeit passports, pirated CDs, pirated videos, pirated software, stolen cars, drugs, money laundering, and arms dealing have turned Ciudad into a $12 to $14 billion annual industry. By contrast, Paraguay's official GDP is only about $9 billion.

It took humans thousands of years to move faster than the speed of a galloping horse. It then took less than a century to move faster than the speed of a train. From there it was only a few decades to move faster than the speed of sound.

Today, satellites, faxes, cellphones, the Internet, and e-mail enable us to send our voices, our images, our ideas, and our money at the speed of light. The planet has been reduced to the size of a computer screen, and the artificial borders which we once called nations have, for all intents and purposes, begun to evaporate. Borders have already become nonentities for transnational organized crime.

During the final years of the twentieth century – a period when we have witnessed the disintegration of Communism and the Soviet Union, the end of the Cold War, and our own abject failure to raise a democratic, free-market Russia out of the ashes – we have lived through the greatest quantum leap in technology since humans invented the wheel. Radical changes in transportation and communication have encumbered governments' ability to exercise controls over the movement of goods, services, people, and ideas. During the final years of the twentieth century we have witnessed both the concluding stages in the globalization of markets and the initial stages in the globalization of crime.

We have also coined a new type of money – megabyte bucks – electronic blips on computer screens that are not tethered to central banks or geography. Money has always been a political force. But never before has it been so easily energized by criminal activity that burrows inside the confusion created by the cross-border flood of goods, services, people, ideas, and of this new money itself.

For much of the half-century that followed World War II, Italian organized crime was, both in practice and in fact, the state. There, as in other parts of the world, the enormous mass of money they were able to launder, to reinvest in criminal activity, to hand out as bribes, and, eventually, to accumulate as profits, replaced the government with a body politic designed in their own image.

Latin America's second-largest export is cocaine. It accounts for 8 per cent of Colombia's GDP, and something like half that of Peru and Bolivia. It is estimated that the industry employs five hundred thousand people, covering every aspect of the business from farming to production, distribution, and financial services.

In Colón, Panama, the world's largest warehouse, there is as much as $2 billion worth of goods stored at any given time; some 60 per cent of those goods come from Asia. The Free Zone turns over $12 billion annually. If transnational criminal enterprise was taken out of the picture, if the counterfeit goods, money being laundered, arms being illegally shipped, goods breaking the Cuban embargo, and those belonging to Italian, Russian, Colombian, Chinese, Japanese, and other Asian organizations were simply erased, the government of Panama and much of the rest of neighbouring Latin America would go bankrupt.

Today, organized criminal groups are the only effective government in Russia. They control 40 per cent of all private businesses, 60 per cent of the state-owned businesses and 80 to 90 per cent of the banks. They exert executive control over key economic sectors of consumer products – including two-thirds of all alcohol sales, estimated to be worth $1.5 billion a year – petroleum distribution, and pharmaceuticals. By its own estimate, the Russian Interior Ministry believes the annual black-market revenues of these groups has now topped $18 billion, about the same sum that Russia was expected to reimburse its creditors in 1999.

Exactly like the multinational corporations they imitate – and, in many cases, have become – transnational criminal organizations realize what many politicians have never come to understand: that this is about one thing, and one thing only – wealth creation.

To maximize their wealth, the underworld needs the upperworld.

Consider the pot-of-coffee analogy. A pot has to be large enough to hold the coffee and, at the same time, there must be enough coffee to fill a pot. Without the professionals – lawyers, bankers, accountants, and company formation agents – to prepare the stage for global criminals, they could never function on a global basis as successfully as they do. And yet, if there was not so much money to be made in global crime, the professionals would not be there to accommodate them. In that sense, a part of the upperworld needs the underworld, too. Theirs is a marriage of convenience.

The merger of underworld groups is much the same.

Both phenomena are based on wealth creation. However, the globalization of crime and criminal enterprises differs from legitimate enterprise in one important area. Where the upperworld professionals who service these underworld groups operate within diminishing boundaries, because those boundaries protect their professional monopoly on services, transnational criminal organizations operate beyond boundaries because that's where jurisdiction no longer applies.

Law enforcement, as we know it today, is a local remedy to local problems. It is a statement of sovereignty – local, state, county, provincial, federal – and therefore confined by budgets and borders, both of which are definitions of sovereignty. It is the state that says, you may not comport yourself in a particular manner here. It is the state that pays the police to enforce the rules and punish those who do not comply. As a result, the state winds up with borders that must be respected with neither the authority nor the money to go beyond them, while the criminals create wealth by purposely functioning beyond sovereign reach.

In San Diego, the border is inundated by Chinese nationals, smuggled into Mexico by Asian organized crime groups, and from there smuggled into the U.S. by Mexican organized crime groups, using the same routes and methods that the Mexicans perfected to smuggle cocaine into the U.S. for the Colombian cartels.

In Turkmenistan, two thousand tons of kerosene – an essential ingredient in the manufacture of cocaine – was sold by an organized crime group there to a company in Argentina, which paid for the shipment entirely in cash. That company was a front for the Colombians. Even though kerosene is a non-controlled substance, they were willing to go that far to hide the transaction's trail. The same company also bought large quantities of kerosene from Polish crime groups, paying for it with cocaine delivered to the groups' agents in Chicago.

In Cyprus, on the south side of the Green Line divide, more than $1 billion arrives every month from Russia. The money is washed through the nearly eight thousand Russian companies and banks that have been formed in Cyprus since 1993. Another twenty-two thousand to twenty-five thousand shell companies belong, mostly, to Eastern Europeans. Once clean, some of that money goes to Britain. One investigation, prompted by the Bank of England, led to the closing of London's Cyprus Credit Bank. On the north side of the Green Line, Turkish heroin is bartered and sold like any commodity. A second investigation prompted by the Bank of England has led to the public disclosure that at least one Turkish bank in London might be directly involved with this traffic.

In Veracruz, on the Gulf coast of Mexico, a group of French organized criminals, with direct links to traditional Italian and Corsican gangs, ran an international stolen car ring. They contracted with Mexican gangsters to carjack luxury models, showing a particular fondness for Chrysler Voyager deluxe vans. They also contracted with a Cambodian organized faction in Florida to steal cars off the streets there. In both cases, cars were shipped to France with newly registered Mexican documents. Bags of cement, lime, and plaster were also sent with the cars, which, considering the presence of the Cambodians, suggests that the idea was to couple car theft with heroin trafficking.

In Ensenada, on the Pacific coast of Mexico's Baja California, Mexican traffickers and their Southeast Asian heroin-dealing partners – in this case, Thai and Laotian – worked out a drugs-by-post scheme. The gang in Mexico shipped bath products to Thailand, where the envelopes were intercepted by Thai gang members working inside the post office. They emptied out the bath products, refilled the envelopes with heroin, and stamped them, "Undeliverable – Return to Sender." The envelopes entered Mexico without Customs inspection because it appeared that they had originated in Mexico. Mexican gang members inside the Mexican postal service then delivered the drugs to their cohorts for smuggling into the United States.

In Washington, D.C., the U.S. State Department's Bureau for International Narcotics and Law Enforcement Affairs, which publishes an annual list as part of their *International Narcotics Control Strategy Report*, points a finger at the most reprehensible money-laundering nations in the world. Among those given "high priority" by the Americans are the obvious offenders: Aruba, the Cayman Islands, Colombia, Cyprus, Mexico, Nigeria, Panama, Russia, Singapore, Switzerland, Thailand, Venezuela, the United Kingdom, and Canada.

In Tel Aviv, the "Law of Return" continues to allow an influx of Eastern Europeans claiming to be Jewish who, in fact, are not. They get into the country with counterfeit paperwork and apply for Israeli passports to substantiate their new identity. Because Israel has no money-laundering laws, these people are able to use the proceeds of crimes to invest in selected politicians who could someday influence the disposition of a government. One group, in particular, is said to be willing to commit $2 billion with just this in mind.

As long as we live in a world where a seventeenth-century philosophy of sovereignty is reinforced with an eighteenth-century judicial model, defended by a nineteenth-century concept of law enforcement that is still trying to come to terms with twentieth-century technology, the twenty-first century will belong to transnational criminals.

Law enforcement could take lessons from these groups, as they open overseas branches to expand established markets, to gain access where they once were forbidden, and to create new markets. Almost as if they themselves have learned their lessons at the Harvard School of Business – in some specific cases, they did – transnational criminal organizations approach logistics, personnel, and accounting in a professional manner. They research and develop new products. They hire experts to guide them through the complex and ever-changing maze of legal issues, marketing techniques, and all things financial. They understand cost flow, reinvestment, franchising, time management, and risk management. They have learned to construct and maintain networks of front companies, to negotiate prices, to decide delivery methods, to set schedules of payment, and to build into all of this a philosophy that takes into account future market developments.

And, like any sound multinational corporation, they also seek out strategic alliances.

In Montreal, Asian organized criminals importing heroin into Canada hand off drugs to an Italian group that ships them to New York in bakery trucks where they are distributed by a Puerto Rican street gang.

In New Zealand, the Mongrel Mob signed a deal to protect Chinese Triad gang members who are serving time in jail there. For their services, Triad members on the outside pay Mongrels on the outside with drugs. Relationships formed on the inside are then translated into joint ventures once members of the two groups get out of jail.

In Germany, seventy Italian organized crime cells deal weapons, traffic drugs, and steal cars. All of them have ties to Mafia groups in Italy. Some of them have also been tied directly to Turkish organized crime which supplies heroin, Colombian organized crime which supplies cocaine, Russian organized crime which supplies weapons, and Asian organized crime which offers them access to their network of Chinese restaurants for money laundering.

In Toronto, an Italian organized crime group ran a strip joint with dancers and prostitutes supplied by a Russian organized crime group, and muscle supplied by an outlaw motorcycle gang.

While their core activities remain the same – drug trafficking, weapons trafficking, car theft, fraud in all its guises, alien smuggling, counterfeit production and distribution, murder, kidnapping, extortion, money laundering, and the smuggling and sale of fissile materials – they flourish in the global markets of transparent borders and meaningless trade restrictions. Unlike their predecessors, they do not limit themselves to single forms of illegal activity, but deal in anything and everything that can make money for them. By broadening their areas of operation and increasing co-operation with other groups, they have enlarged significantly the pot of gold at the end of their rainbow.

The man who pulled into the British Columbia liquor store parking lot that evening had never been to London. In fact, Great Britain was just about the furthest thing from his mind as he got out of his car, locked the doors, strolled into the shop – chimes sounded to announce he'd come in – and thought to himself it was lucky his wife had phoned to remind him about the wine.

The Vietnamese clerk behind the counter at the far end said hello.

The fellow nodded and glanced around.

The place was over-stocked with bottles in all shapes and sizes, with large signs announcing that some of them were on sale, and huge wooden barrels filled to the brim with more bottles.

Eventually the man located a shelf marked Burgundy.

The clerk asked if he was looking for anything in particular.

The man said that he needed some wine for a dinner party, but, thanks anyway, he could find it himself. He perused the bottles in front of him, turned momentarily to the next shelf where the Bordeaux was, did some fast arithmetic, decided that would be too expensive, and returned to the Burgundies.

The six bottles he settled on set him back seventy-eight dollars and change.

The fellow behind the counter loaded them into two bags – explaining that this way they wouldn't be too heavy and break – then rang up the sale.

The customer pulled out his credit card and put it on the counter.

The clerk picked up the card, explained that they had a special on champagne, and motioned towards one of those wooden barrels.

The fellow looked at the champagne.

The clerk swiped the card through a reader under the counter.

After thinking about it for a few seconds, the man shook his head and turned back to watch the clerk put the credit card through a reader on the top of the counter.

When the little receipt churned up, he signed it, took his receipt, took his wine, said goodnight, and went home to his dinner party.

Long before dessert, the number of his credit card, together with the encoded information from the magnetic stripe on the back of it, was e-mailed to Hong Kong. There, magstripe data from several hundred other cards – collected much the same way up and down the west coast of Canada and the United States – was collated and e-mailed to Malaysia.

Within twenty-four hours, a brand new credit card – issued in the name of the man from British Columbia – was bundled along with 199 others, and prepared for delivery to a customer in Italy.

A fresh carton of cigarettes had been carefully opened, as had each packet. The cigarettes were dumped out, and the cards stacked inside. The packets were then resealed – made to look as if they'd never been opened – and replaced in the carton, which was also resealed. At Subang International Airport in Kuala Lumpur, the courier taking them out of the country purchased a bottle of whisky and put the cigarettes in the same plastic Duty Free shopping bag. The following day, he walked straight past Italian Customs – no one cared about duty-free goods – and delivered the specially prepared carton of cigarettes to a gentleman in Milan.

Twenty-five credit cards, including the card that otherwise should have belonged to the man who bought the wine, had been presold to a Russian in Prague. Three days after it was delivered to him, one of the men on the team dispatched to London by the Russian in Prague walked into Harrods and used up nearly all of the twenty-thousand-dollar limit on the Canadian's card.

The designer watches and Hermès scarves that he bought, together with designer handbags, jewellery, more watches, fine leather goods, digital cameras, French perfume, and handheld computers, were all paid for with the Visa, Mastercard, Amex, and Diners Club cards that were in the batch of twenty-five. The goods were packed in team members' luggage and checked onto a regularly scheduled flight to Prague. From there, along with other goods that had been purchased in Paris and Rome and charged to other credit cards controlled by the man in Prague, they were trucked to Moscow.

Within a week, all of those items were on sale in specialist boutiques at the Gum department store, across Red Square from the Kremlin, at prices far beyond those which showed up a month later – total, $18,157 – on the credit card statement of the customer from this liquor store.

Of course, the fellow phoned the credit card company about it right away. And, of course, after looking into it, the credit card company wrote it off. They sent him a new card with a new number. He never had the problem again. As far as he was concerned, it was just some weird mistake. But investigators at the credit card company knew better. It was fraud on a massive, global scale. Although they hadn't yet discovered the specifics – that members of an organized Vietnamese crime gang were being paid to double-swipe cards by a Chinese Triad society, which had sold the cards to a member of the Camorra Mafia, which, in turn, resold some to a Russian organized crime group – they did take a look at the liquor store, but could never prove anything. And without at least one culprit, no law enforcement agency anywhere wanted to know.

Anyway, no one was ever certain in whose jurisdiction the crime had been committed.

None of the diverse law enforcement agencies that might otherwise have become involved was willing to authorize the cost of investigating a Russian in Prague who'd ripped off of some fellow in North America with the help of a gang in Hong Kong that had been in touch with a gang in Italy.

Where national objectives were once defined by a government's ability to protect its citizens, territory, and borders, they are now characterized by law enforcement's inability to defend those citizens and territories from threats outside those borders. Where power and authority were once defined by political polarities, such as East versus West, they are now defined by the control of or influence over markets, such as foreign exchange and essential commodities.

Washington attorney and money-laundering expert Jack Blum is convinced that to fight transnational crime we need transnational solutions. "The idea that jurisdiction is a function of geography does not work in the electronic age. Electrons in cyberspace do not read maps. Few if any international frauds take place solely within the borders of a single country. We will have to change the way nations deal with each other in matters of exchanging evidence, allowing police to work across borders and even the way the international community deals with the question of sovereignty."

Whatever lines once existed between business and crime in many countries have since been rubbed away. Take, for example, the former Soviet Union. There being no job security at institutions such as the KGB, operatives who hadn't socked away a nest egg found themselves on breadlines. The assets they possessed were contacts throughout the world, networks of foreign informants, and the phone numbers of moles planted in the West years ago.

The operatives who stayed on breadlines were the dumb ones.

With global networks already in place, many of whose operatives were abroad, familiar with crime in the guise of Cold War espionage, regearing to function as an organized criminal business became the KGB's pension plan. Many of the dangers that we in the West now face – national security threats that should have passed away with the end of the Cold War – have been placed on life support by the deliberate overlapping of traditional criminal activity with weapons' proliferation and terrorism.

In New York, Greek criminals showed up with five tons of radioactive zirconium for sale. A critical ingredient in nuclear reactors, the metallic element had been smuggled to the West by a Russian organized crime group that used the Greeks as their agents. They also had plutonium and enriched uranium to sell.

In Tokyo, on March 20, 1995, the Aum Shinrikyo religious cult killed a dozen people and injured another five thousand by releasing deadly sarin nerve gas into the subway system. At the time, the group had assets of more than $1 billion in secret bank accounts, $8.25 million in cash, a large quantity of gold bars, a farm in Australia where they'd been testing the gas on sheep and cattle, plus a clandestine chemical weapons factory in Tokyo that was so big it made the group the city's largest private real estate owner. Since then, Aum Shinrikyo began recruiting again, and has reportedly signed twenty thousand new members, all of them discontented Russian soldiers living on military bases in the far eastern reaches of what used to be the Soviet Union.

As it became increasingly evident that the Soviet Union was in the midst of social and political meltdown and would soon disintegrate, a meeting was held at CIA headquarters in McLean, Virginia, to discuss what looked like the very real possibility of criminal nuclear proliferation. Senior managers were concerned that when the system crashed, former Soviet nuclear scientists would be out of work and that to feed their families they would offer their skills and knowledge to the highest bidders. It was known at the time that countries such as Iraq, Libya, and Syria were eagerly seeking Russian expertise. Because the CIA already knew who these Russian scientists were, they created a database to track them. They gave each one a number and set up a system so that they would always know who was where. This, the agency felt, was the best way to protect America from the spread of Russian nuclear expertise.

And while they were zeroing in on the Russian nuclear scientists, no one was bothering with the bio-chem scientists or the crypto guys.

Iranian scientists began working on biological weapons (known as "the poor man's atom bomb") towards the end of the war with Iraq. They'd been able to purchase strains of bacteria from Canada and Holland, plus the necessary laboratory equipment from the Swiss, Germans, Italians, and Spanish. But they'd still not been able to breed the germs into deadly toxins. That is, until the Russians arrived. Within two years their program had leaped from the developmental stage to production and the creation of delivery systems.

In Bulgaria, Russians have been hired to teach at a school where graduate-level students from other countries learn how to create and program computer viruses.

In Cali, Colombia, highly experienced Russian cryptoanalysts are employed in a telephone company owned by a faction of the Cali cartel, their job being to intercept secure phone calls made anywhere in the world by the Drug Enforcement Administration.

In Britain, police computers are not compatible. The Metropolitan Police computer in London cannot talk directly to the Strathclyde Police computer which cannot speak directly with the Thames Valley Police computer. That has prompted one senior officer to hang a sign on the pin board facing his desk which reads, "We're more disorganized than they are organized."

In Ottawa, the Royal Canadian Mounted Police has only just woken up to the fact that many of the computer programs running the Police Information Centre date to 1972 and are, therefore, obsolete. The database, which was designed to handle 60 million requests for information per year, is now handling twice that number, making access to it more difficult and more time-consuming for the fourteen thousand police, corrections, and immigration organizations in Canada who use it. When it's working, it supplies criminal records plus information on arrest warrants and stolen cars.

In Washington, D.C., the computer at the FBI's National Criminal Intelligence Center is also overloaded. A central clearing house for law enforcement across the country, criminals arrested in one state who should otherwise be identified as wanted in other states often slip through the net because many agencies, especially local police forces, have neither the staff nor the budgets to upload information into the system.

In all 140 chapters of the Hells Angels motorcycle gang, whose death's head logo is a registered trademark, and anyone who uses it without permission gets sued, the same way Coke and Microsoft and Nike take people to court for such abuses – computers are linked via a coded intranet. When the Los Angeles chapter does a deal with the Mexicans to deliver methamphetamine to a Chinese gang in Canada, within a few hours of the deal being made, every chapter around the world has been informed and told to stay away.

The Republic of Niue is a two-hundred-beer airplane ride from anywhere.

A chunk of coral rising out of the middle of the Pacific Ocean, Niue is a protectorate of New Zealand, which is twenty-four hundred miles to the southwest. There are no beaches. There is no continental shelf and the weather can be rough. A minuscule self-governing member of the British Commonwealth, the eighteen hundred people who live there are otherwise struggling just to survive. They would like the rest of the world to think of Niue for skin diving. At least one senior law enforcement officer in Hong Kong thinks of Niue as "bird shit, telephone sex, and money laundering."

The birds were there before the people. The telephone sex came much later, imported by the Japanese who took advantage of technology and the international telephone payments system. Someone in Tokyo looking to get turned on dials a number and winds up having his ardour routed through an exchange in Niue, where the local phone company receives a share of the outrageous fees charged back to the poor guy on the other end of the line by the telephone sex company in Japan.

Niue is also into Internet domain names. Anyone who pays a fee to the government there will be granted the right to call their website anything ending in ".nu", like "whats.nu" or "isanything.nu" or "nottoo.nu."

Next stop appears to be Internet gambling. Punters sitting in front of their modem-linked PC can play roulette or poker in cyberspace, with their losses – and presumably their winnings, too – racked up on their credit card by a company somewhere on the planet duly compensating the host nation for the right to be a casino.

Again, those eighteen hundred Niueans have to eat.

The big banquet, however, turns out to be the murky world of offshore shell companies. Since 1994, Niue has been licensing International Business Corporations (IBCs) which, for around a thousand dollars start-up, give anyone the right to incorporate a company in any language, including Russian written in Cyrillic. Those IBCs are permitted to use any suffix that any other company anywhere else in the world can use – such as Ltd., Inc., GmbH, SA, NV, whether or not the company has businesses in Britain, the U.S. and Canada, Germany, the French- and Spanish-speaking worlds, or the Netherlands. To the list of suffixes add A/S, AG., B.V., and Aktiengesellshaft, rendering the IBCs' names virtually meaningless. It is impossible to decipher from the company's name what it does or, for that matter, where it does it. At the same time, it allows a company to pretend that it does something and is somewhere that it doesn't and isn't.

No minimum authorized share capital is required. An IBC is exempt from all local tax and stamp duties. Nor is there any requirement to hold general meetings or file annual accounts. To maximize security of assets, IBCs are permitted to transfer domicile, plus reacquire and reissue shares for cash in any currency, or any other form of consideration. Those shares can be bearer or nominative and, for really good measure, other companies can be listed as directors, meaning that there is absolutely no way anyone can ever find out who actually owns the company.

By charter, there are only a few things that an IBC cannot do. It is not permitted to carry on business with any residents of the island. Nor is it permitted to own property there, except for an office. In other words, the government of Niue will take your money, but they don't want you moving into the neighbourhood or marrying their daughters.

But Niuean IBCs aren't about meaningful relationships. They're about total secrecy and absolute anonymity, and, in some sense, about deception. Which are exactly the kinds of services a money launderer would pay for.

The United Nations got upset enough about Niue to put it on a list of countries where the possibility of money laundering was a real concern. The U.S. House of Representatives got upset enough about Niue to republish testimony from attorney Jack Blum, one of the offshore world's most vocal critics. To wit: "The International Business Corporation, a corporation with anonymous ownership which can do no business in its country of incorporation, has no legitimate place in the international arena. IBCs are now the central tool of money launderers."

The Asia/Pacific Group of the Financial Action Task Force, an agency of the G-8 group of nations, whose sole concern is global money laundering, is worried about Niue; as are the Australian Federal Police, who confirm, "We are monitoring developments in Niue and remain concerned that the establishment of an offshore register will lead to exploitation by criminal groups"; as is New Zealand's Serious Fraud Office, who convinced the government to send a representative to the island to try to explain the dangers of an offshore industry; as is the United States Department of State, Bureau for International Narcotics and Law Enforcement Affairs, who admit to being "very worried" about Niue's offshore industry; as is the Office of the Controller of Currency of the United States, who thought of Niue as the latest "flavour of the month" in the offshore money-laundering business.

The island's affairs, and cases related to it, are also allegedly being looked at, to varying degrees, by law enforcement in North America, Europe, and the Far East.

Although IBCs formed in Niue can be bought over the phone from company formation agents in central London, no one at the Commonwealth Office seems the least concerned.

Adding to everyone else's growing anxiety, however, is the latest dish that the government of Niue has brought to the buffet – banking licences. For less than twenty thousand dollars, you can buy your very own Niue-authorized financial institution, which, as one brochure touts,

"Provides access to the international credits market, as well as to the international mutual funds market and the securities market, [and] allows the bank to conduct FOREX transactions and, with minimal expense, to solve problems of liquidity."

At least three company formation agents easily located on the World Wide Web offer such banks for sale and – hardly by coincidence – list branch offices in Moscow and St. Petersburg.

Because organized criminal groups have come to understand that there is no reason to rob banks when they can own one, Russian "businessmen" are believed to have bought several thousand IBCs and banks registered in Niue.

2

GETTING CONNECTED

Mafia is a process, not a thing.

– Joe Bonanno, *A Man of Honor*

The thing about mobsters in the late 1950s was that you could count on them to be consistent.

They were predictable.

In those days, five crime families ruled New York: Gambino, Lucchese, Colombo, Bonanno, and Genovese. They, in turn, were overseen by a Commission. Nothing happened without the others being kept informed. When the Bonannos shipped heroin into Montreal to smuggle it into the States, the other four stayed away from Montreal. When the Gambinos ran a tax fraud racket on Long Island, the other four stayed away from the scam. When a family negotiated an alliance with hoods in other cities, the other four stayed away from that city. It was a gentleman's business, orchestrated by men who were anything but gentle.

Every now and then, however, there'd be a falling out and two or more of the families would "go to the mattresses." One bunch of idiots would start shooting at another bunch of idiots. Civilians and family members, namely wives and children, were unconditionally off limits. As bodies littered the streets, the New York Police Department would take an unofficial step back. They'd let the bad guys kill each other until the Commission enforced a truce. Someone would declare in the press that, as far as they were concerned, that was twenty-two less gangsters for them to worry about. The NYPD would then count the bodies and pack them off to the morgue.

The badfellas would return to being goodfellas, and everyone would wait patiently for the next time. There was an order to this, a coherence that somehow made sense. It became part of the myth, the stuff of *Godfather* movies.

That's the way it was in the days when being a mobster meant being predictable.

The man who changed his name from Salvatore to Charlie and from Lucania to Luciano, and who once survived such a brutal assassination attempt that forever after he'd be known as "Lucky," was proclaimed by *Time* magazine as one of the most important figures of the twentieth century. "He downsized, he restructured and he used Standard & Poor's as much as Smith & Wesson to change forever the face of organized crime," wrote *Time*.

Born in Sicily in 1897, his family emigrated to the Lower East Side of New York when he was nine. A childhood crony of Al Capone, he dropped out of school at the age of fourteen – still in the fifth grade – to hang out full-time on street corners. He and a bunch of other teenaged Italian hoods had formed a gang they called the Five Pointers and were soon regularly getting arrested for shoplifting and mugging.

It was while terrorizing some local Jewish kids that he met one who stood up to him. Meyer Suchowljansky, a skinny Russian-Polish émigré five years his junior, refused to hand over any of his pocket money. Single-handedly, he defied the Five Pointers, and out of that bravado a lifelong friendship was born. Within a few years the two of them – now with their new names Charlie "Lucky" Luciano and Meyer Lansky – were mocking Prohibition by running whisky from Canada into New York.

Eventually Luciano hooked up with the Giuseppe "Joe" Masseria crime family, where he developed easy relationships with a divers group of other thugs – notably the Neapolitan Vito Genovese and the Calabrian Francesco "Frank Costello" Castiglia – and in them found men who shared his philosophy that business was more profitable than ethnic warfare. At the same time he spurned the old traditions by maintaining his friendship with Lansky, and even extending his circle of Jewish friends to include Benjamin "Bugsy" Siegel and Louis "Lepke" Buchalter.

"Americanized men such as Charlie Lucky," wrote Joe Bonanno, "marched to a different drummer. Luciano never imbibed the true spirit of our Tradition. In his personal life, for example, he was not a family man. He was a bachelor who conducted his business out of a suite in the Waldorf Astoria under the name Charles Ross. . . . Luciano was essentially a loner."

In April 1931, after a protracted war between the old-school eastern Sicilian godfather Masseria and the old-school western Sicilian godfather Salvatore Maranzano, the loner saw profit in confusion and conspired with Maranzano to kill his own boss. In return, when Maranzano divided New York into five families, he rewarded Luciano by naming him head of one of them. Luciano appointed Costello as his underboss and promoted Genovese into a position of responsibility. For good measure, Maranzano crowned himself *capo di tutti capi* (boss of bosses).

The comfy world of North American organized crime might have stayed comfy for a long time, had Luciano not fancied Maranzano's crown. In September 1931, he and some of his pals – ostensibly Siegel and Lansky – knocked off Maranzano. Luciano then solidified power by holding the crime world's first authentic "convention" at the Blackstone Hotel in Chicago. There, Charlie Lucky proffered his vision of a "National Crime Syndicate." He wanted to divide the United States and Canada into twenty-four regions and oversee the regions with a ruling Commission. Seven men, the boss of each of the five New York families plus the bosses of the Buffalo and Chicago mobs, would sit as a board of directors. They would arbitrate disputes, set broad policy, establish a workable code of honour that reflected life in America – for instance, only the Commission could approve an assassination – and enforce the council's mandate with a crew known as "Murder Incorporated" controlled by Umberto "Albert" Anastasia and Lepke.

When the other members approved, the Cosa Nostra was invented.

Fate then provided two twists: the United States Congress passed the Twenty-first Amendment to the Constitution on December 5, 1933, and Japan attacked Pearl Harbor on December 7, 1941.

The repeal of prohibition cut deeply into the syndicates' cash flow, forcing it to look elsewhere for income. That took them into drug trafficking. And that put Thomas Dewey on their backs.

In 1936, as U.S. Attorney for the Southern District of New York, Dewey declared war on the gangsters. To get Charlie Lucky, he presented a dramatic three-week-long case against him for controlling prostitution. No fewer than forty weeping women took the stand to shock the jury with the horrors Luciano had subjected them to. The jurors fell for it. The judge sentenced Luciano to thirty to fifty years in Clinton Prison at Dannemora, New York, a place known in the underworld as "Siberia."

While Luciano was inside, Pearl Harbor was destroyed and World War II happened along.

Legend has it that Luciano was approached by the Office of Strategic Services, precursor of the CIA, to recruit the Mafia in Italy as local intelligence operatives for George Patton's Seventh Army Sicilian landings. A variation on the story is that the U.S. Navy needed Luciano to defend the home front after a troop ship was blown up in New York Harbor. The Navy worried that longshoremen of Italian origin would sabotage the American war effort. They wanted him to guarantee their loyalty. Luciano could have made that guarantee because many of those docks were under mob control. He could, conceivably, have put them in touch with someone in Sicily too. But the idea that the CIA cut him in on the plan for the Allied landings stretches credulity. Besides the fact that no one in Washington would have trusted him, Mussolini had long since purged much of the local Mafiosi. That said, as soon as the war was over, Luciano appealed to Dewey, who was now Governor of New York, and was granted executive clemency on the grounds of "patriotic services" to the nation. Whatever that means.

Luciano was released from jail, then deported to Italy.

Normally, Vito Genovese would have been next in line to succeed Luciano, but he'd been accused of murder and forced to make a hasty exit to Italy. That left Frank Costello to take Luciano's chair on the Commission. Unfortunately for Costello, Luciano's power did not come along with the seat.

No sooner had Luciano unpacked in Italy than he decided it was time to pick up where he'd left off. In October 1946 he flew to Cuba to partner Lansky in his dream of turning Havana into the capital of the underworld. He lived there, on the quiet, until February 1947 when he was arrested because of Frank Sinatra.

The Commission had a five-year, renewable mandate. Luciano missed the meeting in 1946, but then convened the group in the spring of 1947 under the guise of a dinner to honour Sinatra. Among those for whom attendance was mandatory were Lansky, "Joe Adonis" Doto, Bonanno, Costello, Anastasia, and Joe Profaci. Vito Genovese was there as well, having just been exonerated of murder.

If Luciano saw Cuba as the means to renew his control of the Commission, Genovese saw Cuba as the first step in moving Costello aside and taking back what was rightfully his. Oddly, so many gangsters heading for Havana didn't set off any alarm bells. It was the gala for "Ol' Blue Eyes" that made the papers.

When someone in the U.S. Justice Department read that Charlie Lucky was there, the State Department threatened the Cubans that if they didn't stick Luciano on the next boat for Italy, America would embargo medical supplies destined for the island. Luciano was hastily returned to the old country.

Over the ensuing years he built the world's premier drug empire, shipping opium from Turkey to Lebanon, extracting the morphine there, then bringing that to Italy where it was converted into heroin. He contracted with French Corsicans to move the product to Montreal where Carmine "Lilo" Galante, who ran the city as underboss of the Bonanno family, was in charge of smuggling it across the border to other LCN members in Buffalo and Detroit.

In May 1950, Estes Kefauver, a Democratic Senator from Tennessee, opened a series of hearings on organized crime in interstate commerce. One of the first Congressional hearings ever to be televised, Kefauver wanted the public to realize that "modern crime syndicates and criminal gangs have copied some of the organizational methods found in modern business." After listening to the testimony of more than eight hundred witnesses, including Costello, Anastasia, Lansky, Gaetano "Tommy" Lucchese, and Adonis, all of whom denied knowing anything about the Mafia and unblinkingly exerted their Fifth Amendment rights to say nothing more, Kefauver drew several conclusions.

He determined that there was a nationwide crime syndicate known as the Mafia; that it had international ramifications which appeared most clearly in connection with the narcotics trade; that its leaders were found in charge of the most lucrative rackets in their cities; that there were indications of centralized direction and control, although leadership appeared to be in a group rather than in a single individual; that these groups had kept in touch with Luciano since his deportation; that they did business with each other and regularly got together to discuss new opportunities; and that the Mafia acted closely with many persons who were not of Sicilian descent.

He opened a lot of eyes. Curiously, his sternest critic was the man whose life had supposedly been dedicated to fighting crime, J. Edgar Hoover. Not only did he refuse to cooperate with the Committee, the Director of the FBI actually tried to undermine it. And on every possible occasion, he staunchly maintained his long-standing position: "There is no persuasive evidence that a national crime syndicate exists."

In 1956, President Eisenhower signed into law the *Narcotics Control Act*, drastically increasing penalties for drug trafficking. Deeply concerned for their own burgeoning interests, Costello assembled the regular five-year meeting of the Commission. They met on October 17 at the home of Joseph Barbara, a Canada Dry soft drinks distributor who, in real life, controlled mob activities in northeastern Pennsylvania.

Barbara's eleven-room house, built in the late 1940s for the then whopping sum of $250,000, was a long stone building with second-floor rooms under gabled roofs at both ends. There were also five outer buildings on the nearly fifty-acre estate, which was situated in wooded hills north of the Pennsylvania border, fifteen miles or so along the Susquehanna River to the west of Binghamton, in the town of Apalachin, New York.

At that meeting, the Commission members talked about the new law, about heroin, and about how Charlie Lucky would keep them supplied as long as they wanted to be supplied. They talked about how they could count on Meyer Lansky's connections in Cuba to help smuggle drugs into the United States through the southern route and about how Bonanno's Canadian connections would maintain the northern route. But most of all they kept asking themselves, did they really want to be in the drug business? Apparently Frank Costello and Carlo Gambino were both wary of getting involved in any federal crimes that might force Hoover to take action against them. The group stayed at Apalachin for two days. And absolutely no one took any notice.

Seven months later, someone tried to kill Costello. He was just about to walk into his apartment building on Central Park West one evening when a man stepped out of the shadows and shot at his head. Costello was only grazed. The failed assassin was arrested – it was Vincent "the Chin" Gigante, who thirty years later would become head of the Genovese family – but when Costello refused to identify him, Gigante walked.

Vito Genovese led Costello to believe that the hit had been ordered by Anastasia. That made sense to him because he and Anastasia had been at odds. What he failed to realize was that Gigante's day job was chauffeur and bodyguard to his nearest rival, Vito Genovese.

Instead of fighting back, Costello slowly withdrew and slipped into retirement. Over the next several months, two of Anastasia's top advisors got knocked off.

In Italy, the attempt on Costello, the two murders, and Costello's departure from the scene did not escape Luciano's notice. He wanted to make the Italians understand that, despite such hiccups, the LCN organizational model worked in America, and would work for them too. So he called a four-day meeting of the boys. It was held on October 10–14, 1957, at the Albergo e Della Palme, in those days Palermo's plushest hotel.

Some thirty "godfathers" attended. Most were Sicilian. But Bonanno and Galante were there, representing New York and Montreal, as were members of the Magaddino family, which ran Buffalo, as was at least one member of the Priziola family, which ran Detroit. On the evening of October 12, the group moved down to the port, to a restaurant that, in those days, was called Spano's. There, Luciano laid out his master plan for the universe.

He explained to his Italian partners how their American cousins had benefited from having a Commission; he argued that a similar body to manage the Sicilians' affairs would insulate them to a greater degree against internal warfare, and that the two ruling councils could then establish ground rules for joint ventures. He said he wanted both organizations to have a similar structure so that his Sicilian chums could join hands with his American chums and, in effect, create for themselves a heroin stranglehold over North America.

These were radical ideas. Getting everyone to agree required a lot of explanation. It also created a lot of argument. The dinner at Spano's is said to have lasted twelve hours.

While the Sicilians came to see how such a confederation would be the most economical way for them to gain leverage in the North American markets, the Americans weren't as readily convinced. The last thing they wanted was to have their strings pulled from Sicily, even if it was evident that Charlie Lucky himself would be chief string puller.

Interestingly enough, by this time, Luciano had moved his heroin production out of Italy and into France. He'd shifted manufacturing to Marseilles on the advice of his Corsican-smuggler partners, who assured him that they could exert their influence on his behalf. The move created what would come to be remembered as "the French Connection." In the end, through the sheer force of Charlie Lucky's personality, everyone agreed. The dinner at Spano's elevated him to chairman of the Sicilians' Commission, which was dubbed La Cupola (the dome).

One of the people who attended the four-day Albergo convention was Tommaso Buscetta, then an up-and-coming star of Palermo's Porto Nuova family. Some eighteen years later, Buscetta would turn his back on his oath of *omertà* – the code of silence – and testify against his fellow Mafiosi. It would be the first death throe of the octopus that Luciano had created.

"It was the responsibility of the Commission," he explained in an appearance before a U.S. Senate subcommittee, "to rule on disputes between families that cannot be resolved by the family bosses. It is the responsibility of the Commission to rule on the execution of a Man of Honor. Once the Commission has decided to kill someone, the Commission decides who is to carry out its decision, and is empowered to choose its executioners from any family. Organizing the murder is, therefore, the exclusive doing of the Commission."

There is nothing to substantiate the claim that a murder was actually plotted at the Albergo. Only one source claims it was. Clare Sterling, in a book documenting the rise of the Mafia octopus, bases her assertion on a comment by Luciano to the effect that "Albert was really off his rocker." She also contends that two hitmen were then dispatched from Sicily with the contract.

Not so.

The target on Albert Anastasia's back had been drawn in America, long before that meeting in Palermo, and the artist with the crayon was Vito Genovese.

On Friday morning, just after ten, Anastasia and at least one bodyguard walked into the Park-Sheraton Hotel on Seventh Avenue at Fifty-fifth Street. They stopped for several minutes to speak to some people Anastasia knew, then made their way to the barber shop at the other end of the lobby. This was the same lobby where, coincidentally, gangster Arnold Rothstein had been gunned down in 1928.

Although Anastasia was early for his appointment, Tony, who worked chair number four and always cut his hair, motioned for "Don Umberto" to sit down. Two other customers were having their hair cut. Another was waiting. The manicurist was sitting alone at her table along the wall.

The police report notes that Anastasia took his place, loosened his tie, leaned back, and shut his eyes as Tony put a steaming hot towel over his face. The owner of the shop, Arthur Grasso, dragged a short, round stool up to the side of chair number four so that he could talk to Anastasia. The bodyguard sat down in chair number five, also expecting a haircut.

That's when two men stepped into the shop from the lobby.

Both were wearing wide-brimmed fedoras and green aviator sunglasses. The younger of them, widely believed to have been the New York–based thug "Crazy" Joey Gallo, got as close to Anastasia as chair number three. The other man, possibly Joey's brother Larry, hurried to the door that led out to the street. And then, without warning, they both started shooting.

One bullet hit Anastasia in the back of his head and lodged in the left side of his brain. Another hit him in the left hand. A third pierced his hip. A fourth entered from the upper left side of his back and went down, penetrating his kidney, lung, and spleen.

Within seconds, both shooters were gone.

A photo of Anastasia's barely covered bloody corpse was printed on the front pages of New York's evening newspapers that night. And on the front pages of the Saturday morning editions, as well.

The image became one of the most familiar of the decade.

The Lord High Executioner had been responsible for, perhaps, as many as five hundred hits. But Albert Anastasia's time was past. Genovese was taking over.

He gathered together the other New York family bosses at the Livingston, New Jersey, estate of Ruggerio Boiardo, a member of his own crime family. The meeting, which started at noon on Sunday, November 10, lasted until five on Monday morning. The attendees discussed Anastasia's death, ratified Carlo Gambino's elevation to the head of Costello's gang, and, because there were other topics still on the agenda – namely, Genovese's ennoblement as head of the Commission – agreed to meet again, later that week.

Genovese wanted as many out-of-state family bosses as possible to attend his investiture, so he needed someplace both inconspicuous and big. Someone suggested they phone Joe Barbara to ask if they could come back to Apalachin. Barbara wasn't well, having recently suffered a heart attack, but he told his friends that they'd be welcome. He reserved dozens of motel rooms for chauffeurs and bodyguards – explaining that they were for Canada Dry salesmen – ordered two hundred pounds of steak from his butcher, and prepared his house for a two-day conference.

At around noon on a drizzling Thursday, November 14, as gangsters from all over the country drove through rural Tioga County, Sgt. Edgar Croswell of the New York State Police was on routine patrol. One black limousine might never have caught his eye. But thirty of them heading up McFall Road to the Barbara property was too much to ignore.

Apparently Croswell had heard about the motel reservations and the order at the butcher's for steaks. He definitely knew that Barbara was a suspect in three killings. So now he called for backup. He didn't get much, only a few officers, but together they set up a roadblock to keep the cars from driving off the estate. Then, Sgt. Croswell knocked on the door to ask what was going on.

Whoever answered the door assumed that it was a raid, and a cry of "the cops are here" sent everyone scurrying. Some fled through the woods, their dapper clothes taking a beating, their expensive shoes filling with mud. Others tried to drive away, only to find themselves stopped at the roadblock. Some of those who made it to the other side of the woods were rounded up as well.

Under questioning, every one of them told Croswell they'd come to pay respects to their sick friend Joe. The fact that they all happened to be there at the same time, and from as far afield as California, the Midwest, the Southwest, Cuba, and Puerto Rico, was just a how-about-that kind of coincidence.

Although reports vary, it is generally accepted that among those caught in Croswell's net were Genovese, Gambino, his nephew Paul Castellano, Lucchese, Profaci, Galante, Sam Trafficante from Miami, Gerardo Catena and Anthony Riela from New Jersey, Frank Majuri and Louis LaRasso also from New Jersey, Russell Buffalino from upstate New York, John Scalish from Ohio, Frank deSimone from Los Angeles, Jimmy Civello from Dallas, Jimmy Colletti from Philadelphia, and Tony Accardo and Frankie Zito from Chicago. Some of those who escaped included Magaddino, Joe Zerilli of Detroit, James Lanza of San Francisco, and Sam Giancana, the Chicago gangster who would, during the 1960 presidential election, be the crime link between John F. Kennedy and Frank Sinatra.

One of the people who claims to have escaped was Bonanno. He denied getting arrested, although he admitted that he was in town that day. Anyway, his name appears on the police reports.

How many gangsters were actually there has never been established. A Senate investigation set the number at fifty-eight, which is how many were officially rounded up. Robert Kennedy, at the time a Senate lawyer, insisted that over a hundred were in town, which probably included bodyguards, chauffeurs, and anyone else whose name ended in a vowel.

Years later, Croswell would say there were 63, of whom 50 had criminal records, 35 had criminal convictions, and 23 had served time in jail. Croswell also claimed that the mobsters had more than three hundred thousand dollars in cash among them, and were dressed just as he'd imagined mobsters would be: "In expensive dark suits wearing white fedoras." He readily admitted that none of the gangsters had any reason to panic. "If they'd asked us to leave, we would have because they weren't breaking any law by having a picnic."

Known forever as the Apalachin Crime Convention, it is considered a seminal moment in the history of organized crime. When Robert

Kennedy became attorney general in 1961, he announced that organized crime was a priority of his brother's administration. The incident also forced J. Edgar Hoover to concede to Congress, "La Cosa Nostra is the largest organization of the criminal underworld in this country, very closely organized and strictly disciplined." Edgar Croswell deserves the credit for Hoover's about-face.

But it is what Apalachin exposed that really matters: a textbook model of organization, established rules of discipline, a long-term vision of international alliances, and a corporate philosophy that criminals should regularly meet to discuss their affairs and seek out joint ventures.

For that, today's transnational organized criminal groups can thank Salvatore Lucania.

Carmine Galante had just finished lunch at the long table on the patio at the rear of Joe & Mary's storefront restaurant on Knickerbocker Avenue in Brooklyn. A stifling hot Thursday – July 12, 1979 – it was 2:40 in the afternoon when he lit one of his characteristic cigars and sat all the way back in his chair.

Born in 1910 in Castellammare del Golfo on Sicily's northern coast, due west of Palermo, "Lilo" moved to New York as a very young child. He was arrested there the first time at the age of eleven for robbery and assault. A few years later he hooked up with Bonanno, who also came from Castellammare, and began making a reputation for himself as a small-time tough guy, stealing trucks and running booze.

When he was twenty, a robbery went wrong and a policeman was shot, earning Galante a twelve-and-a-half-year sentence. When he was paroled in 1939, Bonanno – now in firm control of his own crime family – brought him back into the gang. Four years later, Galante murdered Carlo Tresca, editor of the New York–based anti-Fascist Italian newspaper *Il Martello*. The contract had been put out by Vito Genovese as a favour to the man who had given him protection in Italy, Benito Mussolini. Although Galante was never charged, he was rewarded for the murder when Bonanno promoted him to *capodecina* (captaincy) within the family. A few years later he was promoted again, this time to underboss, and assigned to manage the family interests in Montreal.

Through a Canadian gangster named John "Johnny Pops" Papalia, who controlled southern Ontario from his base in Hamilton under the supervision of Stefano Magaddino, boss of the LCN family across the border in Buffalo, Galante was introduced to a small-time Calabrian-born crook in Montreal named Vic Cotroni. A friendship grew and after a time Galante brought Cotroni into the Bonanno family. When Galante was tasked with moving Luciano's heroin through Canada, Galante empowered Cotroni to reopen what had once been an old bootleg trail.

In 1963, mob soldier Joe Valachi turned informer and appeared before a U.S. Senate subcommittee investigating organized crime. It was the first time a Mafia soldier had ever violated *omertà*, the first time anyone had ever revealed the inner workings of the empire, and the first time the term "La Cosa Nostra" was used publicly. After months of testimony, interviews, and depositions, Valachi provided enough evidence to indict twenty-four Mafia members, among them Galante.

The world Galante returned to in 1974 was an unfamiliar one. Luciano was dead. Bonanno had been forced into retirement in Arizona. Although Galante was now considered to be the head of the Bonanno family, he felt he needed to reinforce his authority. He struck a deal which named Gambino "boss of the bosses," then set about orchestrating the Sicilian takeover of Montreal.

Vic Cotroni had spent much of the past decade in court. In 1963, the first of a long series of articles had appeared in both English- and French-language newspapers that publicly named him "Godfather of Montreal." Instead of disregarding the articles, Cotroni had sued. After ten years of litigation, the courts decided he had indeed been libelled. They awarded him one dollar for what had appeared in English, and another dollar for what had appeared in French.

Having taken his eye off the ball in this futile litigation, Cotroni, now in failing health, realized that the Sicilian branch of his own family was getting out the knives. He looked to another Calabrian, Paulo Violi, to be his successor. But Galante had other ideas.

Galante had always gotten along with Cotroni. Still, he felt more comfortable in the company of fellow Sicilians, and Violi didn't seem to understand much about the drug business. Or, if he did, he didn't act as if he really wanted to be in it.

First, Violi had been clumsy enough to get enmeshed in an official inquiry into organized crime in Quebec. A bug had been planted in a milk box in his office. With the cops secretly listening in, Violi had spoken openly to associates about organized crime in Montreal and their connections in the States. Then, Vic Cotroni's younger brother Frank got into trouble with the authorities, which raised further doubts in Galante's mind about Calabrians in general. Violi finally put the nail in his own coffin when he complained directly to Galante that his Sicilian partners were not keeping him informed about their drug trafficking. He said he worried that they might be dealing behind his back. He admitted to Galante that he didn't trust Sicilians.

The rising star on the Sicilian wing of the Cotroni organization – which would soon evolve into the Cuntrera-Caruana clan – was Nicolo Rizzuto. He possessed a more international outlook than Violi, having arrived in Canada from Italy by way of Venezuela. He was also less interested in loan sharking, extortion, and labour racketeering. Like Galante, he too felt that drugs was where the money was.

A rash of killings followed, eliminating Violi, his brothers, and many of their backers. Cotroni's heirs struggled to maintain their preeminence as Montreal's first Calabrian family, but Rizzuto and Galante firmly established the upper hand.

Around this time, the Americans had finally pressured the French into shutting down the connection in Marseilles, which effectively eliminated the Mafia's Corsican partners. Rather than retreat, which meant allowing the heroin trade to diminish, Galante raised the stakes by inundating the eastern seaboard with heroin.

Secretly, he deluded himself that he might one day rule the Commission.

Carlo Gambino's death in 1976 left the chair at the head of the conference table vacant. To send out the message that he was the force everyone would have to reckon with, Galante embarked on a killing spree, eliminating several rivals. He even, bizarrely, dynamited the doors off Frank Costello's tomb.

The amount of heroin Galante was importing, the fortune he was earning, the power he was taking, the way he was increasingly relying on Sicilians – soldiers imported from Italy to cut the Commission out of his business – and the killings he was perpetrating made the other bosses extremely nervous. They saw Galante as a greedy man who showed open contempt for them. So they sent him a message to stop the killings. He answered with a warning: "Who among you is going to stand up to me?" A clandestine session of the Commission was called to "rethink" Galante's position.

A few days later, the sixty-nine-year-old boss of the Bonanno family was just finishing lunch at the long table on the patio at the back of Joe & Mary's Restaurant on Knickerbocker Avenue.

It was 2:40 in the afternoon.

Just as he lit his cigar, a blue Mercury pulled up to the curb in front of the restaurant. Three men wearing ski masks jumped out. They stormed through the restaurant to the patio. Two of them had pump-action shotguns.

Lilo Galante died with the cigar still in his mouth.

Many gangland murders only prompt a cursory response from the police. Galante's turned out to be different. Not because the cops shed tears for him, but because when they lifted up the rock that was his murder they found an unexpected mass of maggots underneath. Within two days, the FBI launched what would become, at least to that point, the largest investigation in its entire history.

It had taken the Bureau several years to get to the point where they were even in a position to do that.

Valachi had confirmed what the second meeting in Apalachin had revealed, that organized crime was indeed alive and well in North America. Hoover had reluctantly come to accept that. But the FBI's Director, like so many of his right-wing conservative cronies on Capitol Hill, was still going through a weird sort of denial. Hoover and his ilk were more concerned with the war in Vietnam and the nightmarish prospect of Russian bombers suddenly appearing on Dew Line radar scopes. They still tended to write off organized crime as nothing but "a domestic problem," or a problem that affected only America, Canada, Italy, and, to some extent, Japan. It would take Hoover's death in 1972, Richard Nixon's resignation in 1974, and time for the turmoil that followed both to settle before a fundamental rethinking of FBI philosophy could bubble to the surface among the Bureau's policy-makers.

That controversy is remembered today as "the head versus tail argument."

"It was a huge debate and it was awful," recalls former FBI agent James Moody, who retired as the Bureau's chief of organized crime. "When I first came on the job, agents would be assigned to look after people by name. Some of the names may have already been identified as LCN members. If you weren't sure about a certain individual, you had to find out if he was an LCN member. Once you established he was, you had to keep track of him and find everybody he was associated with. Then you had to determine what it was he was doing and if it was illegal. If it was, you worked up a case against him. It was very difficult because you weren't investigating a crime, you were looking first at an individual and then trying to find a crime."

The FBI got to the point, he says, where they knew just about everything about everybody associated with the LCN, from the name of some bad guy's dog to the measurements of his second girlfriend. "We had a tremendous amount of intelligence. But that's all we had. Not many people were going to jail. The ones who were might be LCN members, but they were the low-level guys. We were taking out the weakest guys, and they were replacing those individuals with somebody smarter who was saying, I'm not going to do what he did. It was like culling a herd. We were taking out the weak ones and making the herd stronger."

Younger agents agreed, but many senior agents held their ground. "In the end, some FBI supervisors lost their careers over it. They were so insistent on hanging onto intelligence that they were removed from their position. It took time but we started changing. We restructured ourselves. We went after the top men knowing that the guys replacing them were not as knowledgeable or as sophisticated. It took a long time but we finally admitted that going after the tail didn't work."

Prior to the Galante killing, the FBI did not specifically investigate drug trafficking. If they stumbled across it, that was one thing, but their main target was organized crime. Now, looking into Lilo's death – thinking heads, not tails – they noticed that Sicilian Mafiosi were living in New York. The more Sicilians they saw, the more heroin they saw. Eventually, they concluded that there was a correlation.

The link that joined the two was a network of pizzerias stretching across the industrial Northeast and into the Midwest. Within a year or so, the FBI established that the Bonanno family – now headed by Salvatore Catalano – had franchised the distribution of heroin to the

Sicilians through these pizzerias and, at least in the beginning, that they were also using the restaurants to launder money.

In fact, with heroin on the menu, there was so much money being put through the tills that the LCN soon had to find other ways to wash their profits. They managed it by carting tens of millions of dollars in cash to investment houses and banks in New York, and, from there, sending the money to Italy and Switzerland. The scheme would have made a great film.

When former fish broker Sal Amendolito lived in Milan, he was involved with a guy named Sal Miniati who smuggled currency out of Italy and into Switzerland for wealthy Italians. When Amendolito moved to the States, Miniati got in touch to say that some clients were building a large resort with American investors, all of whom just happened to run pizzerias. He wanted Amendolito to help get $9 million in cash to Switzerland. Because U.S. law requires that any cash deposit over ten thousand dollars be reported to the Internal Revenue Service, Amendolito had to open accounts in a dozen banks. By slowly feeding a few hundred thousand dollars through the banks, he consolidated the balances in four other accounts, and then transferred the funds to Miniati in Switzerland. But $9 million in cash turned out to be unmanageable.

Unable to squeeze that much into the original twelve accounts, he looked beyond banks to financial investment businesses. When he arrived at a company called Finagest, carrying four small suitcases packed with cash, brokers there suggested he try Conti Commodity Services in the World Trade Center. They in turn referred him to the Chase Manhattan Bank downstairs. An officer at that branch suggested he find a bigger branch. In the end, he wound up leaving the money at Chase headquarters a few blocks away, where it was credited to a Finagest account held at Credit Suisse in Lugano.

The procedure was too haphazard for his taste and Amendolito started smuggling cash to the Bahamas. As the amounts increased, he opened an account in Bermuda. Finally, he gave up and couriered cash directly to Switzerland. Along the way, he succumbed to temptation. When someone in Sicily discovered money was missing, Amendolito vanished.

He was immediately replaced by Antonio Cavalleri, a banker who managed a Credit Suisse office in the alpine village of Bellinzona.

Through Cavalleri, the group created Traex, a company supposedly dealing in property and raw materials. Over the following few months, Swissair unknowingly flew $10 million out of New York for deposit into a Traex account at Cavalleri's bank.

Just as the gang was really getting their act together, Italian Customs stumbled across a suitcase at Palermo Airport containing $497,000. That led to the discovery of five working heroin laboratories in Sicily. The Italians mentioned it to the FBI and the Bureau now started identifying players in the States.

That's when Franco Della Torre moved to New York. As a representative of Traex, he opened an account with stockbrokers Merrill Lynch and, during the first four months of 1982, washed $5 million there. Next he opened a Traex account with brokers E. F. Hutton and, making eleven cash deposits in under ten weeks, washed another $7.4 million. Hoping to avoid undue scrutiny, he opened a second E. F. Hutton account, this one in the name of Acacias Development Company, and a further $8.2 million was funnelled through there in ten weeks. By the time Amendolito resurfaced in 1983 – he was arrested in New Orleans for fraud – the FBI were onto Della Torre. By this time, too, the Bureau had realized they needed help that could come only from Italy.

"We decided to reach out to the Italian authorities," Moody continues, "to establish a working relationship with them in order to investigate this group. But the Italian government was corrupt. Period. Hands down. It went all the way to the premier. Italian law enforcement was corrupt. Period. Hands down. The legal system was corrupt. Period. Hands down. We had to keep looking around until we could identify certain individuals we thought we could work with, both law enforcement officers and investigative magistrates. It took a long time and a lot of effort, but eventually we thought we'd found the right people. We invited a dozen or so to the United States, sat down with them, and worked out a cooperative agreement to investigate the Sicilian Mafia."

In October 1982, at the FBI training school in Quantico, Virginia, senior FBI managers met with Italians representing the National Police, the Carabinieri, and the Guardia di Finanza. Also present were senior supervisors from the DEA, the RCMP, and the Australian Federal Police. The contacts made there were soon reinforced by a second meeting, this one in Ottawa. Three men who attended both were Italian magistrates

Giovanni Falcone and Paulo Borsellino, and a young assistant U.S. attorney working out of New York named Louis Freeh.

Although their missions at home were intrinsically different because the nature of the beast they were hunting was different – in the States, the LCN was a law enforcement problem; in Italy, the Mafia was entangled with the State – Falcone and Freeh developed a close personal friendship. Through that, a bridge of mutual trust was built that would ultimately lead to the Mafia's first near-fatal setback.

With support now assured from Italy, a beleaguered team of prosecutors in New York, headed by Freeh's boss, Rudolph Giuliani, then the brash young U.S. Attorney for the Southern District, created a joint task force to take apart this heroin empire. At the same time, Falcone in Italy was turning Tommaso Buscetta. Following in Valachi's spirit, he talked for ten weeks, giving the Italians all the ammunition they needed to raid hundreds of addresses in Sicily and arrest 364 Mafiosi.

Although a few of the men on the American wanted list were in hiding, including Della Torre and a Swiss jeweller named Vito Roberto Palazzolo – he would be named as the gang's primary laundryman and would reappear many years later in a very unexpected place – Guiliani's task force still arrested twenty-eight people in four states.

The "Pizza Connection" trial charged twenty-two of them for their part in smuggling 750 kilos of heroin into the U.S. with an estimated street value of $1.6 billion. It lasted seventeen months and featured fifty-five thousand FBI wiretaps, most of them in Italian. All of the defendants were found guilty and the five Mafia ringleaders were sent away for twenty to forty-five years. The case also embarrassed Merrill Lynch, E. F. Hutton, and Chemical Bank in New York, Handelsbank in Zurich, and, especially, Credit Suisse in Bellinzona. It was the first drug-trafficking investigation in which the Feds had been able to follow the money.

More significantly, it was the first time law enforcement saw how two otherwise independent groups could come together in a joint venture. Notes William Webster, a former head of both the FBI and the CIA, "This was the beginning of our real awareness of the international character of organized crime."

Now, suddenly, a lot of people were realizing that if it could happen once, it could happen twice.

Pablo Escobar was born in Medellín, Colombia, in 1949, and grew up poor. When he died in a hail of bullets in Medellín the day after his forty-fourth birthday, he was one of the richest men in the world. He had been a minor smuggler, dealing mostly in goods stolen out of warehouses along the Panama Canal, until he drifted into the cocaine business. It was a question of being in the right place at the right time: he and his childhood friend Jorge Luis Ochoa Vasquez established an import-export company called Sea-8 Trading in Miami, then pioneered smuggling routes into the U.S. Before long, Carlos Enrique Lehder Rivas was brought into the group.

The man who prophetically described cocaine as "the Third World's atomic bomb," Lehder understood that any business needs cash flow and reinvestment to survive. While Escobar was courting the press to feed his ego and Ochoa was trying to move into Europe, it was Lehder who set up money-laundering schemes which built a huge financial base and turned the group into what the Medellín cartel would eventually become – the most powerful drug-trafficking organization on the planet.

Escobar made sure it would be remembered as the most violent, too. Over the years he blew up an Avianca airliner and assassinated four Colombian presidential candidates, a Supreme Court judge, and two dozen lower court judges. In 1992 he orchestrated a bombing campaign against government officials and rival gangs, set off three hundred explosive devices, and killed as many people. The following year he sent his men off on a rampage in which they murdered 178 local policemen.

But, there was so much money at stake in the cartel's operation that when he was originally arrested by the Colombians, Escobar bargained with the government to avoid extradition to the United States. He offered that, in exchange for protection from the Americans, he would personally pay off the Colombian national debt.

It's worth noting that Pablo Escobar was never extradited.

Gilberto and Miguel Rodriguez Orejuela grew up in Cali, in the heart of Colombia's agricultural region. Gilberto, born there in 1939, was a pharmacist by trade who once owned the Chrysler Motors franchise for Colombia. Miguel, five years his junior, was a lawyer.

They started by moving cocaine into New York in the early 1970s, then expanded to Los Angeles and Miami. For a while, their taste for gratuitous violence surpassed even Escobar's. Between them, the two cartels were killing ten to fifteen people per day. But the brothers were smarter than Escobar and brought a more sophisticated vision to drug trafficking.

Despite being known as the Cali cartel, it was never a cartel in the same sense that Escobar's group was. The brothers had the vision to distance themselves from the retail side of the business: they gave up smuggling and saw their future in wholesale. Cali was more like a main holding company that franchised out small parcels to a network of independently owned outlets. Because anybody with collateral in Colombia can become a drug dealer, the Cali cartel subcontracted to the mini-cartels. Aspiring traffickers merely had to fill out a very detailed form that listed all their relatives – so that the brothers would know who to kill if someone tried to betray them – then come up with enough cash or collateral to pay for the shipment up front. The brothers continued to buy directly from the producers, but they sold it on to these smaller groups, letting other people worry about the transport, marketing, sales, and money laundering. If cargoes were intercepted, it wasn't their product. If cash was confiscated, it wasn't their money. The deck was stacked in their favour, structured to guarantee that they couldn't lose. And yet as many as three hundred mini-cartels rushed into business with them. Almost as soon as Escobar was taken out, the Cali cartel was racking up annual profits of around $7 billion, more than three times as much as General Motors.

While the Medellín and Cali groups were monopolizing the North American cocaine market, the centre of European heroin traffic moved from Marseilles to Amsterdam. Increased drug competition in New York then forced the LCN to shift some of their operations to Chicago, Los Angeles, and Miami.

By now, the Mexicans had also entered the heroin business and quickly claimed one-third of the market share of North America.

Challenging Mexico, producers in the "Golden Triangle" – Burma, Thailand, and Laos – turned their attention to North America. They relied on various Asian organized crime groups, including Thai, ethnic Chinese, and Vietnamese groups, to handle their distribution.

Not wanting to be left out, heroin producers from the "Golden Crescent" – Pakistan, Afghanistan, and Iran – also offered product to North American distributors. Much of that product was carefully staged in Canada, stored there by Pakistani traffickers for as long as three to six months until appropriate distribution contacts could be established, then driven across the border into the United States. Nigerians were bringing heroin home to Lagos, dividing shipments into smaller parcels and using mules to bring it directly into North America. Lebanese traffickers were also setting up a base in Canada. Couriers would fly out of Toronto and Montreal to the Middle East, pick up their drugs, and transship back through Canada to the States.

Drugs created anarchy in law enforcement, on the streets, and within the traffickers' gangs. What followed in the United States and Canada, all of Europe, Australia and New Zealand, and much of the rest of the world, too, was an era of lawlessness that would make the days of bootlegged whisky and Prohibition seem tame. Worse, the narco-economy bolstered so much of the Third World that, today, dismantling it risks plunging the planet into global economic chaos and depression.

All too quickly, North America became saturated with cocaine. But as the epidemic spread, the Feds racked up a proportionate share of successes. With more traffickers to arrest, they arrested more traffickers. With more product to seize, they seized more product. While Escobar and the Orejuelas, and everyone else in the trade, were far from ready to concede that the arrests and seizures amounted to anything more than the price of doing business, it didn't take a degree from Harvard to spot greener pastures in Europe. Cocaine prices were much higher there, demand was increasing, borders were porous, and very few of Europe's national police forces ever talked to each other.

Escobar already had a minor presence in Spain, which was natural because of the shared language. But he came to understand that anyone trying to force their way into the European market would be stepping on Italian toes, and the Italians' response to that would be violent. So, instead of barging in, he went in search of a partner.

According to Italian sources, in 1987 Escobar dispatched an Italian-speaking Colombian named Edgar Procopio Hernandez Pinzon as his emissary. Pinzon was to contact certain Sicilians to secure their permission to set up cocaine laboratories in Europe. In exchange, Pinzon was to offer them easier access to product for their already-established distribution routes.

Clearly Pinzon had some success, because by the time he was arrested a year later, the Colombians had begun producing cocaine on two windy and otherwise deserted Italian hilltops. In one lab, near Savona, technicians were installed with their wives and children so that neighbours would never suspect that this was anything but a working farm.

Before shutting both labs down, Italian Customs intelligence officers took an interest in a U.S.-based Colombian named Honorio Huertas. The way they tell the story, Huertas had brokered a meeting between his handlers in Medellín and an Italian Mafia group – the Camorra is usually cited – plus one American LCN family. The subject of the meeting was said to be the ground rules for future cooperation. Huertas was subsequently arrested by DEA agents in Miami on an Italian warrant. How fruitful his meetings were has never been fully determined.

The Colombians learned a lot about smuggling from the Mafia. When one of their chemists discovered how to mix unrefined cocaine paste with cellulose to produce cardboard-like boxes, an Italian front company was set up to sell cardboard to a Colombian front company, which filled the boxes with ordinary goods that were then shipped back to Naples, where the cardboard was dissolved to produce unrefined cocaine paste.

They also taught the Colombians about money laundering. The cartel opened Universe Gold Enterprise and Symar Joyeros Mayoristas in Panama while the Mafia formed Aurea International Trading and Eurocatene in Italy. Cocaine cash was smuggled out of the United States, washed through banks in Switzerland, Spain, and Mexico, then sent to Italy, where Aurea and Eurocatene used it to buy gold bars. They shipped the gold to Universe and Symar, who sold it on with false invoices to front companies in Cali. The gold was then sold on the open market and the laundered proceeds were deposited against sales receipts.

In fact, the DEA had stumbled onto Symar, but their investigation was halted when Panama's president, General Manuel Noriega, personally intervened. The scent was picked up again in 1994, after Noriega's departure from Panama, and the Italian police put the ring under surveillance. That was the year this Mafia-Colombian collaboration moved fifteen tons of gold, a shipment of such extraordinary dimensions that for a while it accidentally depressed the world market price.

After three months of watching Aurea and Eurocatene, during which time a ton of gold a month, worth nearly $35 million, was shipped to Panama, the Italians shut down both companies. They arrested eight people, including five Italians, two Panamanians, and Gustavo Upegui Del Gado, the Cali cartel's gold expert.

Giovanni Falcone always believed that no matter what deal the Colombians swung with the Italians, it could never be a marriage, just an engagement. Any arrangement would have to be entirely on Italian terms. He knew how organized crime in Italy controlled nearly 20 per cent of all commercial activities, with interests ranging from drugs and murder to jeans and real estate. He had investigated the Mafia's control over half of the financial holding companies in the country, 20 per cent of the construction industry, and about a quarter of the food distribution business. He had seen first-hand how, despite substantial crackdowns, the Mafia continued to reach into every aspect of national life, wielding influence in every town throughout the country. In Rome, Milan, and Naples, at least half the shops, bars, and restaurants were paying protection money. In Sicily, especially in the capital city of Palermo, all of them were.

There was no doubt in his mind when he proclaimed, "The Mafia will never enter into a deal in which it can't keep the upper hand."

And yet he foresaw the formation of all sorts of alliances. "Crime syndicates are going to become the biggest beneficiaries of a free Europe." He warned, "There should be no frontiers for justice."

His words went unheeded.

Escobar's first partner was the Palermo-based Madonia family. Their first joint venture was a six-hundred-kilo shipment of cocaine from Colombia through Spain to Italy. But until Trans Americas Ventures Associates went into business half the globe away in La Jolla, California, no one quite understood the extent to which Escobar and the Mafia had gotten into bed together.

Operating out of a modern office building of red brick and glass facing the Pacific Ocean, the company was set up to be a financial counsellor. At least, that's what it said on the front door. And in a very real sense, the company did counsel its main client in financial matters. That client was the Medellín cartel, and the company's counsel was how to launder the gigantic amounts of cash they were collecting off the streets of southern California.

On the cartel's behalf, Trans Americas opened leather goods shops in Houston, Miami, Ft. Lauderdale, Chicago, and New York to import merchandise from Colombia. The shops created a legitimate paper trail, which was used to justify getting drug money into the banking system. For each ton of leather that was actually imported, paperwork was forged to show twenty tons.

The Colombians were so happy with the way Trans Americas ran their sink, they asked them to expand, first to Canada, then into the Caribbean, then to Europe. Dozens of dummy corporations were set up as part of the laundry cycle, including a wine export company and an animal-rights group, both based in Italy.

Over a three-year period, from 1989 to 1992, Trans Americas washed more than $53 million of the cartel's money across North America, through Europe, and back into bank accounts controlled by the cartel in Colombia, Panama, Switzerland, and the Cayman Islands. They also effected cash pickups in Britain, Holland, Belgium, and Italy.

While this was going on, Pinzon continued to make new friends in Italy, not just with the Sicilians but also with the Camorra and the 'Ndrangheta. The Cali cartel opened talks with all three Italian groups, too.

What none of the Colombians knew was that Trans Americas was staffed by the DEA and financed under the code name Operation Green Ice.

Undercover agents took careful notes for three years, until they could coordinate one momentous, simultaneous swoop across three continents. On September 28, 1992, police from eight nations – the United States, Great Britain, Canada, Colombia, Costa Rica, Spain, Holland, and the Cayman Islands – arrested more than 200 people, including 112 in the States, 3 in Britain, 4 in Spain, and 34 in Italy. First prize was José "the Pope" Duran, a thirty-eight-year-old Colombian cartel kingpin who'd been arrested in Rome. He was described by the Italian police as the world's most important cocaine distributor. There were dossiers on him in twenty different countries under twenty different aliases to back up the claim.

Additionally, fifteen money-laundering front companies were raided and $54 million in cash was seized, along with three-quarters of a ton of cocaine. One of those companies, an import-export firm in Mantua, Italy, was "managed" by an eighty-year-old woman with no business experience named Vera Romagnoli. Millions of dollars had passed through her company on the way, eventually, to Colombia.

Thousands of files were also confiscated on both sides of the Atlantic. Among them were computerized records taken out of a Cali cartel office that detailed their worldwide money laundering. Other documents identified a Mafia-Colombian joint venture in drug trafficking along the French Riviera and a money-laundering joint venture in Germany.

As a direct result of Green Ice, the Central Operational Service of the Italian police and the Internal Security Service of the Interior Ministry arrested the Mafia's number-two man in Sicily, plus a *capo* in the Camorra, three Sicilian brothers who'd come to be called the Mafia's private bankers, the Camorra's chief laundryman, and, in May 1993, Michele "the Crazy One" Zaza, overall leader of the Camorra. He was nabbed, along with ten members of his gang, on the French Riviera, where they had invested $1.3 billion in hotels, stores, and small industry. Another forty suspects, all tied to Zaza, were taken into custody in Italy, Belgium, and Germany. Also arrested were four men directly connected with Salvatore "Toto" Riina, head of the Corleone clan and *capo di tutti capi*.

Riina had been on the run for more than twenty years, long enough for the Italian authorities to claim they didn't even know what he looked like. Their last known photo of him was said to be for his state identity card, taken thirty years before. The truth has since come out that he'd been living all the time with his wife and children in the hills around the village of Corleone and that, clearly, he could have been found if the authorities had looked for him. After all, when they needed to find him, they did.

But it was Duran's arrest that truly startled law enforcement.

The coalitions Pinzon had forged for Escobar had been reinvented by Duran for the Orejuela brothers. It confirmed everyone's worst fears, that both of the major Colombian drug cartels had orchestrated workable strategic alliances with various factions of the Mafia.

The Colombians had effectively franchised their European cocaine and money-laundering interests. At the same time, they had taken a step towards establishing themselves as franchisees for Italian heroin in the Americas.

In March 1992, the Mafia assassinated Salvatore Lima, an intimate political ally of Italian Premier Giulio Andreotti. Lima also had equally close ties to the Mafia – to the extent that he was in their pocket – and as Giovanni Falcone advanced deeper and deeper into their territory, there was no doubt that he was making a lot of Sicilians apprehensive.

Falcone was a man determined – to the point of obsession – to end the Mafia's thirty-five-year post-war reign of terror. Around 1990 he had uncovered the Cassa Rurale e Artigiana di Monreale, a bank based in a small town near Palermo that had been laundering Mafia money for nearly twenty years. Lima had ties with that bank.

Later, pundits would say that as Falcone closed in on the bank, Toto Riina worried that Lima was the weakest link in the chain. From him, Falcone would be able to follow the money to Andreotti. He had been on the Mafia's payroll since 1968 and owed his entire political career – seven times prime minister – directly to them. Rather than allow Lima any opportunity to save his own skin by confessing all to Falcone, Riina decided he had to be eliminated.

Credence was given to that supposition when, in May, just two months after Lima's murder, the Mafia hit Falcone. He was driving in an eighty-mile-an-hour motorcade on the *autostrada* outside Palermo. A remote-controlled mine exploded under his armour-plated car. Falcone's wife and three bodyguards were also instantly killed.

Originally the media explained it away as revenge. They reported that the Sicilians got Falcone because he had put some three hundred Mafiosi in jail. Then a more complicated theory emerged, in which Falcone's success in Sicily had earned him a promotion as head of an anti-Mafia super-agency. Once in that job, Falcone might be too difficult to kill and impossible to stop. The media didn't know at the time that Andreotti had a very keen interest in making sure that never happened. But Falcone's murder was a major mistake.

The Mafia seriously misjudged the nation's patience with their gratuitous violence. The murder galvanized public opinion against them. The government immediately ordered the roundup of fourteen hundred convicted Mafiosi, many of whom were enjoying relaxed privileges such as house arrest or release on bail. At least two hundred of them were returned to prison. Politicians on Riina's payroll were unable to contain the police, and raids across the country captured more than four thousand people who were then charged with criminal activities. Soldiers were dispatched to patrol Palermo's streets. The sledgehammer approach knocked the Sicilians so far off course that before very long nearly five hundred mobsters were willing to denounce their once-cherished code of silence and exchange information for leniency.

What's more, the Mafia now had to contend with Falcone's successor, Paolo Borsellino. In July, they compounded their original mistake by murdering him and his five bodyguards.

By this point, nothing could save Riina.

The magistrate who succeeded Falcone and Borsellino went after the Cassa Rurale e Artigiana di Monreale. That inadvertently prompted the murder of Mafia businessman Ignazio Salvo, who had been especially close to Lima. But it also brought to justice other Sicilian businessmen and three bank executives. Just as Falcone had known it would, the money trail from the bank brought the authorities right to Andreotti's front door, and eventually to Riina's too.

It turns out, ironically, that Falcone was killed not because he had discovered the Lima-Andreotti-Riina union, but was linked to evidence Falcone was gathering about the Mafia-Colombian alliance. One of the last cases he'd worked on involved that six-hundred-kilo cocaine shipment from Escobar to the Madonias. Falcone discovered the Sicilians had paid for it with heroin and that several Madonia soldiers had been sent to work with the local Mafia in Philadelphia, presumably to supervise distribution of that heroin on behalf of the Colombians. A reasonable assumption is that Falcone alerted the Americans to this transaction, which would account for the fact that within hours of his murder, six FBI agents were on the first flight from Washington to Italy to help in the investigation.

Within a year, Andreotti had been thrown out of power and Riina had been tossed into jail.

Hardly two years after that, Colombian cocaine had surpassed heroin as the Mafia's primary source of revenue.

Yet, it was another event during the Green Ice years, less dramatic and therefore almost completely unnoticed, that would have even greater consequences than those four murders.

The number-three man in the Cali cartel was a violent character named José Santacruz Londono. An engineer by trade, and on the DEA's most wanted list since 1980, he had earned a reputation as a master smuggler by shipping cocaine hidden in crates of frozen vegetables from Guatemala to Miami.

In 1990, he dispatched one of his advisors, José Franklin Jurado Rodriguez, to Luxembourg. A professional money manager with a degree from Harvard, Jurado had already set up Santacruz's personal money-laundering cycle. It started with cash being deposited in a Panamanian bank and wired from there to banks in Britain, France, Holland, Italy, Germany, Monaco, Hungary, Finland, and Luxembourg. Returned to Colombia, it was funnelled through companies owned by Santacruz, his family, and his friends.

While he was in Luxembourg, Jurado got arrested.

In his pocket, he had an airline ticket to Moscow.

3

DETOUR THROUGH THE IN-BETWEEN WORLD

I am a law-abiding citizen. It is the law that makes me a criminal.

– Akwesasne Warrior

The Pizza Connection and Green Ice confirmed that the Achilles heel of the Colombian drug cartels was their need to get huge amounts of cash into the legitimate banking system.

If they could manage that, the first and most awkward step in the money-laundering process, they could then spin that money around the world, in and out of secret banking jurisdictions and across borders, eventually bringing it out the other end freshly washed, looking exactly like legitimate income.

The most widely used method to prevent organized crime groups from doing exactly that is suspicious cash transaction reporting, which requires banks to take notice of cash being deposited that might be of illegitimate origin. The result is that banks and other financial institutions protect themselves from legal retribution by over-reporting. In response, traffickers hire lawyers and accountants to represent their interests, thereby creating a state of "plausible deniability."

As long as a banker can convince himself the cash isn't suspicious – that his client isn't a drug dealer, but a lawyer – nothing has to be reported. The problem is therefore built into the solution. What's more, it's up to the banker to define the word *suspicious*.

The United States, uniquely, went one step further right from the beginning by requiring all cash transactions over ten thousand dollars be reported. And the sum is aggregated annually. If someone pays his dentist four times a year with $2,500.25 in cash, because the total exceeds ten thousand dollars in a twelve-month period, the dentist is obliged to file a report. Those reports are compiled by the Internal Revenue Service, then sent to the Financial Crime Enforcement Network (FINCEN) outside Washington, where analysts look for trends and alert law enforcement when they spot them.

Not only does FINCEN possess the most detailed database of any kind in the world, its effectiveness is manifest. Through it, analysts have traced assets in the West belonging to Iraq, Libya, and Iran, and also financial arrangements put into place linking certain suspects to the World Trade Center bombing. And yet obligatory cash transaction reporting is not the universal model for two reasons.

First, it is an extremely expensive operation to mount and to maintain. Unless the political will to do something about drug cash coming into a banking system is powerful – which, arguably, it is not in Canada, Britain, France, Germany, and throughout the Caribbean and just about all of the Pacific – there will never be a commitment to the necessary funding. Second, instead of solving the problem, more often than not it simply displaces it. Rather than deposit cash in the U.S., traffickers often smuggle it out, for deposit in jurisdictions with little or no reporting requirements.

With so much known about that first step in the money-laundering process, a small group of DEA agents in Atlanta set about trying to find out more about the next step. Operation Dinero was designed to get inside the Cali cartel's money-laundering strategy. But opening a bank and offering it to the cartels as a sink was such a radical notion that when they first proposed it, the various bureaucrats who would have to approve it immediately said no. It had never been done before. And no one knew how to go about doing it.

The DEA team in Atlanta persisted. Over the course of fifteen months, they planned, briefed, and cajoled their way up to the top of the Treasury, Justice Department, and Federal banking hierarchies. They secured the necessary permissions and funding, then went in search of a banking haven from which to operate. The island of Anguilla, a thirty-five-square-mile sandbar in the Leewards, turned out to be ideal. It was close enough to Venezuela and Colombia for the traffickers, and had the added benefit of being a self-governing British crown colony. That meant, if need be, the agents could always turn to British colleagues for help.

Next, they went in search of a bank.

Through various contacts, they located a man in California who had bought a Class B banking licence in Anguilla, the kind that allows private, secret banking, but hadn't gotten around to using it. After making him an offer he couldn't refuse, they wound up owning his licence. They established undercover identities for the agents who would be the bank's officers, outfitted an office in Atlanta, and opened a one-room office on the island, complete with a plaque on the wall and an answering machine that forwarded calls back to Atlanta. They set up subsidiaries in Singapore, in the British Virgin Islands, and on the Isle of Man. They established related offshore accounts at banks in Anguilla, Panama, BVI, Man, Switzerland, and London. They then printed brochures, stationery, and business cards, and at the end of July 1994 they put out the word that RHM Trust Bank Ltd. was open for business.

On their very first day, someone with connections to the Cali cartel called to arrange a money pickup. Within twenty-four hours they had accepted half a million dollars with instructions to wire the money around the world. Within a week, they had laundered over $3 million.

Legitimate accounts were discouraged, which is why, during the entire forty banking days they were in business, RHM serviced only six clients. But all six were tied directly to the Cali mob. Most of the money that came into the bank was routed by the undercover agents, on instructions from their clients, through Europe – mainly Britain, France, and Italy – before being brought back to Colombia or Panama.

Sometime in late October or early November, a request came into the bank from one of its clients to arrange a money pickup in Rome. Bill Malarney, the DEA agent supervising the sting, whose undercover identity was William Rice, Vice President of RHM Trust Bank Ltd., phoned the DEA's attaché in Italy, John Costanzo, about making that collection.

Costanzo, whose first language is Italian, assumed the part of Vicenzo, a freelance laundryman with contacts in Anguilla. Vicenzo's cellphone number was passed on to RHM's client. A week later, a man on the other end introduced himself as Mario and explained that he needed someone to take delivery of 1.32 billion lira, approximately $760,000. Vicenzo said he could handle that and a meeting was arranged at the Palombini Bar in the EUR area of Rome.

Surveillance teams from the Servicio Centrale Opportivo of the Italian National Police were put into place so that everything could be taped for evidence. But the man who showed up was not the man who had originally phoned. He was eventually identified as Mario DiGiacomo, and the money was hidden in an electronically controlled trap in the trunk of his car. He turned it over to Vicenzo's representatives – undercover Italian cops – and Malarney transferred it through the RHM Bank to Colombia.

The Italians, looking at DiGiacomo, were now able to establish that the Mario who had rung Vicenzo was actually a heavyweight trafficker named Pasquale Claudio Locatelli. Born in 1952 in a tiny village near Bergamo, some twenty-five miles to the northeast of Milan, Locatelli was running a small-time stolen car ring and receiving stolen goods when he discovered that there was real money to be made in drugs. It didn't take much to establish a connection for himself in Morocco (that sort of a thing is not difficult for anyone willing to risk making the trip with a pocketful of cash) and began bringing hashish and marijuana back through Gibraltar and Spain into France and Italy.

While doing that, he hooked up with some guys in the Camorra who were interested in his ability to transport product. They too were bringing drugs through Spain and France, so Locatelli added their shipments to his and, in a sense, became their moving van. Through them he met Colombian cocaine brokers and set up a connection for himself, through Morocco and Gibraltar.

Building his transport and trafficking businesses, he noticed that both of his new best friends – the Camorra and the Colombians – had mountains of cash that needed to be laundered. To accommodate them, he set up a string of shell companies in Gibraltar and Switzerland which formed the basis of a complex washing cycle. He continued selling those services to them, until he had so much of his own money going through the laundry that there wasn't any room left for anyone else.

He was arrested in Marseilles in 1990, convicted of trafficking, and sentenced to twenty years. But he had a friend with a helicopter and made a daring escape from prison, although not before getting into a shootout with the cops and killing one of them. Back in Italy, he got into another shootout, this time with the Carabinieri.

Easily convinced that life was safer in Spain, he moved to Malaga. There he oversaw his interests in supermarkets, a car rental agency, and other cash businesses, through which he laundered drug money. He also set about trying to buy a bank in Europe, which would give him access to the international banking community. But his real power lay in his ability to import huge amounts of drugs. He sold some to the Camorra, and moved the rest to France, Rumania, Croatia, Spain, and Greece. He also shipped drugs to Canada, where he soon became the major supplier for the Montreal drug-trafficking family of Pierrino DiVito and his two sons.

In one operation, Locatelli air-dropped nine tons of cocaine onto a ship off the coast of Nova Scotia. Unfortunately for him, the ship foundered in rough seas and five tons sank to the bottom.

He also lost a ship when it was intercepted by a NATO warship in the Adriatic while laden with arms – including ten thousand Russian-made machine guns plus ammunition to go with them – in a run to evade the United Nations' embargo of Croatia. It wouldn't be until much later that the Italian police realized that Locatelli had traded drugs with the Camorra, who, in turn, passed them along to a Russian organized crime group in exchange for the weapons Locatelli was selling in the former Yugoslavia.

By the time he contacted Costanzo, thinking that he was speaking with someone who could launder money for him through Anguilla, Pasquale Locatelli was a career criminal and highly successful trafficker of drugs and weapons with a major reputation that stretched across two continents. Although he was only on the fringe of the Mafia and never a full-blown member himself, he certainly had enough contacts within it to service his needs. That made him all the more dangerous. And as soon as his name came up in Operation Dinero, it elevated the bank sting from an undercover operation out of Atlanta, to an international manhunt led by the DEA in conjunction with law enforcement in Italy, France, and Canada.

Everybody wanted a piece of Pasquale Locatelli.

Needless to say, he was not an easy man to find. It took the Italians quite a while before they located him. But Malaga presented them with a number of difficulties. The town itself was small, populated only by regular residents and tourists, meaning that a bunch of Italian policemen could not just walk around without being noticed. What's more, operating in Spain meant that they had to secure permission from the Spanish national police – and also the police in Malaga – raising the possibility that word could leak back to Locatelli. After all, an international warrant had been issued for his arrest, and yet there he was in Spain, living with impunity. He had obviously paid off some important people. The Italians therefore didn't know who they could trust.

They proceeded carefully, secured the permissions they needed from the Spanish, crossed their fingers that Locatelli would not be told, and dispatched two officers to watch him as best they could for three months. Those officers reported back that Locatelli had twenty-five to thirty people working for him in Spain, that he was operating with thirty to forty different cellular phones to keep his communications secure, and that every few days he would disconnect some of his phone numbers, rotate others, give phones away, and start again with another bunch. It was very tough to intercept his calls, but every now and then they got lucky, like the time they taped him bragging that he had two thousand people working for him around the world. In Rome they still hope he was only bragging because they were never able to identify more than fifty.

Locatelli had a wife and three kids at home in northern Italy – they were separated – and a woman he lived with in Spain, with whom he had another child. Apparently, he kept sending her to health farms in the States, which left him some time for a twenty-four-year-old French girlfriend on the side. The Italians identified her as the daughter of Marc Fivet, a dealer involved with the DiVito family in Montreal.

Then Locatelli disappeared.

He left Malaga and no one knew where he had gone. The only lead the Italians had was his attorney, a short, robust man named Pasquale Ciola, who lived in Bari, the heel of the boot that is Italy. They knew that Ciola was directly connected to Locatelli's arms dealing in the Balkans, and that he was the go-between with Locatelli's businesses in Italy. So they focused on Ciola and before long picked up a phone conversation where they heard Ciola tell Locatelli that his son was going to Spain.

Immediately, special agents of the Servicio Centrale Opportivo, along with a team of electronics technicians, were dispatched to Spain to coordinate the search. Ten other agents set up a command post in Rome. Yet more agents in Italy planted a radio beeper under Ciola Junior's car, and three teams in three unmarked, specially equipped cars, with one Italian officer and one DEA agent in each, were put on Ciola's tail. One of those unmarked cars was a Porsche that the Italian police had confiscated from a drug trafficker. They watched the son load up his car, with his wife, child, and a friend (who turned out to be a magistrate who also had connections to Locatelli), then head north through Italy, west through France, and into Spain.

For two days, three cars chased after the son as he drove, sometimes as fast as two hundred kilometres an hour, to Spain. They didn't know exactly where he was headed, and at one point they lost him. In a panic, they convinced the Spanish police to send up a helicopter to locate him, which they did thanks to the radio beeper.

Instead of going to Malaga, the fellow took his family and friend to Marbella. And they stayed there, vacationing, for four days. The surveillance teams sat in the shadows, waiting. Ciola Junior didn't seem to be in any hurry. The surveillance teams soon decided that Locatelli wasn't there, and grew desperate to find him. Then, the fellow packed up his family and friend, put them in the car, and started driving home. The surveillance teams couldn't believe it.

Suddenly he turned north. Now the cops knew they were on to something. They followed him to Madrid, to a restaurant called the Adriano, where Locatelli was waiting. Before lunch even got started, the Spanish police arrested Locatelli and Ciola Junior, raided Locatelli's headquarters in Malaga, and arrested another four people there, including DiGiacomo.

At this point, Malarney back in Atlanta decided to take a shot at Ciola Senior. Everyone on the team warned him it was too late, that by having arrested Locatelli first, the lawyer would be on his guard. But Malarney argued that Ciola didn't know about the bank's connection with Locatelli's arrest and felt it was worth at least one fax.

The note to Ciola simply introduced RHM and, on the advice of a mutual friend, invited him to use the bank's services. It was a real sucker punch and Ciola fell for it. He faxed back saying he wanted to do some business.

It came just in time because word from Washington was: close the bank and end Operation Dinero. Accordingly, the team in Atlanta moved towards the takedown, coordinating simultaneous arrests in the U.S., Canada, and Italy. Ciola was among the first to get arrested.

Locatelli spent time in a Spanish cell, awaiting extradition to France, where, in early 1997, he was thrown into prison for the rest of his life. If he ever does somehow get out, there are warrants with his name on them in Italy, Greece, and Canada.

The Canadians arrested the DiVitos, father and sons, and Fivet, who now claimed that he'd been working for the French police all along. It turns out that the French had corroborated that to the Italians, but no one ever bothered to inform the Canadians. The Italians were subsequently able to identify the Colombian brokers supplying Locatelli and other people working for him all over Italy.

The final score for Operation Dinero was $110 million seized and more than a hundred people arrested.

The official story, the one the U.S. government puts out for public consumption, is that RHM Bank became too popular too fast, and that by having washed as much as $12 million for their six clients they had arrived at a point where they were becoming part of the problem. That by December 1994, Operation Dinero had accomplished what the RHM Bank had been set up to do. That the DEA had gotten a good look inside the Cali cartel's financial network and now, having managed that, it was time to shut it all down.

The official story, the one the U.S. government puts out for public consumption, is not the whole truth.

That autumn, as the bank sting got up to full speed, the DEA's undercover agents inadvertently started stepping on some important toes. At first, no one in Atlanta realized it. But by November, the people who owned those toes were quietly complaining about the RHM Bank, suggesting it should go away.

If Malarney and his fellow agents know who they annoyed, they're not saying. It is possible that they don't know, because that's the nature of these things. But they definitely got in the way of something important. The obvious candidates are the CIA and the Defense Intelligence Agency (DIA). The obvious reason is that an agency somewhere was mining a vein the agents in Atlanta had tapped into.

Their interest wasn't Locatelli. And it wasn't the bank clients tied to the Cali cartel. No, the object of whatever-agency's interest was on the periphery, minor players in Operation Dinero, but nevertheless players important enough to another agenda that someone was able to shift the government's priority away from a money-laundering investigation to interests with national security ramifications.

In the United States, intelligence agencies are specifically forbidden by law to work in tandem with law enforcement. That doesn't mean they don't, it just means they are not allowed to get caught doing it. If RHM had inadvertently, imprudently, or improperly compromised an intelligence-gathering operation by tapping into a very high level of criminal conduct, that could explain why the Justice Department suddenly decided that they were laundering too much money to justify the results they were hoping to achieve.

Enter here a place called Akwesasne.

Translated as "the land where the partridge drums" – in this case "drums" meaning "flaps its wings" – it is fourteen thousand acres stretching from Cornwall, Ontario, and Massena, New York, along twenty-five miles of St. Lawrence River channels and twenty islands to just north of Vermont. It encompasses territory that the Americans and Canadians jointly recognize as New York State, Ontario, and Quebec.

But that's not the way the St. Regis Mohawk Indians see it. One of the six tribes that make up the Iroquois Nation, they believe that the Jay Treaty of 1794, agreed by the United States and Great Britain, ceded to them a sovereign nation. They do not consider themselves citizens of either Canada or the United States. They believe that theirs is one nation inside two other nations. For them, Akwesasne is an "in-between world."

Three governing bodies operate on the reservation, which is home to around eleven thousand Native people. The St. Regis Mohawk Tribal Council is the political authority, recognized by the Americans, south of the border. The Mohawk Council of Akwesasne is the political authority, recognized by the Canadians, north of the border. The Mohawk Nation Council, which is not recognized by either, claims all of Akwesasne as one geopolitical territory. As such, they insist on the right to move across the U.S.-Canadian border without any controls, transporting goods across the border without paying taxes.

Questions of Native peoples' land rights in general, and St. Regis Mohawk sovereignty in particular, are complicated legal issues, hotly disputed and all too often overtaken by emotion. In the most simplistic terms, the Mohawk are allowed to purchase otherwise taxable items in the U.S. at non-taxed prices for personal consumption on the reservation. Trouble brews when those items are then sold, as if the reservation was one big duty-free shop, to non-Native people, or when those items are transported off the reservation for sale elsewhere.

With this huge hole in the border between the U.S. and Canada, organized criminal groups annually smuggle $1 billion worth of goods, and all sorts of other things, through Akwesasne. Law enforcement on both sides are charged by their own governments to deal with this and are permitted, by law, to go onto the reservation. However, there are very good reasons why they are often reluctant to do so.

Huge painted murals, reminiscent, in many ways, of the murals found during the height of the IRA troubles along the Falls Road in Belfast, pepper Route 37, which runs east-west through the reservation. They show Mohawk braves wearing head-dresses and covered in war paint, warning "NO FBI" and "CUSTOMS STAY OUT" and "WARRIOR SOCIETY TERRITORY."

There is such a thing as the Tribal Police. But the sixteen to twenty-three officers who make up the force are really just neighbourhood cops and not at all equipped to cope with the various connections some of their fellow tribesmen have to organized crime. Especially the Warrior Society.

This militant hard core, numbering two hundred to two hundred and fifty, are pledged to the armed defence of Akwesasne. Funded almost entirely by drug trafficking, smuggling, and other criminal activity, they stockpile enough weapons on the reservation – including automatic weapons, large shotguns, M-14 rifles, AK-47s, and Russian-made rifles – to inflict serious damage to any force short of the 101st Airborne Division.

Extensive public attention was drawn to the Warriors and the St. Regis Mohawk's cause in 1990 when they demonstrated against plans by the town council of Oka, Quebec – thirty miles west of Montreal – to extend a nine-hole golf course into a pine forest. That land was considered by the Mohawk to be a sacred burial ground dating back to the first quarter of the eighteenth century. Several claims had been laid by the tribe for reversion of rights to the land, all of which had been regularly denied by various governments.

What began on March 10 as a simple protest – a small barricade to block earth-moving equipment from coming onto the burial ground – turned sour at dawn on July 11. Just after 5 a.m., a hundred-man SWAT Team from the Sûreté du Québec (the provincial police) stormed the Mohawk camp. Firing rifles, and throwing tear gas grenades and smoke bombs, they were met by Warrior Society return fire.

A police officer was killed.

For the next seventy-eight days, in full view of seven hundred journalists, armed officers from several forces, plus a detachment of soldiers from the Canadian Forces, the Mohawk defended their rights to the area. Inside the camp, around thirty Warriors were dressed in army-issue camouflage with chest webbing, sporting AK-47 rifles and thirty-round banana clips, .357 Magnum pistols and RPK machine guns. At one point, word spread that they also had a 50mm machine gun. With them were twenty-two women and children.

Negotiations were begun, then broken off, then begun again several times. Towards the end, Warriors demanded amnesty for all their previous crimes, full recognition by Canada of Akwesasne sovereignty, and a seat at the United Nations. It wasn't until soldiers in full battle gear took up positions, surrounding the building where the Warriors were holding out, that they finally surrendered. In all, 150 Mohawk were arrested. Only 37 were charged. And only 2 were ever convicted.

The following year, the Warrior Society was one of twenty-one groups to share a $250,000 human rights award named after and presented by Libyan dictator Colonel Mu'ammer Gaddafi. That same year, a sale of nine hundred weapons was made to a group inside the tribe. Investigators eventually traced some of those weapons to drug traffickers, armed robbers, and street gangs across Canada, who used them in robberies, assaults, and attempted murders; the weapons also figured in at least seven deaths. The year after that, the Warriors purchased three hundred weapons, one of which was eventually tied to four killings. Two years later a sale was uncovered to St. Regis Mohawk of two hundred automatic weapons.

The Society has mounted a gigantic sign on the side of the longhouse at Akwesasne. It reads, "WARRIORS 1 CANADIANS 0."

The first high-stakes gambling parlour on an Indian reservation in the United States belonged to the tiny Seminole tribe in south Florida. In 1979 they opened a bingo hall in Hollywood, not far from Ft. Lauderdale. It was an instant success. The Seminoles pushed the state ban on gambling by installing poker and video slot machines. Their claim of sovereignty held up. Today the Seminoles operate a whole bunch of casinos and turn around half a billion dollars a year. Pre-tax profits are apparently running around $120 million, which is the same as after-tax profits, because the Seminoles don't pay tax.

The floodgates have opened. Today there are nearly two hundred tribes in twenty-eight states sharing in the $5 billion Indian reservation gambling boom.

But gambling is one of those industries that attracts strange bedfellows, and the idea of Indian sovereignty being a back door into legalized gambling has not gone unnoticed by a whole slew of strange bedfellows. According to the California Department of Justice, one of the Seminoles' early partners was linked to Sebastian Larocca's crime family in Pittsburgh, which, in turn, was linked to the Genoveses. It now appears that some of the seed money for that first bingo hall might have come from people controlling Meyer Lansky's funds. Categorically denied for years by the Seminoles, Chief James Billie finally acknowledged in 1999 that "there might be some semblance of truth" to the story.

The man in the middle is said to have been the late Stephen Hennington Whilden, a Nixon White House, Harvard-trained lawyer who was the first modern-age General Counsel to the Seminoles when they were bringing in gambling. He is said to have been the one who set up the meetings with Lansky's people. He is said to have been the first one to realize that the Indians were sitting on a fabulous asset called sovereignty. His line was, the tribe reserves sovereignty except where it is expressly abrogated, and therefore the tribe can do things on its land because it is a sovereign nation.

"Wherever you've got jurisdictional confusion," notes Alexis Johnson, a New Mexico attorney who has been one of the most vocal opponents of Indian reservation gambling, "you get 'the guys' surfacing. They understand how confusion works for them, how chaos is their friend. The government can't figure out what the straight line is on how to bust these guys, so they don't get busted. These are not poor Indians running casinos across the country, these are mobbed-up Indians."

As he sees it, gambling is the engine that satisfies all comers. It provides an easy way to say money is happening on tribal grounds. It's an easy way to generate revenue, to create jobs in impoverished tribal economies. But there is a natural relationship between gambling and organized crime, just as there is a natural relationship between gambling and politics. They ride together. Indian casinos allow the mob to run a gambling business in a country where gambling is supposedly controlled and limited to Las Vegas and Atlantic City, while at the same time giving the tribes money enough to buy political influence.

"You can't run a casino without all kinds of ancillary businesses," Johnson continues. "You've got to have all kinds of people who understand how to run the floor, get the employees, how to find the employees who are discreet, how to get the employees that have been buffed up and run past a couple of other regulatory bodies, how to get the limousine services to work, how to get the busses to work, how to get the comped guys here and there, who can go to whose network and launder the money, who can take the casino skim to Las Vegas or the Bahamas or the Caymans, who's got the plane. The whole thing. They need to set up an entire mechanism. All you have to do is look around to see who has that mechanism in place, who knows how to do that. Certainly not the Indians."

Although the Seminoles divested themselves of their earlier partners, they have expanded their operation offshore and own a stake in the Lightning Casino on the Dutch Caribbean island of St. Maarten. Aptly, one travel agent in the Caribbean offers a nighttime gambling package tour to the Lightning Casino, complete with fifty dollars' worth of chips, by boat from the nearby island of Anguilla, home to RHM Bank Ltd.

According to the St. Petersburg *Times* newspaper, in 1995, allegations were made in a federal lawsuit that cash was regularly being transferred by the Seminoles from the Hollywood bingo hall to the Lightning Casino. The implication was that this wasn't seed money for an investment, but that it was, presumably, money laundering. The people involved with those shipments to St. Maarten denied that the boxes they were transporting there contained cash. Nevertheless, St. Maarten is one of the more nefarious money-laundering islands and a well-established transshipment point for drugs. It is also home to the Santapaola crime family whose godfather, Benedetto, is in jail for life in Italy for his role in the assassination of Giovanni Falcone.

That is not to say that there is any relationship between the Seminoles and the Santapaolas. But it does worry some people that wherever the tribes seem to set up a business, the mob shows up nearby.

Recently, the Lightning Casino applied for a licence to open an Internet gambling site. The request was rejected by the Dutch Ministry of Justice. Apparently they didn't like some of the management involved. In response, the Seminoles started looking for another Caribbean base to set up an Internet gambling site, and St. Kitts has been mentioned – yet another island with a reputation for money laundering, drug transshipment, and organized crime. There are already several dozen Internet casinos up and running on the World Wide Web, scattered all over the world, including one fronted by singer Kenny Rogers. Another appears to be based in Australia, although it may not be.

What you see in cyberspace is not always what you get.

The first Indian Internet casino was established by the Couer D'Alene tribe in Idaho, and their Internet bingo game is said to be worth $45 million a year. Even the St. Regis Mohawk are looking for someplace to run an Internet casino. The State of New York would claim that it is illegal for anyone within the State's jurisdiction to gamble that way, but claiming illegality and enforcing State law in cyberspace are two different things.

The beauty of such an operation is that it doesn't take more than a dozen people to keep it running twenty-four hours a day. Also, because money is electronically transferred between players and the casino, it can be banked anywhere, without the government ever finding it. In 1999, Internet gambling revenues were hovering in the $500 to $600 million region. By 2002, one estimate suggests, they will reach $10 billion. By 2005, that figure could easily double, and double again two years after that. The criminal potential in all of this is staggering, to the point that it easily satisfies the wildest dreams of any organized crime family.

"Indians are cover," insists Johnson. "Indians are a geopolitically significant description. Cross out Seminole. Cross out Mohawk. Just talk about stuff. What Indians resemble is transnational stuff. Geopolitical stuff. What do they look like? They look like tax havens. They look like the on-shoring of an offshore concept. They look like law enforcement breakdowns, and we know, axiomatically, they involve jurisdictional conundrum and jurisdictional confusion. Most tribal leaders aren't as smart as the real bad guys, although there seem to be some. Look at the political liaisons, and the lobbying and the lawyering, that's how the deals get brokered. There is always a non-Indian involved somewhere."

In Akwesasne, his name is Larry Miller.

A stocky, chain-smoking, sunburned, middle-aged guy with silver hair, Miller was a Las Vegas–based businessman who had a slot machine business and also owned the Massena Club, a nightclub on the edge of the St. Regis Mohawk reservation. His relationship with the tribe was anchored in his friendship with a fellow named Tony Laughing, who, the year before the incident at Oka, was running Tony's Vegas International Casino at Akwesasne.

There had been a heated debate which split the Native people on whether or not to allow gambling. The success of the Seminole bingo hall had created a huge bandwagon, but jumping on board did not please everyone. At one point, the pro-gambling forces at Akwesasne, supported by the Warrior Society, got into a nightmare of a gun battle with the anti-gambling forces. It was a firefight reminiscent of the war in Vietnam, complete with automatic weapons and tracers marking night skies.

On another evening, when police came onto the reservation to close Laughing's casino – claiming he was in violation of state and federal laws – armed Warriors lined up to stare down the police. Laughing later admitted that he had purchased the assault weapons they had used to protect his business and subsequently made several donations to the Warrior Society.

Among Laughing's Mohawk friends were L. David Jacobs, Chief of the St. Regis Mohawk from 1988 to 1994, who turned out to be his partner in a reservation-based extortion ring; and John "Chick" Fountain, a retired New York State Trooper, who left the force in 1983 with twenty-one years' service to run Fountain Financial Security Services – an armoured-car cash-delivery business – and the Northern Currency Exchange.

Among Miller's partners were the Tavano brothers, Lewis and Robert Sr., with whom he shared the slot machine business, and a company called LBL Importing – as in Larry, Bobby, and Lewis – which imported and distributed cigarettes to Indian reservations.

Robert Tavano had once been chairman of the Niagara Falls Republican Party. But in 1976 he was convicted of insurance fraud after stealing four hundred thousand dollars' worth of premiums from the county and served seventeen months of a five-year sentence. When he got out, he started a travel agency. Louis Tavano also had an arrest record. He'd been nabbed in the 1970s on gambling charges, along with the local godfather, Stefano Magaddino. The case was thrown out because the judge ruled the federal wiretaps were illegal. It nevertheless established that through Magaddino, Tavano had a relationship with the "Johnny Pops" Papalia crime family in Hamilton, Ontario – the same Johnny Pops who introduced Carmine Galante to Vic Cotroni.

Tavano also had a business relationship with the Seneca tribe of western New York State, and through that there are links to a Buffalo-based company that used to be called Emprise. Now known as Delaware North, and by its chairman's insistence totally clean of its previous reputation, Emprise was in the coin-operated concession business at sports facilities, such as race tracks. In 1972, the company was busted on racketeering charges, having fronted for several organized crime figures. There were allegations that Emprise had links to the Detroit mob. There were allegations that Tavano had connections with Detroit. From there, both can logically be linked to Las Vegas gambling interests.

Re-enter Larry Miller.

Understanding the geographic advantage of Akwesasne, he couldn't believe his luck when the Canadian government decided they could prevent young people from smoking by dramatically raising the tax on cigarettes and tobacco. From 1984 to 1993, federal taxes on cigarettes in Canada rose from 42 cents to C$1.93 per pack. Provincial taxes also increased. In Quebec, for instance, they went from 46 cents to C$1.78, and in Ontario from 63 cents to C$1.66.

Referred to in smugglers' jargon simply as "the trade," Miller and his cohorts set up an elementary scam. Cigarettes were exported from Canada tax-free and shipped in bond to warehouses on the U.S. side of the reservation. Invoices were drawn up to show that the cigarettes had been exported to some far-off place, avoiding any U.S. tax obligation, when in fact they were smuggled back to the Canadian side. Sold by the smugglers at high markups, they were still cheaper than cigarettes with the government tax added.

The simplicity of it and the ease with which the cigarettes could be taken back into Canada not only encouraged the smugglers, but made many of them multi-millionaires. Profits were running as high as C$500 per case, which translated to C$500,000 per truckload. In 1989, around half a million Canadian-manufactured cigarettes were legally exported tax-free to New York State. Within four years, that figure had risen to twenty billion. By then, one in three cigarettes being smoked in Canada was reportedly contraband. Cigarette smuggling has always been considerably less risky than drugs, but now – at least for a while – it was also more profitable than drugs.

A large portion of the cigarettes Miller and company were exporting tax-free to the States was a brand called Export 'A'. Its customer base was Canadian; the brand had never been very significant in the U.S. The reason so many were soon being exported was because Miller had been introduced to the right people by the Tavano brothers.

To handle the massive flow of cigarettes being exported, parent company RJ Reynolds of Winston-Salem, North Carolina, set up a subsidiary of RJR-Macdonald of Canada – owners of Export 'A' – called Northern Brands. The parent company then appointed one of their own senior executives, Les Thompson, specifically to market cigarettes to Akwesasne.

His major clients were Miller, the Tavanos, Laughing, and Fountain.

Miller would later claim that the Tavanos also introduced him to Stan Smith, executive vice president of RJR-MacDonald; that in several meetings with Thompson and Smith, the word *smuggling* was frequently used; and that RJR-MacDonald knew full well that the cigarettes they were selling to him at Akwesasne were being brought back illegally into Canada.

Miller bought himself a corporate jet and commuted between his homes in Massena and Las Vegas. He also started spending time in Moscow.

And this is where the plot thickens.

According to an RCMP affidavit, Miller paid $22 million to buy the Beverly Hills Casino near Red Square. His partner in that deal is listed as movie star Chuck Norris.

With so much money to be made, and consequently so many cigarettes crossing the border, "the trade" soon got to the point of being nearly out of hand. As Miller claimed at the time, "You could stand on the river and watch them load the boat with cigarettes stacked up above their head, right out in the daylight." In fact, it reached such a frenzied point that smugglers were even bringing American cigarettes into Canada, stamped with the U.S. Surgeon General's health warning instead of the Canadian Government's health warning.

Eventually, Prime Minister Jean Chrétien realized he had no other choice but to cut the cigarette tax by a drastic C$1.17 per pack. That dried up a lot of trade. But not all of it.

Reacting immediately to maintain his operation, Miller held a meeting at the Sonora Lodge, on the Campbell River in British Colombia. His guests were Louis Tavano, Les Thompson, and supposedly Stan Smith. His bill at the resort, which is accessible only by air and where rooms can start at C$1,000 a night, is said to have come to C$310,000. And again, he later claimed, the word *smuggling* was frequently used.

Since that meeting, and for the next two years, Northern Brands sold tax-free Export 'A's to Miller, through two companies in New York State, one of which was LBL Importing Inc. Papers filed with U.S. Customs by those companies stated that the cigarettes were on their way to Estonia and Russia. Instead, they were stored in one of several prefab warehouses that dot the reservation along the river, until they could be moved north again.

In the warmer months, that meant being ferried by boat across the

St. Lawrence, usually at Cornwall Island. In the winter months, that meant being taken by snowmobile.

Once on the other side, the Akwesasne gangs handed off the contraband to non-native organized crime gangs, including Asian and biker gangs such as Hells Angels, who, as wholesalers, distributed the goods to the black-market outlets. It all too soon became evident that Miller, the Tavanos, Laughing, and Fountain were not the only people involved.

A man named Michael Bernstein, who was a regional account manager for Brown & Williamson – which is the U.S. sister company of Canada's Imperial Tobacco, both of which are owned by British American Tobacco (BAT) – was convicted in 1997 of smuggling cigarettes into Canada from Louisiana. Bernstein has been reported in the press as telling authorities that Imperial Tobacco executives oversaw the smuggling process. None of the companies has yet been charged with being a party to Bernstein's smuggling.

Nor was BAT ever charged with being part of the smuggling operation put together by Canadian Jerry Lui King-hong, at one point export director for BAT in Hong King, who was found guilty of smuggling C$7 million worth of cigarettes into mainland China. In that case, another BAT employee had agreed to testify against Lui. But before he could appear in court, he was found floating in Singapore harbour, stuffed in a laundry bag with his mouth taped shut.

Then again, cigarettes were not the only item being smuggled across the border through Akwesasne. Alcohol was being moved across too, in a mirror tax-dodge scam.

To supply their clients, Miller and the others were bringing whisky up to Akwesasne from several out-of-state locations, mainly Maryland and Virginia but also from as far away as California and Oregon. At the end of 1998 a wholesaler in Santa Barbara was charged with shipping half a million cases of alcohol to Akwesasne, worth about $24 million. Their business partner on the other side of the border was Johnny Pops Papalia.

Laughing, who'd already collected convictions for illegal gambling and resisting arrest, including an assault on U.S. Customs inspectors, was so blatant about this smuggling operation that he once allowed a Canadian television news crew to film it. He has since declared that he and six other Mohawk sold six hundred thousand cases of tax-free liquor to Canadians in 1994 alone, making an average profit of thirteen dollars per case. That comes to $7.8 million.

Needless to say, federal, provincial, and state law enforcement do what they can, but except for the occasional very large bust, it isn't much. The Canadians estimate they seize less than 5 per cent of the goods going through Akwesasne. The Americans, hardly more optimistic, say they get at best 10 per cent.

In late March 1996, the RCMP arrested 170 people after a series of raids aimed at putting a dent in Akwesasne smuggling. They nabbed St. Regis Mohawk, members of a Montreal-area chapter of Hells Angels, organized Vietnamese criminals and Chinese immigrants. They also seized $15 million worth of liquor, cigarettes, cars, and other property. It was their biggest bust to date.

The following night, smugglers were crossing the river again.

A year or so later, a joint task force of RCMP, Tribal Police, the U.S. Border Patrol, the New York State Police, and U.S. Customs raided several locations on the reservation. This time, they hit right at the heart of the Miller-Tavano-Laughing-Fountain cabal.

Announcing that they had cracked a $700 million smuggling ring – one agent described it as "bigger than Al Capone" – they charged twenty-one people with conspiring to defraud the U.S. and Canadian governments. Included were Miller, the Tavanos, Laughing, Fountain, and former chief Jacobs. The two governments also seized alcohol, cigarettes, cash, two of Fountain's armoured cars, three of Miller's boats, two of Miller's homes in Massena, five other homes, parcels of land in Las Vegas, and a pickup truck.

Jacobs was charged under the Federal Racketeer Influenced Corrupt Organizations (RICO) statute with running the tribe as a criminal enterprise. In partnership with Laughing, who was also charged under RICO, the two had been extorting tribal businessmen with gambling interests. Jacobs also admitted that he took kickbacks worth three thousand dollars from Larry Miller for every tractor-trailer load of contraband that Miller moved through the reservation, earning around two hundred thousand dollars. Additionally charged with smuggling and money laundering, he copped a plea.

So did Laughing. His profits on liquor and cigarette smuggling were said to be in the area of $550 million. Faced with so much evidence against him, Laughing agreed to serve eight years and pay a half-million-dollar fine. The Tavano brothers pled guilty for their role in smuggling and the laundering of $50 million. So did Fountain, through whose company much of the money was laundered. So did Larry Miller, who accused RJR-Macdonald of providing him with information on what types of cigarettes were selling in Canada, and therefore co-operating with him in an illegal activity. He admitted to moving about six thousand cases of Export 'A' cigarettes a week, but swore, "The tobacco company knew that the cigarettes they sold me would be smuggled."

At first, RJR denied it. Then they refused to comment. By December 1998, they had seen the writing on the wall, or more accurately, indictments coming down from the Grand Jury, and caved in. U.S. Attorney Tom Maroney announced that Northern Brands International admitted to aiding and abetting others in the avoidance of U.S. excise taxes – specifically taking responsibility for twenty-six truckloads of cigarettes that they'd falsely claimed were destined for Estonia and Russia – and agreed to forfeit $10 million, in addition to paying a $5 million fine.

In addition to cigarettes and alcohol, plenty of Southeast Asian drugs have been coming through the reservation.

Landed in Vancouver by Asian organized crime groups, they are transported across Canada by various outlaw motorcycle gangs, delivered to Akwesasne, taken across to the U.S. side, then handed off to organized crime groups, including other outlaw motorcycle gangs and Asian traffickers.

There is also a thriving market in weapons going in both directions across the border, and being warehoused on the reservation. One story has it that semi-automatic weapons, purchased in the U.S., are smuggled across the border to Canada, where they are converted into fully automatic weapons, then brought back onto the reservation. Another story has it that there is a connection between IRA weapons and the reservation, although investigators who have looked into it have never been able to prove it.

Counterfeit U.S. hundred-dollar bills have been showing up at Akwesasne since 1994. The phony money came from organized Lebanese criminals who passed the notes off to street gangs, which used them to purchase weapons at Akwesasne.

There is a brisk trade in Cuban cigars, both real and counterfeit, Iranian carpets – which are on the U.S. Customs embargo list – various prohibited agricultural products, animals, and skins, and stolen vehicles.

Cars taken off the streets in Canada are driven through the reservation to U.S. ports such as Newark, where they are loaded onto ships bound for the former Soviet Union. There is a definite Russian organized crime connection, which has really taken hold only in the past few years.

"When we send these Native Americans to jail," explains Jeremiah Sullivan, the special agent in charge of the U.S. Customs office in Buffalo, New York, which has responsibility for the U.S. border area that includes Akwesasne, "they interact with all sorts of criminals. They meet members of Russian organized crime groups and traditional organized crime groups. Whoever they interact with in prison, they do business with as soon as they get out."

He says that, in many ways, the service those St. Regis Mohawk smugglers have on offer is really no different from any ordinary moving van business. "They get paid for carrying boxes. In some cases they may not even know what's in the boxes. Anybody who needs someone to smuggle something knows about them. There's a lot of interest out there in what the St. Regis Mohawk have to offer. One smuggler in Oregon, on the other side of the country, once told us, 'All roads lead to Akwesasne.'"

They certainly seem to, even from as far away as Moscow.

A U.S. federal law enforcement informant in a major car-smuggling investigation recently told investigators during a debriefing that he'd been approached by some former KGB officers now involved with a Russian organized crime group. They wanted him to find out what security was like from Buffalo to the Vermont border, what resources the Border Patrol had, what resources U.S. Customs had, what resources the Canadians had, and how often active patrols came through.

Roads definitely lead to Akwesasne from Fujian Province in China.

The Chinese refer to the United States as "Gold Mountain," a promised land where many people hope to join relatives already established and begin a new life. Recruiters in Fujian working for Asian organized crime gangs offer just that possibility. For a 10-per-cent down payment of the total fee, which has been running at a staggering forty-seven thousand dollars, anyone signing on to make the gruelling trip is provided with counterfeit documents that will get them out of China and, eventually, into Canada.

The most popular port of entry is Vancouver, where the aliens, following a prepared script, ask for political refugee status. Canadian Immigration officers, following set procedures, provide them with dates for a hearing. The aliens are then moved by the gang – referred to as "snakeheads" – to safe houses in Toronto and Montreal, where they are stored like packaged goods in a basement until nightfall. They are then trucked to the Canadian side of the reservation, where Mohawk guides get the people to the U.S. side, always at night and often under hazardous conditions.

From the south side of Akwesasne, it is a seven-hour van ride to New York City. In certain instances, aliens have been asked to pay instalments of their overall fee at every staging point. If they can't, or if their relatives back home don't wire the money on time, they are abandoned. In other cases, any monies due once they reach New York are paid off, with interest, through forced labour in garment industry sweatshops, restaurants, or brothels.

For many, it is not only an expensive and dangerous adventure, it can also end in failure or, for some, in death. Granted, it may only be a small percentage who get caught, but those who do are thrown into jail and eventually deported. Or, as has happened all too frequently, something goes wrong, like the time the rubber raft transporting a load of Asian aliens sunk in the St. Lawrence and some of the group drowned. Or the time when an elderly woman died of hypothermia. Or the time when a mother accidentally smothered her eight-month-old child while hiding it under a blanket.

Less frequently, there is the arrest of a snakehead. On one occasion, the Border Patrol realized they'd captured the same man for the third time. Each time, he'd produced different identification bearing a different name. He was taken to court, where a judge demanded thirty-five thousand dollars' bail. Under police escort, the man was driven to his motel room, where he produced enough cash to be set free. He hasn't been seen since.

The big money in alien smuggling goes to Asian organized crime.

The Mohawk guides are sometimes paid as little as fifty dollars per person. At other times they may earn as much as $500 to $750 per load, transporting anywhere from eight to twenty-four aliens. But then, the way they see it, they are simply moving packages.

It took a year-long investigation on both sides of the border to seriously disrupt this particular group. And in December 1998, thirty-five people associated with it were arrested, with warrants issued for another twelve. Of those arrested, twenty were ethnic Chinese, eight were Mohawk.

The ring was believed to have been bringing 150 aliens through the reservation each month and to have been in operation for at least two years. Using the figure of forty-seven thousand dollars, which was released by the U.S. Justice Department in a press conference after the bust, that would mean the gang brought thirty-six hundred aliens into North America and made $170 million doing it.

At that same press conference, the Immigration and Naturalization Service drew a map of the various routes used by the gang. Not all of the aliens, it turns out, travelled on the most direct itinerary. Some were flown from Fujian to Taiwan or Hong Kong and on to Vancouver. Others were taken via Germany, France, Morocco, Greenland, Cuba, or Brazil, before being put on a flight to Toronto or Montreal.

Oddly, while eleven different law enforcement agencies in the U.S. and Canada managed to coordinate a complex investigation into this Fujian–Akwesasne pipeline, they couldn't seem to agree on a name for it. The Americans called it Operation Over The Rainbow II. The Canadians dubbed it Project Othello.

Unfortunately, it's not just illegal aliens from China who are coming through the reservation. More sinister is the traffic in terrorists.

The Canadian Security Intelligence Service has admitted, "Most of the world's terrorist groups have established themselves in Canada, seeking safe haven, setting up operational bases and attempting to gain access to the U.S.A."

Over the past few years several terrorists have been caught. In January 1996, for instance, two vans came across the border on the western end of the reservation. The Border Patrol just happened to have officers in the area, and they stopped one of the vans. Inside was an Algerian, three Pakistanis – who were all Canadian citizens – and one Lebanese gentleman who turned out to be a suspected terrorist. The Border Patrol informed the FBI, who took charge of the five and drove them off somewhere.

No one involved with the original arrests has ever heard about the incident again. And the not-to-be-attributed story from the FBI is, "It happened . . . but, well, it didn't happen."

Over the summer of 1998, three Egyptians with ties to a terrorist organization were picked up by a roving patrol on Route 81 north of Syracuse, having come through the reservation with counterfeit visas that have since been traced back to the British embassy in Cairo.

Around the same time, it is known that law enforcement officers on both side of the border spent three panic-struck weeks searching for a box that was believed to have come through the reservation and into the United States. The best any source will reveal is that it contained some type of "NBC" – a nuclear, biological, or chemical weapon.

If it happened, no one is willing to say whether or not they ever found it.

Rumours have also circulated that the triggering device for the World Trade Center bomb came through the reservation.

If it's true, no one is willing to admit it.

"There is always a Larry Miller type, a non-Indian, involved somewhere," Alexis Johnson says. "Laughing and Fountain are the worker bees. They're part of a network. To understand what's going on throughout the country, you've got to understand the lawyers and the lobbyists. There are some very serious people behind the Indians because this is about big, big money. To have created the jurisdictional breakdown that we see today, you've got to have a serious legal infrastructure in Washington, D.C. The Indians couldn't have pulled it off on their own. What's the probability of the RJR episode just having been a bunch of Indians doing their thing? The answer is some function approaching zero."

None of it could have happened, he says, without the tribal veil of sovereignty. "That's used to say stay away, don't look at us, we get to do what we want because we say so. It's a mask for the Larry Millers of the world. He gets to hide behind the Anthony Laughings and David Jacobs whom he can trot out as Indians. Miller can then do whatever he wants because he's doing it in something that resembles an island in the stream of North America, a tax haven, a jurisdictional confusion zone, a jurisdictional breakdown zone, a place of great confusion, and a duty-free shop. It's about transshipment. It's Isle of Man-ing going on in New York. That's what Indianness is in the U.S. today."

Coinciding with the various busts at Akwesasne came the news that the St. Regis Mohawk were attempting to move their casino rights away from Mohawk ground down to the Catskill Mountains, ninety miles north of New York City.

The tribe wants the U.S. Department of the Interior to take the land in trust for them, which would make a 235-acre tract next to Monticello Raceway in Sullivan County official Mohawk territory, with all the sovereignty that implies, simply for the purpose of opening a casino there. One of the companies that is getting into the deal with the tribe is based in the Bahamas, which means no one can be totally sure who's involved and precisely where the money has come from.

Scoffs Johnson, "Do you really think the idea of a land trust is the Indians'? Come on, this is Washington lawyer talk. A bunch of guys sat down and tried to figure out what to do. They looked at a map and said, what's America's weakest point? Tribal grounds. Lansky's guys figured out this tribal breakdown a long time ago."

Apparently, so did a few people who popped up in Operation Dinero.

Within days of RHM's opening, a courier delivered a corporate cheque in the amount of $676,353 to be deposited into the account of a Cali cartel laundryman named Luis Eduardo Velez-Arias. It had been drawn by a company in Fairlawn, New Jersey, called Compulinx Inc. and was signed "Natalya Kaminer."

A records check revealed that the officers of Compulinx Inc. were Gregory and Natalya Kaminer and that they were associated with two companies, Janus Electronics and Calimont Capital Corporation, that were owned and/or managed by Betty and Benjamin Marcovitch. The DEA had long suspected the Kaminers of being involved with established money launderers in Newark, New Jersey. They'd also suspected the Marcovitches of being involved with money laundering and drug trafficking, their names having cropped up through investigations in New Jersey, New York, Miami, and Colombia.

Betty Marcovitch was Colombian, her maiden name being Rios-Valencia. The other three were of Russian birth.

On the same day that Velez-Arias's representatives took delivery of that cheque for $676,353, Marcovitch – who claimed he was an oil company executive – deposited $666,040 in cash in a Compulinx account at the Citizens First National Bank of New Jersey in Ridgewood, New Jersey.

The bank duly filed a Cash Transaction Report (CTR) with the Internal Revenue Service. Within a few weeks, by the time the processed report reached FINCEN, analysts noticed that it was the seventh CTR accredited to Marcovitch in just about two years. When questioned by bank officials, Marcovitch is said to have told them that the money was owned by Calimont Capital, an import-export business, and that he was its chief executive officer.

Five more deposits quickly followed, totalling just under $460,000.

FINCEN's analysts then noticed that Kaminer, during that same five-week period, had also been the subject of Cash Transaction Reports for several deposits. The first was for $187,000 put into a Compulinx account in New Jersey, followed by a second for $71,380, and a third for $457,464 put into the New Jersey Compulinx account. In addition, he'd deposited four cashier cheques of less than $10,000 each drawn on banks in Montreal.

Investigators were able to establish a large number of phone calls placed from the Marcovitches' Manhattan apartment to numbers in Bayonne, New Jersey, belonging to Anthony Gallagher. A convicted felon who, at the time, was operating a cheque-cashing service, Gallagher has ties with the Genovese family.

An association of any kind that somehow tied Russians, like the Marcovitches and Kaminer, to someone involved with the LCN, while all the time also being associated with Colombians, was precisely the kind of thing that piqued interest.

Soon even more fascinating associations came to light. On September 30, 1994, a cashier's cheque arrived at RHM Bank Ltd. to be deposited into the Velez-Arias account for $995,100. It was drawn on the First National Bank of Northern New York in Massena. Five days later, a second cashier's cheque for $304,551 arrived, also drawn on First National.

This was during a time when Chick Fountain, through Fountain Financial Security Services and his Northern Currency Exchange, was shipping "truckloads of cash" from Massena to Canada. In fact, the Royal Bank became so suspicious at the amount of money coming out of Akwesasne – reliably believed to have been $250 million over a fifteen-month period – that they took it upon themselves to notify the RCMP.

Another link was opened when investigators located a fax that was a copy of a bank wire transfer written in Russian. It translated to reveal that on August 10, 1993, one hundred thousand dollars were wired from the Promstroi Bank in Russia to an account in New York on behalf of Calimont Capital.

Investigators now looked at yet another Marcovitch company, this one called Privat Capital Inc.

A secret "briefing paper" on Operation Dinero notes that the DEA, FBI, and IRS had all been investigating a sophisticated money-laundering operation in the New York area headed by two individuals of Russian extraction who were laundering millions of dollars in the northeast U.S. and Canada. It goes on to say that further information had been developed that suggests, "The New York targets have extensive business dealings within Russia and one is supposedly a former KGB operative who is using his connections within Russia in the money-laundering scheme."

All this time, Larry Miller of Massena, New York, was going back and forth to Moscow to oversee his business interests and casino there.

When the crunch came and RHM was taken down, the Marcovitches and Gregory Kaminer were arrested in Montreal. They waived extradition and were charged in New York: the Marcovitches on four counts of money laundering and two counts of conspiracy, Kaminer on four counts of money laundering and one count of conspiracy.

But unlike almost all of the other people caught in the Dinero sting, these three were not charged federally. Instead, and unusually, they were charged under the laws of New York State. What's more, they waived their right to a jury trial. That, in and of itself, is not rare, but where complex financial dealings are concerned, defence lawyers often prefer to take their chances with a jury – whom they can more easily confuse – than a judge who might understand what the machinations were all about.

The case was heard in New York City, and, despite what the DEA and the District Attorney's office believed to be a mountain of evidence against them, they walked.

All three were found not guilty by the judge on all counts. The judge then ordered that all of the evidence against them, plus trial transcripts, be sealed.

Whatever the relationship might have been between the Marcovitches, Kaminer, and Larry Miller – and anyone else at Akwesasne – is something that a few people in Washington truly do not want anyone else to find out.

4

THE BIG STING

They were too busy washing money to care about the cameras.

– Yvon Gagnon, RCMP

Officially it was called "Operation 90-26C," but the main part of it got called "Projet Compote," which was the French name, although they used that as the English name too, even though it wasn't nearly as romantic as the translation, "Operation Applesauce."

It all came about as the result of a failure.

For the last three years of the 1980s, drug money was gushing through Montreal's many *bureaux de change* in staggeringly huge amounts. Information was also regularly coming in to the Mounties from the Drug Enforcement Administration and U.S. Customs that cheques issued by money exchanges in Montreal were showing up in their money-laundering investigations, specifically in Panama.

Canada's stature as an integral part of the world's drug-money-laundering cycle had been growing for years. Now, from their high-rise offices in Westmount, RCMP officers in the Anti-Drug Profiteering Section couldn't help but think that the country's reputation was dangerously close to America's caricature of Canada as "the Maytag of the north."

It was time, they decided, to target those *cambios*, to disrupt the money-laundering cycles of Canada's major traffickers. One man in particular who'd been in their sights for a very long time was Pierrino DiVito, an old-fashioned Mafioso drug dealer. Well connected with the mob throughout Canada, his name kept popping up in all those foreign investigations. They launched an undercover operation that managed to turn someone inside a *bureau de change*, and with their informant's help, over a twenty-six-week period in 1989, they tracked more than $52 million. But everything fell apart when, at the last minute, the informant refused to testify.

Getting to DiVito was now impossible. And twenty-four hundred kilos of cocaine had been imported while they sat around and watched. But the Mounties didn't exactly walk away empty-handed. They'd identified around twenty different criminal organizations that depended on these money exchanges. It was now more apparent than ever that the way to attack the traffickers was through the *bureaux de change*.

Without their informant, however, the Mounties reckoned they only had two options. They could try to find another informant – and even if they did, there was no guarantee that this time it wouldn't also end in tears with no one willing to testify – or they could become money launderers themselves.

Which is how Sgt. Yvon Gagnon, RCMP, became Yvon Richard, laundryman.

Money laundering is sleight of hand, a magic trick for wealth creation. It is the lifeblood of drug dealers, fraudsters, smugglers, kidnappers, arms dealers, terrorists, extortionists, and tax evaders. It is perhaps the closest anyone has ever come to alchemy.

According to myth, the term was coined by Al Capone, who used a string of coin-operated laundromats scattered around Chicago to disguise his revenue from gambling, prostitution, racketeering, and violation of the Prohibition laws.

A nice story, but fiction.

It's called "laundering" because that perfectly describes what happens – illegal, or dirty, money is put through a cycle of transactions and comes out the other end as legal, or clean, money.

Interestingly enough, it wasn't until 1973 that the term "money laundering" actually appeared in print for the first time. It was during Richard Nixon's 1972 presidential campaign. Four cheques – illegal contributions totalling $89,000 – were made payable to a Mexico City lawyer. He in turn forwarded the money to Miami, where it was deposited into the bank account of a local real estate salesman named Bernard Barker. He withdrew the money as cash and handed it over to Nixon henchmen Maurice Stans and John Mitchell.

It was a thoroughly amateurish scheme. Today, there are as many methods of washing dirty money as there are villains with dirty money to wash. Yet four factors remain constant in the process.

First, the ownership and source of the money must be concealed. There's no sense laundering money if everyone knows who it belonged to and where it originated when it comes out the other end.

Next, the form it takes must be changed. No one wants to wash $3 million in twenty-dollar bills only to wind up with $3 million in twenty-dollar bills. Changing the form also means reducing the bulk, which is a real problem with drug dealers and their street cash. A $1 million stack of hundred-dollar bills stands over five feet high and weighs more than twenty-two pounds.

Third, the trail left by the process must be obscured. This is what Stans and Mitchell thought they were doing. And this is where "Deep Throat's" advice to Bob Woodward and Carl Bernstein of the *Washington Post* – "follow the money" – led back to the Oval Office.

Finally, constant control must be maintained over the process. There are plenty of people looking to steal illegal cash knowing that there's little the original owner can legally do about it.

That said, there are three distinct stages to the washing cycle.

The first is immersion. A drug dealer who amasses $5 million in cash might have a million or more pieces of paper to put into the banking system. He wants to consolidate the stash, making it as small as possible. He then relies on bank accounts, postal orders, traveller's cheques, and other negotiable instruments to funnel the cash into the world's financial system as fast as possible.

The second step is heavy soaping. This is where the laundryman disassociates the money from its illicit source. By moving it through as many accounts as he can – in and out of dummy companies that he's set up around the world for just this purpose – and by relying on bank secrecy and attorney-client privilege to hide his own identity, he creates a complex web of financial transactions that frustrates any audit.

The last stage is the spin dry. Here the washed funds are brought back into circulation, now in the form of clean, and often taxable, income.

Until recent money-laundering legislation was proposed – and its effectiveness remains to be seen – Canada was a near-perfect laundromat. It offered laundrymen a firmly established democracy, a sound banking infrastructure, highly advanced communications, and easy access from the United States, the world's most important drug market. The five-thousand-mile stretch that separates the two countries is the longest undefended, and mostly unpatrolled, border in the world. Where there are checkpoints, traffic in both directions – at least for American and Canadian citizens – passes largely unhindered. The only thing that unequivocally stops at the border, as far as U.S. law enforcement is concerned, is federal jurisdiction.

Every now and then, someone does get caught at the border. A few years ago Canadian Customs nabbed some Mexican laundrymen crossing at Surrey, B.C. Because these two were such a long way from home and didn't look like your average tourists, they were asked to open the trunk of their car. When they did, an especially alert officer happened to notice that the spare tire didn't fit the car. He ripped it open and found eight hundred thousand dollars.

But that's the exception.

A spare tire that does fit, in a well-maintained car with New York State plates and skis lashed to the roof, driven by a well-dressed young couple heading for Mont Tremblant on a Friday afternoon might attract someone's attention in July, but never in a month of Friday afternoons would anyone think twice about it in January.

Before 1989, when money laundering finally became a criminal offence in Canada, hardly anyone thought twice about cash at all. The Mulroney government attempted to change that by introducing currency transaction reporting. But it wasn't mandatory. Banks voluntarily agreed to ask depositors about cash. And because no one was going to prosecute them if they didn't, they sometimes "forgot." Combining the kind of laxity that is built into all voluntary systems with a modern, internationally networked financial services industry, it's no surprise to discover that Canadian banks have for years maintained a major commercial presence in tax havens such as the Caribbean.

Bruce "Peewee" Griffin, a convicted drug smuggler from Florida, had a well-established relationship with the Bank of Nova Scotia. According to the FBI, from 1975 to 1981, he laundered more than $100 million through Scotiabank Nassau, almost a quarter of it during one hectic four-month stretch in 1979. He kept several accounts there in the names of Bahamas-registered shell companies. To consolidate his holdings, he wired money to Scotiabank Cayman Islands and into an account it held for a Caymans-registered shell, Cobalt Ltd. From there, the money travelled through Scotiabank New York before being dispersed into several U.S. companies controlled by Griffin. When Griffin was finally indicted in 1983, along with a hundred associates, his assets included racing cars, racing boats, and a Texas ranch where he bred horses.

In those days, the Bank of Nova Scotia was famous for not asking questions about large cash deposits and also for ignoring normal banking practices. Among other things, it purposely kept minimal records to hide the identity of its depositors. What's more, some Scotiabank employees in the Caribbean actually received tips in the thousands of dollars from their clients for their help in washing drug money. In 1984, a U.S. federal court in Miami fined Scotiabank $1.8 million for refusing to turn over to a federal grand jury records which they'd subpoenaed.

One of Griffin's associates was a Bahamian lawyer named Nigel Bowe. It was Bowe who introduced Griffin to Bahamian Prime Minister Lynden Oscar Pindling. Hardly by coincidence, the Bank of Nova Scotia was also where Mr. Pindling washed his money. Then under investigation for allegedly receiving one hundred thousand dollars in monthly drug bribes, Pindling owed much of his success to his old friend and mentor Meyer Lansky.

Having the right friends can yield dividends. If you can get a politician, a lawyer, and a bank manager on your side, you can launder any amount with ease. But then, many laundrymen work wonders with only one of the three.

When the drug-dealing Cuntrera-Caruana family stumbled across the ever-affable Aldo Tucci at the City and District Savings Bank in Dollard-des-Ormeaux, Quebec, they couldn't believe their luck. He was so anxious for their business that he was willing to do just about anything. They invited him to administer six of their companies and in the first year alone they put $13 million through his branch. To keep such clients happy and encourage more of their business, Tucci took it upon himself to make special arrangements for the group to deliver their cash-laden tote bags at the bank's back door. In fact, the gang and Tucci got along so well that when he was transferred to another branch in Montreal, they moved their accounts to his new office.

The clan got lucky again when they opened accounts at a rival bank. The manager there became so concerned with the amounts of cash they were bringing into his branch – in just over a year they'd delivered to him $14 million stuffed in suitcases and paper bags – that he asked them please to be kind enough to tie the money into five-thousand-dollar bundles. Naturally, they obliged.

And then there was Gary Henden, a Canadian lawyer who became a legend in his laundryman's lifetime by having a fifteen-year-old boy on a bicycle deliver parcels of cash to banks around Ontario. For some bizarre reason, a child carrying $250,000 in small bills eluded the bank managers' suspicions. The RCMP later claimed the banks should have questioned the teenager's deposits. The banks maintained it was none of their business.

Employed by drug traffickers, Henden set up a company called Antillean Management and opened foreign bank accounts in that name. He then created one called Rosegarden Construction. When he found property to buy, money would be wired from the Netherlands Antilles company to the M&M Currency Exchange in Canada, yet another Henden shell. From there it would go into Cencan Investments Ltd., also a Henden invention, which would loan it to Rosegarden. Cencan would issue a cheque which would be deposited by Henden, as the attorney acting for Rosegarden, into his client account. Henden then paid for the purchase, but registered the mortgage in favour of "Gary Henden, Attorney at Law, In Trust." Needless to say, those mortgages were never repaid.

Henden eventually admitted to having washed $12 million over a three-year period for a drug-trafficking syndicate. The police feel a more accurate figure might be five times as much. Still, had they not been able to establish a direct link between Henden's assets and drug trafficking, they could never have broken through the screen he'd erected around attorney-client privilege.

It was much the same for the Vancouver attorney working on a flat percentage when he deposited $7.4 million in cash between March 1985 and July 1987 into his client account at a local branch of the now infamous Bank of Credit and Commerce International (BCCI). In a single eighteen-month period, he also turned $3.1 million into U.S. dollars, walking into the bank with anywhere from $56,000 to $396,000 in his briefcase, pre-sorted into piles of $20 and $50 notes. When the bank manager asked about the money, the man explained that he was a lawyer acting for a client and refused to say anything more about it. The bank manager reassured the lawyer that he understood attorney-client privilege and that his business was welcome.

Yvon Gagnon confesses that his golf game isn't as good as he wishes it was. Nor is the *vin de table* he makes at home – bottled with his own labels – ever going to be confused with Château Lafite. But he loves playing golf and he loves his homemade wine, and there are plenty of drug traffickers he's busted over thirty years who wish he had spent more time with his golf and his wine, too.

A sturdily built, friendly man with dark hair and a dark moustache, he says there is something very basic to understand about drug trafficking – that it is a business – and the way to get to the traffickers is by going after the money. So when the informant at the *bureau de change* bottled out and refused to testify, setting up an undercover *bureau de change* sounded to him like the perfect sting.

Gagnon and a small staff of officers in Westmount then put together a proposal. The idea was that they would establish a company, open an exchange office in the middle of Montreal, staff it with trained undercover officers – which eliminated the problem of worrying about civilian witnesses – offer a money-laundering service, and wait to see who walked in.

In July 1990, they submitted their proposal. RCMP headquarters in Ottawa approved it on August 13 for a six-month trial. Gagnon assumed the identity of Yvon Richard, a European businessman with a Montreal address who circulated on the fringes of international finance. A company was set up in his name with a $750,000 loan from an RCMP undercover operations fund. Everything was done exactly the way anyone would establish any business in Quebec. Lawyers were hired. All the proper paperwork was put into place. Richard's company then set up a *bureau de change*, again going through all the proper procedures. At the same time, Gagnon and his team started looking for trained undercover officers who might have worked in a bank on summer vacations when they were in school or before joining the Mounties, or who had experience with complicated banking investigations. Four were eventually selected, all of them from out west, none of whom could be traced easily back to the RCMP. They were set up with false identities and all the necessary background, just in case anyone checked, then sent into a bank for some last-minute, on-the-job training.

The commercial banking relationship that the *bureau de change* needed was established by Gagnon through the president of the National Bank in Montreal. Because of the nature of the undercover operation, and the amounts of cash they were planning to put through their accounts, the Mounties knew they couldn't jeopardize a bank's legal position by using the bank without their knowledge. So they let the bank president in on their secret and secured his co-operation. They also wound up using premises owned by that bank.

The Centre International Monétaire de Montréal – CIMM for short – moved into a corner office at Peel and de Maisonneuve West, a neighbourhood surrounded by about eight or nine competing *bureaux de change*, several of which had been identified in the previous operation as being used by traffickers. For all the obvious security reasons, the sting was classified top secret. Only around thirty people knew about it. That included four undercover officers working inside the CIMM and another dozen or so who worked surveillance and security from across the street in office space they rented to film the entrance. Others with knowledge of the sting were divided between a small group in Westmount, a few trusted bankers, brass at RCMP headquarters in Ottawa, officials in Ottawa who oversee the Mounties, and some people at the Office of the Solicitor General, which ultimately had authority over the sting.

Because the CIMM was going to handle so much money, security cameras were installed throughout the tiny offices. They recorded all the really good stuff, like the main targets showing up, opening suitcases filled with cash, and handing over the money. The cameras were in evidence, peering down from every angle in every office. Amazingly, none of the suspects ever objected to being videotaped. Gagnon shrugs philosophically, "They were too busy washing money to care about the cameras."

With everything in place, the CIMM opened its doors for business on Sunday morning, September 30, 1990. The very next day, the first of a long succession of money launderers stopped in to do business.

In the beginning, all the traffickers wanted to do was get out of Canadian dollars and into American dollars. They started coming in with Canadian dollars – twenty-five thousand to thirty thousand dollars, mostly in small bills – looking to consolidate their street-level cash by turning it into large-denomination American banknotes. The CIMM charged them the usual 1 per cent commission. Before long, the traffickers were in the fifty-thousand- to hundred-thousand-dollar range.

"One of the most amazing things," Gagnon says, "is that, maybe 90 per cent of the time, our clients themselves didn't know how much they were bringing us. We kept very good books, counting everything, recording everything, being very precise. But they didn't bother with that. They'd walk in with bags full of cash, tell us how much they thought they had, and most of the time they were wrong. Most of the time it was more."

Besides American dollars, they also occasionally exchanged money for Dutch guilders or Swiss francs, depending on their business requirements. After a time they started asking for a second service, buying cashier's cheques from the CIMM, drawn on an account in New York that Gagnon had established there. Because cheques leave a money trail, the Mounties were able to follow those cheques – which four years later totalled around $40 million – as they were deposited into accounts at 200 different banks, 150 of them just in Panama.

All of those accounts were owned by the Cali cartel.

The cheques that the CIMM issued were all in phony names. The traffickers would make them up on the spot. On one occasion, they simply went down the roster of players from the Montreal Expos. It didn't matter which names got put on the cheques as long as they didn't use any single name too often. The idea was, in case anyone ever looked at the CIMM's books, to make it appear as if all these different people had simply walked in off the street.

The cheques were then sent by courier or delivered by hand to South America. They went to Brazil and to Venezuela and, towards the end of the sting, directly to Colombia. The cartel's accountants credited the amounts on the cheques against the monies owed by the traffickers in

Canada. Once that bookkeeping had been accomplished, the cheques were sent off to be deposited in those two hundred different banks.

Some of the money went to the cartel leaders. Some of it went to paying off government officials and banking officers in Panama and Colombia. Some of it was funnelled through import-export companies in the Canal Zone, to be reinvested in drug trafficking. Two companies that were eventually uncovered were Symar Joyeros Mayoristas and Universe Gold Enterprise. They were the Colombian end of the cocaine-for-gold joint venture with the Mafia's Aurea International Trading and Eurocatene.

Gagnon and the others didn't know it at the time, but the money they were helping the CIMM's clients funnel into Panama was affecting the price of gold in the international markets. It also represented one of the most successful strategic alliances ever constructed between Sicily and Cali.

As trust continued to grow between the traffickers and the CIMM, a third service was requested and provided. Now the traffickers wanted to deposit money directly into the CIMM's bank accounts in Montreal, then have it wired out to other accounts on their behalf around the world. Before long, the CIMM was moving $1 million to $2 million at a time, most of it destined for Luxembourg and Switzerland.

Three specific groups emerged. The first was run by Giuseppe "Joseph" Lagana, then thirty-eight, an attorney whose main client was Vito Rizzuto, the suspected head of the Canadian-Italian Mafia. Lagana's office was directly kittycorner to that of the CIMM. His expertise was moving money out of Canada and through Switzerland. On several occasions, he told his new best friends at the CIMM that if it wasn't for his money-laundering skills, he wouldn't be making a living.

As a student in Montreal, Lagana had worked in a bar and befriended a young Brazilian his age named Jorge Luis Cantieri. Lagana now introduced Cantieri to the CIMM. Cantieri had been trafficking in Canada probably since the 1970s, had gotten caught in 1985 – he was charged with trafficking 20 kilos of cocaine and 8.2 kilos of hashish, worth $14.5 million – and was supposed to have been sent away for twelve years. When he got out on early release, he flew straight to Colombia to get connected again, set himself up, and went back into business. He first walked into the CIMM with cash in early 1991 and remained one of the exchange's best and most loyal customers, making his final $1 million deposit the day before Gagnon and the others took down the operation on August 30, 1994. Believed to be connected to Vito Rizzuto and beyond him to Vic Cotroni, Cantieri spent most of his time out of the country, travelling through South America and Europe, organizing drug deals.

The second group was headed by an importer-exporter and bar owner named Dominico Tozzi. Ten years older than Lagana and Cantieri, he was associated with both. In fact, it was Lagana who assured the undercover agents that Tozzi knew everything about everybody and that if he ever got arrested and decided to talk, half of Montreal could wind up in jail. The undercover agent reportedly observed that Tozzi might someday find himself at the bottom of the St. Lawrence River. Lagana reportedly responded, "I'm surprised it hasn't already happened."

According to the Mounties, Tozzi told one of the undercover agents that he'd personally carried an eight-hundred-thousand-dollar bribe to Venezuela to secure the release from prison there of the aging Mafioso boss Nick Rizzuto.

He'd fled Montreal for Venezuela with his family in the 1970s – Paolo Violi had put out a contract on him – seeking protection there from the Cuntrera-Caruanas. At the age of sixty-nine, in 1989, Rizzuto was thrown into jail by the Venezuelans for being the middleman in a coke-and-money-laundering joint venture between the Sicilians and the Cali mob.

When Tozzi's comments got published, after the sting was shut down, the Rizzuto family denied that anyone had been bribed or that Tozzi was in any way involved. Tozzi himself also then denied saying it or being involved. But the Mounties insist he said it, although there is no proof that he did in fact make the payment.

What is known, however, is that Tozzi was in Venezuela around the time the bribe was reputedly made. Returning from an overseas trip, Canada Customs stopped him – at the request of the RCMP – and checked the stamps in his passport. They revealed that, in just under three years, he'd travelled to Nigeria, Colombia, Luxembourg, Italy, the United States, Thailand, Costa Rica, Switzerland, and Venezuela.

Tozzi's main connection was a heavyweight character named Vincenzo Dimaulo. A close friend of Frank Cotroni and a convicted murderer,

Dimaulo had been sentenced to life in a 1970 shooting death that followed a robbery. His lawyers argued for years that Dimaulo never knew his partners were armed and shouldn't be held responsible as an accomplice to the killing. He served around fourteen years before being paroled. When he got out he went into the real estate development business, allegedly backed by Rizzuto. One of his projects in the suburban Montreal community of Saint-Léonard turned out to be, ironically, building the local courthouse.

Through contacts with Tozzi and by following transactions he was making at the CIMM that they believed to be on behalf of Dimaulo, the Mounties learned that the two were planning a twenty-five-hundred-kilo shipment of cocaine from Haiti. The plan was to buy a ship in Jamaica – Tozzi directed two payments from the CIMM for the purchase of the *Tromso* – sail drugs up to Halifax, sink them, and let fishing vessels recover them. But it never happened because the *Tromso* sank en route to Haiti.

The third group was run by Samy Sabattino Nicolucci. The RCMP had been tracking him since the early 1980s, trying to nail him as a courier for Vito Rizzuto. At one point they followed him all the way to Aruba, where he stayed at the local Holiday Inn. Except when they checked with the management there, he wasn't registered. His room had been booked in the name of, and had been paid by, Pasquale Cuntrera. They finally nailed him for $2 million worth of cocaine staged in Vancouver and destined for the States. He was convicted in 1985 and sentenced to fourteen years.

Released from prison just in time to get involved with the CIMM, he worked as an all-around laundryman, sharing an office with Tozzi. Some of the cheques he asked the undercover team to write on behalf of his clients turned up in New Jersey, received there by an individual under investigation for ties to both the LCN and the Colombians.

As the Mounties laundered more and more money, and worked their way deeper inside the main three groups, Projet Compote branched out. Gagnon and the others turned for help to the Americans, Italians, Swiss, French, and even the Panamanians. They followed money through those Italian-Colombian alliances, identified back-to-back loans made through Switzerland for the purchase of real estate in Canada, and located property held by the suspects in the south of France and Florida.

The six-month trial period that put the CIMM in business was extended six more times. About halfway through, the undercover team was so busy that they put a sign on the door announcing "By Appointment Only," to keep additional business from coming in off the street. They also raised their commissions, making them the most expensive *bureau de change* in Montreal. Their customers complained, but kept doing business there.

"The day we shut it all down," Gagnon notes, "we arrested fifty-two people. Of those, forty-three were tied into Italian organized crime. The nine others were part of a French-Canadian gang trafficking hashish from Jamaica. During those four years, we laundered $160 million. That doesn't include the legal business we did, such as the money we changed for tourists. What's more, we ran the business at a profit, making around $2 million. So this operation didn't cost Canadian taxpayers anything."

The takedown included most of the major players, plus four in England. The RCMP also seized property, cash, cocaine, and two hundred accounts in twenty-nine banking institutions. It was Canada's biggest money-laundering bust to date.

Behind the scenes, it was also one of the RCMP's most criticized undercover operations.

Four years after the CIMM was shut down, Solicitor General Andy Scott demanded that the RCMP inform him of what had been going on.

Scott's interest was piqued by a week-long series of solid investigative reporting by Andrew McIntosh in the *Ottawa Citizen*. Among McIntosh's revelations were that, due to manpower shortages, only three of more than twenty identified groups had been brought to justice by the sting; that one Mountie working in the sting grew so frustrated after complaining about the lack of support from headquarters that he asked to be transferred out of the operation; that none of the sting's original targets ever did business with the CIMM; that they only seized $17 million; and that the money washed by the CIMM had served to help put close to five tons of cocaine on the streets of Eastern Canada, with a retail value of more than $2 billion. McIntosh also claimed that the sting hadn't been properly approved by the solicitor general before it was launched and that Mounties had come precariously close to being charged with money laundering in the United States.

RCMP Commissioner Phil Murray responded to Scott in a secret ten-page report dated June 24, 1998. In it, Murray formally acknowledged what Gagnon and the others had been complaining about throughout the operation: that a lack of resources – including staff shortages and logistical problems – had seriously hampered the investigation.

Personnel and equipment were so overstretched, Murray conceded, that some of the drug groups that should have been investigated, weren't. While Murray denied that there had been anything illegal about the sting, he was willing to admit there had been serious problems. So serious, in fact, that the Mounties had taken notice, changed several procedures, put new procedures in place, and consolidated all of their undercover activities in one office.

He also denied McIntosh's most serious charge – that security breaches had taken place. That charge concerned the RCMP officer who, when the CIMM first went into business, was head of the drug squad in Montreal. Inspector Claude Savoie became the target of an internal affairs investigation for taking two hundred thousand dollars in bribes from the mob. Transferred to Ottawa in 1991, the following year, as the investigation moved in on him, he shot himself in his office at RCMP headquarters.

The immediate worry was that he'd sold out his men in Montreal. The undercover team held its collective breath. And despite denials by the investigators – they wouldn't want to have had an officer's death on their conscience – they didn't breath a collective sigh of relief until the sting was taken down.

There had also been a problem with funds diverted to an ancillary operation that had to be written off. Tozzi had approached the guys at the CIMM with a deal. He said he had $40 million that he needed to get to Europe and asked if they could move it for him. Gagnon, as Yvon Richard, assured Tozzi that wouldn't be a problem.

The original idea was to set up a clandestine Canadian company in Holland, but the RCMP rejected it, worrying that the Dutch police would get very annoyed if the Canadians acted behind their backs. The alternative was to do this in conjunction with the Dutch. That joint venture went into business during the summer of 1993. But Tozzi never came up with the $40 million.

In the end, the *Ottawa Citizen* series raised serious points and it is still not clear that either the RCMP or the solicitor general's office ever fully addressed them.

If nothing else, too many bad guys got away.

But the bad guys who didn't get away mattered. And two major drug deals were busted up in the interim.

Luis Cantieri had some customers in Montreal who'd put in a big order for cocaine. They wanted one thousand kilos, about $10 million worth, delivered to the U.K. Cantieri said he could handle it, but he said his customers would have to come up with the front money. His customers easily came up with $4 million. The deal was that they would pay him the rest once they sold it. That brought up several areas that needed to be negotiated, like what would happen if the coke was seized before it got to England, or on arrival by British Customs, or while it was in storage by the police.

Cantieri's shipping guy was dispatched to Colombia to supervise the on-loading. He wound up getting stuck there for six weeks, while Cantieri and his customers worked out the rest of the contract.

In the meantime, through information obtained by the CIMM, the Mounties were able to get to some of their own people on the inside of the deal. Cantieri was off in France, so one of the undercovers was able to negotiate directly with Rosenblum, while the other negotiated back in Montreal with Lagana. That exposed all of the people involved.

When it finally came off, the Mounties were able to arrange the seizure of 558 kilos off the coast of Colombia. And the British were able to arrest Cantieri's customers – Pierre Rodrigue and David Rouleau – Canadian Hells Angels who'd gone to help the British Hells Angels take over the U.K. cocaine market.

The other deal was even sweeter, especially for Gagnon's group in Westmount.

Through Cantieri, the undercover team learned about a huge shipment of more than five hundred kilos of cocaine that was going to be brought into Canada. The way the Mounties worked it out, they had someone on the inside there, too.

The ship carrying the drugs, the *Pacifico*, sailed north from Colombia, tracked at all times by the Canadian Coast Guard. The plan was that it would rendezvous off the coast of Halifax with a smaller fishing vessel and off-load the drugs. Once the transfer was made, the Coast Guard arrived to arrest both ships, including the *Pacifico*, which it stopped outside Canadian waters.

The man who had shipped the cocaine from Colombia was Pasquale Locatelli. The man who'd paid to get it into Canada was none other than Pierrino DiVito.

Tozzi went away. So did Dimaulo. So did Cantieri. So did Lagana. So did DiVito. So did almost all the others who came through the CIMM to wash money for the three groups.

For a while, it looked as if Samy Nicolucci might be beyond the Mounties' reach, but only because he was otherwise occupied. Around spring 1994, he'd negotiated a deal with a Colombian supplier in Miami for 150 kilos of cocaine. But by the time the shipment reached Montreal it was damaged by humidity and was no good. The Colombians in Miami blamed Nicolucci and his trucker for ruining the drugs. They wanted their $1.6 million. Nicolucci refused to pay. In August, a bunch of Colombians showed up and kidnapped Nicolucci and held him in Miami for several weeks. Tozzi managed to raise the money, which was paid through the CIMM. Gagnon alerted the Montreal police, who went to see Nicolucci's wife to say that they'd heard he'd been kidnapped and to ask if it was true. And they were assured it wasn't true.

The Mounties knew he was still being held in Miami and could be there for a while, because when they shut down the CIMM, one of the cheques that didn't clear was Nicolucci's ransom money. The Colombians got him out of Miami and into Colombia, where he was put to work to pay off his debt until the summer of 1995, when he was arrested by the police and, eventually, deported back to Canada. And he, too, joined his friends in jail.

5

THE *MAFFIYA*

We Italians will kill you, but the Russians are crazy.
They'll kill your whole family.

– John Gotti, Mafioso

In the beginning, the *Maffiya* created driver's licences.

They came to New York, huddled masses yearning to be free, what few belongings they owned tied with rope into old suitcases and wooden crates. But it didn't matter what they could carry in their arms because in their minds they carried their future. They were doctors, physicists, and biologists. They were chemists, sociologists, and geologists. And each of them, as they waded ashore, counted on their knowledge and skills to help them make their way.

Filled with hope they arrived in Brighton Beach, Brooklyn, where the ones who had come before had settled but, one by one, they learned the hard way that in the New World their Old World diplomas didn't count. Their university degrees were not even a minor curiosity.

They were forced to turn to what is sometimes referred to as "entry level immigrant" work – jobs that have always been open to the newest arrivals – like waiting on tables and cleaning offices and driving a taxicab. But to get a job as a cabbie, they needed a driver's licence. The problem was that many of them had never owned a car back in Russia, and didn't have a licence. At least not until the *Maffiya* found out there was a market for them.

Traditionally, Russians are good at many things, but they are absolutely superb at counterfeiting. Years of Soviet oppression taught them that if they wanted something, they could either wait for officialdom to get around to it – which often meant it never happened – or they could forge whatever official documents they needed. It wasn't long before a few ingenious wiseguys got into the driver's licence business.

Bathed in the spirit of their new-found capitalism, they produced their own absolutely perfect copies of Russian licences – heavy cardboard, 5 ¾ by 4 inches, folded down the middle, red on one side, salmon pink on the other, with just enough room on the pink side for a photograph, a name, an address, and a date of birth written in by hand, with plenty of official-looking stamps banged on top. They were absolutely perfect copies, although in the end that hardly mattered because no one at the New York State Department of Motor Vehicles knew a real one from a phony one anyway. They simply exchanged the bogus Russian licences for valid New York State licences.

Which is how the *Maffiya* put so many doctors, physicists, biologists, chemists, sociologists, and geologists behind the wheel of New York City taxicabs.

Popular belief has it that Russian organized crime rose out of the ashes of the former Soviet Union, a consequence of chaotic social, political, and economic transformation.

Not true.

The implosion of Communism merely let the genie out of the bottle. Organized crime was one of the best-kept secrets of the Soviet era. We in the West never had a printed program to tell us who the players were because the Soviets had always refused to admit their existence. But once that genie popped out of the bottle, it headed West with the fervour and passion formerly reserved for the wildest dreams of the Red Army's strategic planners.

Bred to flourish under the command economy of the old system, the criminal element trekked through a seventy-five-year apprenticeship, mastering every necessary skill – corruption, extortion, black market trading, blackmail – to circumvent the state and beat the system.

Criminals survived under Stalin and persisted under Khrushchev, but they thrived under Leonid Brezhnev, who unofficially empowered them because the Party needed them to manage the black markets.

Where central planning was failing the State, Brezhnev saw them as the safety valve – he brought them in as full partners in the fraud that was Communism – an essential element to keep the masses under his thumb. But in tacitly endorsing thief power as the engine of the underground economy, Brezhnev and his cronies inadvertently created a subculture of entrepreneurs. And they dominated the post-Brezhnev years the way heroin commands a junkie.

Mikhail Gorbachev couldn't control them. Boris Yeltsin never tried. When the country disintegrated under the weight of its own ineptitude, no mechanisms were in place to deal with the black economy. The intense rush of Western business to get in there, to take advantage of commercial opportunities, only served to exacerbate the problem.

"Like everything else in Russia, criminality is an emerging process," says Matty Maher, now a consultant on global organized criminality but previously Director of International Operations for the DEA. "It has become entrepreneurial too. But they are not yet as structured and ordered as the Colombians, Italians, or even the Mexicans. While the forces in Russia are focused more on survival than stopping criminals, the criminals in Russia are struggling to develop an infrastructure that will support more sophisticated levels of criminality. Ironic, no, that criminals are building their infrastructure and the Russian government isn't. In a way, that becomes our responsibility. The Russian government is dressed for a banquet but the only thing on the table is peanut butter and jelly. We have to teach them how to cook."

Communism vaporized overnight and the only people left standing were empowered criminals. They were the ones who took over. By the time "privatization" – a euphemism for plunder – rolled around, criminals had become Russia's most powerful special interest group. They were the only ones with the money to pay for State industries. They were the ones who also had the business skills to milk those industries dry.

Maher continues: "Something like 70 per cent of the commercial activity is today conducted with barter. A company supplying cement is paid in tires because that company was given tires by another company building apartment houses. Another company pays for steel with oil. And the company who gets the oil uses that to pay for food. So the economic foundations of the country do not support the free exchange of currency. In doing things by barter, you not only defeat the tax system, you expose the country and its whole economic and political system to corruption. The people who wound up with all this black money looked for ways to hide it and to reinvest it in something which would return a larger profit." They found that first in state industries, then in the government. Once they owned both, they owned the nation.

The day Yeltsin stood on the top of that tank in front of the Moscow White House to defy the Communists in their final hours, there were already three thousand criminal organizations spread across the eleven time zones that make up the nation. Within two years, that figured had doubled. At the end of the millennium, there are nearly twelve thousand groups, boasting a membership of perhaps one hundred thousand or more.

In the most general terms, Russia has been consumed by a four-headed monster.

First, there are the *vory v zakone*, the criminal version of Boy Scout troop leaders. The term translates to mean "thieves professing the code," but for the convenience of the media the *vory* have been dubbed "thieves-in-law." Moulded out of pre-1917 Revolution traditions, they are a fraternity of organizers – Fagins, if you will – who inspire criminal acts and take a cut. They are the troop leaders who motivate their scouts to rub two sticks together then hog the campfire.

Almost without exception, they do their apprenticeship in prison. The respect they command is in direct proportion to the jail time they serve. And that's where they are awarded the title. The initiation ceremony is formal and many of them traditionally wear tattoos, kind of like Boy Scout merit badges. They also have a set of rules to live by. But theirs is hardly a code of honour.

"The old-time Mafia used to talk about honour," explains Roger Urbanski, Director of Foreign Relations in the Office of Investigations at U.S. Customs. "There's none of that with the Russians. They have no honour. Just seventy-five years of 'Let's beat the system.'"

Rather than call it a code, it is perhaps more like a Masonic pledge of brotherhood: Fellow thieves-in-law are to be treated exactly like family, supported and protected; they must earn their livelihood exclusively from criminal enterprise; they must never co-operate with the authorities; they must preach their code to younger thieves, who, in turn, must be willing to take a fall for an older thief; they must fulfil all promises made to other thieves; when differences arise, other thieves must be called in to resolve them; the decision of the arbitrators is final and punishment, which usually means death, must be swiftly carried out.

Estimates vary wildly. There may be anywhere from fifty to five hundred thieves-in-law operating today. No one really knows because they don't publish a mailing list. They do occasionally get together. One well-documented jamboree took place in Tbilisi in 1982. They met specifically to argue the merits of actively seeking more political power. Within a few years, one of them became "politically significant" to Georgian President Eduard Shevardnadze.

The second head of the monster belongs to those former Communist Party members and government officials who saw what was happening, took advantage of their position to salt away fortunes, reinvented themselves in the new age, and now steal on an even grander scale. As most of the bureaucrats in power today once served Communist masters, rising through the ranks of a system in which corruption was a way of life, it's hardly surprising that corruption remains a way of life. Old habits die hard, and then only when they have ceased to serve their purpose.

Neither democracy nor capitalism, honesty nor civil responsibility, was ever postulated as a suitable alternative. After all, if the average income is a mere few thousand dollars a year – and even that might seem high in a nation where, reportedly, one-fourth of the population lives below the poverty line – then a job offering fringe benefits to double, or treble, or quadruple that figure is something to strive for.

A licence to steal is redefined as a privilege of rank.

For example, when Russian troops were withdrawn from East Germany, the Bundestag authorized a payment to the Russian army specifically to construct five hundred thousand apartments in Russia so that those troops would have somewhere to live. Approximately three thousand apartments were built. The money for the rest of them has since disappeared. Furthermore, the sheer number of wealthy men in

Russia's government more than attests to the fact that civil servitude is a means to financial security.

The monster's third head comprises ethnic and national groups – Chechens, Armenians, Azerbaijanis, and Georgians – who filled the void left by the Communist Party and, literally, became the criminal state. In 1993, two Chechens were murdered and dismembered in a luxury flat in London's West End. The hit men were two visiting Armenians. It all had to do with illegal arms shipments – the foreign relations of a criminal state – and who had the right to sell what to whom. Clearly there was a lot more at stake than just a few rifles because the dead men, both mere pawns in this game, left estates worth more than $2 million.

Finally, there are the so-called organized crime groups, which are really just loose-knit conglomerations of criminals. They may be referred to as the *Maffiya* because that is a convenient term to describe a criminal organization, but they are not at all like their Italian cousins. There are no pyramid organizational structures, no family ties to unite them, no Commission to oversee their activities. Instead, these groups are more like collections of friends and associates who band together for certain crimes, going their own way for others. As a group they may target a specific industry, or just hold on to a specific territory. The term they use is "zones of influence."

Typical is Solntsevo.

Sometimes known as Solntsevskaya, sometimes translated into English as the "Brigade of the Sun," they originated in a large Moscow neighbourhood, where they monopolize prostitution, drug trafficking, political corruption, extortion, and murder.

On March 1, 1995, assassins killed journalist Vladislav Listyev, the Lloyd Robertson of Moscow television news. He'd just taken on the job as head of the country's main public television station and announced that one of his first acts would be to suspend advertising on the channel. His contention was that the advertising industry had been infiltrated by criminal organizations – to wit, Solntsevo – and that before commercials came back to his station, he was going to get them out of the business. So they whacked him.

The following day, Boris Yeltsin was quoted saying, "The merging of the *Maffiya* with commercial structures, administrative agencies, interior ministry bodies, city authorities – nowhere else in Russia do the authorities turn a blind eye to these things as they do in Moscow."

Because this was such a high-profile hit, the police issued composite sketches and, based on those, soon announced with great fanfare that they had two suspects in custody. But the identification of those suspects proved faulty and, rather quietly, they were released.

Shortly thereafter, the newspaper *Izvestia* linked the murder to a power struggle within Solntsevo. But such is their power and the depth of their reach inside the tangled and confused bureaucracy that is Russian government that no one has ever been charged with the crime. Then again, for the eight-year period between 1991 and 1999, not a single widely publicized contract murder – of which there have been literally thousands – was successfully investigated and prosecuted. There is no political will to bother with them.

Russia is today a full-fledged mafiocracy.

At least six groups operate from Moscow. The Tstentralnaya, Ostankinskaya, and Avtomobilnaya are Chechen and count as many as two thousand members between them. The Solntsevo and Podolskaya are Russian, as is the Twenty-First Century Association. There are four main groups in St. Petersburg and apparently nine in Vladivostok.

Complicating matters, the groups either break down along ethnic lines, are based on territorial control, or split along generational divides. Some have links with bureaucracy, others are strictly anchored in specific industries. Chechen groups, for example, are strongly based in the petroleum business. Kurganskaya have set themselves up as the Murder Inc. of Russian organized crime, offering their professional hit men to other groups around the world, including the Mafia and the Colombians.

As soon as groups such as Solntsevo acquired a headlock on Russia's banking and financial institutions, they set up affiliates and branches outside Russia, creating for themselves a magic wand. They wave it and $200 to $300 billion a year disappear into the secret world of offshore banking.

Flexing their muscle, they orchestrated the rouble crisis of 1997.

Their carefully planned and very sophisticated shorting of roubles and shift into dollars sent the Russian economy into a nose-dive and created a tidal-wave effect throughout Western financial markets. The profit they made buying back those same roubles refinanced criminal activities inside Russia and earned them more money, which, once the economy straightened out, they turned into hard currencies and made a second sizable profit.

According to the Global Organized Crime Project of Washington-based think-tank the Center for Strategic and International Studies (CSIS), Russian criminals launder about $1 billion a month just through Cyprus – where some eight thousand Russian shell companies have hung their shingles – and another $1 billion a month just through Israel. The Swiss are finally, albeit reluctantly, willing to admit to having helped Russian crime organizations launder $40 billion since 1991. That said, by 1994 Russian organized crime had wired enough money outside Russia to finance its own operations throughout the world.

Law enforcement in Russia is either unable or unwilling to do real battle with either organized crime or political corruption. The legal system is equally impotent, so much so that Transparency International – a Berlin-based democracy watchdog – considers Russia the fourth most corrupt country in the world, after Colombia, Nigeria, and Bolivia. A Yeltsin-commissioned report noted that hardly anyone trusts the police, hardly anyone has any faith that laws passed by parliament will be enforced, and, perhaps most startlingly of all, that nearly 80 per cent of all businesses in the country are forced to pay extortion. With roughly two-thirds of the nation's economy under the sway of crime syndicates, even Yeltsin himself has had to concede that "Russia is the biggest Mafia state in the world."

In the days when the Party owned everything, its members knew what was for the taking and subsequently helped themselves to whatever they wanted. Today, criminals are full partners. A businessman trying to run a small factory might be faced with taxes amounting to 80 per cent of his profits. He defends himself by double bookkeeping, showing tax inspectors a bottom line indicating profits of 10 to 20 per cent. Because the university-educated leaders of Solntsevo and other groups understand what the government doesn't – that is, how a free-market economy works in the real world – they come onto the factory floor and demand 50 per cent of the profits. The Russian term is *krysha*, roof tax. For the rest of the world, it's just the old-fashioned protection racket.

Not every company succumbs to it, even when the requests aren't particularly subtle. In 1993, Coca-Cola's bottling plant on Solntsevo's turf was gutted by a rocket-propelled grenade. But when smaller businesses are targeted and threats are made against family as well as assets, many businessmen convince themselves that paying the *Maffiya* is still cheaper than paying the Kremlin.

Some people argue that groups like Solntsevo are simply the ultimate capitalists – businessmen, unregulated by law, with no moral code, whose only aim is to accumulate wealth. Out of that comes the suggestion that Russia's crime leaders are just a modern version of America's "robber barons" – the Morgans, Goulds, and Vanderbilts – suspect entrepreneurs who, in return for being allowed to bilk the system, left a legacy of transcontinental railroads, massive industries, and schools, libraries, and hospitals.

The difference is, the Russians have reversed the process. They started with massive industries and, in exchange for having pried them loose from government ownership, have taken for granted their right to bilk them.

One scam, resulting in the systemic rape of the nation's assets – gas, crude oil, petroleum products, coal, steel, tin, aluminum, timber, copper, zinc, nickel, cobalt, diamonds, antiquities, weapons, and fissile materials – revolves around the illegal shipment of resources to the West, where they are unloaded at bargain-basement prices.

Typically, a business is set up with a facade of legitimacy, then accepts huge amounts of internationally negotiable goods. Disposition of assets is fraudulently manipulated with double sets of banking and business records. Behind the scenes there are corrupt officials, bent businessmen, and the constant undertone of violent retribution for anyone who doesn't follow the script.

Which is pretty much the way it happened in late 1993 when a young man in his early thirties named Andrei Kozlenok arrived in San Francisco to process precious gems and import diamonds from Russia. Together with two Armenian partners – Ashot Shagirian and his brother David – he named the company after the initials of their first names and called it Golden ADA.

It was an off-the-rack, golden-calf, model scam.

So that everybody knew there were new kids in town, Kozlenok made himself very visible by throwing around a lot of cash. He paid $11 million for the firm's headquarters at 999 Brannan Street – way over the owner's original $6 million asking price – $1 million for a Rolls-Royce and a matching pair of Aston Martins, $1.2 million for three boats, $3.8 million for three homes, $18 million for a corporate jet, and $4.4 million for his weekend retreat at Lake Tahoe. He also bought six gas stations in San Francisco and eighteen other properties around Northern California. Then, just in case there was any doubt remaining about the depth of his pockets, he ferried over a $1.7 million Russian Kamov Ka-32 military transport helicopter and presented it as a gift to the San Francisco Police Department.

It was, to say the least, a very splashy diamond merchant's introduction to a city that had never been a diamond market. Diamonds are London, Antwerp, and New York. But then, Kozlenok's background was not diamonds. Whatever money he'd made back in mother Russia came from flogging cognac and tires to Russians and gas masks to Kuwaitis. What's more, according to the FBI, the brothers Shagirian had, only two years before they became partners in Golden ADA, been painting sidewalks.

The source of the company's extravagance was "the closet," more formally known as the National Treasury of the Russian Federation. An enormous labyrinth of huge underground vaults in Moscow and others hidden somewhere deep in the Ural Mountains, they are filled to the brim with precious stones, coins, jewellery, silver, platinum, and hundreds of tons of gold. Its precise contents and total worth are labelled an official state secret. But that's likely nothing more than an excuse for not having to admit that no one knows.

A man who might have been able to provide a good guess, one of the few people believed to have had access to "the closet," was Yevgeni Bychkov. He'd served as head of the State Treasury, as chairman of the Committee on Precious Metals and Gems, and was a close personal friend of Boris Yeltsin. In his spare time, Bychkov was a father figure to Kozlenok.

It was Bychkov's idea to set up Golden ADA. Publicly, he intended to challenge the DeBeer Corporation's control of the world diamond market. Privately, he was putting nearly $100 million worth of diamonds and literally tons of assorted other treasures into Kozlenok's control.

Assets that arrived in San Francisco were quickly turned into cash. For instance, several tons of antique gold was melted down and sold far below its intrinsic value as scrap. Money was then wired to Russia, Belgium, Liechtenstein, Switzerland, and Israel, where most of it has since disappeared. One allegation, denied by Bychkov, is that those assets paid for his new dacha. One allegation, not denied by anyone, is that those assets paid for Kozlenok's $5 million Bermuda home.

As more and more of the nation's riches arrived in San Francisco, Kozlenok's extravagance increased. He acrimoniously shoved his partners out of the business – they claimed he'd threatened to put a $5 million contract on their heads – and then, suddenly, found himself on the run. He was next seen in Belgium, penniless, insisting that he'd been kidnapped and lost his interest in Golden ADA.

When the IRS knocked on the door of Golden ADA's office, looking to collect $63 million in back taxes, they found automatic weapons, ammunition, bulletproof vests, and explosives. In the meantime, the FBI says that $178 million went through Golden ADA and that they've now been able to trace $40 million of it back to Russia, 10 per cent of which, they believe, might have wound up paying to print copies of Boris Yeltsin's autobiography.

Another popular way of bilking the system is through fake contracts. Companies in Russia simply have to produce documents to show they're importing something in order to transfer money out of the country to pay for the goods. Like contrails in the sky marking the path of a high-flying jet, these days there are literally hundreds of money trails coming out of Russia. And one of the most popular destinations they lead to is Great Britain.

Money bundled out of Russia is washed through the City of London, sheltered in the Channel Islands, and spent on fashionable real estate. Britain also offers expensive private schools for Russian children, art and antiques at auction, and elite shopping.

The City of London Police set up a specialized Financial Investigation Unit in 1995, and since then it has carried out an average of fifteen major investigations a year. The crimes they're looking at average $3 to $4 million, although there was one that saw £3 billion come through the City over the course of several years.

Not all of it is Russian-sourced money, but a lot of it is, especially in the larger cases. London seems to be a pivotal point linking Moscow with the Channel Islands, the Caribbean, Cyprus, and Israel. And the reason is obvious. It's like that liquid you add to the dishwasher to make your glasses shine. Once dirty money has been put into the cycle, a rinse through the City gives it an extra sparkle of legitimacy.

The Russian financial newspaper *Kommersant* noted, "Tens of millions of dollars have left the former Soviet Union, specifically bound for Britain." By now, the figure is several hundreds of millions.

In one case, British police intelligence officers had indications that led them to believe three people in England had laundered $50 million for a Russian organized crime group. But intelligence information is not the same as hard evidence that can be presented to a jury, and so no prosecutions resulted.

In another – this one still ongoing – a police fraud squad noticed two Britons living in a rural part of the country who were marketing promissory notes on behalf of a former Soviet state-owned industry. The men had approached various European banks looking to discount the notes. Initially, investigators believed they were either dealing in forgeries, or that the notes behind the trades were false. It turned out that the notes were real and, under closer scrutiny, that the scheme was very complex.

Among the notes the police saw early on, one had a face value of $2.7 million and was purchased by a major British bank. Another, worth $5 million, was taken up by a British-based company that appears to be legitimate, although investigators aren't totally sure. A third, for $4.3 million, had been sent through Britain to a subsidiary of the main company in Russia. Another, for $8 million, was picked up by a major Swiss bank.

It seemed that the men, one of whom has Russian family connections, were simply moving the funds they received to companies and accounts overseas. For their efforts, records showed what looked like commissions ranging from thirty thousand to eighty thousand dollars per transaction.

But a second circuit then appeared. This was money coming out of St. Petersburg and going into a British company which purported to be in a very specific industry, while in reality it turned out to be nothing more than someone's back-bedroom. Soon there was a third circuit, this time a Moscow–Antwerp connection, through which police traced $200,000 and about which they know nothing else. Then a British–Cyprus link came to light. Payments of up to £300,000 at a time, plus several of $30,000 and at least one of $170,000, have gone through there.

Following that, additional monies came into a British company controlled by the two men. There were payments from a foreign bank in the City of London for £100,000; from a Swiss company for £300,000; from a company that may or may not exist – police still aren't certain – for £300,000; from one of several Isle of Man companies apparently controlled by one of the two Britons for £110,000; and from a company in Moscow, which may or may not represent a legitimate business, for $160,000. Some of this money left the British company for distribution elsewhere, notably $5.9 million, which was purported to be payment to a U.S.-registered company that, police claim, does not exist.

Since then, even more promissory notes have appeared – including one for $11 million and another for $25 million – which have been picked up by a company in the Middle East seemingly linked to the two Britons. One of the two has further associations with a second company in the Middle East, which in turn has associations with a company incorporated in the United States but that has bank accounts in one of the Baltic states. Police have traced nearly $6 million going through that link. What's more, there is an "arrangement" between the Russian company and a company outside Russia, which is linked to one of the two Britons, and records there indicate movements of $8 million.

Enter now a U.S.-based businessman associated with both the Britons and the man in Moscow whose name appears on the privatized company's contracts. It is believed that several payments have been made directly to him, which he has used to invest in legitimate American business ventures. The income arising from those investments will appear perfectly clean by the time it is deposited back into the bank accounts of whoever it is in Moscow authorizing the systematic pillage of that particular company.

Succumbing to world pressure in 1970, the Soviets reluctantly allowed Jews to emigrate from Russia to Israel. Many of these people had been trying to get out for years. Now, finally free, they started on a journey that would take them – in some cases by way of Vienna and in others through Cyprus – to the Promised Land.

But not everyone wound up in Israel. Some settled in Vienna, others in Cyprus. In both cases, Russian émigré communities developed, and before long they would become extremely significant in the world of transnational crime. In yet other cases, they journeyed instead to the United States, to settle in Brighton Beach, Brooklyn.

It was standard U.S. policy in those days not to ask for criminal background checks on anyone applying for refugee status. Two reasons are officially given. One is that the additional paperwork required to check on the average fifty thousand applicants a year was far too much for Washington to handle. The other is that the delay created by background checks would at best deter applicants from applying, at worst expose them to reprisals when Moscow was informed that they wanted out of the country.

The Russians now say they warned the Americans that dangerous criminals might emigrate, pretending to be Jews. But apparently those warnings got lost somewhere in the translation. When word spread that the Americans weren't doing background checks, Russians who hardly knew what a Jew was claimed Jewish heritage. Hidden among the thirty thousand to forty thousand Russians who showed up in New York in those early years were hundreds, if not thousands, of Russians who were not Jewish. Some had simply forged papers to get out. Others were refugees from gulags who'd served time for a variety of offences, some of which were political, many of which were decidedly criminal.

Over the next twenty years, Russian immigration to the United States would come close to three hundred thousand people. When the Soviet system finally shredded into a mass of rubble, travel barriers were relaxed and hundreds of thousands of non-Jews also emigrated.

Today, Brighton Beach – known to New Yorkers as Little Odessa-by-the-Sea – is the largest Russian community outside the former Soviet Union.

Old men play dominoes on the boardwalk, in front of cafés with Russian names and menus printed only in the Cyrillic alphabet. Two blocks north, the elevated subway tracks that run above Brighton Beach Avenue shade the entrances to nightclubs and restaurants and food stores with Russian names. Above the storefronts, in scores of one-room offices that face the tracks, Russian names on the windows spell out marriage broker and dating service and immigration service, mostly fronts for prostitution and other frauds that have become cottage industries here. The D-trains and Q-trains that rattle back and forth all day and all night drown out car horns and loud voices, and easily cover the sound of gunfire, which has also become part of the local folklore, as the murder toll slowly but steadily mounts.

But Brighton Beach is not the only vibrant Russian settlement in North America. Russians have settled throughout New Jersey and in Philadelphia, Baltimore, Detroit, Cleveland, and Chicago. There are Russian enclaves in Toronto and Montreal, in Miami, Los Angeles, and San Francisco. According to a U.S. Justice Department report on the growing presence of Russian organized crime groups, they are even settling in relatively obscure places, like Lincoln, Nebraska.

And as the Russian émigré population has increased, so has crime. There is extortion, counterfeiting, loan sharking, and a variety of frauds. Russian criminals have targeted the health insurance industry by creating hundreds of paper companies that bill insurance companies for examinations and procedures never carried out, and in one scam they stole $125 million. They've targeted Medicaid, selling cheap shoes to patients needing orthopedic shoes, stealing a couple of hundred thousand dollars from the government in a few weeks. They've targeted jewellery manufacturers, in one case scamming gold worth $54 million. One group simply aimed a high-powered scanner out of a window at cars driving by, collected peoples' cellphone numbers, and sold them to other crime groups. It's known as "phone cloning," and before they were stopped, they'd deciphered eighty thousand numbers.

As one law enforcement officer summed it up, "The Russians just add a zero to anything that anyone else thinks of."

According to another, senior FBI agent Hardrick Crawford, Jr.: "They're experts at perpetrating frauds of all shapes and sizes, very violent, very intelligent, and computer literate. They hire ex-intelligence officers who are familiar with the ways of Western law enforcement. They hire computer specialists who can hack their way into any business. They hire lawyers and bankers who are conversant in international law and finance. They hire other business professionals who can manage their assets once their money has been laundered and reinvested in casinos, hotels, and resorts."

The problems they then present to law enforcement are totally different from, say, those of La Cosa Nostra. "Our New York office has long been studying the LCN," Crawford goes on. "We can tell you about a particular *capo* for a crime family, who his aunt was, who his brother is, where his father was born. Now, we look at the Russian organized crime groups and first of all we can't pronounce the name of the organization. When you tell us that the individual came from a certain region in the former Soviet Union, we didn't know that it existed. The difficulties presented by such a scenario are staggering. We're always playing catch-up."

Realizing that so many of these émigrés would have a natural fear of law enforcement – a phobia reinforced on a regular basis under the Communists – the FBI in 1994 established the first of several Russian squads. The New York Police Department also has one. Both squads began with the premise that Russian criminals are more adept at white-collar crime than their LCN counterparts, and that their world is more difficult to penetrate. Both advertised in Russian-language newspapers, hoping to encourage locals to come forward with tips and gossip about crimes, to talk about murders, extortion, fraud, drugs, and counterfeiting. They reached out to newly arrived Russians, hoping to convince them that America was not like home and that the police would protect them.

But Russian fear runs deep and the results were underwhelming. People were simply too afraid of retribution, too scared to testify at trials. They couldn't bring themselves to trust a state system, especially a federal police force. Even promises of witness protection programs fell on deaf ears.

No one had to remind the Russians of Brighton Beach that by talking to the authorities they put their entire family at risk. If they didn't get killed, their children, or even their relatives back in the mother country, might wind up paying for their indiscretions.

No matter what the FBI or the NYPD said to them in their own language, at least in the beginning, the newly arrived Russians opted for survival according to the rules they knew. They were convinced that they couldn't survive unless they lived in a Russian community, and they couldn't live in a Russian community if the local crime bosses suspected them of siding with the authorities. Consequently, as the Russian émigré population increased, so did murders and violence and extortion and prostitution. And the locals stayed silent.

"I've often thought that Russian organized crime guys have seen too many old gangster movies," says Tom Kneir, the FBI's Deputy Assistant Director of the Criminal Investigative Division, "because they pattern themselves after the strong-arm stuff. They're not at all shy when it comes to putting out a message. If someone needs to get whacked, they get whacked. You see some very sophisticated criminal activity, stock manipulations, the looting of precious metals, and surrounding it is all that violence. Most of our home-grown, white-collar, high-level criminals do not resort to violence in any form or fashion. They live by their wits, not by their brawn. But with the Russians, no matter how sophisticated the scheme is, if a message needs to be sent to a witness or to someone who is co-operating with law enforcement, they go with that option."

At the same time that the wave of Russians was coming ashore in the early 1980s, but absolutely unrelated to it, the State of New York changed the way it collected excise taxes on fuel. They shifted the burden from the retailers, who'd been responsible for paying the tax, to the wholesalers, who would now owe the tax as soon as they sold the fuel. In so doing, the state inadvertently opened the floodgates for untaxed trading between wholesalers which came to be known as "the daisy chain scam."

It was precisely the sort of scam that Evsei Agron found especially appealing.

A tiny, balding man with a furry black moustache, Agron's visa papers listed his profession as jeweller, but he told people he was vice president of a Brooklyn health club. The place couldn't have been too healthy because it was a front for the Colombo family and the scene of a 1982 gangland killing. In a previous life, Agron was a convicted murderer from Russia who'd served seven years' hard time before Leonid Brezhnev emptied out his gulags, allowed all sorts of psychopaths to claim Jewish heritage, and shipped them off to the West.

After leaving Leningrad in 1971, the thirty-seven-year-old Agron went first to Germany, where he ran a gambling and prostitution ring.

Four years later, he arrived in America to find that Brighton Beach's sidewalks were paved with a kind of gold – the hard-earned income of those immigrants who'd come before him – and set about filching his share. He installed himself in an office above the El Caribe Country Club Restaurant on Strickland Avenue in Mill Basin, surrounded himself with a crew of almost five hundred goons, carried a cattle prod under his arm like a swagger stick, and oversaw a reign of extortion terror that, by 1980, was netting him fifty thousand dollars a week. Among his more celebrated stunts was extorting fifteen thousand dollars from a man by threatening to murder his daughter at her wedding. Not nearly as intelligent as he was ruthless, Agron was, however, smart enough to align himself with Marat Balagula.

A black-marketeer from Odessa, Balagula was thirty-four when he arrived in Brooklyn at around the same time as Agron. But unlike his boss, he had two advanced university degrees – one in math and one in economics – and had already put together a chain of fourteen gas stations. Now, with Agron's muscle and his intellectual skills, they created a series of fictitious cash transfers through shell companies. They filed false invoices with the government along with fraudulent tax-exemption forms to show tax accumulating on the books of one company, while banking that money in the offshore accounts of another. When the taxman came looking for his share, the company supposedly holding the government's money – known as the "burn company" – turned into smoke. Its address was either a phone booth or a vacant lot.

What made the scheme so attractive was the staggering amount of money involved. The average fuel tanker holds about eight thousand gallons. Federal and state taxes hover around forty to fifty cents per gallon, depending on the state. It wasn't long before Agron and Balagula were selling $150 million worth of fuel every month and pocketing $30 to $40 million a month in unpaid state and federal taxes.

Around the same time, Lawrence "Sal" Iorizzo – a 450-pound independent wholesaler who ran three hundred gas stations on Long Island – had also worked out the daisy chain scam. But Iorizzo's cash-heavy operation had inadvertently attracted unwanted attention. A couple of wiseguys showed up one day having decided they were going to be his partners. To protect himself, Iorizzo turned to Michael Franzese, an up-and-coming member of the Colombo family. In exchange for taking care of Iorizzo's problem – which was done swiftly and effectively with one menacing visit – Franzese and the Colombos became Iorizzo's partners.

A few months later, Franzese was introduced to three Russian gas wholesalers in Brooklyn – Michael Markowitz, David Bogatin, and Lev Persits – who were having problems getting their scam off the ground. To begin with, they were owed some money. Then, they were finding it difficult to arrange certain licences from the state. Franzese explained that debt collection was a Colombo specialty and, also, that the family had someone inside the state capital who could help with the licences. The Russians quickly realized this was an offer they couldn't refuse.

Franzese merged the Russians' wholesale business with Iorizzo's retail outlets, took 75 per cent for himself – which he then spread around the rest of the Colombo family – and left the Russians with 25 per cent. But that wasn't necessarily a bad deal for the Russians because in four years the scheme defrauded New York, New Jersey, Connecticut, Pennsylvania, and Florida, as well as the federal government, out of nearly half a billion dollars.

As Franzese later testified, "It was not unusual for me to receive $9 million in cash per week in paper bags from the Russians and Iorizzo. Our profits ran anywhere from two to thirty cents per gallon, and at one point we were moving four hundred to five hundred million gallons per month."

Before long, the Russians expanded the joint venture with Franzese and the Colombos to include securities and insurance fraud, and loan sharking. They also went into the banking business. Iorizzo had contacts in Panama, where he'd formed several offshore companies, and Bogatin had contacts in Europe. So Iorizzo, the Russians, Franzese, and the Colombos pooled some money, constructed a web of offshore shells, and bought themselves a bank in Austria.

Then someone tried to kill Agron.

In January 1984, a lone gunman walked up to him outside his apartment at 100 Ocean Avenue in Park Slope, Brooklyn, and shot him in the neck. He survived. While he was on the operating table, doctors pulled bullets out of him from a previous shooting. Later, he told detectives that he couldn't identify his attacker, and anyway, he intended to take care of the matter himself.

Apparently he didn't. Sixteen months later, on May 4, 1985, when he walked out of the front door of his fifth-floor apartment on his way to the elevator, someone put two bullets in his head. This time he didn't survive.

His bodyguard and chauffeur, an ex-wrestler named Boris "Beeba" Nayfeld – who'd been waiting downstairs to drive him to his daily steam bath – suddenly drove away. When the police caught up with him he told them he just couldn't imagine how anything like that might have happened. The very next day, Marat Balagula moved into Agron's office above the El Caribe and Nayfeld went to work for Balagula.

It wasn't long before Balagula also got connected with Italians – in this case the Lucchese family – cutting them in to collect debts and acquire the proper licences. It turned out to be a relationship that saved his life. A fellow named Vladimir Reznikov who had decided he wanted to be Balagula's partner strolled up to Balagula one day in a Brighton Beach restaurant, stuck a gun in his head, and said that the price for not pulling the trigger was part of the gas-tax action and six hundred thousand dollars' walking-around money. Marat convinced Reznikov that the offer sounded perfectly fine, then phoned his Italian pals. They took the threat against Balagula personally, got the hit okayed, and eliminated Vladimir.

The State of New York then tried to plug the loophole through which the scam worked, by changing the way fuel was taxed. It had no real effect, however, as the Russians and their Italian cohorts reacted by changing the way they ran their daisy chains, switching from gasoline to diesel fuel, which was still being taxed in the old way.

By this time, Iorizzo was also in trouble. He'd first appeared on law enforcement's radar screens in early 1984. As soon as he heard they were closing in on him, he fled to Panama. But in a rare show of co-operation with the United States, the Panamanians sent him home. So Iorizzo spilled the beans on, among others, Franzese. At the age of fifty-seven, Iorizzo was installed in the witness protection program under the name Lawrence M. Harrison. As Harrison, he almost immediately violated his deal by getting back into a fuel-tax scam, and wound up being sent away for fifteen years. Franzese was also convicted, also decided to co-operate, and gave up several of his former Colombo associates.

Franzese's three Russian partners now decided they didn't need the

Italians any more and struck out on the their own. Proving them wrong, the Colombos had Markowitz shot and killed. Persits was also shot, although he survived, permanently disabled. Panicked, Bogatin decided Austria offered a healthier climate than Brooklyn and made a run for it. The Feds got to him before the Colombos, dragged him home, put him on trial, convicted him, and shipped him off to prison.

As is often the case where loads of money are at stake, Balagula's scam also, inevitably, turned to mayhem. Everyone was skimming off the top, essentially stealing from one another. It was too big for any one person to control, and anyway, Balagula was too busy juggling his businesses and acquired assets. Among other things, he owned a New York mansion decorated in pink marble and his own private island off Africa.

Through two fuel distributorships that he ran – one was called Mallard, the other Energy Makers of America – he dealt with the R&R Cab Corporation. That was owned by Nayfeld and his brother Benjamin, who also shared interests in arms and drugs trafficking.

When the cops finally closed in on Balagula, he fled the country, hooking up in Africa with his chum Shabtai Kalmanovitch, a "businessman" with access to a supply of Israeli passports. Kalmanovitch was wanted in the United States, and was widely believed to have close ties to the KGB. One of his main bases of operation was Sierra Leone, where he had enough political clout to wind up owning, personally, most of the nation's diamond wealth.

Together, Balagula and Kalmanovitch imported gas to Sierra Leone, a deal supposedly brokered through a company controlled by fugitive U.S. businessman Marc Rich and financed with a guarantee by the Luccheses. Balagula and Kalmanovitch also put together deals in South Africa and Bophuthatswana. Later Balagula's friends would claim that they lost money on every deal they did with Kalmanovitch. True or not, eventually, the Israelis caught up with Kalmanovitch, accused him of selling state secrets to the Syrians, tried him as a spy, and sent him to jail. But he stayed locked up only for a few years, suggesting that some of his reputed KGB connections might, in fact, have had some pull.

On the run again, Balagula got arrested in Germany. Whatever connections he had proved useless as the Germans sent him back to the United States, where he was tried for a 1980 credit card fraud he'd put together with the Nayfeld brothers. They'd matched counterfeit cards to a list of clients' names stolen from stock brokers Merrill Lynch and managed to steal three hundred thousand dollars on the cards before anyone could put a stop to it. The judge sentenced him to eight years.

Then the government put a gas-tax fraud case together against him – for evading $85 million in federal taxes on nearly a billion gallons of fuel sold between 1983 and 1988 – and rebooked his cell for an additional ten years.

Then the Lucchese crowd, which was still running Balagula's gas-tax scam, heard that the Genovese family also had Russian partners in a gas-tax scam. So Tony Casso, the Lucchese underboss who had been Balagula's immediate partner, set up a meeting with underbosses from the other two families, plus their Russian partners, and suggested everyone work together. He argued that by combining their efforts, they could run a mega-scam across the entire eastern seaboard. That sounded pretty good to everyone else, so that's what happened.

Then the Gambino family came along.

Some Russians in New Jersey had decided to set up a scam and had gone to the Gambinos, and for the privilege of working in Gambino territory, showed respect and cut them in. So now Casso and the others invited the Gambinos and their partners to sign on.

Needless to say, an operation of this magnitude did not escape attention. By 1992, the FBI and the IRS were working a sting that came to be known as Operation Red Daisy. From a base in Newark, New Jersey, they were able to get inside several fuel distributors and begin picking apart various Russian-Italian joint ventures. The four-year investigation focused on the theft of over $140 million in Federal motor-fuel excise tax revenue and "tribute payments" made by the Russians to their LCN partners, including money that made its way up to Gambino boss John Gotti.

After considering the evidence, which included more than twelve hundred taped phone conversations and enough surveillance film to fill a thousand square-foot storage area, a federal grand jury returned indictments on twenty-five people, including fifteen Russians. Included in the charges was money laundering, as profits from the scam were hidden in Greece, Switzerland, Latvia, Aruba, and the British Virgin Islands. The biggest fish caught in this particular net was mobster Anthony "Fat Tony" Morelli. He was convicted of racketeering, extortion, interstate travel in aid of racketeering, money laundering, mail fraud, wire fraud, and tax evasion, and sent away for twenty years.

As more and more daisy chains have been shut down, the Russians and the Italians have moved on to "cocktailed" fuel scams. By blending non-taxed products such as kerosene, waste oil, and toxic wastes with taxable fuels, they've been able to increase the volume of product on which they can collect tax. The fact that these mixtures are highly polluting and, at times, decidedly dangerous, is beyond their concern. They now also move fuels around interstate, otherwise arbitraging taxes. Buying fuel in New Jersey, where state taxes are lower than in New York, then selling it in New York, can make a difference of two, three, or four cents per gallon.

In their simplest form, these deals are simply classic sales-tax scams, the likes of which get worked by small-time crooks in dozens of countries every day. In the European Union, motor fuel is taxed in a different manner so organized crime hasn't bothered with it. There are some instances where crooks have worked similar scams with diesel fuel. In the U.K., there is one where the chemical colouring of untaxed fuel is removed so that it can be sold as taxed fuel. It's particularly prevalent in Northern Ireland and known to be one of the many money-spinners used by the IRA. There is also active smuggling of non-taxed diesel fuel across the Northern Ireland–Republic of Ireland border.

FBI Director Louis Freeh says that there are fifty-four countries around the world that have an active Russian organized crime presence. Top of the list is the United States, where several dozen groups operate. Nearly as many have appeared in Canada. Russians are also showing up in great numbers in Australia, New Zealand, and throughout the Pacific. But after North America, Europe is their main target. And the Europeans are playing right into their hands.

In the past, ethnically defined immigrants have always moved into well-established ethnic communities – the way the Russians moved into Brighton Beach – where their presence naturally took root. That is no longer the case.

Furthermore, unlike the massive immigration of the nineteenth century, or even those Europeans who flooded into North America prior to World War II, this wave is not agrarian. Russians on the move today are educated and technologically competent. The don't need land to farm, just cities with telephones that can accommodate modem plugs.

They have swarmed into Eastern Europe – familiar territory after so many years of Communist occupation – to "recolonize" Hungary, Poland, the Czech Republic, and Slovakia. From there they have headed west, starting with the city they knew best, Berlin. Today Russian organized crime groups are operating in Germany with near-impunity.

Because of the damage done by the Nazi SS and other secret-police organizations, the newly unified Germany legislated wide-ranging privacy rights, placing strict limitations on police search-and-seizure powers. For instance, it has only been within the past few years that police there have been given the right to use wiretaps, and then only under very specific circumstances. The issue remains highly emotive.

"It is as if," one senior German law enforcement official said, "the Russian mafia is using computers while we German police are stuck with an abacus."

Cocaine comes into Europe by sea from South America, arriving at Rotterdam, Genoa, and Barcelona, and increasingly into the coast of Galicia. Marijuana enters Europe mainly from Morocco. It is ferried into Gibraltar and Spain for distribution across the rest of the continent. Russian organized crime groups are, however, trying to attract activity into Baltic ports, both to ease importation into Russia and also as a transshipment point for the rest of Europe.

The former Soviet Union is the major transshipment point for Afghan drugs coming into Europe, and even though most of the heroin that arrives in the U.K. is manifested in Turkey, the scale of Russian criminal activity is staggering. According to the Office of National Statistics, the income of organized crime in Britain is so huge – approximately £8 billion – that by not including it in the nation's published accounts, those accounts give "a distorted picture of the British economy."

Britain is an especially prime target for synthetic drugs – tipped as the nightmare of the next millennium – because they have become, for all intents and purposes, legal. Easily made in basement laboratories and often referred to as "club drugs," they are so widely distributed at raves and parties and in clubs that more than one million ecstasy tablets are reportedly consumed every weekend in Britain.

Synthetic drugs are often manufactured in the country where they are sold. Smaller groups, such as outlaw motorcycle gangs, get involved precisely because all that's needed are the base ingredients and someplace to cook them. But here, too, there are indications that Poland has become a major source of ecstasy and that both Russia and Latvia are also sources of supply. If that's the case, then look for Russian organized crime groups to bring club drugs into Western Europe as well.

The Russians have established themselves in London neighbourhoods like Maida Vale, Swiss Cottage, and Hampstead, where once only the British lived. They've invaded the French Riviera and bought up the largest properties, where once only wealthy Brits, Americans, and Arabs lived. They've gone to Paris and moved into the choicest *quartiers*. They've bought big villas in Rome as well. They've moved into Toronto. And wherever they settle, there is Russian organized crime.

Not all of it is immediately visible. Only some of it is commanded locally. Much of it is run by remote control – men sitting on sunny balconies, overlooking a beach somewhere, with cellphones, e-mail, and fax machines. After cutting their teeth on the indignities of Communism, in a society where breaking rules and survival were all too often synonymous, the Russians have found that life in the West turns out to be dead easy.

The West is their candy store.

6

THE B TEAM

They come from the most disorganized country in the world, how do you want them to become organized just like that?

– Former NYPD detective Peter Grinenko

Beeba Nayfeld thought he had a really good idea.

He'd arrived in America in 1978 at the age of thirty-one, to find that the openness of capitalist society was like a printed invitation to fraudsters. He couldn't believe the abundance of opportunities, wherever he looked, everywhere. What he hadn't counted on was getting arrested so soon.

Nabbed on Long Island in 1980 for having worked that credit card scam with Marat Balagula, he was charged with grand larceny. But thanks to clever lawyering, he was allowed to plead guilty to petty larceny. It was a first-hand lesson that the American justice system could be beaten. He served no time.

By 1985, the cops were looking at him again, this time because of the murder of his boss, Evsei Agron. They suspected Nayfeld of having been involved, and indications are that he was, but they could never prove it, so he walked.

It was just after that, while working for Balagula as his *consiglieri*, that his really good idea came to him. He reckoned that if the Russians and Italians could do gas-tax frauds together, they could do other business together as well. And when one of the Gambino gang mentioned the word *heroin*, Nayfeld was sure he'd found his niche.

He put together a consortium of ten Russians and six Italians to finance a connection through Eastern Europe, which essentially made Boris "Beeba" Nayfeld the first Russian to form an international strategic alliance with the LCN.

Heroin was acquired in Thailand – an easy enough stunt to manage – and packed inside television sets. Picture tubes were sheered in half, the drugs stuffed inside them, and the tubes then resealed. Even the wiring was put back in place, making it almost impossible to detect any sign that the sets had been tampered with.

According to the bills of lading, the televisions were destined for Singapore. But they were shipped first to Poland. Oddly, no Customs officers along the way ever wondered why these TV sets were taking such a circuitous route to their destination. The drugs were off-loaded in Poland, then couriered to New York in parcels weighing three to five pounds, where the LCN took over.

Because U.S. Customs and the DEA normally looked for drugs to come in from the Orient and South America, it was quite a while before they cottoned on to this route. Yet word of Nayfeld's huge success had easily reached other Russian gangsters, who decided they wanted in. One of them was Monya Elson.

Another graduate from the Evsei Agron crime school, Elson had also come to America in 1978, but without a criminal history. Nicknamed "Kishinevsky," a reference to the Moldavian town where he was born, Elson worked for a clothing designer and a jeweller before joining Agron's brigade. But he found that as an employee he wasn't feared, and because he yearned to be feared – to make a name for himself – he moved to Israel, to try his hand at drug trafficking. Within a few months he was arrested and convicted for selling cocaine, and sent away for six years. By the time he returned to Brighton Beach in 1990, a lot had changed. Agron was dead, Balagula was in jail, and Beeba was now a big shot.

Jealous of what Nayfeld had accomplished, Elson established his own crew, known as Monya's Brigade, and with some muscle behind him, set about trying to take over Brooklyn. He threatened and extorted anyone he thought had money. He got into drugs and co-sponsored a number of multi-kilo deals with members of the Genovese gang. He ran insurance scams. And he tried to establish himself as a *rukovodstovo*, a sort of godfather who mediated underworld disputes. From his Rasputin headquarters – a gaudy nightclub on Coney Island Avenue where the walls are rose-coloured marble and, true or not, customers bragged that there were bulletproof doors in the toilets – he listened to other crooks voice their complaints, then pronounced a settlement in exchange for a cut of their action.

Still, he wasn't making the kind of money Nayfeld was making, which was the kind of money he wanted to make. Eventually, Elson decided that the way to strike fear into potential rivals and move in on Nayfeld's territory was by murdering him. What he never understood was that his reputation for irrational violence would get in the way of his master plan because enemies were beginning to line up.

"The problem was," says former cop Peter Grinenko, "Monya was a moron. He only got people mad. He kept pushing people. And sometimes he pushed the wrong ones too far."

In January 1991, Monya pushed Beeba too far. He ordered a bomb planted under Nayfeld's car, which at the time was parked in front of a local school. The police later explained that the weather had been too cold and had frozen the detonator. Had it gone off, there is no telling how many children would have been killed. However, the incident did not go unnoticed by Nayfeld.

Elson next moved on Vyacheslav Lyubarsky who had been associated with Elson's Italian partners. When some drug money went missing, Elson decided that Lyubarsky had switched sides and was plotting against him with Nayfeld. Elson shot Lyubarsky in early March of that year, but merely wounded him. This time, Nayfeld responded.

In May, a group of gunmen attacked Elson. Except that they botched the job and Elson lived to play another day.

Round two came in January 1992. Lyubarsky, his wife Nellie, and their son Vadim were just coming home after dinner, when assassins appeared in the hallway and liquidated father and son.

Nine days after that, one of Elson's lieutenants, Efrim Ostrovsky, was rubbed out in Queens by Alexander Slepinin. Word on the street was that Slepinin worked for Nayfeld and that Elson was the next name on his contract hit list. So in June, Elson launched a pre-emptive strike and murdered Slepinin.

Two weeks later, another Nayfeld associate, Elbrous Evdoev, was shot but only wounded. That particular missed hit troubled Elson enough to resolve that perhaps the weather was better in Los Angeles. It's not sure when he actually moved there, or how long he planned to stay, but Nayfeld located him there and, in November, tried yet again to kill him.

Elson was shot in the arm and driven to the hospital by his associate Leonyard Kanterkantetes. Two days later, someone tried to plant a bomb under Kanterkantetes's car, and was killed when it accidentally went off. Now, Elson dropped out of sight, and he stayed out of sight. He didn't reappear until he heard that Nayfeld had hurriedly left the country.

On Monday, July 21, the police in Brooklyn received word he was back in Brooklyn. Nayfeld, hiding in Belgium, heard the same news.

Five days later, on Saturday afternoon, Oleg Zapinakmine – who was Elson's bodyguard and also his nephew – parked the new Lexus in front of Elson's home on East Sixteenth Street in Sheepshead Bay, then got out to open the rear door for his uncle Monya and his aunt Marya.

As they stepped onto the curb, a brown car drove up. The Elsons only managed half a dozen steps towards their home before three men jumped out with shotguns, and started shooting. Elson was hit in the ankle and the thigh. Marya was shot in the back. Zapinakmine suffered a graze wound in the stomach. The gunmen fled.

Ambulances arrived and rushed them all to Coney Island Hospital. Marya was in serious condition when they got her into the operating room, but she pulled through. Monya and Oleg were declared stable and treated, and the pair of them walked out several hours later.

When they interviewed the victims at the hospital, the police were interested to learn that Elson was carrying three hundred thousand dollars' worth of watches and gems. One shotgun was found at the scene. The getaway car and a second shotgun were found a block away. However, none of the victims was eager to help the police with their investigation and, because the cops knew who Elson was, none of them spent much time pursuing the possibility that robbery was the motive. Later that night, the police speculated that this was someone's way of telling Elson he was no longer welcome in Brooklyn. To reinforce that message, someone killed nephew Oleg, and then killed Elson's friend Alexander "Sasha Pinya" Levichitz.

Now Monya decided that Mediterranean weather was even better than California weather. Word on the street was that he was hoping to find safety among the tens of thousands of Russian immigrants in Israel.

Nayfeld had felt the heat too.

He'd heard that the DEA was closing in on his heroin ring, and was worried that Elson might be getting closer as well. So he took himself to Egedem, Belgium, a suburb of Antwerp, and the safety provided by friends. One of those friends was Rachmiel "Mike" Brandwain. Another was Riccardo Fanchini.

The Russians had established a community in Antwerp even before they began populating Brighton Beach. The city was the home of an international diamond market and a port well-known for smuggling. The refugees who settled there, especially those who arrived in the 1970s and early 1980s, added money laundering to the list of local attractions.

Brandwain had gotten in on the ground floor. Born in the Ukraine, he was ten when the family emigrated to Israel in 1959. He did his military service in the merchant navy, which was when he first saw Antwerp. As soon as he got out of the navy he moved to Belgium and started his hustle.

He dabbled for a while with textiles, but it was thanks to the slow demise of Eastern Europe and the creation of a huge black market by Russian soldiers in East Germany that he really scored. The soldiers stole whatever wasn't nailed down and un-nailed whatever was, so they could steal that too. Brandwain strolled into the middle of this mayhem and picked up mountains of stuff – including electronics gear and military hardware – at fire-sale prices. He then marketed it through his company, M&S International. He earned the confidence of senior officers who, when they found themselves with bulging pockets and no knowledge of the western financial markets, turned to Brandwain to become their laundryman.

Operating out of a house on Heren Street, in the heart of Antwerp's diamond district, he had contacts with certain diamond merchants who had established a money-laundering operation that linked them to diamond merchants in London and Israel. He began by feeding the Russians' money through that existing setup. As the black market grew and the amounts needing to be washed increased, he constructed a network of offshore companies, designed specifically to shift millions from East Germany and Moscow into secret bank accounts in Geneva, New York, and Tel Aviv.

When Nayfeld arrived, he found everything he needed to maintain his drug trafficking, including the web of companies surrounding M&S International. Within weeks, a metric ton of cocaine, sourced in Antwerp, showed up in Vyborg, Russia.

Later, Brandwain would publicly deny ever having anything to do with drug trafficking. But it simply wasn't true. Interpol claims that Brandwain was definitely involved in drugs, and arms trafficking as well, and had also discussed murder with Nayfeld and specifically with reference to Elson.

Oddly, it's down to Israeli intelligence (Mossad) to partially defend Brandwain. They say that while Nayfeld was in Antwerp, the drugs were his, and that Brandwain was merely the financier who did for his mate Beeba what he'd been doing for years for the Russian army. The situation changed when Nayfeld went back to the States to renew his passport and never returned.

Brandwain was facing extortion from a Moscow crime faction that had moved in on M&S International, so he called some friends in the diamond business to help him take over Nayfeld's business. Eight years before, he'd been involved in a smuggling ring with local jewellers. They'd been short-circuiting the taxman by moving gold and diamonds to jewellers in London's Hatten Garden and New York's Forty-seventh Street. British Customs somehow got inside this very closed Orthodox Jewish community – members usually conduct all their business in Yiddish – and wound up arresting several people for Value Added Tax (VAT) – the equivalent of GST – fraud.

Because the smuggling process is the same whether the contraband is gold, diamonds, dirty money, or drugs, resurrecting that earlier connection gave Brandwain a way to move heroin into Britain. And despite the fact that the North London Jewish communities of Stamford Hill and Golders Green roundly and with one voice condemn drug trafficking, Brandwain was able to find a few people to help him move product.

It didn't last long, however. In 1996, a thirty-four-year-old Israeli living in Antwerp was arrested at Ramsgate with fifteen kilos hidden under the rear seat of his car. He got eleven years for it. The drugs were ultimately destined for the Glasgow market. They had been paid for by a Scottish trafficker named David Santini. He was arrested in a separate incident and got thirteen years for that. The Israeli's contact was a Russian Orthodox Jew whom he was to meet in North London. An intelligence operation keyed on him led to the arrest of several other Orthodox Jews, including a man from Antwerp stopped at Dover with ten kilos of heroin hidden in a rental car; an American living in North London arriving from Antwerp at the French side of the Channel Tunnel with heroin and cocaine in his car; and a Talmudic scholar in Israel who'd run a private bank, laundering money through a charity.

Brandwain would have also been arrested had he not been gunned down in mid-July 1998 in broad daylight on an Antwerp street. The contract is believed to have been put out by those people in Moscow who'd elbowed their way into M&S International and were now trying to get into the middle of his heroin ring.

Nayfeld's other friend in Antwerp, Riccardo Marian Fanchini, had also been on to a good thing when Nayfeld first arrived. Polish by birth, and not Italian as his name suggests, Fanchini was chairman of Kremlyovskaya, a company making Belgian vodka and selling it, duty free, to Russia. While the money was rolling in, Fanchini hung out in Monte Carlo and followed the Formula One Grand Prix racing circuit. Through Kremlyovskaya, he even sponsored racing teams for a while, including Jordan Peugeot in 1995, with drivers Eddie Irvine and Rubens Barrichello.

Fanchini and Nayfeld went way back, to the early days in Brighton Beach, along with a third friend, Yakov Tilipman, who now ran Benitexes, the Moscow importer of Kremlyovskaya vodka. In 1987, Tilipman had been arrested in New York in connection with some major jewel thefts. His accomplice was named as Jerzy Bank, who turned out to be Fanchini.

Now high on the FBI's list of suspected Russian organized criminals, Fanchini's company was being looked at as a money-laundering front. But before anyone could shut him down, the Russians repealed the law permitting the importation of tax-free vodka, effectively pulling the plug on Kremlyovskaya. By the time the 1996 Monaco Grand Prix rolled around, Eddie Jordan and the management of Peugeot realized who they'd been dealing with and bailed out.

The Belgians didn't like the way Kremlyovskaya had gone bankrupt, and arrested Fanchini on fraud charges. The FBI also put in their bid for his time once the Belgians were through with him. In the meantime, Nayfeld's passport ran out.

Fearing that no U.S. embassy or consulate would renew it for him, he snuck back into the United States to do it himself. He managed it quickly, without any hassles, and was on his way to Kennedy Airport, with a one-way ticket to London, when the DEA grabbed him.

One of the first things he did when he realized he wasn't leaving the country again for a very long time, if ever, was to settle at least one old score. He grassed on Monya Elson, implicating him in heroin trafficking and murder.

Until 1995, the only Russian criminals the Italian National Police had seen were some independent operators trying to pass off counterfeit money, and prostitutes showing up on street corners. In February, they received word from the DEA that a man they wanted for extortion, drug trafficking, and murder was believed to be living in the country. It was Monya Elson.

Asked by the DEA to keep an eye on him while they prepared extradition papers, the Italians became concerned, mindful of the threat Elson posed. So senior managers at the Italian National Police ordered the elite "Second Bureau" of the Service Centrale Operativo to target him.

Under the command of a driven and successful Mafia hunter, Dr. Alessandro Pansa, the team operated out of a secret – no signs – modern fortress-like location in a working-class district of Rome, where heavily armed guards patrol the perimeter gates and strict security inspections control who comes in and who leaves. With the wealth of sources built up over years of pursuing Italian organized crime, Pansa's men launched Operation Rasputin, located Elson living in the Hotel Angela in the Adriatic coastal village of Fano, and placed him under surveillance.

They knew they could arrest him whenever they wanted to under Italy's "Mafia association laws," which made it a crime to have organized crime affiliations. It was also evident that he was living in Italy illegally, so even without the DEA's extradition request they could deport him back to the States. But Pansa had too many questions and wasn't going to interrupt Mr. Elson's life until he had all the answers.

They listened to him speaking on the phone to Shabtai Kalmanovitch and also to a Russian living in Budapest named Semion Mogilevitch. Little did they realize at the time that Mogilevitch would soon be described in the West as the most dangerous man in the world.

Pansa expanded the intelligence gathering to determine what Elson was doing in the country and, especially, whether or not he was there on his own. What Pansa's men unearthed astounded their bosses.

Heavyweight Russian criminals had been operating openly in Italy for over two years, making major real estate investments in Sardinia and laundering money on a massive scale. Others had established export businesses all over Italy, to purchase goods for cash, then ship them back to Russia. Still others had shoved a number of highly suspect financial transactions through the Italian banking system. A small group had settled quietly in Italy as early as 1981–82, implanted there for no other reason than to lend logistical support to another group working out of Moscow. And yet other Russians – these unassociated with the ones living in Italy – were flocking into the country, opening bank accounts, filling them with cash, then wiring the money out of the country, typically to havens like Switzerland, before closing the accounts and never being seen again.

For the Italians, now greatly worried, Elson looked like a minor player. They knew about his Brooklyn past, and that he often commuted between Israel and Italy. They knew he was shipping furniture to Russia and dealing in gold. They also discovered that he was laundering a lot of money.

On March 8, 1995, Pansa gave the order to arrest him. They grabbed Elson in Fano and locked him up. They held his wife for a while, too. And after all the usual rigmarole of extradition, the Second Bureau handed him over to the DEA who brought him to the States, where he will be a permanent resident at a federal facility until he dies.

Pansa's men moved on to bigger fish, one whose name appeared in Elson's money-laundering scheme. Yuri Essine had an export business just like Elson's, sending consumer goods, foodstuffs, and furniture back to Russia. It's become a typical way of masking tax fraud and, through double-invoicing, capital flight. Essine, too, invested in gold, an obvious way to launder the funds he was stealing through his export business.

But Essine was not the insecure fool that Elson was. Born in Russia's easternmost port, Vladivostok, in 1951, he'd been a gang member there before moving to Moscow and joining a group called Primorskaya. Over the years, he'd earned a reputation as a cunning and ruthless criminal. When his friend Sergei Timofeyev – nicknamed "Sylvester" because he fancied himself the Russian Rambo – assumed command of the group, Essine contracted with Kurganskaya to have him murdered, and duly took Sylvester's place.

He'd arrived in Italy in 1994. The Second Bureau found him living with his wife in a huge estate in Santa Marinella, on the coast northwest of Rome. Surrounding him was a ring of Russian nationals, many of them Sylvester's former henchmen and bodyguards, who now protected and worked with Essine.

Over time, the Bureau was able to tie this group into crimes being committed outside Italy, including extortion, kidnapping, arms dealing, alcohol smuggling, and car theft. Inside Italy, they linked Essine to the Mafia: he was supplying their clubs on the Adriatic coast with Russian prostitutes. He was also extorting an Italian businessman with interests in Moscow, making him pay a *krysha* of four thousand dollars a month. Essine's name surfaced in connection with two kidnapping cases in Italy, although both victims were Russian nationals. One was said to have stolen $3 million from Solntsevo and Essine wanted it returned. The Italians later heard on a wiretap that the man had been killed. The second owed Essine a personal debt and he wanted it settled.

Unlike Elson, Essine was a major player, not just because he had heavyweight crime connections, but also because of his dealings in oil.

In the mid-1990s, there were around forty joint-venture Russian oil companies operating in Europe, the Middle East, and North America. Most of them were set up to pilfer the nation's assets and move money out of Russia. Essine's was Globus Trading, which operated both as a buyer and a broker of oil and petroleum products. To handle the brokering side of the business, he brought in Alberto Grotti, a vice-president of the Italian oil company ENI. Essine held a 30 per cent stake. Grotti secretly had the same.

Together they used Globus to launder money from Russia, through Austria, Great Britain, and Switzerland. Globus also dealt in counterfeit currencies, importing forged U.S. dollars from Russia in thirty-thousand- to fifty-thousand-dollar parcels.

Their investigation of Globus led the Second Bureau to a forty-nine-year-old former KGB agent who lived in Rome named Dimitry Naumov. Already deported from France and Austria for his questionable dealings, in addition to being part of Essine's counterfeit currency ring he also dealt in other false paper, including passports. He moved some of Essine's oil through his own company, Dimex, and had worked out a scheme to ship $20 million worth of frozen meat to Russia. The paperwork was made to look like a bogus foreign aid program so that he didn't have to pay European duties.

More importantly, he too had ties to Semion Mogilevitch and was known to be dealing in fissile materials, particularly the dubious substance red mercury. He'd lived in Vienna and knew the Averin brothers – Viktor and Aleksandr – who were suspected of being senior officers in the Solntsevo. And he also knew their boss, the man said to be the head of the group, Sergei Mikhailov.

The Second Bureau now believes that it was in Vienna that Naumov first encountered the Russian businessman Grigory Loutchansky, whose company, Nordex, had been based there. Loutchansky has also been suspected of dealing in fissile materials – he has been described by *Time* magazine as "the most pernicious unindicted criminal in the world" – and apparently wound up owning Dimex.

Not surprisingly, Naumov was an especially interesting link for the Italians because it tied Essine directly into all these other players. What they didn't yet know was just how strong those links were. Then, in April 1996, for some still unknown reason, Essine and Naumov went their separate ways. And it was an acrimonious separation.

After months of surveillance on the pair, plus thousands of hours of wiretaps on forty different telephones they used, the Second Bureau decided that by arresting Naumov – on charges of illegal weapons and document forgery – they might learn more about Essine, Mogilevitch, the Averins, Mikhailov, and Loutchansky. So in June they grabbed him.

During the search of his apartment, they found documents detailing arms trafficking between Russia and Austria, and evidence that pointed to Naumov's involvement with the trafficking of radioactive substances, and scams centring around red mercury.

For whatever reason, they didn't hold him very long, and once released, he fled home to Russia. On September 23, ten days after he arrived in Moscow, he was sitting in the bar of the Hotel Tverskaya when two men walked up behind him and put eight bullets in the back of his head.

As their investigation continued to broaden, the Italians now came across a name that gravely worried them – Aleksandr Solonik. A former Russian policeman who'd been fired after he was accused of committing rape, he was a hired killer and a charter member of the infamous Kurganskaya Brigade. The Russians had issued a warrant for Solonik's arrest as the prime suspect in the Timofeyev murder. Shortly thereafter he was identified in a routine police identity check. A gunfight followed, during which Solonik used a seventeen-round Glock pistol to kill four officers. It took a bullet through his kidney to stop him.

Under questioning, he confessed to being a contract killer, but declined to go into detail and categorically refused to name his employers. There was a brief trial. He was sentenced to life and installed at Moscow's maximum-security Matrosskaya Tishina prison. He escaped in June 1995.

The story is that his employers, in gratitude for his silence, paid his guard half a million dollars to plant a dummy in Solonik's bunk and help him crawl down a drainpipe. The breakout added to the Solonik legend that had long been building in the Russian underworld. Stories abound of him jumping out courtroom windows, of disappearing in the nick of time, of two-handed two-gun shootouts, of South American plastic surgery to change his face.

The Second Bureau discovered that he'd been living in Rome for two years using the name Vladimir Kesov and that he travelled regularly between Italy and Greece. They were able to locate an apartment he used, watched it for two months, and when he didn't show up, broke in. They found it stocked with three Kalashnikovs, two small Scorpion machine guns, seven pistols, two shotguns, twenty-five hundred rounds of ammunition, silencers, laser aiming devices, knives, wigs and other disguises. They also found documents indirectly connecting Solonik to Essine. Oddly, the two associated with many of the same women, but the Second Bureau was never able to establish a connection more direct than that.

The Greek authorities were notified and the search for him centred on Athens. They located him living in a large, rented seafront villa – they claim he was dealing weapons and running a string of prostitutes from there – and notified the Russian authorities. An elite team was dispatched from Moscow to bring him back. It arrived a day too late.

On February 2, 1997, Solonik was found wrapped in black plastic garbage bags in the woods twelve miles north of Athens. The thirty-seven-year-old had been strangled from behind with a wire. After two weeks, when no one claimed the body, the Greeks buried him in a pauper's grave.

A woman's body was found only three hundred yards from the villa. It took some time to identify her because she'd been chopped to bits, stuffed into a suitcase, and buried. She turned out to be Solonik's girlfriend, a former Miss Russia and a one-time student at Britain's Lime House boarding school – nineteen-year-old Svetlana Kotova.

No one has ever been charged with the two murders, nor is anyone ever likely to be. The Greeks put it down to an underworld settling of scores. Sources say that Kurganskaya owed Solonik a lot of money for previous contracts, that they weren't paying him, and that he'd been threatening the killers who had hired him to murder others.

In Italy, some investigators have proposed an alternative theory. They claim that the team of Russian police who went to Greece to bring Solonik home was a decoy, and that another team preceded it. It was the first group of cops who exacted revenge for Solonik's killing of the four policemen and then dismembered Kotova to send a message to others that cop killers – especially when the killer is a former policeman himself – would not be tolerated.

The Italians then learned that Solonik had been planning to come to Rome that same week to fulfil a contract. His target was to have been Yuri Essine. So the Bureau's attention now refocused on him. Pansa ordered Essine's arrest and a daring plan was set into motion.

In mid-March, a group of Pansa's men moved surreptitiously into the little ski resort of Madonna di Campino. Essine was holding court there, in the Golf Hotel, celebrating his forty-sixth birthday with a dozen associates. The police skilfully gathered the intelligence information they needed, and put officers into the Golf as tourists and waiters. On the afternoon of March 15 and throughout the day on March 16, the rest of the team, nearly eighty officers, furtively moved into place. Some of them hid in the next village. Others hid in the hotel next door.

At precisely 4 a.m. on March 17, police invaded thirteen rooms. The entire raid lasted fifteen minutes. Essine and his friends were awakened and arrested, their rooms were searched, and then they were hustled out of the hotel. By 5 a.m., everyone was on their way back to Rome. And not one of the hotel's regular guests ever realized what had happened.

Globus was promptly dismantled, and Grotti would have been sent to jail, had he not already been there, serving a three-year sentence for corruption. Unfortunately, the wheels of Italian justice ground too slowly, and after a very long time of waiting to come to trial, Essine was allowed to bail himself out of jail. Naturally, he skipped. The Italians don't know where he is – they presume he's back in Russia – but are certain that he's no longer operating in their country. He has since been tried in absentia, found guilty, and will spend the rest of his life in jail if they get him back.

The void left in Brooklyn by Nayfeld and Elson had been more than filled. A heavyweight had moved in. Or, at least, a 150-pound guy with bad skin whom everyone believed to be a heavyweight.

Vyacheslav Kirillovich Ivankov also hailed from Vladivostok but was Essine's senior by eleven years. He arrived there on New Year's Day, 1940. The shape of his face and the cast of his eyes gave him a slightly oriental look, which led to his nickname, "Yaponchik," meaning "the little Jap."

The beginning of his criminal career can be traced back to the early 1960s when, as a follower of a thief-in-law called "the Mongol," he provided muscle for the gang's extortion schemes. His ruthlessness earned him a reputation both inside and outside criminal circles. It led ultimately to his arrest by Soviet law enforcement and a five-year sentence. It was during that stretch in jail that he became a *vory v zakone*.

When his time was up, he returned to the streets and formed his own gang, made up mostly of ex-athletes. But with each act of violence he merely called attention to himself, and by 1981 he was back behind bars, this time to serve a fourteen-year stretch in a Siberian gulag.

Released after ten years – thanks entirely to political and judicial connections corrupted by other *vory v zakone* – he was picked up at the prison gates by limo, flown by private jet to Moscow, and welcomed home by his friends with a huge champagne reception at the Metropol Hotel. Shortly thereafter, he left Mother Russia for Germany. From there, he made his way to New York.

The state security force (MVD) in Moscow warned the FBI about Ivankov, and based on what the Russians were saying, the Bureau labelled him the most powerful Russian organized crime boss in the United States. One line was that he'd been sent to Brooklyn by the men running the Solntsevo organization with a mandate to take over their interests there and put rival groups out of business. Ivankov himself was telling people that a group of thieves-in-law had sent him to America "to bring order here in émigré circles."

The Russian media gave him credibility in early 1993 when they tagged him one of the country's most important thieves-in-law. The American press picked up on that and basically constructed a reputation that suited him. There are various versions of the myth. One has him as a wrestler who was sent to prison the first time for beating up someone in a bar. Another has him running the black market under the Soviet system. Then there is the story that he was sentenced to fourteen years in prison after he committed a string of robberies disguised as a cop. Yet another has him shipped off to a gulag in 1982 for robbery, forgery, arms trafficking, and drug dealing.

"Who sent him over here?" Jim Moody, then the FBI's organized crime boss, shrugs. "Good question. We didn't know who Ivankov was. The Russians told us he was a thief-in-law and that he was in the U.S. We then had to identify where he was, which was quite difficult because he kept moving around and using all sorts of aliases. It took us a while to pin him down. When we arrested him, he had seven passports from seven different countries. I think he may even have had an American passport."

But Peter Grinenko, the former New York detective and supervising Russian expert for the Brooklyn District Attorney's office, says the whole thing was nonsense, that Ivankov never deserved the reputation of a major Russian bad guy. "He was a car thief who got arrested in Russia when he went to the fellow whose car he stole and tried to sell it back to him. And he wasn't sent here to take over anybody's North

American organization because there is no such thing. Russian organized crime is anything but organized. The key to understanding the Russian *Maffiya* is to realize that they are not actually a mafia. They have no defined organizational structures like the Italians. They're individuals who are into scams and shakedowns, individuals who operate in small groups in order to make money any way they can. There is no pyramid structure, there is no central control, there is no Commission. They don't fit the definition of organized crime because they're not organized. They get involved with people they know and use each other to commit crimes. And once they've done that, they rip each other off."

If the FBI didn't buy Grinenko's theory it was either because they knew better or because it suited their purposes not to. And Moody remains convinced of Ivankov's star status. "He was so important that shortly after he came to the United States, there was an editorial in *Pravda* requesting he be brought back home so that he could get control of the street crime in Moscow. He was an infamous figure in Russia."

He entered the U.S. with a visa, sponsored by a company in New York called Twelve-LA Inc., one of several he hid behind. He claimed that he was in the film business. Within a matter of months after having paid fifteen thousand dollars to marry a Russian woman who'd already become a U.S. citizen, he secured a green card permanent resident's visa.

Once they located him, the FBI put him under surveillance. They watched as this man with a stubby grey beard covering his acne scars settled into life in Brooklyn with his wife. They watched as he regularly cheated on her with several girlfriends, as he bought himself a place in Denver and as he set up a string of shell companies. Media Waves was supposed to have been his drug-trafficking front. Slavic Inc. was supposed to have been his money-laundering front. The chairman of Slavic was a Russian hockey star, Vyacheslav Fetisov, who played in the National Hockey League for the Detroit Red Wings. Fetisov has always denied any wrongdoing. And they watched, with ever-increasing interest, as he travelled to Los Angeles, Miami, Denver, and Boston, to Moscow, Monte Carlo, and Vienna. Especially Vienna, where Ivankov met with friends, where he stashed money, and where one of his two sons was living.

He also travelled to Belgium, where investigators have since found records of a company in Moscow that transferred millions of dollars to Slavic Inc, which links Ivankov to both Brandwain and Nayfeld.

Another place he spent a lot of time was Fairfield, New Jersey, where he frequented the Troika Restaurant. No doubt he was fond of the cooking there but, intriguingly, his cellphone bills, averaging between five thousand and six thousand dollars a month, were sent there to be paid by the restaurant.

Yet, while Ivankov might have somehow managed to fit into the new Wild West that Moscow was fast becoming, he was decidedly out of place in Brighton Beach. It wasn't merely his lack of sophistication, it was also his ego. His clothes, in imitation of a man he clearly admired, New York Mafia boss John Gotti, were much too flashy. And he soon became too visible as a high-roller at the Taj Mahal casino in Atlantic City.

To help the FBI understand who he was, what he was doing, and how they could stop him, they called on the Russian MVD, who sent agents to New York, the first time Russian and American law enforcement had ever co-operated on this level. They analyzed tape recordings, identified photographs, and went onto the streets with the American agents to spot some of the people the FBI didn't know. But it wasn't until Ivankov began extorting money from two Russians on Wall Street that the Bureau could build a case against him.

Alexander Volkov and Vladimir Voloshin had set up a financial advisory firm in New York called Summit International Trading and Investment Corp. Sometime around late 1994, they received a wire of $2.7 million from someone they knew at Moscow's Chara Bank, a licensee of the Central Bank of Russia. So the story goes, the banker was facing difficulties at home and had been especially adept at making certain that the money he was entrusting to Volkov and Voloshin couldn't be traced. There was a run on his bank and he somehow wound up dead. The pair in New York presumed they'd just inherited a fortune.

But the assistant director of the bank also knew about the money, and he wanted a piece of it. He was accused of hiring Ivankov to help collect it.

Ivankov sent word that the deal was going to cost Volkov and Voloshin $3.5 million. They refused to pay. To make them understand how serious he was, in April 1995 Ivankov sent another message, this time in the form of an attack on Voloshin's father in a Moscow subway station. An unknown man beat him to death.

The killing drove the two Russians into the arms of the FBI. They helped the agents come up with a cellphone number – which also revealed Ivankov's interest in the New Jersey restaurant – and added those phones to the list already being tapped.

The final meeting with Ivankov was to happen in the main restaurant at the New York Hilton on the Avenue of the Americas on May 25, 1995, except Ivankov wasn't there. The two bankers were sitting at a table when a number of very large men in dark suits appeared in the exits of the restaurant. Once they were in place, another man approached the bankers and explained, in Russian, that there were only two ways they were going to leave the hotel. One was to get up and go to their car, in which case their safety could not be guaranteed. The other was to walk out with him. They chose option number two.

He drove them, with the men from the exits, to the Troika Restaurant in New Jersey, where they were held captive for twenty-four hours, until they signed agreements to hand over $3.5 million to Ivankov.

While Ivankov was plying his trade in New York, his brother-in-law, Vyacheslav Marakulovich Sliva, was installing himself in Toronto.

He'd told immigration officials that he was coming to see a friend, and specifically named hockey star Valeri Kamensky, who was then playing with the Quebec Nordiques. Kamensky has since denied knowing Sliva. Whether they knew each other or not, what Sliva did not tell immigration officers was that he had a criminal record in Russia, because that would have precluded his entry into Canada. His first arrest was in 1961, at the age of sixteen, when he stole a watch. He went away for three months. Two years later he was jailed for refusing to go into the army. He did four years for that. Then, in 1982, he was arrested for robbery, sent away for eleven years, and served nine. At least, that's what he eventually admitted to. With those omissions, plus false information he did provide – including his sister-in-law's name where it asked for his wife's, because he didn't have a wife at the time – he was granted a visitor's visa and arrived in Toronto in 1995.

Sliva was smart enough to maintain a low profile in Toronto, but he nevertheless became the key to getting Ivankov. It was information the RCMP developed in their wiretaps on him that provided the FBI with the probable cause they used in their affidavits to obtain wiretaps of their own against Ivankov.

From what both forces heard, it sounded as if Sliva had been sent to Canada by Ivankov and their mutual friends back in Moscow to take over all Russian crime activities in the country. The RCMP says they overheard Sliva make death threats, and also discuss with Ivankov how the two of them intended to divide extortion payments coming in from Russian players in the National Hockey League.

Sliva had targeted a number of players – including Alexander Mogilny, Vladimir Malakhov, Oleg Tverdovsky, and Alexei Zhitnik – threatening them and their families with violence if they didn't meet their demands. Apparently, Moligny went to the cops and Sliva's henchman was arrested. Presumably several other players paid. The NHL took its time before admitting that there was a problem. And then, a fifteen-month investigation by the United States Senate suggested that the extortion of Russian players in the NHL was more widespread than the league was willing to fess up to. Since then, Senate investigators have looked into claims of extortion of Russian basketball players in the NBA and Russian tennis players on the professional tour.

The Canadians learned that Sliva had been forced to flee Russia after threats had been made on his life there. They easily tied him to a man in Denver who had a long personal association with Ivankov, a man suspected of being a senior thief-in-law. Despite regular contact between the two, however, the RCMP never overheard them plotting criminal activity, the way Sliva had with Ivankov. Some senior people in the RCMP were convinced that Sliva was the number-two man in the Russians' North American organization.

Even those who agreed with Grinenko that there was no Russian criminal organization, wanted Sliva out of the country. But putting together a case against him was never going to be easy, and it certainly wasn't going to be cheap. So the Canadians settled on the most cost-efficient and swiftest method. They arrested Sliva at his high-rise condominium at Finch and Bayview avenues in Toronto in July 1997 and charged him with failing to disclose his criminal record on his visa application and being criminally inadmissible to live in Canada. For a couple of days Sliva maintained that he was innocent, until he understood that there was no way he was going to be permitted to stay in the country. He then agreed to be deported and was promptly returned to Moscow.

It was a better fate than Ivankov's.

In many ways, the same rules that governed life during the heyday of the LCN in the streets of Little Italy – the traditional Italian neighbourhood to the west of New York's Chinatown – apply today in Little Odessa-by-the-Sea. Rules which say that seeing stuff that doesn't concern you can be hazardous to your health.

Oleg Korataev was forty-four years old, an ex-boxer, and an ex-con too. Convicted in Russia for robbery and assault, he came to America in 1992 on a visitor's visa, found someone in Brooklyn to marry – which got him his green card – and went to work for the U.S. branch of the organized crime gang he'd known back home, called the Valiulins.

At 3 a.m. on January 12, 1994, after bringing in the Russian New Year at the Café Arbat, Korataev walked outside onto Brighton Beach Avenue with a man who took a .38-calibre pistol out of his pocket and shot Korataev in the head, killing him.

Most of the hundred witnesses questioned by the police said they hadn't seen anything. The few who admitted they had said that they'd seen the man shoot the boxer, go back inside the restaurant, then leave a few minutes later with a woman. But no one in the restaurant knew anything about the murderer, or the woman.

Despite Korataev's reputation for being a brutal enforcer with criminal connections in Brooklyn, Toronto, and Russia, everyone the police spoke with that night, oddly, seemed to come from Boston – decidedly outside NYPD jurisdiction – and otherwise suffered from amnesia.

The FBI believes that the contract on Korataev was taken out by a Moscow drug dealer named Dzhemal Khachidze as a warning to Ivankov to stay away from his market. The message must have been clear enough because three days later, Ivankov flew to Puerto Rico to meet with several other thieves-in-law, including Khachidze's people, in an attempt to work out their differences. The FBI knew about the meeting and not only taped what they could of it, but also sorted through everyone's hotel room garbage.

One of the topics discussed in San Juan, out of Ivankov's earshot, was how to eliminate him.

Reporters from the New York *Daily News* somehow learned about the summit meeting and asked Ivankov about it. He denied that he had ever been to Puerto Rico. He claimed that in four years of U.S. residency, he'd never left the country. But the FBI had enough of his Puerto Rican garbage to prove that he'd been in San Juan for seventeen days that January, and a subsequent search of his apartment uncovered a number of fake passports, all of which had foreign immigration stamps in them.

Now, with Volkov and Voloshin willing to testify, plus the mountain of wiretap evidence that the FBI had accumulated, the U.S. Attorney's office in Brooklyn decided they had enough to make a case.

On June 19, 1995, a few minutes after seven in the morning, armed FBI agents banged on the door of an apartment in Brooklyn belonging to one of Ivankov's girlfriends. Ivankov answered the door and the agents dragged him out kicking and screaming. Later, they were obliged literally to uncurl his fingers so that they could get his prints. Needless to say, he was held without bail.

"We were kind of surprised when we arrested him," Jim Moody confesses. "Most high-level organized crime guys have a persona about them. They conduct themselves in a certain way. They have some sophistication. They know how to deal with people. This guy was a scumbag. All the way through. That surprised us. No class at all."

Through confidential informants, the FBI then learned that two of their agents, who had helped to track him down and arrest him, were the object of a contract. Ivankov, who was said to be paying two hundred thousand dollars a month to a pair of "brigades" to protect him, allegedly asked them to liquidate the agents. Affidavits later produced in federal court apparently showed that one of the brigade leaders was a former KGB agent who had already murdered half a dozen Russians on Ivankov's behalf. The two FBI agents were immediately placed under protective watch.

When he was arrested, Ivankov had a slip of paper in his wallet containing information about a bank account in the Bahamas. But then there was another one, the account where he'd intended to stash the money he was extorting from the two Russians on Wall Street, and that was only just across the Hudson in New Jersey.

He was charged with extortion and conspiracy, and also with fraudulently marrying the woman for his green card. At his trial, Ivankov's attorney insisted that his client was a freedom fighter, a man unjustly framed by the former Communists simply because of his outspoken anti-Communist stance and, especially, because of his devout faith in the anti-Communist Russian Orthodox Church.

The jury didn't buy his story, and neither did the judge. She sentenced him to nine years and seven months on the main two charges and to nineteen months for the bogus marriage. Prosecutors had attempted to get him on the murder of Voloshin's father in Moscow, believing that he'd personally ordered it. But the judge would not consider crimes attributed to Ivankov outside the United States.

Caged in a tiny cell near Lake Placid, New York, Ivankov still protests his innocence and insists that he will neither forget nor forgive the people who put him there.

When he finally gets out – a man in his late sixties – the U.S. government intends to deport him back to Russia. What little remains of his organization today will, by then, be non-existent. The fear he can spread these days is already minimal. By then it will be hardly detectable.

For some of the agents who helped track him down, he was a cartoon cutout, an exhibitionist who did not understand that by boxing toe to toe with American law enforcement he was only setting himself up for a severe beating. For others, especially the agents who finally took him out, Ivankov was a dinosaur, an old-school thug who didn't understand that the old ways didn't work in the New World.

For Tom Kneir at the FBI, "Ivankov was an idiot. He put himself out there saying, I'm going to show you that I'm the biggest, baddest guy on the block. All he did was make himself a pretty easy target. He stood up in front of everybody and threw out a challenge. So the FBI and the U.S. Attorney's office said, Okay asshole, you're next."

The Russians who came after Ivankov are anything but idiots.

7

THE FOUR HORSEMEN

There will be no frontiers for crime. There should be no frontiers for justice.

– Giovanni Falcone

According to German intelligence sources, Grigory Loutchansky was born in Tbilisi, Georgia, in 1946, raised in Latvia, served two years in prison for embezzlement, became an academic at Riga University, and in 1989 formed a company called Nordex. Its startup costs were paid for with money stashed in Europe by the KGB.

Nordex became a conglomerate dealing in oil and petroleum products, chemicals, metals, fertilizers, and foodstuffs. Within five years it was reporting a turnover in excess of $2 billion, and by the end of the decade that figure is said to be above $3 billion. The company supposedly trades within the former Soviet Union as well as operating in several other countries, including the United States, Canada, and Britain. One of Loutchansky's business contacts was the late British media baron Robert Maxwell.

Originally based in Vienna, Loutchansky moved Nordex to Moscow – more accurately, the Austrians encouraged him to leave by deporting seventy of the company's eighty employees – where today it ranks in the top ten of Russia's largest private companies. Nordex is also said to be the largest of about three dozen firms active in the West as fronts for Russia's foreign intelligence service, or for former intelligence officers who were smart enough to feather their pension funds.

Loutchansky likes to tell people that the secret to his success is in the high margins that Nordex realizes on its trading activities due to the substantial difference between domestic and world prices. An example might be the deal he managed some years ago in the Ukraine. The Kremlin had cut off oil supplies because the government in Kiev owed them too much money and wasn't making much of an effort to pay it. Nordex bought $120 million worth of oil from Russia for hard currency – the Ukraines only paid in roubles – and bartered it in Kiev for sugar, wheat, and other commodities, which they then turned around and sold to the Russians, a classic middleman's swap. It is not, however, for commercial tight-rope walking that Loutchansky has attracted attention. He made the American headlines in July 1995 when he was invited to a Democratic fundraising dinner with President Clinton at the Hay Adams Hotel in Washington and, rather suddenly, the invitation was withdrawn. To the embarrassment of the Democratic National Party, solid investigative reporting by the Pittsburgh *Tribune-Review* revealed what the intelligence services claimed to know about Loutchansky – that beneath the veneer of a globe-trotting businessman, he was the planet's most important dealer in black-market nuclear materials.

What's more, he had already attended an October 1993 fundraiser with the president, at a time when the National Security Agency was said to have seen firm indications that Nordex was a front for weapons smuggling.

Photos taken at that dinner show Loutchansky with Clinton and a New York real estate operator named Sam Domb, who had secured Loutchansky's invitation. At one point, Domb denied having known Loutchansky before the dinner. However, the *New York Post* reported that he admitted to them he had brought Loutchansky along as his guest, and that he had hoped to do business with him. While it is not entirely clear if Loutchansky himself ever contributed to Clinton's campaign, he did receive a thank-you letter from the president for his support.

By the time the invitation arrived for the 1995 affair, Loutchansky was already barred from entering England, Canada, and Hong Kong – he was unable to satisfy immigration authorities about the source of his funds – and is quoted as admitting that he feared he would also be stopped from entering the U.S.

Previous to that, Loutchansky's name came up when a huge cache of arms – twenty-seven thousand Russian machine guns, five thousand

Czech pistols, and seven million rounds of ammunition – was intercepted en route from Panama to Croatia. No charges were lodged, nor was any evidence ever publicly put forth that either Loutchansky or Nordex were involved. Since then, however, Nordex has been tied to the transport of Scud missiles from North Korea to Iraq. That stems from a report out of the Ukraine that in the spring of 1995 officials inspected a cargo plane – Loutchansky's privately owned Antonov 124, said to be the largest aircraft in the world – that had stopped to refuel on its way from Pyongyang to Baghdad, and discovered the warheads.

Loutchansky has also been suspected by intelligence services of being associated with Russian criminal activity – in particular, money laundering. British intelligence sources say that through Nordex he controls nearly forty businesses in the West plus another sixty inside the former Soviet Union. One of his companies appears to be Dorotel AG, registered in Switzerland, which is alleged to be a front for "discreet payments."

Following his appearance as a friend of U.S. Democrats, Israeli interest in Loutchansky heightened. Various stories circulated suggesting that he had met high officials in Israel and offered to peddle influence in Moscow. At least some of the Israelis' suspicions were confirmed in a report passed along to them by an American intelligence agency. It is said to have detailed Loutchansky's attempt to buy favour with Boris Yeltsin through several large campaign contributions.

Time magazine went even further, claiming that he has long since bought his way into real power. *Time* connected Loutchansky and Nordex with former Russian prime minister Viktor Chernomyrdin. Before assuming his post in the Kremlin, the authors of the article wrote, Chernomyrdin had frequently visited Nordex in Vienna and those visits were tied to a lucrative commodities deal. After his appointment as head of the government, Chernomyrdin ordered Russian Customs to waive licensing requirements and export fees on a shipment of thirty thousand metric tons of electronics-grade copper, a Nordex deal.

It was further reported by *Time* that, in 1993 and 1994, American intelligence had intercepted Nordex communications that led them to believe the company was supplying fissile materials and other nuclear bomb-making components to both North Korea and Iran. As a consequence, the State Department pressured the U.S. Export-Import Bank to scotch a loan that would have backed a Kazakhstan joint venture between U.S. Steel and Nordex.

Mossad has apparently located Chernomyrdin's Swiss bank accounts and established that his personal fortune – said to be worth in excess of $5 billion – was built on the back of Gazprom, the Russian oil conglomerate that he once headed. Today, Gazprom has ties leading directly to Loutchansky.

John Deutch, Director of the CIA, stated categorically in June 1997 that Nordex was "an organization associated with Russian criminal activity." Added James Woolsey, who preceded Deutch at the Agency: "While we have slain the dragon of the Soviet empire, we now find ourselves in a jungle filled with a bewildering variety of poisonous snakes."

In Vienna, Police Commissioner Peter Stiedl confirms that when the company was based there, they were particularly concerned about funds in one Nordex account that they suspected to be the proceeds of crime. They asked their counterparts in the former Soviet Union for information about those funds, the company, and Loutchansky.

"That information was never forthcoming," Stiedl says. "We even froze the money and held it because we felt that we could establish probable cause. Four different teams in Russia said they would help us. The first group showed up, said they would get us what we wanted, and went away. A second team showed up, but they were totally different people who didn't have any of the information. So we requested it again. By the time we were dealing with the fourth group, it was too late. There was a huge amount of conflicting information, but the Russians never confirmed to us what we needed to know, so we had to return the money."

Loutchansky has always denied any and all allegations against him and his company. He says he does not traffic in arms or drugs, nor does he launder money. He says he is merely a successful businessman who is being victimized by the press. He labels stories tying him either to organized crime or the intelligence services as outrageous and false. He has frequently been quoted saying: "None of the statements about links of this group of companies with the criminal world is corroborated by facts or by the results of the numerous investigations which were carried out both by the Russian and foreign secret services, including Interpol."

Which seems an odd thing for him to say, in light of the fact that in 1995 an eleven-nation, two-day conference was hosted by Interpol, and the sole subject of the meeting was Mr. Loutchansky.

The second horseman had also once been based in Vienna.

Sergei Mikhailov didn't get into crime until late in life – it was in 1984, when he was twenty-six – by reporting his motorcycle stolen and attempting to collect on the insurance. It cost him six months.

A sports fanatic, he'd wanted to be a trainer, but somehow sidestepped into hotel management and even worked for a time as a waiter in a restaurant. However, what he learned in jail must have suited him because as soon as he got out, he gave up working for a living to string together the loose-knit group that would rule southern Moscow under the name Solntsevo.

He was arrested again five years later and charged with extortion. The main witness against him suddenly decided he couldn't remember anything and the case was dropped. In 1993 he was arrested a third time, suspected of killing someone in a casino. Again, witnesses failed to provide evidence.

Around that time, a gang war broke out in Moscow and bodies were strewn around the streets. Mikhailov applied for passage to Israel and was granted a passport on the grounds that his wife was Jewish. One story has since surfaced that the woman wasn't his wife. A second, that she wasn't Jewish. Mikhailov, meanwhile, moved on to the peace and quiet of Vienna.

Not satisfied with just Russian and Israeli passports, he got himself named Honorary Consult for Costa Rica, a title which came with a diplomatic passport. He increased his collection of IDs with papers from Greece, Belgium, and Portugal, as a CNN correspondent and as a member of the Kremlin's security detail.

While his business interests have always been cloaked in mystery – by design – it is widely believed that by 1992 Solntsevo had gained control of the Russian Exchange Bank and that he and his friends were using that as a conduit to get money out of Russia. Certainly by mid-decade, the Russian banking system had become the world's most important money-laundering sink, snatching the title away from the equally corrupt financial world of Panama.

It is known that Mikhailov got involved in gas and oil deals in Russia, a five-star hotel project in Budapest, and bananas in Costa Rica. Along the way, he managed to get himself banned from France indefinitely and from the Czech Republic for ten years. It is suspected that hidden behind his businesses, and his *persona non grata* status, were Solntsevo's extortion rackets, arms and drug trafficking, and money laundering.

Two years after arriving in Vienna, with his name linked by the Austrians to Russian organized crime and to Loutchansky, Mikhailov moved again, this time for Switzerland. On June 21, 1996, he purchased a large house in the village of Borex just outside Geneva for SF 1.3 million. He installed his wife and two young children there, and began shifting some of his business interests to neighbouring Belgium.

He hooked up with Mike Brandwain, and along with his right-hand man, Viktor Averin, registered one of his main companies there, MAB (as in Mikhailov-Averin-Brandwain) International. Through that company, negotiations were opened on several construction contracts. One was for a sewer system in Moscow. Another was for a gas pipeline in Turkmenistan. Whether MAB International was involved with Vyacheslav Ivankov is not clear. There was a relationship somewhere but it might have been either personally with Mikhailov or through Solntsevo as his sponsor.

Regardless of the identity of his silent partners, Swiss authorities were beginning to take an anxious look at him. Because they didn't like what they saw, less than four months after the Mikhailovs moved into their new home, the cops arrested him at Geneva–Cointrin Airport.

Mikhailov spent the next two years in jail, awaiting trial. While he was there, the Swiss ambassador to Russia received several death threats; a Moscow magistrate interrogated him as a suspect in the still-unsolved murder of television journalist Vladislav Listyev; a scandal broke out in Israel over identity papers, implicating Mikhailov, Averin, and several others along with someone inside the Ministry of Interior who supplied the papers; and his own lawyer got arrested for smuggling letters between Mikhailov and Averin past the jail censor.

It wasn't until December 1998 that the Swiss finally tried him on charges of being the head of Solntsevo.

The stage for this drama was Geneva's Criminal Court, an imposing building located opposite some tiny boutiques along a narrow and winding street on a hill in the heart of the old city. Such was the powerful reputation of the defendant that police SWAT teams wearing flak jackets and carrying automatic weapons drew a tight security cordon around the *quartier*. Mikhailov arrived every morning in a bulletproof Mercedes wearing a grey suit and bulletproof vest. He was safely delivered inside the building before he was permitted to get out of the car. He was always handcuffed and always under heavy guard. To follow the proceedings, which were held in French, the bulky Mikhailov had an interpreter constantly whispering in his ear.

Two star witnesses were scheduled to appear. Only one lived to see the trial.

Vadim Rozenbaum, who was said to have first-hand knowledge of Mikhailov's criminal activities, was murdered in Holland in 1997, only days after his name appeared on the witness list. The second witness, Nikolai Oporov, the former chief of the Moscow Police Organized Crime Bureau, received so many death threats that the Swiss took the rare step of granting him political asylum.

Testifying from another room at the courthouse via closed-circuit television, Oporov told the jury that the first time he'd heard Mikhailov's name was in 1987, when Solntsevo was working a small-time protection racket, extorting money from people operating street kiosks. He tied Mikhailov straight to the leadership of the gang. So did Geneva's special anti-Russian crime squad. A witness from the squad produced photos and other evidence of meetings between Mikhailov and leaders of various Eastern European organized crime gangs. So did Swiss police inspector Patrick Scheurer, who testified to finding all those identity papers, plus Mikhailov's various passports, and to tapping telephone conversations where Mikhailov himself told others that he was running Solntsevo. Scheurer also produced evidence that Mikhailov possessed a shell company in the Channel Islands through which he had laundered tens of millions of dollars.

Robert Levinson, the retired FBI agent and Russian organized crime expert, also put Mikhailov at the head of the gang. He said that Mikhailov controlled two "combat brigades," or assassination squads, that would commit murders in Russia and other countries in Europe, then go to Miami to cool off. He said that under Mikhailov, Solntsevo ran nightclubs in Brighton Beach and in Los Angeles and had a car dealership in Houston, Texas, all of which were fronts for drug dealing. He told the jury, "The organization was engaged regularly in the extortion of businesses, the distribution of drugs including cocaine, counterfeiting of currency, and trafficking in arms."

When the defence presented its case, the picture it painted was of a highly successful businessman – they needed to explain away more than $4 million the Swiss had frozen in his bank account – who exported gas and oil from Russia, bought bells for churches, and donated money to orphanages. One of their star witnesses was former U.S. attorney general Ramsey Clark, who testified that what Levinson had said was hearsay and would never be permitted in a U.S. court of law. In all, there were around eighty witnesses, the majority of them called by the defence.

After eight days of trial stretched over two weeks, the jury had to come to a decision on four charges. To the horror of many – and the shocked delight of Mikhailov – they found him not guilty of belonging to the Solntsevo crime group; not guilty of controlling the crime group from Switzerland; not guilty of using forged documents; but guilty of violating the law that prohibits foreigners from purchasing real estate in Switzerland.

The prosecutors had failed to prove their case. Their mistake was in attempting to prove that Mikhailov was a *Maffiya* godfather instead of taking the more direct route and aiming at specific crimes. The problem was that they had not found any specific crimes committed in Switzerland – except his purchase of Swiss property. The Russians failed to provide enough incriminating information about him and no other country had requested Mikhailov's extradition.

He was kept in jail overnight before being deported on the single guilty verdict. He objected. He wanted to stay in Switzerland. They loaded him onto a regularly scheduled Aeroflot flight to Moscow. He objected to that too.

He wanted to go to Budapest.

Averin was in Budapest.

But Averin was second string.

In the back of his mind Mikhailov must have worried about being killed in Moscow. He'd been out of circulation for two years, young guys had moved up, there was discontent with him among the Solntsevso foot soldiers, and the streets had become even more violent. Budapest was where he would be safest. Budapest was where he could count on the protection of, arguably, the most dangerous man in the world.

Semion Yudkovich Mogilevitch, horseman number three, was his friend, benefactor, and favourite business partner.

Two years older than Mikhailov, the Ukrainian-born Mogilevitch – who held a graduate degree in economics from the University of Lvov – had been able to parlay thin air into a seemingly invincible business empire. And like Loutchansky, he found that his protestations of legitimacy, all too often, fell on deaf ears.

According to several intelligence and law enforcement sources, including the National Criminal Intelligence Service in London and the FBI in Washington, Mogilevitch is into everything, from weapons to money laundering, from prostitution to art smuggling, from extortion to drugs. There are even some people who claim he is into murder.

Notes one senior FBI agent, "Mogilevitch is involved in more bullshit than you can shake a stick at."

Even Mogilevitch's pal Monya Elson has described him as "the most powerful mobster in the world."

Supposedly, he has a headlock on freight passing through Moscow's Sheremetyevo International Airport. (The Lucchese family invented that gimmick when they took over Idlewild Airport, long before it was renamed JFK.) He is believed to have bought a bankrupt airline from one of the central Asian republics. It is known that he bought one of Hungary's bankrupt armament industries, and that his name was linked to a multi-million dollar cache of Warsaw Pact weapons that got sold to Iraq. The arrangement is said to have included surface-to-air missiles, which brings up the hypothesis that he is linked to Loutchansky's alleged arms dealing and the SCUDs.

In the 1970s, when that first wave of émigrés was allowed to leave

Russia for Israel, Mogilevitch was a member of a street gang working petty thefts and counterfeiting. But he saw opportunity in the exodus, and convinced people who were leaving immediately that he could sell their belongings for them and would pay them in hard currency when they got to Israel. Of course, he collected the goods, sold them, and kept all the money for himself.

He must have been connected with the bureaucrats because he got into oil and gas – he could not have secured contracts in those early days if he hadn't been paying someone off – and pushed everything through a company registered in Alderney, Channel Islands, called Arbat International. There has always been a rumour that the Channel Islands is where Mogilevitch is linked to Vyacheslav Ivankov. It is known that there are Channel Island links to Sergei Mikhailov.

In 1993, Mogilevitch also fled the gang wars, opting first for Israel, where he obtained a passport, then leaving for Budapest, which was just starting to happen. He was married to a Hungarian woman, which allowed him to take up legal residence there. The Hungarians were selling off state industries, the police didn't have a clue about transnational organized crime, he had money to buy muscle, he knew that muscle could buy him respect, and he proved that respect could produce all sorts of opportunities.

A second company appeared on the registrar's books in Alderney, this one called Arigon.

Among the deals that Mogilevitch is believed to have godfathered are a joint venture with the Genovese to ship toxic waste from the United States to Chernobyl; the movement of stolen art works and religious artifacts through the Western auction houses; the purchase of a jewellery factory in Hungary to produce counterfeit money, financial instruments, and Fabergé eggs; and the establishment of a chain of nightclubs and strip joints, through which he could presumably push prostitutes, drugs, and dirty money.

"Black and White Nightclubs" were opened in Budapest, Riga, Kiev, and Prague. But that world can be violent, and the deeper he got into it, the higher he raised the personal stakes. In 1994 a Frankfurt brothel owner was killed, along with twelve of his prostitutes. Suspicion fell on Mogilevitch. The murders were assumed to be a grisly warning to any groups thinking of moving in on his patch. A German television crew went to Budapest to interview him about the incident and later claimed to have been apprised of what awaited them if they didn't leave town immediately. They left. Shortly thereafter Mogilevitch was involved in a shootout in Budapest, said to have been an attempt on his life by a rival gang, either to avenge the killings or to muscle in on his clubs. He was not charged in either case.

In May 1995, Mogilevitch travelled to Prague, where Viktor Averin was hosting a birthday bash at the Uhaluba Club. Just before going to the party, someone tipped off Mogilevitch that during the evening he was going to be murdered. Mogilevitch turned around and went home, but not before calling the police. They raided the party and interviewed all two hundred guests. They never found out if the assassination story was true. But Mogilevitch thought it was, and that seriously spooked him. These days, he spends most of his time well-guarded in Budapest. Anyway, by 1995 he was onto a new way to make a huge fortune – long distance and by remote control.

A Russian émigré named Jacob Bogatin, who had been an engineer in a Soviet military research institute, had started a small magnet-manufacturing company near Philadelphia called YBM. A few years before, while buying privatized companies from the government in an end-of-Communism fire sale, Mogilevitch had also picked up a magnet business called Magnex Rt. Still, the twain might never have met, had it not been for Marat Balagula's fuel-tax scam in Brooklyn.

One of the people involved with Balagula had gotten arrested, was tried and found guilty, then allowed out on bail to await sentencing. Instead of sticking around, he jumped. Arrested in Vienna, he was held there for a year until the Austrians decided they didn't have enough evidence against him in a money-laundering scheme related to the Balagula fraud, and let him go. Rather than return to Brooklyn, where all sorts of warrants were piling up, he made his way to Poland, where he wheeled and dealed and wound up owning a bank – he called it the First Commercial Bank of Lublin – which he set up as a money-laundering sink for any crime group willing to pay his fee.

Mogilevitch knew that man, who happened to be Jacob Bogatin's brother David. Consequently, Jacob Bogatin also spent time in Budapest.

The plot Mogilevitch then hatched was one worthy of someone with an economics degree.

He took a shell company called Pratecs, floated it on the Alberta Stock Exchange – where little or no due diligence happened because little or no information was required – and folded YBM and Magnex into it. Behind the scenes, Mogilevitch hid some of those shares in Arigon and Arbat and set up a string of shells in Hungary through which he could use the newly created YBM Magnex to launder money.

Pratecs started life as a penny share, but Mogilevitch oversaw the cooking of the books for months. He then brought it to the Toronto Stock Exchange. No one bothered to look too closely, and it fast became one of the darlings of the TSE 300. At one point, around March 1995, word came from London that someone involved with the company was under investigation. The sale of the shares was suspended. The company then issued this rebuttal: "The allegations were aimed at two companies in the U.K. and the attorneys of these two companies. The companies are in no way related to YBM or its subsidiary, Arigon. However, because the companies are owned by an employee and a former director of Arigon, and the companies' monetary affairs were handled by the same solicitors that Arigon used in the past, it had put Arigon also under scrutiny."

Such double-talk seemed to satisfy the powers that be in Toronto. Further double-talk satisfied the investors.

The company announced that while producing magnets in Hungary, it had discovered a residue powder called neodymium, which, when added to crude oil, significantly cut refining costs. It then explained how the company was buying crude oil on the spot market, treating it with neodymium, and making a lot of money selling it to the government of the Ukraine under a long-term contract. The best thing about this, the company said, was that the more magnets they made, the more powder by-product they had for their oil interests.

They might as well have been selling snake oil.

Market analysts could see that since its inception, YBM Magnex's net sales had quadrupled, net income had jumped by a multiple of nine, and earnings had increased by a multiple of five. With all sorts of influential people on the board – and many of those same people touting the shares to fund managers – the stock took off. It moved up to $10 and continued to rise from the summer of 1997 to March 10, 1998, hitting a high of $20.15. The company was now valued at $1 billion.

In the midst of the excitement, YBM Magnex acquired Crusteel Magnetics in Sheffield, England, and the following year two other magnet firms in Lancashire. The three were joined together into YBM's British subsidiary, Crumax Magnetics.

But along the way, the company's auditors, Deloitte & Touche, didn't like the fact that there were all sorts of strange things going on and that, in certain cases, there was no paperwork to back up accounting entries. According to its own accounting, YBM's turnover had risen from $90 million in 1996 to $138 million in 1997. Their version also suggested the company's main market for magnets was the U.S. Deloitte discovered that YBM shipped most of their magnets to Russia and the Ukraine. The auditors were refusing to sign off the 1997 accounts. Rumours abounded and warning signs were conspicuous. Several large blocks of shares were discreetly sold by people inside the company.

By Tuesday afternoon, May 12, the stock had slipped from its all-time high and was hovering around $14.35.

On Wednesday morning, May 13, at precisely 10:30, some sixty officers of the Organized Crime Strike Force – composed of agents from the FBI, IRS, Customs, Immigration and Naturalization Service, and the U.S. State Department – working out of the U.S. Attorney's office in Philadelphia, walked into the company's Newton, Pennsylvania, headquarters, presented their search warrants, and proceeded to cart away tons of documents and computerized records. Exactly twenty-three minutes later, the TSE halted trading on YBM Magnex.

Just like that, shareholders were looking at $635 million of worthless stock. For all intents and purposes, the company was dead.

Just before Pratecs went public, the British authorities had become curious about a man called Konstantin Karat, whose name appeared as managing director of Arigon Ltd. They suspected Arigon was laundering money through London. They were able to connect Karat, Arigon, and Arbat to Mogilevitch, and laundered funds back to him. But the people apparently doing the wash for Mogilevitch were not Russians. They were a pair of English solicitors.

Officers at NCIS compiled dossiers on Mogilevitch, Arigon, Arbat, Karat, and the solicitors until December 9, 1994. At that point, believing they had indeed uncovered criminal activity, they passed along a "development package" to the Southeast Regional Crime Squad (SERCS) for further investigation.

Officers on the SERCS money-laundering investigation team promptly focused their attention on the relationship between "Moguilevitch" – spelled that way in the development package – and the small firm of London solicitors known as Blakes.

The two partners at Blakes were Adrian Bernard Churchward and Peter Blake-Turner. They had been the ones who set up Arbat and Arigon for Mogilevitch in Alderney. They had also set up other Channel Islands companies for him, including Createbury Ltd. and Limegold Ltd. On closer inspection, it turned out that Mogilevitch and Churchward were linked with a company called Pendosi and, closer still, through Churchward's wife, Galina Vassilyevna, who was the mother of Mogilevitch's son.

With additional intelligence developed through contacts in Hungary, Russia, the Czech Republic, Austria, the United States, and Canada, the SERCS team became increasingly convinced that Mogilevitch was running an organized crime group that dealt in extortion, prostitution, arms dealing, and drugs trafficking. They also came to believe that the solicitors were washing some of Mogilevitch's criminal profits through accounts they controlled at the Royal Bank of Scotland on Lombard Street.

Overall, SERCS officers spent five and a half months investigating the three men and their business interests in several countries. One conclusion they drew was that money banked in the solicitors' client accounts was not properly scrutinized by the money-laundering reporting officer of the Royal Bank.

The bank had assumed that because solicitors were regulated by the Law Society, it was therefore up to the Law Society to look into clients' accounts and their use as conduits for dirty money. In this respect, the bank was hardly unique. It knew its clients and, as so many banks still do, had every excuse to wipe their hands of the matter. What's more, banks have also discovered that when they do question lawyers about their clients' accounts, the answer customarily forthcoming is that information is protected by client-solicitor privilege. Which is why lawyers' clients' accounts make for near-perfect money-laundering sinks.

The SERCS officers eventually concluded that, over the course of three years, as much as $50 million had been moved through the solicitors' client accounts for Mogilevitch. They came to believe that Arigon was Mogilevitch's private holding company, while Arbat – which, among other businesses, ran a funeral parlour in Moscow – was the laundromat. Neither company appeared to be trading, but money was moving through Arigon, then into and out of Arbat and the funeral home.

The problem investigators now faced was exactly the same that the police in Vienna faced when they looked into Loutchansky's money. It's the same problem police investigators all over the West face whenever Russian or Eastern European money is involved. They needed to prove, beyond a reasonable doubt, the criminal origin of the funds. And without information coming from police in the East, that would be extremely difficult.

With patience and by using the relationships they'd been able to build on a cop-to-cop basis with the Moscow police, the officers constructed a convoluted but nevertheless interesting hypothesis.

A man known to the British police only by his last name, Mysinkov, had been operating an advanced-fee-fraud scam – bilking the Moscow city government out of $3.2 million with 111 contracts for sugar – using a company called Perigey. That money was showing up in the Pendosi and Createbury accounts, and then disappearing. When the British cops asked the Moscow cops to put them in touch with Mr. Mysinkov, they were informed that he had died in unknown circumstances and that, just prior to his death, his wallet and passport had disappeared.

Back in London, the SERCS team had reason to believe that the targets of their investigation were, if nothing else, handling stolen funds, although they couldn't identify specific crimes. Based on that assumption, they made applications for warrants to search the solicitors' office and homes.

Churchward, his wife, and Blake-Turner were arrested on May 16, 1995, and the searches carried out. All three were then released on police bail, awaiting evidence from Russia that could be used in a British court. According to the police, the search produced "extensive intelligence relating to financial transactions conducted by the Mogilevitch Organization." They were also able to ascertain that the Royal Bank of Scotland held just over $2 million in three separate Arigon accounts.

They now moved against Mogilevitch and Karat. Warrants for their arrest were issued and the funds were seized.

In the meantime, the Russian authorities didn't appear to be in much of a hurry to help SERCS. The Moscow police had passed their request on to the prosecutors' department, and that's where the paperwork sat, awaiting a decision. Officers from SERCS and NCIS tried to move things along, stressing to their Russian counterparts that time was of the essence, but to no avail. They asked again about the Mysinkov case. They were told it was closed. They used what political pull they could to obtain the paperwork on the Mysinkov matter. The answer came back: It's all gone.

In the absence of any evidence from Russia, the charges of conspiracy to handle stolen goods against Churchward, his wife, Blake-Turner, Mogilevitch, and Karat had to be abandoned. The only way still left open for the SERCS team was to pursue a prosecution for a minor money-laundering offence. Under the 1993 money-laundering laws, however, the clause they might have used only applied to new clients. So that course was not pursued either. The money sitting in the Arigon accounts was unfrozen and legal costs were awarded to the Churchwards and Blake-Turner. No application for costs was made by anyone else.

Mogilevitch himself placed a phone call to someone at NCIS. The officer wasn't there at the time and Mogilevitch left a message asking why he was being chased by the British police when he was a legitimate businessman trying to earn a legitimate living. According to the officer at NCIS, the call was not returned.

Officers at NCIS who worked on the intelligence-gathering side of what came to be known as Operation Sword described Mikhailov and Averin as "thugs" who depend on Mogilevitch's business skills.

When Mikhailov got locked up in Switzerland, they say, Averin ran scared and headed straight for Budapest, where Mogilevitch could protect him. Back in Moscow, the Solntsevo foot soldiers were unhappy that Mikhailov was still getting his share of the profits while locked up and unable to earn money for the group. The man who was supposedly the paymaster for the combat teams was named Arnold Tamm. And he allegedly cut off payments to Mikhailov. Mogilevitch is said to have stepped in and was funnelling money to Mikhailov, and also to Averin, through the Channel Islands companies.

While this was going on, the officers say, Mrs. Mysinkov came to see Mogilevitch about her husband's money. She had been told that Mogilevitch had done her husband a favour by allowing him to launder his advanced-fee-fraud profits through Pendosi and Createbury, and now that her husband was dead, she wanted the money back. Apparently, she was met at the airport in Budapest as she got off the plane, told in no uncertain terms that the money now belonged to Mogilevitch, and was bundled onto the next plane home.

There is also the strong belief around the intelligence services that the Hungarians are well aware of who Mogilevitch is and what he's doing – how could they not be? – and allow him to live there because they've come to an understanding with him.

It's the "devil you know" syndrome.

The arrangement is, in exchange for his get-out-of-jail-free card, Mogilevitch has pledged to the government that he will not commit crimes in Hungary and also that he will personally keep out other, more violent and, therefore, less controllable groups.

The deeper investigators burrowed inside Arigon and Arbat, the more they unravelled about Pendosi and Createbury to solve the mystery of the Mysinkov money. His $3.2 million – the profits from his fee-fraud scam – had been wired from a Lithuanian bank to a Hungarian bank, from there to accounts held by a Swiss bank at Chemical Bank in Buffalo, New York. Six days later the sum total was wired out again to several accounts in Europe, including one the investigators believed to be controlled by Mikhailov and another they believed to be controlled by Averin. They also traced money from the Channel Islands to Philadelphia, and accounts that appeared to be controlled by Josef Bogatin. That's how they stumbled across YBM.

British officers travelled to the States and, accompanied by an FBI agent, drove to the company's then headquarters in Hatboro, Pennsylvania. What they found was an old school, with tiny offices where classrooms had once been. A piece of paper was taped to a door that led to what used to be the cafeteria. In handwritten letters it read "YBM." They knocked but no one was there.

That was what YBM looked like when NCIS first heard about it.

Because none of this fit together, and was all so obviously suspicious, they kept an eye on the company and its banking relationships with the

Channel Islands, until word came that Pratecs was being listed on the Alberta exchange and that YBM was being folded into it. Horrified British investigators sent a warning to the exchange officials in Alberta.

They explained the connection to Mogilevitch and outlined the implications of him being permitted to float Pratecs – that he'd be floating YBM, Magnex Rt, and Arigon at the same time – and that if he got away with this he'd be out of control. They prophesied that his next step would be the purchase of a bank. At that point, they argued, he might also be beyond reach.

Security officials at the exchange asked for evidence.

The officers at NCIS tried to make them understand the difference between intelligence information and evidence, especially evidence that could be presented in court: they only had intelligence. But, they insisted, their information was sound. They urged the Canadians to realize that "the directors of this company are connected to Russian organized crime and indeed the main individual, Semion Mogilevitch, is considered to be the leader of Russian organized crime in Hungary and the Czech Republic."

Even the FBI pitched in with their fears: "Semion Mogilevitch runs an extensive prostitution operation out of the Black and White Nightclubs in Prague and Budapest. Foreign law enforcement agencies have documented Mogilevitch's prostitution operation as the centrepiece of his operations in Europe. Arigon is a central element of the Mogilevitch Organization."

In Alberta, exchange officials turned a deaf ear.

And Pratecs was floated.

The British Operation Sword produced 545 files of records and 1,325 exhibits, including a record of every financial transaction conducted on behalf of Mogilevitch and other Russian organized crime figures by Churchward over a five-year period.

The SERCS' final report concluded, "Mogilevitch is one of the world's top criminals who has a personal wealth of $100 million. He is a target of Law Enforcement Agencies and Security Services in several countries and as a result of the effect of his financial impact on the City of London he clearly falls in the category of an NCIS core criminal."

If nothing else, the officers had the minor satisfaction of closing down every company they found to be controlled by Mogilevitch. Bank accounts in Britain were also shut. And on August 10, 1995, an order was signed by the Home Secretary forbidding Mogilevitch's entry into the United Kingdom. A similar ban on entry has also been posted in the United States.

In the days following the raid on the YBM Magnex headquarters in Pennsylvania, it was discovered that Arigon had resurfaced in the Cayman Islands under the name of United Trade Ltd. Forensic accountants were brought in and their report, on file with the Alberta Court of Queen's Bench in Calgary, describes a tangled web of mysterious bank accounts, unexplained money transfers, and unusual transactions, all indicating that money laundering had been taking place.

Documentation to support the transfer of millions of dollars, the report says, was non-existent. The relationship between YBM Magnex and a Bahamian subsidiary, United Trade, was highly suspicious because the bank account didn't seem to be under corporate control.

They wrote about "several transactions effected by United Trade involving the movement of substantial amounts of money through bank accounts controlled by United Trade. These transactions . . . have several indicia of money laundering."

United Trade was also shown to be associated with the movement of millions of dollars around various bank accounts in Eastern Europe, and all sorts of suspicious trading. There were indications that oil, wheat, and magnets had been moved in and out of companies, most of them associated in some way with United Trade, but there was insufficient documentation to explain what it was all about.

Forensic accountants also found that Mogilevitch controlled a company in Budapest called Technology Distribution, which was the sales agent for United Trade. Woven around that was a web of other companies, at first glance independent of him, but ultimately all connected back to him through various interrelationships, such as shared addresses and shared directors. By having signature authority on various bank accounts – namely, Technology Distribution and United Trade – it was then child's play for him to move product and money through all these companies and, effectively, make everything disappear.

Since the fall of YBM Magnex:

Crumax Magnetics was forced into receivership.

NCIS and SERCS were left to conclude that YBM Magnex had been created for a single purpose, "to legitimize the [Mogilevitch] criminal organization by the floating on the stock exchange of a corporation which consists of the U.K. and U.S.A. companies whose existing assets and stocks have been artificially inflated by the introduction of the proceeds of crime."

Both the FBI and the RCMP have alleged that there were links from Arigon back to Brandwain's old group in Brussels. U.S. Customs has gone further, suggesting that Mogilevitch is tied to everything Brandwain was doing, including narcotics trafficking, money laundering, extortion, murder, and the smuggling of stolen auto parts into the former Soviet Union.

And Tamas Boros died.

On July 2, 1998, a car bomb, said to contain as many as twenty sticks of dynamite, exploded in the middle of a shopping district, killing Boros and three innocent bystanders. He'd been a well-known restaurateur, owned a nightclub, and was said to be co-operating with Hungarian police in an investigation of Semion Mogilevitch.

No one has been charged with the four murders.

Israel's "Law of Return" is set in stone.

One of the pillars of the Jewish state, it guarantees the Diaspora that any Jew, from anywhere in the world, regardless of his or her country of birth, will be welcomed "home" and automatically provided with citizenship. Considering how some Russians abuse that law today, it seems almost naïve of the founding fathers to have enacted it.

Since Israel's founding, there have been three main waves of Russian emigration to Israel. In the 1970s, the immigrants were high profile, intellectuals and dissidents, rejected by the Soviets for their political views. And they were easily absorbed into Israeli society. In the late 1970s and early 1980s, there was an influx that included many Russians from Georgia, and inside that group were some professional criminals. They ran extortion, gambling, and prostitution rackets, but there was no one group, or any one person, who seemed to be in charge. Then came the 1990s.

In the final decade of the century, over eight hundred thousand Russians have arrived in Israel. How many of them were really Jewish is anyone's guess. In many cases, they only stayed long enough to get their passport, then left, and have never come back. It was this third wave that brought the Mogilevitches and the Mikhailovs and the Loutchanskys. It was this third wave that proved that an Israeli passport was not just a window into the United States, it was an open door.

Of course, not all of those non-Jewish Russians left the country. Police in Tel Aviv have drawn up a list of thirty people they believe to be organized criminals, and only one is definitely Jewish. The problem with putting labels like "Russian immigrant" on people is that in Israel – a country where emotions about everyday issues already run strong – the issue of Russian immigration and organized crime produces emotions in spades.

A senior Israeli police intelligence officer explains, "Some people left Israel a long time ago because all they ever wanted from us was citizenship. Others never came back because we've been able to embarrass them. The ones who stayed did so because Israel does not extradite its citizens. That may be changed one day, but as of now, an Israeli can be indicted by a foreign court and, in certain instances, can even be tried in Israel under that indictment. But they are not extradited. It essentially gives some of these Russian organized criminals a free pass to commit crimes outside Israel."

Statements like this, and the implication that among Russian Jews a significant minority is engaged in criminal activity, make some people upset. Decries one Russian Israeli, "If you took the same things said about us in this country and said them about Jews or blacks or any other ethnic minority in any other country, you'd probably be arrested."

Stereotyping is always unfortunate and politicians tread on such thin ice at their peril. As citizens, all of these recently arrived Russian immigrants may vote. As their numbers have increased, so has their real political power. Still, a 1997 investigation into how some Russian immigrants had avoided their obligatory Israeli military service uncovered a network of organized criminals, sixty-three of whom got into the country with forged documents.

Enter here the fourth horseman.

Gregory Lerner arrived in Israel as part of the third wave, in 1990 at the age of thirty-nine. He became a citizen and took the Hebrew name Zvi Ben-Ari. A former journalism student at Moscow University, he had supposedly hawked black-market razor blades to earn a living in the mid-1970s. By 1982 he'd worked his way up to fraud and had served two years in prison. But by the time he got to Israel he was telling people that he was a banker who'd been running a company called Lomus International. He said that under the Soviets, he'd been given government backing to establish commercial banks, that in 1988 they'd advanced him seventy million roubles in the form of a three-year loan, but in 1989 – along with the first signs of the social and economic changes that were about to happen – some of his backers tried to call in his loan. Again, this is his version of the tale.

While he was on a business trip to Austria, he said, the KGB set him up by raiding his offices, taking away all the paperwork that mentioned the loan, and substituting in its place paperwork that did not mention the loan. By 1992, he was living in Switzerland, running an import-export company. That's when the Swiss arrested him on a warrant from the Soviets, and deported him back to Moscow. It was the first and only time the Swiss ever honoured an extradition request from the Soviets.

Back in Russia, Lerner stood trial for embezzling funds, stealing his employees' salaries, and taking bribes. When he was finally allowed to leave the country, eighteen months later, he headed straight to Israel.

Over the next few years, he went about building an empire of shell companies scattered around the world that, on the surface, appeared to justify his luxurious lifestyle. By maintaining visibility, he created an aura around him that fooled a lot of people, including the press, which often referred to him as "Israeli millionaire Zvi Ben-Ari." At one point, a survey of Russian immigrants in Israel named him among the four most popular. Eventually his name surfaced in the papers as a possible candidate for a Knesset seat. Secretly, the police suspected that Lerner had bought his way into Israel's Russian-language press, but they were never able to prove it.

What they now knew for sure, however, is that Lerner was connected to Solonik and also to Vyacheslav Ivankov. The story they tell – one that remains unconfirmed by the FBI – is that the Bureau's wiretaps on Ivankov's phones in Brooklyn caught him talking to Lerner on several occasions. After listening to conversations with thousands of people, the Bureau's investigators concluded that Lerner is the only person who ever dared talk to Ivankov as an equal.

If it's true, it says something about Lerner. If it's not, it says a lot about the image that Israeli law enforcement has of him.

In 1995, Lerner founded the Israeli-Russian Finance Company, in partnership with Russia's Promstroi Bank. At the end of November 1995, the Bank of Israel granted him a limited permit to handle security transactions but with the proviso that he could deal only in overseas funds controlled by non-residents. In other words, they didn't want him to become an Israeli banker. It was, at best, naïveté, at worst, sheer stupidity. In this day and age it doesn't matter where the bank is located – it can be on the moon – as long as there's a way to wire money to it.

Although Lerner was never far from their radar screens, a formal investigation into his banking affairs was not opened by the Israelis until the following year after a man purporting to have been his former partner filed a complaint against him in Russia. The man claimed that Lerner had defrauded him. With help from law enforcement in Britain and the United States, the Israelis were able to take a close look at all those shell companies Lerner had sprinkled around the globe: in Panama, throughout the Caribbean, in Mauritius and Luxembourg. But the one that caught everyone's eye was in Cyprus. It was a bank.

Since the end of World War II, Vienna has been the historical pivot point between Russia and Israel. But secret banking, the availability of shell companies, and good weather prompted the Russians to make Cyprus their "bus station" into Israel.

Limassol in Cyprus has become a Mediterranean suburb of Moscow, St. Petersburg, Kiev, and Tbilisi. What used to be an inexpensive fishing village has, thanks to the Russians, now joined the list of the world's fifty most expensive cities. In streets where a few thousand drunk British tourists used to raise hell on Saturday nights, now there are twenty thousand Russians with offshore companies and laundered money in their bank accounts, and Greek lawyers who speak Russian and make themselves available as facilitators.

In Cyprus, forged identity papers are on sale to anyone with cash to pay for them. Russian birth certificates that show a Jewish mother can be purchased for under five thousand dollars. Papers that show a Jewish name cost a little bit more.

Across the fence, still patrolled by United Nations troops, that cuts through Nicosia and divides the island into Greek and Turkish halves, the north side has also been washed with a wave of Russians. There are said to be 150,000 to 200,000 living there, some for the weather, others for the "safe passage" on offer because Northern Cyprus is not recognized by, nor does it have extradition treaties with, any other country, except Turkey. No matter who you are or what you have done, if the police in Istanbul don't want you, no one can bother you in Northern Cyprus.

From either side of the island, it's only a few hours on a plane to Israel.

The shell companies Lerner was using in his elaborate money-laundering scheme all revolved around that bank in Cyprus. Money coming out of Russia was going through the various shells and eventually coming back through Cyprus. What's more, the bank's money-laundering facilities were being made available to Italian organized crime and the Colombian cartels. Lerner had become the mobs' banker.

He was helping himself to more than his fair share, particularly of the monies he procured through his Promstroi Bank partnership in Russia. Contracts were forged, then used to back loans from other Russian banks, which upped the balance sheets of his Israeli-Russian Finance Company, which helped to keep the Bank of Israel from looking at Cyprus. Lerner channelled money into Israel, after it had been laundered, because other Russian criminals were paying him to do their bidding there. They needed him to buy influence.

There are some politicians who say that influence cannot be bought in Israel. There are others who maintain that it can. Lerner proved that, if nothing else, it's fairly easy to rent it.

One story floating around Israel is that organized Russian criminals are planning to spend in excess of $1.5 billion – some have put the figure as high as $4 billion – over the next few years to secure political power.

Although campaign contributions to political parties are not permitted within nine months of an election, there are very few conditions restricting contributions to individual candidates. Anyway, in a society oriented towards cash – as the entire Middle East traditionally is – it's little wonder that in recent elections men like Lerner have offered bribes to politicians. When one party refused his cash outright, he volunteered to pay for their political broadcasts. That too was refused.

Although the story was initially denied, it now turns out that Soviet dissident turned Israeli Trade and Industry Minister Natan Sharansky accepted one hundred thousand dollars from Lerner. Sharansky insists the money was passed along to an organization that sponsors Russian Jews planning to emigrate to Israel. It later came to light that Lerner also made approaches to, among others, former prime minister Shimon Peres.

The case opened a very sore point with Israeli police intelligence. A senior officer laments, "Political infiltration is a strategic threat to any nation. It is all the more critical in a country like Israel, where coalition governments are so fragile. We know of instances where certain Russian criminals actually debated whether or not to work their way into one of the two main parties or to target one of the smaller parties."

As early as 1996, Israel's chief of internal security, Moshe Shahal, had publicly raised serious questions about the nation's political safety. He claimed that "elements of the Russian *Maffiya* are effectively trying to control Israel." He based his assessment on the political ambitions of fifteen different organizations – likening them to American-style crime families – that the security services had identified. These groups, he believed, were branching out from prostitution, gambling, and extortion to drugs and politics. "The gangsters are now trying to buy and influence politicians."

Shahal was widely criticized as a cowboy firing from the hip, and of insulting Israel's Russian population. But if Shahal is right, as there is every reason to believe he is, the ramifications are enormous.

For example, Israel does not have money-laundering laws because the founding fathers wanted to remove all bureaucratic stumbling blocks facing immigrants who wished to import capital. In other words, Jews seeking refuge in Israel should not be impeded by laws that would prevent, or even delay, them from being able to arrive with their assets.

"Anyone can bring money here," the police intelligence officer goes on, "put money into the banking system and no questions are asked. It makes Israel a prime vehicle for laundering dirty money. There is a feeling, now, that money-laundering laws will have to be implemented. Russian organized crime has a huge stake in preventing us from making changes. Now consider that coalition governments in Israel often hang on very thin majorities. A few votes either way by a minority party can have disproportionate influence over the entire population. And yes, there is clear evidence that certain Russian immigrants have been seeking just that disproportionate voice."

The single thing that currently keeps the Russians and others from turning Israel into one of the world's major sinks is that the economy is not large enough to accommodate the sums of money they would want to put through it. The problem is that as the economy has grown and in the absence of money-laundering laws, drug trafficking has grown too.

There had been a few drug cases before 1995. In a notable one, a ton of cocaine had been shipped from Venezuela to St. Petersburg. The drugs were hidden in cans labelled meat and the final destination was Belgium. The shipment was discovered and the case has been used ever since as an example of the link between Russian organized crime and the Colombian cartels. According to one Israeli source, however, the Russian involvement came from Israel and had the backing of former KGB operatives. The Israelis tried to pursue it but they could never get any evidence out of Moscow. The only solace the Israelis could muster was in the knowledge that the drugs were never destined for Israel.

But the game changed in 1995 when heroin began showing up in the country. Asian heroin, known as "rock heroin," comes into Israel from Holland. Turkish heroin comes in through the Lebanon. At the same time, a marijuana problem developed in the Sinai Peninsula and coke now arrives in discernible quantities from Latin America. Russian organized crime is suspected to be at the heart of it, but that doesn't necessarily mean that any of the traffickers are living in Israel.

Lerner was arrested by the Israeli police on May 12, 1997, at Ben Gurion Airport, just as he was stepping onto a plane for the United States. He had fifty thousand dollars in cash on him plus two satellite telephones. At his various homes – he owned six villas and three apartments – police found a further four hundred thousand dollars in cash, an unlicensed rifle, and forged passports. They wanted him for fraud and bribery. They wanted him in order to discuss with him the murder of several Russian bankers and the attempted murder of a senior banker at Promstroi Bank. And they also wanted him because the Russians were accusing Lerner of having stolen $85 million from them.

He spent ten months in jail, most of them denying his guilt. While he was stuck there, more than 120 investigators worked on his case. They interviewed three Israeli government ministers and seven members of the Knesset. By the time they finished, they had built a strong enough case against him that he agreed to a deal.

Lerner pleaded guilty to thirteen charges, including fraud and attempted bribery. In exchange, the prosecutors dropped their investigation into murder and attempted murder, fined him five million shekels ($1.4 million), and sent him away for six years.

He is the only one of the four horsemen to be put temporarily out of circulation.

Concludes the police intelligence officer, "The fact that criminals not living in Israel were able to get someone inside the Ministry of Interior to facilitate passports for them, the way Mogilevitch did, shows how inefficient our warning systems are. This is not really about Russian immigrants and street crime, this is about upper-level organized criminals. About men like Mogilevitch, Loutchansky, Mikhailov, Kalmanovitch, Lerner, and others. This is about men who are connected to each other through culture, language, and businesses, who are always looking for new opportunities and enterprises. They don't have a sense of humour. They see everything as black or white, friend or foe. There is no grey. They have no fear. They have no shame. Only Lerner is here."

The others are alive and well in the rest of the world.

8

REMAPPING THE EARTH

The more open the world becomes, the more vulnerable people become to those who have organized and have weapons, information, technology, and the ability to move.

– William Jefferson Clinton

There are many different kinds of maps of the earth.

As kids in school we all knew the pull-down kind that hung just above the blackboard – the one that showed the British Empire in pink so that everyone could plainly see how the sun never set on it – and that's how we learned that the world is divided into political boundaries.

Sometimes there was also a topographical map, showing the continents in relief. You could trace the path of the Amazon River all the way into the rain forest and tell right away that America's western mountain ranges stretched all the way from Alaska down through Canada and Mexico and along the west coast of South America, almost to the very tip.

The older you got the more complicated the maps got. Then they threw in a Mercator projection, which is how we discovered that an airplane ride from London to Los Angeles takes you over Canada and not straight across the Atlantic via New York, the way it looked on that pull-down map at the top of the blackboard.

But it took higher-level classes in economics, geology, demography, meteorology, and the like to get to maps that showed plate tectonics or climate, vegetation or population, and then maps that divided the planet into languages, religions, standards of living, standards of education, sources of energy, mineral production, transportation, public health. . . . Whatever the subject, somebody somewhere can draw a map of the world and assign colours to it to describe a variety of properties and relationships.

Someday, someone will draw a map describing transnational organized crime. They'll colour in spheres of influence. But as soon as they do, the map will be obsolete.

Austria shares borders with eight countries. The only other nation in the world that has more is Germany, with nine.

If you were to redraw that map on the blackboard, colouring in the two with most of their neighbours – forming a sort of Hapsburg Empire minus Spain – you could show that, during the 1990s, this was the centre of the transnational criminal empire. This is where all the gangs came together.

A year after the Easter 1990 meeting at the City Club (described in the Prologue), Italians and Russians returned to Vienna, this time checking into the Marriott Hotel. And this time, the Austrian Ministry of Interior was tipped off. They put agents into the hotel. But the Austrians didn't have legislation in place permitting them to do proper surveillance. They couldn't bug the rooms. So they were never able to establish who was there – people were registered under false names – and what was discussed.

As a direct result of that meeting, both the Austrian National Police and Vienna Police demanded new legislation that would permit them to carry out the proper surveillance of such meetings. They'd been fighting the politicians for years to get new laws. It was the Marriott gathering that clinched it for them.

Over the next few years, similar meetings were held around Europe – notably in Warsaw, Berlin, and Prague – but they were irregular, the participants kept changing, and intelligence was difficult to collect.

When the European press cottoned on to the idea that mobsters were having conventions, meetings seemed to pop up everywhere. Sightings were reported in Gyöngyös, Hungary, and in Beaune, France, and in the middle of the Mediterranean on chartered yachts, far from prying eyes. In a few instances, the Russian newspaper *Izvestia* even listed the topics that were being discussed – casino gambling in Moscow, relations with non-Russian gangs, and murder – as if their reporters had been there.

No fewer than eighteen European crime group conferences were reported in the press over the period from 1991 to 1998. Most of them definitely took place; a few of them probably didn't, at least not the way they were reported. It is highly unlikely, for instance, that Ivankov and Sicilian Mafia head Tito Riina co-hosted a meeting in a tiny rural French village, as one paper had it. There may have been some sort of meeting there, but Riina had been in hiding for decades and, in all probability, would not have left Sicily, while the Brooklyn crowd would never have been permitted to cut the LCN out of the loop by going directly to Riina.

It is a fact, however, that during a homicide trial in France in the mid-1990s, in order to place the defendant at the scene of the crime, the police were forced to reveal their certain knowledge of two meetings, both of which they had secretly observed. They claimed there were Russians, Italians, Colombians, and Turks, yakuza and Sun Yee On Chinese Triad members in attendance.

Accepting that it happened the way the French police said it did, a group like that could have discussed all sorts of criminal activity – the permutations are frightening – but it's a sure bet that, at some point, they talked about narcotics trafficking. The drug market was big enough for everybody, and by co-operating with each other, groups minimized their risk, eliminated competition, and maximized profit.

The Russians and Colombians discussed drugs at meetings in Vienna in 1991 and again in 1995. Subsequent conferences took place in the Caribbean, where the two groups continue to meet regularly on the islands of Aruba, St. Vincent, and Antigua. One agreement has the Colombians bartering cocaine for distribution inside Russia, in exchange for whatever commodities they need. In a few instances, that commodity is Afghan heroin, which the Colombians then market in North America. More often, however, it's surplus Soviet military equipment, especially helicopters and light aircraft, which the Colombians use to fly drugs around the world.

Further discussions have focused on the Russians' capacity for moving money. Colombians now ship drug cash back to Mother Russia for laundering. Deposited in *Maffiya* banks, the money is wired through centres such as Cyprus before being brought into the Western financial capitals – Zurich, London, Frankfurt, New York – and finally bedded down in the Caribbean. Intelligence sources believe that Russian-controlled Colombian drug money comes through the City of London in amounts approaching several million dollars per week.

The Russians and the Italians have also entered into joint ventures. When the two of them sat down in Warsaw a few years ago to meet with Colombians and a group of smaller Eastern European traffickers, one result was a Russian marketing concession of Italian refined heroin to gangs in Bratislava. Another was cocaine, paid for with heroin by the Italians and shipped from Peru to Moscow and then on to Poland.

Once the relationship was established, at least two Russian-Italian-Colombian meetings took place subsequently at the Vienna Marriott. The first was in May/June 1994, the second the following year. Among the people known to have attended both are Sergei Mikhailov, Viktor Averin, and a man named David Sanikidze.

That second meeting happened just after news of Ivankov's arrest in New York. At some point, either before the Colombians arrived or after they left, the Russians discussed Ivankov's fate. If he was acquitted, worrying about who his successor would be was academic. But if he was found guilty, they all had their own interests to protect. It was decided, in the event of a guilty verdict, that Sanikidze, who was a Georgian businessman, would go to New York to take over.

In all, the Austrian police have substantiated some fifteen conferences in the city, mixing and matching groups. Russians from Moscow have met with Poles and Czechs, an Italian group from Milan has met with Russians and Hungarians. At the end of 1998 a delegation from the Ukraine showed up to speak with some Sicilians.

"They come to Vienna," explains Michael Sika, Director General of the Austrian Interior Ministry and an expert on transnational organized crime, "for the same reason that spies came to Vienna during the Cold War. It's geographical. Austria is neutral turf. This is where the KGB met with the CIA. There is a certain tradition. They meet here to discuss deals in other countries, and by deliberately not committing crimes in Vienna, they hope to avoid police attention."

They come as businessmen. No fedoras. No violin cases. No obvious shoulder holsters. Just a lot of men in suits with attaché cases, looking more like accountants than anything out of Al Capone's Chicago.

"Take the Italians as a good example. Local police pressure has forced the Sicilians to seek new markets, to look further into Europe. They're especially prevalent now in Germany and the Czech Republic, where they do money laundering, prostitution, and drug trafficking. Organized crime needs an ethnic base. Italian organized crime, in particular, only exists in countries that have a firm Italian community base. We don't have that in Vienna, so they come here to meet, not to commit crimes."

There are, he says, three types of so-called organized international criminal groups. "The first is a Mafia, a group with a strong hierarchy and structure, with central control and discipline, with technical experts, legal experts, business experts. Then there is a quasi-mafia, a group based on a family structure, such as the Camorra or Hells Angels. Finally, there are groups like the Russians. No real structure. They co-operate for only one or two crimes, then go their own way. And when they form these alliances with other groups, that's the kind of entity they create."

This, he insists, is precisely what makes them both so dangerous and so difficult to police. "When the crime is over they disappear. They form another alliance for the next crime. Conspiracy used to be co-operation of two or three people for a long time. This definition no longer holds because the conspiracy is only just long enough to do a crime. That's why we don't call this organized crime, we call it professional crime. It's fluid, always moving. The Sicilian Mafia and the Camorra are static. The yakuza is static. The Russian gangs are static. But the alliances they form are fluid."

Even though the Austrian police know that these alliances are being formed in Vienna, he unhappily concedes that there is very little they can do about it. "It's no crime for them to meet here. It's true that conspiracy to commit a crime in another country is a crime in Austria. But proving it is the problem. The conspiracy is hatched in Vienna, but the crimes are committed in Germany, the money is sitting in the Cayman Islands, the Italians are in Sicily, and their Russian partners are living in Hungary. The only way to stop that is through solid international co-operation among police."

He notes that while Austria has a very good relationship with the

Italian police, it is impossible to develop a similar link with Russians, Czechs, Hungarians, and Slovaks. "Whenever you deal with police in the East, there is always a lingering suspicion about them. I wouldn't say they're all corrupt, although the Russians are and the Czechs can be. Hungary is better than Slovakia, but neither is great. Police officials change too often. It's difficult to know who to trust, difficult to build up any sort of long-term relationship because a year later those people have been moved on to another job. We have real problems establishing genuine trust."

It was long believed by law enforcement in the English-speaking world that Vienna's main appeal was as a money-laundering centre. The existence of the infamous *sparbuch* – a bearer passbook savings account that guarantees anonymity – helped to create this reputation. And the Austrians' staunch refusal to end *sparbuch* fuels the fire.

The Financial Action Task Force has reproached Austria for not doing away with *sparbuch*. The European Union claims that Austria is in breach of its anti-money-laundering rules by maintaining it. A few years ago, the Italians strenuously objected as they watched traditional Mafia money move from Switzerland and Liechtenstein to less obvious financial centres, such as Vienna and Salzburg. In a formal report, the Anti-Mafia Commission in Rome complained, "Austria absorbs illegal money from all over the world like a sponge."

While *sparbuch* remains, other banking rules have been updated. There is now an obligation on banks to report suspicious sums over two hundred thousand schillings. *Sparbuch* is only available to Austrians although, needless to say, there are ways around that. And cash deposits in excess of one hundred thousand schillings have to be explained by the depositor to a banker's satisfaction.

There is no doubt that *sparbuch* continues to be used to some extent by criminals, but it is too cumbersome to be a primary device. To open fifty or sixty accounts – which is what it would take to put large sums through the system – would be difficult, if not impossible. That's why Russian groups and Italian groups have formed Austrian companies. There are thousands of them on the register. On close inspection, thousands show no real business activity. They're used for nothing more than moving money into the Caribbean or next door to Liechtenstein and Switzerland.

Asian organized crime groups have opened restaurants for much the same reason. There are 550 Chinese restaurants in Vienna. Police report that perhaps fifty of them have enough customers to sustain a regular business. The other five hundred appear to have no legitimate source of income. The money coming through the tills belongs to Asian organized crime groups, and, increasingly, to Russian and Italian groups who are paying the Asians to wash their money.

As Peter Stiedl puts it, money coming through Austria these days is no longer black, it is grey. "That's become a real problem for us. The crimes that produce the funds are not committed here, so investigating them is difficult. In 1989, when the Communist governments of Eastern Europe crumbled, many people who had access to funds brought them to Austria. Some of that money was quickly moved out of the country, but it wouldn't have mattered what happened to it because we had no mechanisms prior to 1992 to freeze accounts, no way to get inside those accounts. We knew the money was here but didn't know the source of it. That's been changed. However, it's still difficult for us to do anything about this grey money because there is almost no police co-operation with anyone in the Eastern bloc. If someone commits a crime in the former Soviet Union, we need information about that crime. Someone has to tell us that the funds here have been created by a crime. But we can't get that information out of the Russians. So there's not much we can do from our end about the money here."

To guarantee that the welcome mat will always be out, the crime groups have created what might be called a "*Pax Viennoise*."

And it is clearly visible. Along the Danube in Budapest, there are sixty to seventy organized crime-related homicides a year. In Vienna, over the five-year period 1994–99, there have been three.

Achmedov Hodscha was a fixer. He combined a talent for being at the centre of Russian activity in Vienna with good connections back in Moscow. He was in a position to do favours around Vienna for other Russians, but he was never tied to the big guys. He was a petty player who earned a living as an exporter of spare auto parts and a smuggler of prostitutes. He sent the spare parts to the Czech Republic and Slovakia and brought the women in from Rumania and Bulgaria.

He had to pay his suppliers in Eastern Europe ten thousand Deutschmark for each woman he "bought" from them. In 1994, his clients in

Vienna paid up front for nine women. The people in Eastern Europe gave him extended terms. He jilted them both. There was no way he was going to get away with it, and it's amazing he ever thought he could.

On the night of September 19, the thirty-four-year-old was in front of his house when he spotted some guys coming down the block. He must have recognized them because he ran to his car and tried to get it started. They put eleven shots through the car window with a machine pistol. The killers – whether they were acting for his Austrian clients or the Eastern European suppliers – were never caught.

Nearly four years passed before the next killing.

Israel Laster was a hustler. Born in Poland in 1928 and very much a part of the old Russian community that lived around Mexicoplatz, he dealt in whatever he could. Sometimes arms. Sometimes counterfeit goods, including currency. He had a police record and was well known to the cops, but he wasn't connected to anything major. He was strictly small time.

On June 16, 1996, he was shot by a Bosnian man who'd pretended to be a house painter. At first, the gunman told the police that he'd killed Laster because Laster hadn't paid him for painting his apartment. It didn't sound right to the murder squad. They suspected that the Bosnian had been hired by an organized group outside Austria, possibly because of a weapons deal that somehow touched on the former Yugoslavia. But the Bosnian never changed his story.

Exactly three weeks later, just two days after Ivankov was convicted in Brooklyn Federal Court, two men murdered David Sanikidze. The figurehead front for Orbis – Georgia's state airline – Sanikidze owned a company called ABV which, among other things, owned hotels in Russia. He also controlled a construction company in Vienna, developed real estate in Florida, and was a close personal friend of Georgian president Eduard Shevardnadze. He was Ivankov's business partner in several criminal activities, although he was never thought to be a *vory* himself. A man with contacts in high places, he had access to people that Ivankov never could have met and provided him with something that he could never have otherwise obtained – respectability. Both Sanikidze and Ivankov stashed shell companies and money in Austria. Sanikidze was also a surrogate father to one of Ivankov's sons, who lived in Vienna.

At first, the police were certain that organized crime was behind the killing. They learned about a deal in France that was worth $170 million. Money had been transferred to New York for Ivankov and Sanikidze. But another group claimed they were owed a part of it and demanded their share. It's possible that when it wasn't forthcoming, they looked to the two principals to get it. With Ivankov out of circulation, Sanikidze became the prime target. So the motive was business. But the two men arrested for the shooting had another story.

A fellow named Richard Dzhavakhadze was the chief of security at Sanikidze's ABV Hotel in Tiblisi. He'd been on the take, big time. Sanikidze caught him and demanded restitution. When it wasn't forthcoming, Sanikidze ordered his murder. In May, the contract was carried out in Moscow. One of the two men who killed Sanikidze was Richard's son, Popov. So the motive was revenge. But the second man – the one there with Popov – had his own reasons. He was Grigory Oniyani, the brother of a powerful Georgian gangster who just happened to be Sanikidze's primary rival. So the motive was business, too.

The press used the case as a wake-up call to remind politicians that organized crime was a reality in Austria. It also was a reminder to men like Mikhailov and Averin that even in the safe city of Vienna, they weren't totally safe.

"They can never be safe anywhere in that business," says Max Edelbacher, Chief of the Serious Crimes Squad of the Vienna Police. "But they appear to be safer here than elsewhere. They come for two reasons. Eastern Europeans have traditionally used Vienna as a staging post between Moscow and Tel Aviv. And they come here because of our banking secrecy. We found that more than 40 per cent of the suspicious cash transactions reported by our banks involve funds from the Eastern bloc countries. But they are generally careful not to commit crimes here. The Russians in Vienna don't even work extortion of other Russians, the way they do in Brooklyn. They use Austria to launder their money and for recreation."

He believes that transnational organized crime groups generally migrate in three stages. Initially, they introduce themselves into a country, bring money, set up businesses, and buy real estate. Next, they move soldiers into the country to protect their businesses. In the final stage, they try to take over the local organized crime groups and impose their will.

"We may be in the second stage in Austria," he goes on. "So far, they like the hospitality, they like the banking conditions, and they're trying to stay invisible. But we've observed that the leaders are leaving Austria and going to the south of France. That has created a vacuum for younger groups to move in. They're doing joint ventures with the local Austrian criminals, bringing in girls for the brothels and smuggling aliens. They also smuggle art. They steal it in Poland and the Czech Republic, get it into Vienna, then sell it throughout the rest of Europe. So far, they're staying quiet. We are starting to see some minor operational disputes here. If they lose control, or if other groups try to elbow their way in and turn the rest zone into a crime zone, then everything will change. But if the murders don't escalate, and they haven't so far, then that means somewhere a deal has been struck."

Sika agrees. "The Russians buy property here. Not just in Vienna but throughout the country. They come here because this is a pleasant country. They come here because it's safe for them. And the reason it's safe for them is because they don't commit crimes here."

He says that Mikhailov still has connections in Vienna. Viktor Averin is believed to be living full-time in Budapest but his family is in Vienna and he apparently spends weekends there. Mogilevitch has connections in Vienna as well.

"He is a dangerous and important man," Sika confirms. "We believe he is protected by the Hungarians and by the Russians. He doesn't come here often, as far as we know, but if he did come to Vienna, he wouldn't be arrested. There is no international warrant for him at this time."

In Germany, Russian criminals are responsible for one-third of all crimes. They deal in drugs, arms, prostitution, computer fraud, extortion, and auto theft. Working out of Berlin, they launder money through more than two hundred gambling parlours they own or control. They smuggle both illegal immigrants and radioactive materials across borders.

Surrounding all this is an extreme level of violence. "Crimes are being committed with a brutality that we have not seen before," says one German law enforcement official, on the record. He then adds – and this is not for attribution – "We're five to ten years behind the criminals. We're only starting to put in place means to come to grips with them now."

When the Kremlin agreed to pull Russian soldiers out of what had been East Germany, those same soldiers decided they suddenly faced a bleak future. The command and control element of the army had all but broken down, and without the state to help feed their families, many of them took the opportunity of their final year or so in Germany to build a nest egg. They put together a huge black market in everything they could steal, from cigarettes to Kalashnikov rifles. They expanded operations to include stolen cars: BMWs and Mercedes taken off the streets of Berlin at night were loaded into military aircraft and delivered within hours to their organized crime partners in Moscow, who just as quickly sold them to the only people in Russia who could afford such luxuries, other criminals.

While all of this was going on, the German police could do little except watch. Surveillance cameras were set up outside Russian bases. Police saw the cars being driven onto the bases and then being air-freighted out. But without legal authority to enter the Russian bases, they were helpless. Of course, they tried setting up roadblocks to prevent the cars entering the bases. But the Kremlin officially objected every time they tried to seal off a base, and so the business flourished.

The problem was not solved even when the Russians finally closed those bases. Many of the soldiers, now well connected to organized criminal groups, simply moved east. They established operations in Hungary, Poland, Slovakia, and the Czech Republic, where Russian ties to the former Communist states were still very strong. Now, instead of relying on military immunity, they live in their former satellites, protected by the long-established corruption of the political and legal system. There is more money involved now, and, thanks to improved communications and ease of travel across the German border, the systematic bilking of the country is rife.

Expensive automobiles are still regularly stolen off German streets. These days, however, they are raced across the border, mainly into Poland, where they are either sold for cash, which is fed back into drug trafficking and arms dealing, or traded for young girls, who are smuggled back into Western Europe – Germany and Holland are prime destinations – and held as white slaves for prostitution.

The world has never looked so small.

Russian gangs run prostitution rackets in Paris, co-operate with Colombian cartels to launder money through *bureaux de change*, and are believed to have invested with some Italian gangs in businesses along the Riviera. Asian organized criminals are using their traditional base in Holland to ship amphetamines to groups established in Australia, which include Lebanese, Rumanians, and the much-feared 'Ndrangheta. Czech mobsters have forged alliances with criminals in the Middle East to ensure a constant supply of heroin, which they then move through Austria into Germany, France, and, increasingly, Great Britain. Some of these same Middle Eastern criminals – usually Lebanese – have become middlemen, linking Eastern European criminals with Balkan drug-trafficking organizations.

Once, drugs from Turkey, Afghanistan, and Pakistan travelled freely through the former Yugoslavia, trucked in and out on the way into Western Europe by Turks and their ethnic Albanian partners. Slobodan Milosevic put a stop to all that. Not because he wanted to keep drugs out of what's left of Yugoslavia. He just wanted to keep out the Turks' and Albanians' drugs. Cutting them off meant choking the currency supply that the Kosovo Liberation Army was using to pay for their weapons. And anyway, there were plenty of other criminal gangs who would pay handsomely for such transshipment privileges.

Closing the Balkan route forced the Turkish and ethnic Albanian traffickers to sidestep Serbia and move through Bulgaria, Rumania, Hungary, and into the Czech Republic. From there, heroin is divided into parcels destined for Switzerland, Germany, France, and Great Britain. The hard currency these gangs earn in the West is spent in the East on weapons. They buy arms from Russian organized criminals and Abkhazi separatists in northern Georgia, or do deals directly with them, swapping heroin for weapons. Whatever it takes to maintain the flow of arms back to the Balkans.

Closing the Balkan route also opened a trafficking highway through Macedonia and into Albania, then across the Adriatic to Bari, Italy. That's where the Kosovars have joined with traditional Italian organized crime groups to trade drugs for arms. Along with heroin, the two groups smuggle illegal Albanian aliens into Italy, and non-Albanians, too – Kurds, Pakistanis, and Sri Lankans – who get brought along only because they've paid the Kosovo Liberation Army the money the KLA needs to buy the heroin that starts the cycle.

Slovakia has been turned into a transit territory. The size of the shipments coming through was highlighted in early 1998 when Colombian-grown marijuana was seized. Originally shipped from Panama to Florida, it was loaded onto a container ship bound for Bremen, Germany, and trucked from there to Bratislava. The load weighed thirteen metric tons.

Meanwhile, the Serbs have financed their activities by counterfeiting currency, which they feed into the world's financial markets through a reported two hundred private banks and currency exchange offices under their immediate control. They also allow other groups, notably the Mafia, to launder $1.5 billion a year through those same sinks. And they have reportedly opened up the Balkan route to Middle Eastern organized crime groups that now have a way to get marijuana up to Slovenia and, from there, easily into Austria.

War, bloodshed, and political instability are good business for transnational organized crime. Then again, these days, so is peace and prosperity.

Bulgarian criminals steal luxury automobiles to feed Russia's black market with product. They are then often paid with drugs now being cultivated throughout the former Soviet Union. Polish gangs do exactly the same thing. One report notes that the average life expectancy of a new Mercedes in Warsaw is under three months.

In Switzerland, at the beginning of 1998, Federal Prosecutor Carla Del Ponte – who has relentlessly pursued dirty money in Switzerland to the great annoyance of Swiss bankers – claimed that Russian organized crime had stashed more than $40 billion in the nation's banks. At the same time, the Swiss identified ninety companies plus more than 680 Swiss and foreign nationals living in the country as having direct links to Russian organized crime. From Switzerland, those companies and those individuals can be connected to Russian and other organized criminals throughout the world.

In Britain, direct links have been exposed between Russian organized crime and prostitution, illegal immigration, and fraud in international football transfer fees. British companies operating in the former Soviet Union pay protection money to extortionists as an accepted business expense. Kidnapping of businessmen in places like Chechnya has become all too common. From the criminals' point of view, hostage-taking serves a double purpose. Gangs take the payoff money, and then come back to sell the company protection against kidnapping.

In New York, where Chinese gangs have decided they need help distributing drugs outside their ethnic neighbourhoods, street-level alliances have been formed with other groups, including the LCN.

In Thailand, criminals co-operate with ethnic Chinese gangs to smuggle illegal aliens out of Asia and into the United States, Canada, Germany, France, and Britain. They claim to have a success rate near 90 per cent, and even station their own agents at the arrival side to facilitate immigration controls. It is believed that one particular Thai group has used the LCN in North America, traditional Italian groups in Europe, and the yakuza in Japan to collect debts for them. Illegal aliens who can't pay are then forced either into prostitution or heroin trafficking.

In the United Arab Emirates, planeloads of Russians arrive on charter flights almost every day of the week, mostly at Sharja, and are then bussed into Dubai, where they swarm through the gold market with crisp new hundred-dollar bills, buying up just about everything they see.

In Rimini, Italy, the scene is repeated. But here, instead of gold, the Russians buy leather goods at the wholesale market just outside of town. And in both cases, the goods are shipped back to cities across the former Soviet Union, building up import-export businesses that buy drugs to earn money to launder in goods to earn money to build up import-export businesses.

A recent DEA estimate suggests that while Asian opium production is up, heroin shipments coming into the United States from Asia have declined. The assumption they make is that the Asians have simply opened new markets. In a sense, they're right. A foreign intelligence service with a strong interest in tracking Asian heroin says that the traffickers are sidestepping the DEA by joining forces with the Colombians. They ship raw opium to the cartels, which refine it in the jungles, then franchise it out to the LCN and the Mexicans for sale in North America.

Co-operation between Chinese law enforcement and Western law enforcement has improved slightly over the past few years; then again, since the "goldfish fiasco," it could only get better. In 1988, the Chinese tipped off the Americans about a huge heroin consignment bound for San Francisco. The drugs were stuffed inside dead goldfish and controlled by a local Wo Hop To Triad society. The gang leader, William Mui, was arrested. In return for the favour, the Americans told the Chinese about Mui's associates in China. The Chinese arrested one of these associates, Wang Zongxiao, and shipped him off to California to testify against Mui. For a few weeks, it actually seemed as if the two countries were building a firm law enforcement friendship. That is, until Wang's lawyer convinced him to defect and ask for political asylum in the United States. It has taken the Chinese a very long time to trust Western law enforcement again.

Vietnamese gangs have carved out a niche for themselves in Europe, running massive cigarette-smuggling businesses in Germany and France where there are strong ethnic communities. The original sources of the cigarettes were Poland and Hungary, where many of them were manufactured under licence, and some were simply counterfeit. As they expanded their operations and required more product, they began importing cigarettes from the United States, shipping them to Rotterdam, them smuggling them into the markets. Their profit comes from cheating on the excise duties. Their de facto licence to operate was granted by the larger Eastern European gangs, who feel contraband cigarettes are too small a business to bother with. German police indicate, however, that in the wake of increasing violence against their street sellers from small gangs trying to elbow in on their pitch, the Vietnamese have turned to one of the Chechen organized crime groups for protection. One estimate out of Belgium suggests that of the nearly one trillion cigarettes that are exported annually to warehouses in Antwerp and Hong Kong, about 30 per cent – that's 300 billion – go missing. Black markets thrive in Britain, Spain, and Italy.

The same Lebanese gangs trafficking in Europe have had a presence in Australia since the 1970s. Originally they imported heroin and marijuana from the Syrian-controlled Bekaa Valley. There now is evidence that they failed to finalize deals with the Chinese, were rebuffed by the Vietnamese gangs, and have finally settled into partnership with the Colombians. The 'Ndrangheta has also had a longstanding relationship with Australia. So have Rumanian gangs. Rumanians once tried to get into the heroin trade, were stopped from becoming importers, and have had to settle for a role as resellers. They also work social security frauds. The yakuza also see Australia and New Zealand as markets worth cultivating.

And, of course, the Russians have landed, as well.

Nigerian criminals have invaded Japan, married local women so they can't be deported, and done deals with yakuza gangs that see them as partners in typical advanced-fee-fraud schemes.

In spring 1999, Australian police wound up an eight-year undercover operation and broke up what they described as the nation's biggest ever drug ring. They arrested 135 people and seized enough chemicals to flood the Pacific with $200 million worth of heroin, amphetamines, cocaine, and marijuana. Operation Phalanx coordinated the efforts of sixteen police task forces, shut down three operating drug labs, identified a dozen already dismantled labs, and took out a huge chemical storage facility. The major players were native Australians, but the bust emphasized that the group had working alliances with other organized crime groups in Vietnam, Hong Kong, and Amsterdam.

As the globe shrinks, the danger posed by transnational criminal groups increases proportionately. The world has never been so dangerous. Atomic weapons, which have been remapping political boundaries since 1945, are now remapping the transnational criminal boundaries.

During the 1990s, there have been fifteen hundred to two thousand incidents of fissile materials known to have been offered for sale. The figure depends on who's counting and what criteria are being used. But by everyone's count and by any yardstick, given the intricate and complex nature of nuclear physics, it is indisputable that almost no one in this market has a clue what he's dealing with. Technological ignorance runs rampant. It is that fact alone which explains why, thankfully, all but a handful of the materials offered for sale have been totally useless to anyone attempting to manufacture a nuclear device.

Putting aside – but not discounting – the obvious health hazards to the idiots who are running around with radioactive materials in jam jars, law enforcement bodies have three basic and extremely disquieting concerns. The first is, the number of incidents of trading in illegal atomic materials continues to increase each year – in some years more than doubling – while the quality of materials offered for sale has been improving. This is an ongoing and unmistakable danger. There is no such thing as a minor nuclear bomb. The second is, with each incident, the odds shorten on an educated seller meeting an educated buyer. The third is, unlike other crimes, you only hear about the trade in nuclear materials when the bad guys fail. When – not if, but when – the bad guys finally succeed, it may not make the papers until after someone lights the fuse.

Four incidents, all of them in 1994, demonstrate how close they've already come.

In May, sixty grams of radioactive powder, which included one-fifth of an ounce of weapons-grade plutonium – that's Pu-239 at 99.75 per cent purity – were found in Tengen, Germany. The powder was in a lead canister, hidden in the garage of Adolf Jaekle, a fifty-two-year-old businessman who got caught only because he was under investigation for counterfeiting. He reportedly had been guaranteed up to $100 million from a rogue state – speculation centres on Iraq and North Korea – to purchase enough material for a bomb.

In June, as a result of a sting operation, 0.3 grams of weapons-grade uranium – that's U-235 – were discovered in Landshut, Germany. The police also seized a small quantity of enriched uranium tablets. They arrested one German, four Slovaks, and a Czech.

In December, 2.72 kilos of near-weapons-grade uranium – U-235 enriched to 87.5 per cent – were found in Prague. Acting on a tip, Czech police stopped a Saab driven by a Czech scientist and found the material in two metal containers on the back seat. American investigators were able to help the Czechs trace it back to a ten-kilo theft of enriched uranium from a Russian nuclear research centre at Obninsk. Buyers who were known to have been approached included a Nigerian crime group that offered heroin in exchange for the uranium, Spaniards rumoured to be linked to the Basque terrorist organization ETA, and North Koreans. The operation fell apart when the sellers offered the uranium to a German undercover agent at two hundred thousand dollars a pound. It was the largest amount offered to date on the black market.

A few arrests were made, but the smugglers and their suspected Russian partners are still at large. At least one of the criminals had promised his contacts in the Czech Republic that he could guarantee delivery of five kilos of this material a month, and forty kilos immediately.

The fourth, being the odd one out, took place in August 1994. A steel suitcase arrived at Munich Airport off a Lufthansa flight from Moscow. It contained twenty ounces of radioactive material, three-fifths of which was near-weapons-grade plutonium – sometimes referred to as "weapons capable" – Pu-239 at 87 per cent pure. There were also two hundred grams of lithium – Li-6 – another necessary component in the manufacture of a thermo-nuclear device. It was announced at the time that three men, caught up in an undercover sting, had promised to deliver up to nine pounds of material. But the operation took place on the eve of national elections in Germany, when law enforcement and nuclear trafficking were election issues. It is now clear that the German government manipulated this one to bolster votes.

Still, two salient points came out of it. The first was the message sent to the rest of the world, that radioactive materials were readily available. Explains David Kyd at the International Atomic Energy Agency (IAEA), "The Russians said it didn't come from them. And this stuff is not easy to fingerprint. It's not easy to know the origin of fissile material. The German official explanation was inadequate. German security agents were waiting at the airport. That's just too slick. But even if it was a hoax, it opened eyes. It was a wake-up call and has had a salutary effect."

The second point to emerge from the incident was the nationality of the three men arrested. Two were Spanish and one was Colombian. The moment you mix Colombians into a criminal equation, somewhere, somehow, there is a connection to cartels and drugs.

"One of the real problems with nuclear materials is that they are not easy to detect," Kyd continues. "Contrary to public opinion, there's not a lot of radiation that comes off a nuclear device. Any group of terrorists competent enough to know how to set off a device will know how to shield what little radioactivity comes off of it."

He says that if he were a nuclear trafficker, he'd hand off his materials to a drug dealer. "I'd contract it out to the drug lords and let them move it. Look at how much drugs cross our borders. If you're talking about a bomb, you need grapefruit sizes of plutonium. If it's uranium, a bowling ball size will do. One or the other would be just as easy to hide in a bale of marijuana."

Nuclear trafficking is still in its infancy. But there might be some comfort in knowing that in most instances, the goods offered for sale are useless. Uranium pellets enriched to 3 or 4 per cent are of no interest to Iraq, Iran, Syria, Libya, North Korea, Pakistan, India, or South Africa, among many others. Research quality, which is enriched to 20 per cent, doesn't hold much attraction either. There have been cases of criminal groups brokering "dual-use" materials, which are non-radioactive metals that have industrial applications but which are also found in atomic weapons. These have created some interest. But it is "the big-bang stuff" that really opens wallets.

Anything available at more than 80 per cent would get looked at by everyone in the market because it can be used as feedstock in the enrichment process. Anything enriched to over 90 per cent is what makes a bomb.

According to the IAEA, the Iraqis have been using a 1940s process in their bomb development program. The blueprints are available to anyone for free at the Patent Office. Manufacturing such a bomb would be a messy and inefficient process. And even if the Iraqis somehow acquired weapons-grade plutonium, they wouldn't automatically have a bomb. But they would be a lot closer with those materials than they would be without them.

Saddam Hussein had already made significant progress at the time of the Gulf War. The CIA discovered just how much progress thanks to the human shields he installed at his Tuwaitha nuclear research centre. As soon as they were freed, the Agency bought their clothing and, through forensic testing, established the presence of highly enriched uranium.

It takes around twenty-five kilos of uranium enriched to 90 per cent to build a bomb. And where uranium is concerned, it's an easy process to hide. A plutonium device only needs eight kilos of highly enriched materials, but it's a much more complex process, and more easily detected because of the unmistakable shape of the building where it's done.

Saddam is reasonably believed to have spent in excess of $10 billion and still hasn't gotten a bomb for his money. No one doubts that he is willing to spend a lot more.

In recent years he's shifted slightly the emphasis of his research program, away from looking for materials at any price, but instead going in search of people who can speed up his development and manufacturing processes. The risk of detection is higher when dealing in the black market for uranium or plutonium than it is when dealing in the employment market for out-of-work Russian physicists. If he were to put another billion or so on the table for experts and materials – a sum he could certainly afford – it probably wouldn't take the world's organized criminals very long to start looking at ways to get their share.

But then, Saddam is the one who originally created the awareness that sellers could find buyers. On both sides of the Gulf War, the call was answered by subcontractors and freelancers who now thrive in Europe. And in Japan, too, where affiliates of U.S. companies have illegally attempted to sell fissile materials. The market there has not escaped the attention of the yakuza, who, like their Russian organized crime counterparts, have also explored the lucrative possibilities.

The marketplace has created joint ventures. Russian organized criminals, mainly working out of Vladivostok, met with yakuza members in an effort to find and steal weapons-grade materials in the Pacific region that can then be offered on the black market to the highest bidders. The Russians have the contacts in the Middle East. The yakuza have their own people inside industries based in Japan. So have the murderous members of the Aum Shinrikyo cult.

When police searched their various premises after the sarin nerve gas attack on the Japanese subway in March 1995, documents were found at the cult's "Science and Technology Agency" detailing the mechanics of uranium enrichment. Highly technical and marked "Internal Use Only," the documents dealt mostly with specialized experiments using lasers to enrich uranium. They were sourced back to a Japanese heavy machinery company. It was also discovered, through information obtained in other documents, that an Aum member was on the staff of the Kurchatov Institute, Russia's most prestigious nuclear physics laboratory.

As the market in what is sometimes referred to as "the poor man's equalizer" has expanded, criminals feeding it have grown more sophisticated and peripheral markets have grown up too. Prime among them is the market for "red mercury."

Touted by some as an essential ingredient in pure-fusion weapons, the Russian-invented substance has also come to be known as a magic potion that can be almost anything, including a shortcut to the creation of a nuclear device.

Around 1990 or so, the story circulated that Soviet scientists had come up with a powerful new explosive. The version generally taken to be official noted that it was "red and semi-liquid, of pure mercury and mercury antimony oxide, irradiated for up to twenty days in a nuclear reactor. It can then yield enough energy to fuse tritium atoms." That would be a nuclear bomb. Except that many physicists are sceptical that a compound of pure mercury and mercury antimony oxide would be sufficiently stable to be used as an explosive. And anyway, apparently no one of genuine repute has ever seen the stuff. According to the FBI, every time they've looked into it, they've either found a small amount of low-grade nuclear material that wasn't red mercury, or hot air.

In other words, there is no reliable evidence that red mercury exists.

But that's never stopped organized criminals from selling it to purchasers who want to believe they're buying the real thing. The Austrians have recorded several instances of red mercury sales, including a significant one matching a Russian organized criminal seller with a Saudi government official. By the mid-1990s, red mercury had shown up in Hong Kong and Macau, then quickly spread to all the major Australasian markets.

A certain folklore has grown up with it. One theory is that red mercury was invented by the Western security services. The idea was to bait a hook and see who bit. Another theory is that the Soviets cooked it up because they needed the money. A more likely rationale is that some scientist came up with the theory and some criminal decided he could sell the possibilities. And that is exactly what happened. Word got out that red mercury could solve the problems bomb designers in the Third World found most vexing, and deals were done. The going price was three hundred thousand dollars per kilo.

Even without red mercury there is enough unaccounted-for fissile material that once belonged to the Soviet Union to turn much of the developed world into an uninhabitable moonscape. Perhaps as many as a thousand sites within the U.S.S.R.'s former borders still house enriched uranium and plutonium. But no one knows how much is there, or even how much used to be there. It seems the Soviets couldn't be bothered to keep detailed records. And anyway, what remains of the records they did keep are, today, in disarray. It would take decades to work out the true extent of what's missing, if anyone wanted to take on the task. At the moment, no one does.

If the submarine base at Murmansk is any indication, then nuclear accounting, storage, inventory controls, maintenance, and security at other sites is not just seriously inadequate, it is almost non-existent. What's left of the Soviet nuclear fleet is rusting away, its fuel reactors still on board. Some years ago, two Russian naval officers simply walked into the base, sawed through a padlock on a door at Fuel Storage Area 3-30, and walked out with four kilos of fresh submarine fuel – U-235 enriched to 20 per cent. It was six months before they or the fuel rods were found.

In May 1993, Lithuanian police, acting on a tip, searched the basement vaults of the Joint-Stock Innovation Bank and found twenty-seven wooden crates of beryllium. Valued in the open market at around $600 a kilo, the cache of 4.4 metric tons was officially worth $2.64 million. Used in missile-guidance systems and precision optical equipment, beryllium is known to physicists for its ability to reflect neutrons. That means it is also used in nuclear bombs. Sort of a fuel additive, beryllium helps to create a bigger explosion with less fissile material.

What the Lithuanian police didn't know was why it was in the bank vault, and who had put it there. What they did know was that, suddenly, all previous bets were off.

Up to this point, doomsayers were warning that because Russia's atomic stockpile was so easy to pilfer, it was only a matter of time until enough fissile materials to build a bomb fell into the hands of the *Maffiya* and terrorists. Authorities in Moscow and Washington were understandably anxious to pour scorn on those kinds of statements. They insisted that safeguards were being put into place to protect the atomic stockpile and that, in any case, the only thefts of fissile materials to date were not weapons-grade and were managed by amateurs.

Typical was the butcher in St. Petersburg who had a relative working at a plant with access to uranium-235. The relative put some in a jar, took it home, and the butcher tried to sell the stuff at the local street market. But that was one jar's worth. This was 4.4 tons.

The mystery took years to unravel, but basically came down to this: a man said to be connected to Russian organized crime was able to buy the beryllium from a former Soviet factory where the workers were starving because they hadn't been paid. The purchase was made in the name of a karate club in Moscow. They had it shipped to a laboratory in Vilnius, while waiting to sell it to a Russian in Austria. At the lab in Vilnius, someone realized that included in the beryllium was 19.8 pounds of highly radioactive cesium. One of the more deadly by-products of nuclear fission, there is a black market for cesium that would have paid around eight hundred thousand dollars for that much. So the cesium disappeared.

The Russian in Austria was paying $2.7 million for the beryllium, having pre-sold it to a Swiss company with an address in Italy for $24 million. That company had a client for the beryllium with "interests" in North Korea. The police in Vilnius killed the sale.

When Interpol heard about it, they went to see the Swiss company's office in Italy. But the company had moved and left no forwarding address.

Working on a tip from a discontented member of an Italian organized crime gang, prosecutors in Italy dismantled a Mafia ring in 1998 that had offered a cache of nuclear materials for $170 million.

For sale were seven bars of uranium, each weighing 1.33 kilos, controlled by the 'Ndrangheta. They are thought to have been brought into Italy from Zaire, where the Russians had originally shipped them in 1972. It is believed there were several potential buyers in the Middle East. Only one of the bars has been found. Among the fourteen individuals arrested was a member of the Santapaola family, the same clan that operates out of St. Maarten in the Caribbean, where Russians meet Colombians and the Seminole Indians have an interest in a casino.

Perhaps even more chillingly, at the end of 1998, a U.S. federal court indicted terrorist Osama bin Laden on grounds that he "made efforts to obtain the components of nuclear weapons."

Over the past several years:

Police in Tanzania arrested a man with radioactive cesium.

Police in Rumania arrested two men in possession of eighty-two kilos of non-weapons-capable uranium. In unrelated incidents, they arrested seven people offering to sell seven kilos of uranium and strontium-90; four others trying to sell four kilos of uranium-235 and uranium-238; several more attempting to sell 4.5 kilos of uranium tetrachloride; five Rumanians with 2.6 kilos of uranium; and three more with three kilos of uranium pellets.

Police in Switzerland arrested a man with low-enriched uranium. Acting on information obtained in that case, police in Turkey then arrested eight people with another 1.13 kilos of the same material. In unrelated incidents, they arrested an Azeri with 750 grams of uranium; seven Turks with 12 kilos of weapons-grade uranium; and five people in connection with 22 pounds of uranium discovered in Istanbul.

Police in the United Arab Emirates arrested a man in Dubai offering to sell three kilos of red mercury.

Police in Poland arrested a man coming into the country from the Czech Republic with eleven small containers of strontium-90. In an unrelated case, they seized eight kilos of radioactive americium-241 and cesium-137.

Police in Hungary arrested four Slovaks with 1.7 kilos of depleted uranium in a fruit jar on their way into Austria. In unrelated incidents, police discovered 26 kilos of various radioactive materials in the trunk of a car; arrested two men with 4.4 kilos of fuel rods stolen from a reactor in Russia; confiscated 2 kilos of uranium fuel rods.

Police in Tehran arrested five Iranians for being in possession of uranium.

Police in Bulgaria arrested a group of Russians and Ukrainians in possession of "materials of strategic value," some of which were radioactive. In unrelated incidents, Bulgarian police found four lead capsules containing radioactive materials on a bus going to Turkey; and they arrested six Bulgarians carrying nineteen containers of radioactive material.

Police in Slovakia arrested three Hungarians, four Slovaks, and two Ukrainians with 18.4 kilos of radioactive material. In unrelated incidents, they arrested four people trying to smuggle in one kilo of non-weapons-grade uranium.

Police in Italy arrested a man for a murder committed when the victim couldn't pay for five grams of plutonium. The nuclear materials were never found.

Police in India arrested four people trying to sell 2.5 kilograms of uranium extracted from ore.

Police in Germany discovered a flask of radioactive material sitting in a railroad station. In unrelated incidents, they arrested a Polish man for trying to sell one kilo of uranium; a Zairian man for smuggling in 850 grams of uraninite; and confiscated 800 milligrams of uranium coming in from the Czech Republic.

Police in South Africa reported that 130 barrels of enriched uranium waste went missing from a storage facility.

Police in Canada reported that non-radioactive isotopes worth $350 million were brought into Toronto by a Swedish-Russian joint venture, for smuggling into the United States.

And in a slight twist, police in Russia arrested two Lithuanians for smuggling uranium-238 into Russia.

More than five hundred metric tons of U-235 and three hundred tons of Pu-239 have been extracted from dismantled Russian warheads and are stored somewhere in Russia, waiting to be disposed of. Enough to create sixty thousand nuclear weapons, that material represents only what they've recovered through disarmament agreements. This is not their regular stockpile.

The Russians have consistently denied that any of their weapons-grade, or even near-weapons-grade, materials has turned up in the West. They have, however, admitted that quantities of highly enriched uranium have gone missing inside Russia. But they conveniently ignore the residue from the collapse of the Soviet Union.

Nearly five thousand scientists got stuck in Kazakhstan. Unable to earn a living because the Russians don't want them back and there isn't much for them to do in Kazakhstan, it takes only one to hire himself out and bring his own fissile materials along. Life in the Ukraine for ex-Soviet physicists isn't much rosier than for those in Kazakhstan.

But then, no one has to go that far to find dangerous merchandise. When the Russian military pulled out of East Germany, they left behind a whole pile of atomic junk.

Not long ago in Washington, seventeen of Russia's most senior military officers were asked how they rated the chances of "nuclear migration" to a Middle Eastern country. In other words, on a scale from one to ten, how likely was it that some country in the Middle East would soon come up with the technological know-how and the source materials to build a nuclear device.

All seventeen said, "Ten."

9

CONNECTING IN CALI

There was this guy, there are others.

– Homicide detective Billy Ahern, NYPD

Vladimir Beigelman fancied himself a contender.

At thirty-six, the dark-haired, husky Russian with a thick gold chain around his neck was a man intent on making the right connections. Always on the prowl for the next scam, he was looking for a way to break into the big leagues. He was convinced that with the right connections he could become a player, and being a player meant money.

His pal Oleg Zapinakmine had the right connections. He was Monya Elson's bodyguard. And after Nayfeld attempted to kill Elson on that Saturday afternoon in July 1993 – when Elson, his wife, and Oleg all lived to tell the tale – Monya and Oleg became just like father and son. Being friends with Oleg gave Vladimir a line to Elson, and because Elson had heavyweight connections with the Genovese family, this could be his line to the Italians. But before Beigelman could milk that connection, Oleg's luck ran out.

On September 24, 1993, as he was getting into his car, which was parked right in front of his house in Brighton Beach, the twenty-five-year-old Zapinakmine noticed one of his tires was flat. He bent down to take a closer look. He never saw the man with the gun who came up behind him and put a single bullet into the back of his head.

Understandably, Oleg's death shocked Beigelman. However, looked at in a harsher light, it didn't necessarily shut the door to the Italians.

There might still be ways to get connected through Elson. In the meantime, he had a steady earner with the Colombians.

They had rented a big house for him in Mill Basin, an upmarket neighbourhood where many Russians, newly arrived and stuck in Brighton Beach, aspire someday to be. Not far from King's Plaza, just north of Brooklyn Marine Park, the house had a private dock along a small inlet which leads into Jamaica Bay – waterfront access that made smuggling easy. And the Colombians were paying Beigelman enough in cash to live better than he had ever lived before. So now, with Larissa expecting their second child, keeping the Colombians sweet – at least until something better came along – was a worthwhile occupation.

The Colombians, too, were pleased with the way things were working, or so he thought. After all, when he complained about the Ford Arrow-Star van they had bought for him, they promised, albeit reluctantly, to get him a better one.

Then, in a turn of events as sudden as Oleg's murder, it looked as if his luck was running out as well. Vladimir never had to do much to earn his keep with the Colombians. His contact, Enrique, merely asked him to hold onto a couple of thousand kilos of coke whenever they landed it. Beigelman stashed it safely in his house until one of them came to pick it up. The problem was, somewhere along the line, a few hundred kilos went missing.

They accused him of stealing it. He accused them of stealing it. The quarrel got worse. They cut him off. They said they would never give him any more work. They said that he was in serious trouble if he didn't come up with either the coke or, at least, the money to pay for it. He continued to protest his innocence. They stopped paying his rent. Bills piled up. He blamed them.

He had hustled all his life and knew that he could always, somehow, find a way to make a living. Ducking and diving was what he did best. But now, the combination of Oleg's death and the missing drugs had thrown a serious monkey wrench into his game plan.

Enrique had promised to make it all right again. But until Thursday night, December 2, 1993, when a call came in to Beigelman's home, he didn't know if or when his luck would ever change for the good again.

It was a quarter to nine. Larissa Beigelman answered the telephone. A man with a Hispanic accent asked, "Where's the Russian?" She handed the phone to her husband. Vladimir didn't speak for long, a couple of minutes at most, before hanging up and saying to her, "I'll be back in a little while. I'm going out to Queens to get a new car."

He fetched his keys, pulled a blue winter coat over top of his "Save the Planet" T-shirt, stepped into his track shoes, put on his N.Y. Giants cap, and grabbed a pair of driving gloves. He took neither his wallet nor his gun.

Leaving his wallet behind might not have mattered and Larissa might not have noticed, but it was strange that he didn't slip his gun into his pocket, because Beigelman always carried a gun whenever he left the house. Maybe he didn't bother taking it because all he was going to do was pick up a new car, because he wasn't expecting any problems, because he thought to himself, if Enrique is giving me a new car it means we're back in business together.

The drive from Mill Basin to the meeting point in the middle of Queens took about forty minutes. Two Colombian teenagers were standing on the sidewalk, waiting for him, right where they were supposed to be. They instructed him to park the van and leave the keys in the ashtray, explaining that they would take him to the new car and come back to pick up this one. He did what he was told to and walked around the corner – with one kid on each side of him – into the 9200 block of Fifty-sixth Avenue.

The neighbourhood is residential, made up mainly of apartment houses. Towards the middle of the block there's a playground behind a chain-link fence. They were on the playground side. Just as they got to a street lamp, two other guys came up to them. If Vladimir Beigelman hadn't figured it out yet, he was never going to. The shooter fired from only eighteen inches away.

Billy Ahern is built like a halfback – compact enough that you know he can move well, big enough that you know you don't want to get in his way.

Brought up on Long Island, he joined the New York Police Department in the early 1980s and by December 1993, after a dozen years on the force, he had seen it all – street gang warriors, stickup men, stickup children, con men, child abusers, hookers, knife slashers, bank robbers, rapists, muggers, husbands who beat up their wives with their fists, wives who slammed their husbands to death with hammers, drug dealers, murderers – but mostly drug dealers and murderers.

When he started his shift that Friday morning, doing general detective work at the 110th Precinct in Corona, Queens, the talk was about how a Russian had gotten dusted the night before. The neighbourhood was Colombian, so a white man's body on the sidewalk was worth talking about.

The call saying someone had been shot came into the precinct at 10:20 p.m. Uniformed officers arriving at the scene found a Caucasian male in his mid-thirties, 170 to 180 pounds, lying dead on the sidewalk, shot numerous times. Detectives showed up a few minutes later and counted five bullet holes – one in the man's left cheek next to his nose, one in the left side of his nose, one in the left side of his neck, and two in his left shoulder. From the size of the wounds, they could tell he'd been shot at very close range. Billy Ahern would later remark, "They definitely wanted this guy dead when they shot him."

Surprisingly, the street was not covered in blood. In fact, the crime scene photos show there was very little blood. When your heart stops as suddenly as Beigelman's did, blood stops flowing just as abruptly.

When the detectives searched the body, they couldn't find any ID – no wallet, no credit card, no driver's licence – nor could they find any car keys. But the dead man's pockets weren't turned out, which said to them that the motive probably wasn't robbery. Not that robbery was ever much of a possibility. A dead white guy in this neighbourhood, shot the way he was shot, had all the signs of a drug-related murder.

There was a second baseball cap not far from the body, a blue scarf nearby, and a few witnesses, including an off-duty cop. He told the detectives, "There were two males, possibly Hispanics, twenty years of age, running from the scene. Also a dark-coloured car. Two male Hispanics confronted the victim, shots went off, the dark car came up, one of the male Hispanics jumped into the car, the other ran off on foot." He said one of them threw something into the yard. It turned out to be the scarf. Thinking the gun was wrapped inside, he picked it up. But it was empty.

Other witnesses put four people at the scene – the two guys who walked with Beigelman, the shooter, and someone with the shooter. They said that one of the two guys walking with the victim jumped into the car – identified as a dark Buick Grand National, which is known for being very fast – while the other ran down Fifty-sixth Avenue towards Ninety-fourth Street. The shooter and the guy with him just disappeared. The only thing the detectives could safely conclude was that they didn't know for sure who went where.

Then someone said that the victim had gotten out of a van that was parked around the corner. So the detectives walked around the corner and found a Ford Arrow-Star with keys in the ashtray. They ran a check on the licence plate. It turned out to be registered to a false name with a false address. Then they called for a drug dog, which sniffed its way through the van and discovered false walls built into the panels where drugs had once been hidden.

They had to rely on fingerprints to ID the victim, which took several hours, and later that night, once they had a name and address, officers drove to Mill Basin to notify his next of kin. Larissa took the news badly. The detectives asked her questions but she refused to answer. No matter what they said, she would not co-operate. And shortly after the murder, she moved away.

But Billy Ahern didn't know anything about her when he showed up for his shift that Friday. All he knew was the morning scuttlebutt, that some Russian had been whacked the night before in a Colombian neighbourhood. It sounded to him like just another dead drug dealer. Still, the detectives had to go through the motions, fill out the appropriate forms, so the lieutenant in charge of homicide – knowing that Ahern had worked on cases with the Drug Enforcement Administration – asked him to make a few phone calls.

Billy rang the Manhattan office of the DEA, mentioned the victim's name, and heard the agent on the phone shout out to other guys in his office, "Hey, the Russian's dead."

The agent then explained to Billy that they'd just started working a case on Beigelman, based on information from a DEA office outside New York. His name had popped up because he was purportedly sitting on a multi-kilo shipment. By coincidence, a few nights before, they'd actually installed a pole camera to watch his residence. Ahern duly reported back to his lieutenant.

Deep down, he had a gut feeling that, given time, this was a case he could solve. But all he'd been asked to do was make one phone call. Anyway, he had his own cases to worry about. So this one was duly shoved into the recesses of his mind under the heading of someone else's unfinished business.

For the detectives working the Beigelman murder, there were never any indications of who did what or why. The witnesses' statements were too vague. And the off-duty cop who'd been at the scene was never spoken to again. The file was officially sent away to gather dust on December 21, 1993.

The only published record of the murder appears to have been in New York's *Newsday* newspaper. A small box in the December 4 issue was labelled, "The homicides by gunshot reported by city police during the twenty-four-hour period ending at 6:00 p.m. yesterday: 10:19 p.m. Thursday. Vladimir Beigelman of Brooklyn shot to death at Ninety-second Street and Fifty-sixth Avenue, Queens."

Normally, that would have been the end of the story.

As Billy Ahern later explained, "A guy dealing drugs is dead and if you can find the guy who did it, you do the community a great service because you lock him up and get two off the streets for the price of one. Nobody gives a fuck about dead drug dealers." In NYPD jargon, those murders are referred to as "misdemeanour homicides."

Some faceless bureaucrat in "time management" decided that there should be a general rule for these things and settled on four days. That's how long a New York City homicide detective can devote to any one murder.

Except in rare circumstances, either the case gets solved in four days or it gets dumped. The only reason the Beigelman murder didn't meet the four-day rule was because the folder sat on desks a couple of weeks longer than it should have.

The four-day figure wasn't plucked out of thin air. Most murders that get solved, get solved within four days. But then, most murders are committed by people known to the victim, so the cops don't usually have to look very far. Perhaps as many as 80 per cent of the murders that don't get solved within four days are written off simply because the detectives haven't enough time to do what they need to do. They have to move on because other cases are piling up. A few years ago, some senior officers wondered what would happen if an elite team were given enough time to do whatever they have to do to solve those cases. And by late March 1995, Billy Ahern had moved from the Corona precinct to one in Jamaica, Queens, where a homicide lieutenant named Phil Panzarella was running a "cold case squad."

Known to his men as "Sundance," Panzarella is legend around the NYPD for his photographic memory. He and his team of seasoned homicide investigators were assigned to search through the archives for unsolved murders and solve them. Panzarella offered the newly arrived Ahern a ton of cases to choose from. On March 30, 1995, Ahern elected to reopen the Beigelman murder.

After getting the records up from archives and going through them in minute detail, he phoned a DEA agent he had worked with on other cases – a highly experienced, six-foot two-inch, 210-pound street narc named Brian Crowell. They had met back in 1991 when Ahern was dealing with one of his first homicides. A Colombian woman in Queens, a real estate agent, had been murdered in her office. In broad daylight, the shooter boldly walked in, strolled past several people sitting at their desks, went up to her, and blew her away. During the course of that investigation, Ahern stumbled across Crowell, who'd been targeting restaurants and money remitters through which the Colombians were laundering drug cash. Ahern would later say about Crowell, "Ninety-nine per cent of the people are talkers. Only one per cent are doers. Brian is a doer." And Crowell would later say about Ahern, "Billy knows a lot of those guys hanging out on street corners, who they are, where to find them, how to talk to them. He knows what he's doing."

Now Ahern reminded Crowell that the DEA had recognized Beigelman's name the morning after the murder and asked him to run it through their system. The name didn't ring a bell to Crowell. But that wasn't surprising because he wasn't dealing at Beigelman's level. His team was targeting Colombian cell heads. He was aiming for the guys at the top of each sales and distribution team, the guys who oversaw particular territories.

When Crowell first got into the business, Colombians only dealt with Colombians. Then they started handing off to Dominicans, but only at the street level. Now he was seeing cell heads dealing directly with

Dominicans, who, in turn, had achieved significant influence in New York's cocaine trade. Dominicans not only controlled entire neighbourhoods, such as Washington Heights, but they had also found a niche for themselves in transport, staging shipments in the Dominican Republic.

A Colombian-Russian link was, nonetheless, out of the ordinary.

Crowell ran a check and reported back to Ahern that Vladimir had been a bagman who'd been set up in Mill Basin, in what the trade calls a mid-level stash house, for the purpose of receiving two thousand to three thousand kilos of coke at a time. He said that a DEA office out-of-state had made Beigelman's name, address, and phone number, had come up with a pretty good idea about what and who he was involved with, and, based on that, had set up a surveillance camera. They even had footage of Vladimir leaving his house on the night of his murder.

Ahern tracked Beigelman's wife down to Brighton Beach and tried to reach out to her. He explained that he'd been assigned to look into her husband's death and that he was genuinely interested in finding the perpetrators. She responded by giving Billy the name of her attorney. That struck him as odd. She wouldn't elaborate, except to say that from her experience with the detectives who had originally investigated the case, she wasn't interested in co-operating.

Ahern convinced the lawyer to set up a meeting. And on April 4 – just five days into this investigation – Larissa, her lawyer, Billy, and Brian sat down in the lawyer's Manhattan office. The two cops assured Larissa that they were only interested in finding the people who'd murdered her husband. They knew about his drug dealing but they had no interest in any involvement she might have had.

After making their pitch, Billy and Brian left the room to give Larissa and the lawyer a chance to talk. Five minutes later the lawyer invited them back in and announced that she would co-operate.

She began by telling them a lot of things they already knew. Next she said that shortly before her husband's death, he had gotten a call from a Colombian arranging a pickup for two hundred to three hundred kilos. The two guys who came for the stuff – the same two who always made the pickups – later claimed it never happened. Beigelman insisted that the Colombians had ripped it off. Finally she admitted that Beigelman had gotten involved with the Colombians through her.

In those days, they were living in New Jersey and he was a low-level hustler working gas-tax frauds for the Russian mob. She had a job in a clothing store, where she became friendly with a Colombian woman who also worked there. The two couples started going out to dinner. It was the Colombian woman's boyfriend, Enrique, who connected Beigelman to the cartel. During the course of their friendship, Enrique got into trouble and was locked up in New Jersey for dealing drugs. Bailed with money wired from Cali, the minute he was out, he jumped. Around that time the Beigelmans had moved to Brooklyn.

Back in Colombia, Enrique went to his boss and told him he knew a white guy who was married with a kid, and who was looking to get connected. Enrique's boss liked what he heard about Beigelman. He knew from experience that white couples were less suspect than Latinos. He said to set it up. He made Enrique "Beigelman's rabbi," the guy who oversees the deal, makes sure it works, and gets held responsible if it doesn't.

When the two pickup men – who happened to be Enrique's cousins – complained about missing two hundred to three hundred kilos, Enrique immediately shut off shipments and payments to Beigelman. But he was still in trouble with his own boss. He was kidnapped and held hostage, and made to understand – in no uncertain terms – that because he had put it together, it was his problem. Using what little credibility he had left, Enrique convinced his boss that he could resolve everything by going to New York. His boss agreed. Left unsaid was what would happen if he failed.

If there ever was a code of honour among thieves, it certainly doesn't exist where the Colombians are concerned. Before going into business with any Colombian national, the cartel bosses insist on knowing where the employee's family lives. They may try to reach out to a guy who steals from them. They may be benevolent enough to ask once what happened. But when their patience runs out – and historically it's in very short supply – they go for the family. Consequently, they don't often get ripped off by their own. Nor, for that matter, do many of their own dare to testify against them.

So with more than just his own neck on the line, Enrique headed for New York. But the outstanding warrant in New Jersey meant he couldn't fly direct. Instead, he travelled first to Mexico, crossed the U.S. border at Tijuana, and made his way to Brooklyn. He slept at the

Beigelmans' house for almost three weeks. Later, Ahern and Crowell would see from phone records that he regularly reported in to his boss in Colombia.

During Enrique's visit, Beigelman reminded him about the van. He said it just wasn't up to standard and that he wanted something nicer. Enrique promised to correct that problem as soon as they had resolved the matter of the missing two hundred to three hundred kilos. Enrique tried to get in touch with his cousins, but he never managed it. And Beigelman refused to put Enrique in touch with them, all the time insisting that he didn't have anything to do with the missing drugs and that he didn't want to have anything to do with them. Enrique returned to Colombia in November, after consoling Beigelman that as soon as everything was squared away, they'd set him up again.

Ahern and Crowell now turned to the out-of-state investigation where Beigelman's name had first appeared.

The officers handling it had an informant whom they were willing to share. At the beginning of April, Ahern and Crowell travelled to see the informant. He admitted to knowing the Russian, confirmed Larissa's story, identified Enrique, and added that he'd even had a conversation with Enrique about the murder. He maintained, "Enrique told me, Beigelman caused me a problem. Somebody had to go. He was the most likely candidate. Better him than my cousins. So he went."

By July, Ahern and Crowell were still trying to identify Enrique's cousins. Separately, Ahern was having difficulty locating the off-duty detective who'd been at the scene. That's when a Colombian gang war broke out in Queens.

A group called Los Tusos was shooting it out with a group known as Mono's Crew. Bodies were dropping on a daily basis. One day the 110th Precinct would have two. The next day the 108th would have three. Then the 115th would have one. Then the 110th would have two more. Word on the street was that the leader of Los Tusos used to work for Mono, that the two had a falling out, and that this would go on until one side eliminated the other. Although there were some people left standing at the end, the war went on for months and cleaning up the mess cut into a lot of police time.

Ahern was no further along in collaring the people who had killed Beigelman, except that the name Chino kept popping up. Ahern's contacts were telling him they didn't know if Chino was involved, but Chino took a lot of contracts and Chino was a real bad guy – so bad, in fact, that nobody was willing to identify him. Then, just after Christmas, Billy learned that Chino was the leader of Los Tusos.

Based on information obtained during the gang war, Ahern got a plate number for Chino's car. With two other homicide cops, Joey Miles and Rueben Martinez, Ahern climbed into an unmarked van and, on the long shot that they might get lucky enough to spot Chino's car, headed for Chino's known hangouts. The long shot not only paid off, but against all odds, it happened within thirty seconds. Chino drove by.

The cops followed him until he pulled over. They also pulled over, a safe-enough block behind. At least, they thought it was safe enough. Chino and two others got out of their car. They were eating Chinese take-out. Almost too casually, they started walking towards Ahern and his partners. When Chino got to within one hundred feet, he was staring at the three cops.

Billy announced, "We've been made."

One of the others asked, "What do you want to do?"

Billy answered, "We take them."

They didn't know if Chino and his pals were armed. Nor did they have time to worry about whether arresting Chino might somehow compromise the murder investigation. The three cops merely bailed out of their van, guns drawn, screaming, "Down on the ground . . . down on the ground . . . ," taking Chino and his two pals by surprise, and at the same time shouting on their radio for backup.

Squad cars from all over Queens responded with sirens blaring.

Less than a minute after the takedown began, Chino and the other two were cuffed and in the process of being carted away.

Born in Medellín, Colombia, twenty years before, Juan Dairon Marin Henoa, a.k.a. Chino, liked to brag that as a teenager he'd killed people on assignment for Pablo Escobar and that once he'd reached majority, when he could be tried as an adult for his crimes, he skipped the country. In the States, he freelanced, working for anyone who would pay him. Since the demise of Escobar and the Medellín cartel, that meant the Cali crowd.

Normally, kids like Chino stay quiet, but as soon as he and Ahern sat down to talk, Chino suffered a case of verbal diarrhea. He admitted to doing several hits in New York – eleven in all – and when Ahern asked why, Chino shrugged, "Because I had contracts."

Ahern got him to account for each of those eleven murders, going into details about how much he was paid, who paid him, and even which gun he used. For the record, it was a 9mm Glock, a favourite of Colombian hit men because the barrel can be removed, thrown into a river somewhere, and a new barrel put on. Effectively, it becomes a new gun that can't be traced to the last hit.

Ahern also asked how each of the eleven victims died. Chino said they'd been shot in the head because, "I shoot you in the stomach or in the chest, you might live. I shoot you in the head, you're dead."

After all that, Chino swore he didn't know anything about the Beigelman murder. But he knew a lot about the gang-war killings, and volunteered three names. Billy hunted those guys down, locked them up, and from them, got five more names. None of those guys was willing to say they knew about Beigelman, although Ahern noticed a common thread running through their stories: the Apollo Bar on Corona Avenue.

The gang members told him that was where they used to muster up, meaning that when a hit was contracted, the fellow holding the contract – a guy like Chino – would go to the bar to ask if anyone wanted to come out with him. He'd negotiate a price, usually a couple of thousand dollars per man, and recruit a crew.

Word on the street is that the contract on Beigelman went for seventy thousand dollars, although some people contend it might have gone for ten times as much. While it's true that in the world of Colombian drugs, killing a white guy costs more than killing a Colombian – which can be arranged for a few grand – the one sure thing is that the fee didn't last long. The guys who take these contracts are all alike. Chino, for example, is believed to have picked up several hundred thousand dollars in murders in 1995, and yet, Ahern notes, "He spent everything on drugs, cars, girls, guns. Didn't have a cent left. Nothing. Didn't have a pot to piss in."

So the Apollo was the "employment agency," which really piqued Billy's interest because it was only five blocks from where Beigelman had been murdered. Ahern and Crowell started making the rounds and asking questions. Their hunch was right.

Someone at the Apollo told them, "I was hanging out on Roosevelt Avenue and two guys came by and asked me if I could take them for a ride, cause I had a car. So I said sure, they got in and told me where to go. I wanted to know why they wanted to go there and they said, 'Cause we just shot somebody and we want to make sure he's dead.' They get to the block, it's lit up like a Christmas tree with cops' cars, and that's how the hit men knew they'd done their job."

Another came up with a name for the fellow who'd picked up the contract. Someone else suggested word had come directly from Cali that Beigelman needed to be killed because he was an undercover DEA agent. That was the cover story, the line they invented to make it easy to find a crew and someone to pull the trigger. Informants at the bar also bandied about four nicknames. Ahern and Crowell were able to put photos to the nicknames and last names to the photos. But the fourth man on that list, they were assured, was dead.

The problem became one of separating real from phony names because these guys changed their names all the time. One day someone was Juan Gomez. The next day he was Manny Garcia. The day after that he was José Gacha. Dealing with addresses was no easier. These guys lived in one room with three pairs of pants, two shirts, one pair of sneakers, and a paper bag to carry their clothes in when they moved to a new location, which they did every few days.

Locating the dead guy was a little more straightforward. The DEA came up with a death certificate for him. "Otherwise," Ahern said, "I wouldn't believe he was dead."

Billy had not given up looking for the off-duty cop who'd been at the scene – earning his nickname from Panzarella, "the Energizer Bunny" – and kept on going until he found him. The off-duty cop said to Ahern, "I told the cops at the scene, I'm available. If you need me I'm in. But no one ever bothered to call me after that." It turned out they'd gotten his name wrong. More importantly, the off-duty cop added, "I can ID these guys."

On March 6, 1996, eleven months after Billy and Brian first interviewed Larissa, and two and a quarter years after the murder, they got a major break. Ahern received a phone call from Florida, where a DEA agent had locked up a guy who was talking about a Russian getting killed in New York. Ahern was on the next plane heading south.

That man admitted to knowing the shooter, plus the names of the other guys on the crew. He ID'd the two who had met Beigelman around the corner and confirmed that the fourth guy was dead. From what he heard in Florida, Billy was no longer sure he knew who'd picked up the contract. But whoever it was, Ahern still wanted him. And even more so, he wanted the guy who'd put out the contract – Enrique's boss.

Back in New York, on March 21, Ahern and Crowell and two other cops went to a location in Queens and arrested Neil Matos, whose street name was "Baby Face," one of the two who'd walked Beigelman to his death. At the time of the murder, Matos was just thirteen years old.

When Ahern informed Baby Face that he was under arrest for a murder in 1993, Matos responded, "What took you so long?" He admitted it was his baseball cap and blue scarf that were found at the scene, and confirmed the names of the others.

At this point, Crowell left Billy to get on with the case alone. He returned to his regular duties at the DEA, where today he's still out on the street, giving cell heads a lot to worry about.

The shooter was easier to locate than Ahern ever imagined. His name appeared on the system. His current address was listed as a nearby federal prison. Concluding that the shooter wasn't going anywhere for a very long time, Ahern decided to hunt down Baby Face's partner. Matos claimed he too was already in jail. But Ahern couldn't find him, at least not under the name he was using in 1993. Then Ahern stumbled across an informant who gave him the name of the money man in the States who'd paid for the hit. He too was already in federal custody on other charges.

By spring 1999, Baby Face's partner had still not been found. The shooter was about to be charged with three other contract murders. And there was still some doubt as to who, exactly, had picked up the contract. Enrique was in Colombia and his cousins – who'd almost certainly stolen the two hundred to three hundred kilos – were somewhere in hiding. The U.S. Attorney's office in New York was, however, planning to put a number of people away for life.

The odd one out was Baby Face. He was treated as a juvenile and placed on probation. Shortly after his eighteenth birthday he was arrested for crack distribution, treated this time as an adult, and is back in jail. His only lament is that he never got paid for his part in Beigelman's death.

The fate of Enrique's boss is a different matter.

That out-of-state DEA investigation connected Beigelman to Enrique's cousins and, in turn, connected the coke he was storing to a rising-star drug baron in Colombia named Juan Carlos Ramirez Abadia.

Known as Chupeta – "Lollipop" – because of his boyish looks, he was raised in a middle-class Colombian family and trained as an industrial engineer. He learned the drug business under the tutelage of brothers Ivan and Julio Fabio Urdinola Grajales, who ran the North Valley cartel, a sort of subsidiary of the Cali cartel.

By the early 1980s, Chupeta – who was born in 1963 – was already starting to see where the organization's weaknesses were and to postulate a suitable strategy to compensate for them. He recognized how an Urdinolas' joint venture with the Italian Mafia had turned them into Colombia's primary heroin traffickers. Slightly further afield, he noticed how the Medellín cartel was beginning a minor flirtation with the Mexicans.

One of the traffickers associated with Escobar in Medellín was a Honduran named Juan Ramon Matta Ballesteros. Through contacts, presumably in Spain, he'd befriended a Mexican trafficker named Alberto Sicilia Falcon. When Ballesteros introduced Falcon to his friends in Colombia and Falcon returned the favour by introducing Ballesteros to his friends in the Guadalajara cartel, they did what new friends sometimes do – they went into business together. The deals that followed, however, were minor. Ballesteros supplied small amounts of product for the Mexicans to smuggle, even though the Mexicans weren't terribly interested in trafficking coke and Ballesteros wasn't terribly keen on running drugs through Mexico. They didn't need each other. The Mexicans had marijuana, a product they were very adept at handling, and the Colombians had the Caribbean, an efficient, cost-effective, and well-established thoroughfare into the States.

Another Medellín cartel member, Gonzalo Rodriguez Gacha, also took advantage of Ballesteros's friendship with Falcon. Again, not because it was a necessity but because Gacha – who relished his nickname, "the Mexican" – happened to love all things Mexican.

For much of the 1980s, these early ties were little more than a hobby and never anything like a serious, big-money business connection. It was almost ten years later before the Cali cartel upped the stakes.

Because the Caribbean was becoming too dangerous, the Orejuela brothers negotiated a relationship with Juan Garcia Abrego, the trafficker who controlled much of the border with Texas through his Gulf cartel, ensconced just across the Rio Grande from Brownsville in Matamoros, Mexico. But in between Ballesteros's deal and the Orejuelas' deal, the pact that bridged the way from hobby to business was Chupeta's.

In the mid-1980s he had deduced that the future of Colombian trafficking was no longer in running a business like a major international oil conglomerate – that is, by having a hand in every stage from oil well to gas station – but to consider the operation itself as a commodity. Taking a lesson straight out of the McDonald's Hamburger School of Business, they moved into franchising. It was a lesson he learned the hard way.

In 1987, Chupeta was in charge of running cocaine in tractor-trailers across the U.S. for the Urdinolas. He hired Jamaicans to drive the loads, a radical departure from the golden rule, which had always been to never trust anyone except another Colombian. When a half-ton shipment was busted in Loma, Colorado, the Urdinolas insisted he pay for it. So Chupeta started a sideline business for himself. He decided it was better to take a smaller profit by wholesaling to someone else – thus guaranteeing much-needed cash up front – in exchange for minimizing his risk. The most obvious candidates were the Mexicans, because smuggling anything and everything across the U.S. border was what they did.

He brokered a relationship with the Juarez cartel, then paid a retired Colombian air force pilot upwards of half a million dollars to fly thirteen hundred pounds of coke in a King-300 to an unpaved airstrip in Chihuahua, Mexico. Initially, he agreed to pay his Mexican partners around $3 million per shipment. Then they demanded 35 per cent of the take. Before long, they were insisting on half.

Chupeta might not have liked the percentages, but the strategy was working. He soon was involved in similar joint ventures with the Guadalajara cartel.

At the time he ordered Vladimir Beigelman's death, Juan Carlos Ramirez Abadia had opened the door wide enough for the Mexicans to control all cocaine sales on the West Coast and to begin moving east to secure strongholds from the Rockies to Chicago. In doing that, Chupeta had become one of the top five most powerful cocaine traffickers in the world, ruling a mini-cartel with as many as two hundred franchised agents. By his own admission, Chupeta says that between 1987 and 1995 he smuggled at least thirty tons of coke through Mexico into the United States. By their own calculation, the DEA says the figure could be two or three or four times higher.

It was just after the hit on Beigelman, but in no way related to it, that a series of events occurred which changed his life.

Under pressure from the United States, the Colombian government finally cracked down on the Cali cartel. As a consequence, civil war broke out among the traffickers. Both Urdinola brothers went to jail, although that didn't stop either their trafficking or their attempt to move in on the wounded Cali cartel. Chupeta was forced to take sides and wisely chose Cali. The Orejuela brothers also wound up in jail, although that didn't curtail their drug trafficking or impede their ability to fight off the Urdinola takeover.

The infighting left a void. And Chupeta was there to fill it. With the remains of the Cali cartel crumbling around him, he emerged relatively safe, the best and brightest of the younger generation.

One of the senior Cali members, José Santacruz Londono, had also been put in prison, but at the beginning of 1996 he escaped. In early March, the Colombian police found him in Medellín and, under the rules of engagement for someone resisting arrest, they killed him. That was followed by a brutal two-day crackdown in Cali by the national anti-narcotics squad. Now Chupeta was thrown into a panic, fearing that he too might be accused of resisting arrest.

Under the allegedly corrupt regime of President Ernesto Samper, whose election campaigns are said to have been largely financed by drug money, the Colombians had created a lenient system of surrender. Chupeta opted to make it work for him, and ten days after Londono's death, he gave himself up to government prosecutors in Cali. Nine months later, he was condemned to twenty-four years in prison, the stiffest sentence yet to a Colombian drug trafficker. But in Colombia, twenty-four years doesn't necessarily mean twenty-four years, and it was quickly reduced to thirteen. Leniency was administered based on his surrender and an agreement to forfeit assets worth, perhaps, as little as 10 per cent of the money he'd made by drug trafficking.

Like the brothers Urdinola and Orejuella, Chupeta is believed to still be in the drug business, running his interests from mobile phones in his cell. But in Colombia, thirteen years doesn't necessarily mean thirteen years.

In 1997 Chupeta turned against his partners, outlined for the Colombians how his Mexican franchise operation worked, and contended that it never could have happened without a thoroughly corrupt Mexican government. The following year he turned state's witness again, this time testifying before a Mexican judicial panel. He accused several senior officials with ties to former Mexican president Carlos Salinas de Gortari of having been on his payroll. Among them were Mexico's former deputy attorney general for narcotics matters and a former commander of the judicial police. Chupeta even insisted that no drugs moved through Mexico without their permission. Apparently that was good enough to cut the thirteen years down to seven or so.

But in Colombia, seven or so doesn't necessarily mean seven or so. He could be out, with most of his assets still intact, in under five.

Billy Ahern and Brian Crowell would love to see him brought to the States to stand trial for the murder of Vladimir Beigelman. But that's not going to happen.

Anyway, Chupeta – the player who made it into the majors by franchising his drug business like hamburger stands – probably wouldn't even recognize the contender's name.

10

THE NEW MELTING POT

The traditional Mafia is saying, We're watched but we can fly in Russians who are not known to the authorities and get them to do some heavy lifting. They're able to function because we don't know who these guys are.

– Former FBI agent Bob Levinson

Miami was where they decided to get together.

The weather was good. They had friends there. They had business there too.

It was 1993.

Ivankov came down from New York. Mikhailov and Averin flew in from Vienna. Essine came in from Italy, and Sergei "Sylvester" Timofeyev flew in from Moscow.

A few other minor players might have been there. No one ever published the attendance list. But notable by his absence was Monya Elson. He would have come, except they didn't invite him.

That was the meeting where they decided that Essine would have exclusive control over Italy, and where Ivankov and Mikhailov, with Averin in tow, divided up their interests in Moscow's most important hotels. Ivankov claimed a full-third share. Mikhailov agreed, taking a third for himself. The rest would go to the others.

That was the meeting where they decided that Vienna would be declared a crime-free zone. That was the meeting where they planned future meetings with the Italians and Colombians. That was the meeting that Monya Elson didn't get invited to because they planned to murder him.

Instead, with Elson furious at having been excluded, it was Sylvester who was gunned down in Moscow.

In the days before drug money, Miami had far fewer banks than it does today.

Then, suddenly, there were oceans of drug money.

Then, suddenly, there were more banks in Miami than any other North American city, except New York.

Nowhere else in the world has the natural alliance of drugs and money manifested itself in quite this way, transforming an American city into the capital of South America. Walled estate by walled estate, security camera by security camera, marina by marina, golden-reflective-glass-fronted bank by golden-reflective-glass-fronted bank. Miami was built by white powder Foreign Aid.

The LCN had colonized the south way back in the days of Luciano, because the weather was better than up north, because Meyer Lansky was using it as a staging point for Cuba and the Bahamas, and because airplane travel was creating business opportunities in real estate and the leisure industry. By the 1960s, even the five New York families had developed strong ties with Miami. They were well ensconced when the Colombians arrived in the late 1970s and the early 1980s. But as the Latinos waded ashore, they were greeted with silence.

In the past, whenever one group moved into another group's neighbourhood, there would be stern warnings, and if the warnings weren't heeded, there would be gunshots. But in Miami, as those oceans of drug money washed over the entire peninsula that is south Florida, it was almost as if the long-established LCN guys didn't mind.

Then, in the late 1980s and early 1990s, the Russians arrived. And again, there was silence. Again, it was as if neither the LCN nor the Colombians cared if new kids set up on the same block.

Those people in law enforcement who understood what such silence meant started to get extremely nervous.

The Russians knew the LCN from New York. The Colombians knew the LCN from the Caribbean. It was now just a matter of forming stronger bonds between the Russians and the Colombians, which wasn't difficult because the Colombians were a one-crop shop – if you wanted to deal serious amounts of cocaine, you had to do business with them – and the former Soviet Union was just sitting there, crying out to be exploited as one of the world's foremost cocaine markets.

Miami is perfectly suited as a melting pot for gangsters. The international airport is the main hub for Latin America. You can get anywhere south from Miami. Because it is also a main hub for North America, you can get away north from Miami as well. You can get to Europe easily, and to the Orient too. It is also the feeder point into the Caribbean and the world of offshore banking.

The port of Miami is one of the largest and busiest in the western hemisphere. Nearly nine hundred thousand full-size cargo containers move through Miami every year. It is categorically impossible for U.S. Customs to inspect even a fraction of those containers. So drugs easily sail in and drug cash easily sails out in the same containers. Whatever tiny percentage winds up getting seized is written off by the drug barons as the price of doing business.

Telephone and satellite communications are as good in Miami as anywhere in the world, and with so many banks vying for business, finding a crooked banker is only slightly more difficult than opening the Yellow Pages. In fact, judging by the precedent set by the BCCI affair in the 1980s, there's no need to bother with the Yellow Pages. Inventing a bank is actually easier.

Drug traffickers were bringing mailbags full of money into the BCCI office in Miami. To cover the arrival of all this cash, which the bank could never otherwise have explained, managers there created a non-existent branch in the Bahamas. The cash deposits were then logged onto the books of the non-existent branch. Next, the managers in Miami filed appropriate forms with U.S. Customs to import that cash from the Bahamas to Miami. Once those were filed, the cash was deposited in another Miami bank, representing a shipment from the Bahamas branch.

That the branch never existed, except on the hard drive of a computer in Miami, tells a lot about how banking in Miami has sometimes worked. It also speaks volumes about the kind of world we've created for ourselves, where any banker in any corner of the globe can log any transaction onto the books of any bank in any other corner of the globe, without ever leaving his own office.

Then too, in the world of Miami banking, the Yellow Pages is only worth bothering with if it's closer than the nearest computer.

"The same thing that attracts tourists to Miami is the lure for the criminal element," notes Hardrick Crawford Jr., assistant special agent in charge of the FBI's Miami Field Division. "The weather is great. The beaches are great. It is the gateway to the Caribbean. At the same time, it is an uncontrolled and uncontested market. You have the LCN and the Russians and the Colombians here, and cocaine flooding in by the ton. Using Miami as a hub, it's easy to supply a willing market in Europe, Canada, and the rest of the United States."

Unlike New York, he says, where geographical boundaries have been clearly defined, there are no staked-out political subdivisions in Miami. Nor are there any real conflicts between organizations. "The cocaine wars in the Miami area in the 1980s were a result of Colombian organizations having violent shootouts with one another. These shootouts even extended back to Colombia itself. The various criminal organizations, particularly the Colombians, learned that it is counterproductive for them to be shooting at one another. They became more organized and less confrontational. Today they all see Miami as a free market. They've decided there is plenty for everybody. There's a lot of money to be made. They've decided there's no need for violent conflicts which only draw the unwanted attention of the media and, of course, state, federal, and local law enforcement. Instead, they get together."

Bob Levinson couldn't agree more. He worked with Crawford at the FBI in Miami, and by the time he retired from the Bureau in 1998, he was recognized as one of the most knowledgeable experts on Russian organized crime in Western law enforcement. Today, in private practice, he is arguably one of the most respected such experts in the country.

"South Florida is palm trees, open territory, nice people, nice beaches, and the bad guys all want a piece of that. They also see south Florida as a place to invest money and a good place to live. So a variety of criminal organizations have built bases of operations in Miami. But what we started seeing while I was still working for the Bureau were alliances between Russian organizations and traditional LCN. And this was a very alarming trend because before this, everyone was just operating on their own turf. No one bothered anybody. There was a mutual respect. Now, alliances are being formed. It means that where the Russians can't get something done, the Italian-American groups will go for it, and vice versa."

As an example, he cites that group of Georgians who have set themselves up as enforcers. "The Kurganskaya is running around New York and Miami doing the dirty work for some of the Italian-American organizations. The traditional Mafia is saying, we're watched but we can fly in Russians who are not known to the authorities and get them to do some heavy lifting. They're able to function because we don't know who these guys are. That's what's going on now. And I think that's significant."

Over the years the FBI has painstakingly documented criminal migration between New York and Miami, New York and Los Angeles, Miami and Los Angeles, and back and forth between those cities and Toronto, too. They've also watched Russians making the commute between Miami and San Francisco, which they believe is the link to Far Eastern Russian money and people.

They've watched couriers carry money that has been collected from extortion payments in San Francisco and Los Angeles to New York, stop there for a few days, then travel on to Moscow and St. Petersburg. They've also watched Russian criminals who operate in San Francisco, coming to Miami to cool off.

The principle centre for Russian organized crime in the Far East is Vladivostok, which used to be a closed city and which now has at least four formal organized crime groups. Many of the people who normally operate out of there have been seen in the United States, setting up joint ventures along the West Coast. These same people have formed drug-trafficking alliances with the yakuza and alien-smuggling alliances with Asian organized groups in China. But the bulk of their proceeds are laundered in the U.S. – the cycle starts in San Francisco and Los Angeles – and, more often than not, at some point the money and the mobsters, too, pass through Miami.

The FBI aren't the only ones who are anxious. Other U.S. law enforcement is just as concerned, as are the Canadians, the British, the French, the Germans, and the Italians, all of whom have active-duty law enforcement officers stationed in Miami. This isn't a liaison desk job. These are investigators who work alongside U.S. law enforcement to protect their own national interests in a critical part of the world. No country can hope to understand its own cocaine and money-laundering problems, and by extension those of the Caribbean and South America, without first coming to grips with Miami.

That almost universal sense of growing disquiet over organized criminals getting together was precisely why an ad hoc collection of Miami-based law enforcement officers also decided to get together. From their own perspectives, they'd each seen the trend developing. Comparing notes, they reckoned, could prove very useful.

A small clique of officers from the DEA, the FBI, the Immigration and Naturalization Service, Metro Dade Police, Broward County Sheriff, North Miami Beach Police, and the State Department's Security Branch, which handles passport fraud, began to meet regularly, but always informally, in late spring 1994.

They decided that the most convenient place for everybody, centrally located, with plenty of parking and totally secure, was a training room at the DEA's Miami Field Division headquarters. After the second or third gathering someone thought it would be amusing to put a flag bearing a likeness of Lenin in the room, and after that they started referring to the venue as "the Odessa Room."

Because they all knew each other and most of them had worked on cases together, they were able to shove aside the usual inter-agency rivalries and share information. Sometimes, in those meetings, when good information came up, one of the agents acted on what he or she had learned. Like when it was mentioned that a couple of Lithuanian guys were looking to trade Russian-made surface-to-air missiles for white powder. An undercover sting was developed and played out over two years. Agents posing as drug traffickers met with the targets in Miami and in London, and tried to sort out a deal. The targets finally came up with a plan to supply their clients with Bulgarian surface-to-air missiles. They could deliver the goods into the United States, and would make certain that no one traced the arms back to the source. They showed the undercover agents all the paperwork and all the forged signatures they needed to convince them that for $330,000 the weapons were real.

The undercover agents asked if these missiles could blow an airliner out of the sky. The targets assured them that's exactly what the missiles could do. And both were very quickly locked up.

Sometimes, in those Odessa Room meetings, when the same name got mentioned a lot, then all of the agents took notice. Which is what happened with Tarzan.

Born in the Ukraine with the name Leonid Fainberg, he apparently trained as a dentist before emigrating to Israel. Then he moved to Germany and in the early 1980s, with an Israeli passport that gave his first name as Ludwig, he came to the United States.

He settled in Brighton Beach, where he worked in a furniture store delivering stuff. Then he tried his hand at running his own furniture store. Next, he ran a video-rental shop and a coin-operated video-game business. By then, Tarzan was closing in fast on thirty and fancied more action. Miami was happening, so he moved there. He opened a discount clothing store. Before long, he was able to hustle enough out of that business, and supplement his income through contacts with the growing Russian underworld, that he could buy himself a strip club. Located in Hialeah, not far from Miami International Airport, he named it Porky's.

From the very first day he opened the doors in 1991, the place earned a reputation for sleaziness that was notable even by Hialeah strip club standards.

Tarzan knew enough Russians in south Florida and back in Brooklyn to assure a constant flow of young Russian girls to work his club. Because his customers were willing to pay for such things, he encouraged the dancers to make contact with the customers, getting them to go as far as they possibly could without actually engaging in public sex.

He didn't have much of a record, just some minor stuff. There were misdemeanours for lewd and lascivious behaviour at Porky's, and one case – although charges were never filed – where he acted as muscle for a guy from Moscow who was extorting two Canadians in Miami. They were running a successful bagel shop, the Russians moved in, took over the business and frightened the Canadians back to Toronto. But that was all.

The guy from Moscow was scary, however. His name was Anzor

Kikalischvili, and he was a major player. A self-described businessman, he was one of the people always rumoured to have been at that 1993 Miami meeting. If he wasn't there, the reputation he's helped build for himself suggests perhaps he should have been. Fainberg had turned to him for protection.

Word reached Tarzan that some people were saying he was too independent. That he was overstepping boundaries. That he wasn't authorized to get into the areas that he was getting into. That some powerful Russians didn't like him. The story on the street was, Tarzan's marked.

He ran to Kikalischvili, who, as they say in the movies, made a few calls and made everything right. Fainberg therefore owed him. When Kikalischvili was looking for muscle to help him shake down those Canadians, Tarzan could not refuse.

It was well known that Kikalischvili was a close friend of Josif Kobzon, the Russian version of Frank Sinatra. Kobzon was the man who went to Israel to bring his friend Grigory Lerner back to Russia. Kobzon is also known to have been tight with Ivankov. So Kikalischvili's friendship with Kobzon links him to Lerner and Ivankov.

Sometime after he and Tarzan moved in on the bagel shop, Kikalischvili was caught on tape telling someone that he was setting himself up in south Florida as the man in charge. He said it was important to have someone like him taking control of things. And then he bragged, "I already have over six hundred people here." To stop him before he could fulfil his ambition, the Immigration and Naturalization Service cancelled his visa and stuck him on a list of undesirables.

But neither Kikalischvili, nor Porky's, was the reason Fainberg's name kept popping up at those Odessa Room meetings. It was, instead, because along the way Fainberg had earned his own reputation as a "facilitator."

His name was out there as someone available to help other Russians looking for action in Miami. Witnesses in other cases kept telling these law enforcement officers that whenever anybody in New York – and sometimes even as far away as Russia – said they were heading down to Miami, they were told to look up Tarzan. He could hook them up with girls, or dope, or sell them whatever it was they were looking to buy. Tarzan was the local Welcome Wagon.

He looked sinister enough. He was pumped up through steroids and weightlifting, had a goatee, a blond ponytail, and a business card with a caricature of himself as Atlas holding the world in the air with one hand.

He was precisely the sort of character the agents in the Odessa Room wanted to know about.

Through some of the backers he'd lined up to open Porky's, Fainberg had become friends with some local Cubans. One in particular was Juan Almeida.

Almeida owned the Fort Apache Marina, a boat storage and repair operation in North Miami Beach, and was known to have connections in Colombia.

Around the same time that Porky's opened, he mentioned to Tarzan that some of his Colombian pals were looking to buy surplus Russian military aircraft. Getting into this game would be pretty good, Fainberg decided, and immediately sent word back to the Colombians that he had all the right contacts. Even though he didn't.

The Colombians were anxious to believe him and said they wanted to do some deals. To make them happen, Fainberg began travelling on a fairly regular basis to Russia. Sometimes he went alone. Sometimes he took Colombians along. He translated for them, made contacts for them, and helped them buy some bulletproof limousines and six surplus military helicopters.

In the fall of 1994, Fainberg opened a supper club called Babushka at 3363 Northeast 163rd Street in North Miami Beach. It was a cute little place, where he served good Russian food and featured music on weekends. It quickly got to be a hangout for Russians with money or Russians just passing through town who, for whatever reason, wanted to meet Tarzan and felt that Porky's was too down-market. But running two places, and working all his scams on the side, soon became too much for Fainberg. Word went out that he was looking to hire a manager for Babushka. It was repeated in the Odessa Room.

One of the DEA agents thought about it, saw the opportunity to take on Fainberg, and realized that he knew exactly the man for the job. A fellow who once ran the Gem furniture shop on Coney Island Avenue in Brooklyn. The same fellow who'd once given Tarzan a job.

Mr. Roizis was yet another Russian émigré whose first name got changed along the way. Sometimes he was Josef. Sometimes he was Aron. And sometimes he was Gregory. His friends always called him Grisha, but back in the old neighbourhood, in Brighton Beach, they still remember him as "Cannibal." It's a handle he's had a hard time shaking off.

Born in Russia in the late 1940s, Roizis wound up in a reform school at the age of fifteen after severely beating up a man who'd crossed him. A dozen years later, he took his wife and two young children to Israel, where he fought in the Yom Kippur War. Two years after that, he moved his family again, this time to Brooklyn. He worked as a house painter, a salesman, and occasionally as a drummer and singer in a nightclub band. But the prospect of making a fast buck was more than he could resist, and as a result, he found himself getting arrested a lot, albeit for minor stuff.

On one occasion, he was taken into custody by police – they say it was for being an all-around jerk – and was being booked when a cop referred to him as "a fucking Jew." Still handcuffed from behind, Roizis flew off the bench where he was sitting, knocked the cop to the ground, and bit off the end of his nose. Other cops then beat the crap out of him. And "Cannibal" became a legend in the old neighbourhood.

He had that furniture store for a while. It wasn't a bad business, but it wasn't good enough either, because Roizis had a minor heart condition and, unlike Russia, where medical bills didn't exist, treatment in the States required money. There wasn't enough coming in from the furniture business, so he turned for help to someone he'd met while working in the nightclub, Marat Balagula.

He'd seen for years how heroin had lifted other people – Boris Nayfeld and Monya Elson among them – out of the boardwalk tenements and into palatial houses in exclusive, non-Russian neighbourhoods. He asked Balagula to please set up a connection for him. Balagula duly introduced him into Nayfeld's consortium of ten Russians and six Italians – their Golden Triangle heroin connection that moved drugs out of Thailand, through Poland, and into the States – which in 1991 brought in more than enough to keep Grisha's medical bills from backing up. But a year was all it was worth.

Grisha was on a furniture-buying trip in Rumania when word reached him that the DEA had busted up his heroin ring. The others either had been or were about to be arrested. For the sake of his heart problem, he suddenly decided that life in Rumania would suit him fine. Except it didn't.

An international arrest warrant was issued for him through Interpol. In September 1992, once the Rumanians realized who he was, they complied with the warrant, kicked out his front teeth, and tossed him into jail. They eventually notified the DEA that he was available for collection. And that, the Rumanians decided, was the end of that. They did nothing else.

Or, more precisely, nothing at all.

Their excuse was that he was not their prisoner, they were just holding him for the Americans, so there was no reason for them to spend their money on him. They didn't bother to feed him. They didn't bother to give him his heart medication. They just left him in a cell to wait.

Grisha's wife arrived in Bucharest in a hurry, which may be the only reason he survived. She fed him. She medicated him. She also helped get a DEA agent from the U.S. embassy in Vienna to interview him. Understandably, Roizis was now in a total panic. He told the DEA agent, "I don't care what you're charging me with, just get me the hell out of here. I'll waive any fight over extradition. Please, just get me out." The DEA brought him home and, for good measure, stuck him in jail in Otisville, New York. While he was there, they worked out a deal with him.

Using his heart problems as a cover for splitting his trial away from that of the others in the heroin consortium, Roizis secretly pled guilty. Then, just as secretly, he began testifying before several grand juries about everyone he'd ever met and everything he ever knew. He talked about the ten Russians and the six Italians. He talked about Elson. He talked about Nayfeld. He talked about Balagula. By the time he was finished, Grisha had helped to put away some of the biggest names in Brighton Beach.

Satisfied, the DEA cut their ties with him.

Now, with Tarzan a target, they found themselves going back to Roizis, asking if he'd be willing to work for them undercover. It turned out that the offer from Tarzan was for more than just a job. He had explained to Grisha that if he would invest some of his own money in the restaurant, to pay off back rent, take care of some unpaid bills and finance needed repairs to the air-conditioning system, Grisha could come in as a partner. The Miami Field Division convinced some of the hierarchy in Washington to come up with seventy thousand dollars to finance Grisha's investment in Babushka and, just like that, they had someone inside Fainberg's organization.

Their original plan was to bug the restaurant. They figured that a few well-placed listening devices would come in handy when it came to dealing with Fainberg and also, given the restaurant's clientele, lead them to a lot of other people. Making this even sweeter, because Roizis was one of the owners, they could wire the place without going through all the red tape of court orders. This would be consensual taping. Totally legal.

But totally unworkable.

They wired Grisha's office and a couple of the booths where some of the gangsters were known to hang out, then set up a system where they could turn the bugs on and off, depending on who was there. Unfortunately, the band was always playing and the place was too noisy. They couldn't hear a damn thing. In the end, they were forced to wire Grisha himself from time to time with a miniature tape recorder.

The next thing that happened was that Brent Eaton, the DEA agent who worked the case alongside FBI Special Agent Tony Cuomo, heard about a Russian-speaking DEA agent named Alexander "Sasha" Yasevich. He was born in Odessa, on the Black Sea, and came to America with his parents when he was fourteen. He grew up in Brighton Beach, drove a taxicab to put himself through school, joined the Marines, and was what Eaton calls "a real rough and tumble guy." Fluent in Russian, Hebrew, street lingo, and crime lingo, Eaton and Cuomo knew right away that he was the guy to bring into the operation.

Yasevich agreed and they hooked him up with Grisha. The story they settled on was that Sasha was a guy from the old neighbourhood, which was true. In fact, they'd lived in the same building and had known each other as kids. Sasha also knew Tarzan by sight but had never known him personally.

On January 27, 1995, Yasevich strolled into Babushka's, sat down, ordered a meal, and started eating. Grisha walked by, did a double take, and they recognized each other. There were several minutes of the usual hugging, kissing, shaking hands, then Grisha brought Tarzan to the table to meet his old pal Sasha. They talked about the old neighbourhood and went through all the usual did-you-knows. The undercover relationship took instantly.

Tarzan became Sasha's buddy. They hung out together. Sasha told Tarzan that he dealt heroin and arms. Tarzan told him that he wanted to open up a separate strip club and suggested that if Sasha gave him 150 grand they could be partners and Sasha could launder all his money through the club. He insisted it was a great way to wash dirty money and explained how he avoided taxes by skimming cash.

They spoke about all sorts of criminal activities, then Tarzan confided, "Those same people I sold helicopters to, they talked to me the other day and said they want a submarine."

Neither Sasha nor the agents listening to the wire he was wearing could believe it. Fainberg went on, "They're talking about a big military submarine, with a crew of twenty-five or more, that they can purchase or lease or something for a couple of years. They want to sneak it underwater to Colombia and use it to deliver drugs up and down the West Coast of the United States." He confessed that it was so big it scared him. A startled Yasevich, playing his role perfectly, gently encouraged Fainberg to tell him all about it.

Like many crooks, Fainberg had a penchant for cloned cellphones – the ones that work off stolen numbers – so that he didn't have to pay for calls. The DEA arranged with the Secret Service to get some phones set up that could be passed as clones. Every now and then, Sasha, who explained he had a connection, would give one to his pal Tarzan as a gift. Those were the phones that he used to call Russia and South America. In fact, he phoned everywhere on them. He couldn't thank Sasha enough for them. He never suspected they were tapped.

As the possibility of a submarine deal developed, Tarzan turned more and more to Sasha for advice. Sasha kept saying that, because he had been in the military, he had a lot of the right contacts. He hinted that he was hooked into military intelligence. He told Tarzan that the best thing they could do was have everything checked out, so that they'd sound really intelligent when they talked about stuff like submarines. He said, that way they could both make some money out of it. Over the course of two months, Sasha was Fainberg's number-one advisor.

Tarzan would go to Russia, then come back and tell Sasha what was going on. He would ask for more advice. Sasha would promise to check on things with his military contacts, then come back a few days later with an answer. Then Fainberg would go off to Russia again, and come back seeking more advice.

On March 19, 1995, Fainberg introduced Sasha to Juan Almeida. The cautious Almeida interrogated Yasevich for half an hour. He passed muster because Almeida told him, "Okay. I need you to help us move the submarine from point A to point B." He warned him that this was very confidential, so he mustn't tell anyone about it. He said, "My buyers have unlimited funds, price is not a problem, but they do require security because they're going to use this for illegal purposes. They're going to find gold off the coast of the Philippines." Then he laughed, and winked.

Sasha never met Almeida again.

The Colombians, through Almeida, had provided funds for Fainberg's various expenses – the middleman was a fugitive in Florida named Nelson "Tony" Yester – and guaranteed that they would have enough money sitting in Switzerland to make the purchase when the time came. They budgeted up to $35 million for the deal.

By this point the DEA had picked up a lot of information about Fainberg. They knew that he was dealing in drugs, counterfeiting, prostitution, extortion, and car theft. One day, when Fainberg told Roizis that a Russian military plane he'd sold to Colombian coke dealers had been seized by the DEA in Bogota, they added arms brokering to the list.

They'd also known for some time that he was trafficking in stolen cigarettes. When they learned that two of his truckloads had been seized by the police – one in Georgia and one in New Jersey on its way to New York – they decided to cut in some other agencies. They got the Bureau of Alcohol, Tobacco and Firearms involved. They sold Tarzan some untaxed liquor. They got Customs involved too. Sasha introduced an undercover agent to Tarzan, saying that he'd laundered money through him.

Along with Yester and Almeida, Tarzan was shipping coke from Ecuador to St. Petersburg in fresh iced-down shrimp. He talked to Sasha about the deal and told him that the St. Petersburg guys were looking for a ten-kilo sample. Tarzan said he couldn't send it with the shrimp deal, and asked if Sasha would take it over there for him.

The DEA immediately said no. With hindsight, they regret the decision. They could have come up with a million reasons why Sasha got there and the drugs didn't. Meeting with Almeida's and Yester's contacts in St. Petersburg would have gotten Sasha more involved in the dope end of the thing.

After a while, with all this other stuff going back and forth, the submarine deal seemed to stagnate. Through Sasha, the DEA had photographs of Fainberg climbing all over diesel subs in Kronstadt and Murmansk. He continued travelling to Russia every week or so, staying for up to a week on each trip, coming back to tell Sasha that he would find a submarine soon. But it just wasn't happening.

By that summer, it came to light that Yester had misappropriated a few hundred thousand dollars. That created a lot of friction. The undercover budget to keep Grisha in the restaurant business was also starting to run out. What's more, Yasevich's home office in Washington was getting testy about him constantly being in Florida, working on this project, when they had things for him to do. So the operation slowly wound down.

Grisha decided that if the DEA wasn't going to support him any longer, he was going to get out, because he just couldn't stick around on his own. Babushka folded. He moved back to New York.

Sasha went back to Washington, although he stayed in touch with Tarzan. Every now and then he'd remind Tarzan that he was always looking for a heroin deal, if one ever came along. The DEA had settled on heroin because coke was too easy to arrange.

On July 3, 1995, Tarzan phoned Sasha to say he might be able to make a heroin connection for him – that is, if he was still looking for some. Sasha said he was. Tarzan told him this was heroin base being sold by Russians. Sasha said he wanted to meet.

What he didn't know at the time was that Fainberg was under pressure from the Colombians to come up with the misappropriated money. Yester had left the country and was living between Panama and Caracas. Fainberg was also still running back and forth to Russia. He and Yester were supposed to meet in St. Petersburg, so he couldn't make the scheduled meeting in New York between Sasha and the heroin traffickers. It got cancelled and was never rescheduled. Tarzan did, however, come up with a submarine.

He found a Tango-class diesel submarine in Murmansk and negotiated a price of $5.5 million. The deal would be run through a civilian government agency that would rule the submarine to be surplus and approve the sale to Fainberg's people for "oceanographic research." Fainberg later told Sasha that the Russians were giving submarines away because money was so short and the military guys were broke.

He also found a retired admiral who, along with his crew of twenty-five, would sail it. Fainberg guaranteed them two years' employment.

The problem now became how to get the sub to Colombia. The admiral didn't want to sail across the Atlantic because the boat would need a complete overhaul as soon as they got into port. His idea was to tow it. But a submarine in tow is pretty visible and someone might wonder what was going on. That prompted several more meetings. Tarzan, the admiral, and the Colombians got together in Switzerland to discuss it. The Colombians even flashed their bank book with the $35 million in it to prove they could afford this.

Apparently, the more the admiral talked, the less enthusiastic the Colombians became. Submarines – even if they are pretending to be research vessels – simply attract too much attention. So, after a time, they said thanks anyway. They decided they'd rather find a surface ship that might be more suitable for the oceanographic research cover.

When the DEA found out that the Colombians had walked and mentioned it to some people in other agencies, a senior manager in one of those other agencies sighed, "Too bad. I wish they'd gotten it. They come at us with everything to smuggle drugs. From speedboats to container ships to aircraft of all sizes to balloons to microlights, they use them all. Those get through. They even use semi-submersibles between Colombia and Puerto Rico. Very small, fibreglass, with small engines, virtually impossible to track. Those get through, too. We should have done whatever we could have to encourage them to buy that sub. Just imagine, they could have filled it up with four hundred tons of drugs. We should have let them do that and come at us fully loaded. Because submarines we can find."

As it happens, the entire coast of North America is ringed with special sonar devices designed specifically to detect submarine penetration. Furthermore, the U.S. Navy has a huge library of soundprints – engine and other noises given off by submarines that are particular to each boat. From the soundprint alone, Naval Intelligence can tell not just the class of sub, but its name and number. The Colombians might not have known that. Fainberg almost certainly didn't. It's possible that the Russian admiral mentioned it. He would know.

Anyway, that was the end of that, but Fainberg was still in business.

He had swallowed the bait from U.S. Customs and in the fall of 1995 decided to nurse his sorrow over the failed submarine deal by laundering money for them. Sasha had introduced him to an Italian agent who played his part very well, took Tarzan out on a yacht, and filled his head with all sorts of promises. Fainberg handled the first shipment of cash just fine. But the second time he was handed forty-five thousand dollars to put through the washing cycle, he helped himself to it. That brought things to a head with Sasha. He berated Tarzan, said that he'd already paid the Italians their share, adding, "Now you owe me."

Just after that conversation, agents Eaton and Cuomo learned that some local television people had been shooting an exposé on Russian organized crime, filmed inside Porky's, spoken with Tarzan, and said some things that had frightened him. They had talked about undercover operations. Tarzan suddenly began to wonder about Sasha. Eaton, Cuomo, and their bosses agreed that nothing else could be done undercover, so Sasha was pulled out. But the DEA and FBI still had some scores to settle.

It wasn't until January 1997 that they took down Fainberg, for no other reason than that it took the FBI that long just to translate all the calls and conversations they'd recorded – more than fifteen thousand – and then to make some sense out of them.

Eaton and Cuomo made the arrest.

Yester was gone, but was indicted and is wanted.

Almeida hid for a while in Russia, then just gave himself up.

Unusually for an operation like this, especially with the DEA's involvement, they wound up with no dope and no seizures, but an awful lot of evidence.

After hiring and firing at least six different attorneys and, at one point, defending himself, in February 1999 Tarzan finally decided he'd had enough. He settled for a plea bargain, admitted his guilt to racketeering, agreed to testify against Almeida and Yester, and resolved to co-operate with the Feds in their ongoing investigation into Russian crime groups.

In exchange, he's been admitted to the Witness Protection Program. They'll change his name and give him an entirely new identity and he'll spend the rest of his life hoping – possibly even praying – that neither the men he's implicating, nor any of their various friends, ever find him.

11

THE CANADIAN CARIBBEAN

Just think of them as dandelions.

– Ben Soave, RCMP

The Caribbean, a collection of former colonies or current protectorates, is living testament to the money-laundering cesspool that is the British Commonwealth.

Shame on the British.

Shame too on Canada, because the largest foreign banking presence is Canadian.

Not only are the banks there, but the shell companies are there and the Colombians are nearby and the Italians are there and the Russians are there too. Dirty money and drugs have turned the Caribbean into organized crime's version of the warm-water port the Soviet military could never establish.

Bank secrecy is a service many people are willing to pay for, but that is hardly an excuse for its existence. To claim that selling such a service is the sovereign right of any government, as long as no laws are being violated locally – in total disregard for laws that are being violated elsewhere – is disingenuous. Most people who hide money are doing so for reasons which, at best, are questionable, at worst are blatantly illegal. For a government to shut its eyes to these realities is deceitful.

Start, then, with the Cayman Islands.

The Caymans have one bank for every forty-nine residents. A recent survey suggested that their assets totalled almost $500 billion, which works out to nearly $20 million for each resident.

In the Caymans, they tell you right from the get-go that everything is above board. They don't want money launderers and they reject dirty money. They say they have cleaned up their act and are no longer a sink for the world's drug cash. But that is not the same as saying there's no dirty money coming into the Caymans.

In reality, what the authorities have done is build "plausible deniability" into the equation. Their clients aren't Russian drug dealers, not at all; their clients are well-established Panamanian lawyers with whom they've been dealing for years. But who are the Panamanian lawyers working for? That doesn't matter. No one really needs to know the beneficial owner of the money, because no one really wants to scare the money away. So today in the Caymans, bankers, lawyers, and government officials all sing from the same hymnbook: we've sorted out the laundrymen and will not allow dirty money to pollute our otherwise sterling reputation. They claim to have strict anti-money-laundering laws in place. They say the bad old days of men with dark sunglasses arriving by private jet carrying suitcases filled with hundred-dollar bills are long gone. They are right on both counts.

They do have strict anti-money-laundering laws. Except that those laws are frequently overlooked. And the days when men with dark sunglasses and suitcases fly in are over. Today the money is wired in from someplace else.

Like many similar songs sung in that part of the world, it is off-key enough that you know they can't carry a tune.

Money-laundering expert Jack Blum remembers going to the Cayman Islands in 1970 and seeing one to two dozen offshore banks along a beach. "Now that sandbar is a city. And it's all been built on offshore money." Growth in the Caymans during the 1990s has been spectacular, due in part to two political phenomena.

The first was the fall of the Soviet Union and the huge amounts of capital that has come to the West. Russian money has poured into the Caribbean. How much of this capital comes from businessmen hiding money from the tax authorities, and how much of it is being siphoned out of the economy by organized criminals is impossible to say. It would, however, be total nonsense for anyone in the Caymans to suggest that while up to 10 per cent of the world's drug money – around $50 billion – is being laundered by the Russians through the Caribbean, none of it washes ashore in the Caymans.

The second, less obvious source of Cayman prosperity, was the Chinese takeover of Hong Kong. In fear of what Beijing might do, a great deal of cash was shipped out to be bedded down in the Caymans for safekeeping. Some of it was legitimate money. Some of it was owned by Asian organized criminals. But by the time it got to the Caribbean, it was all squeaky clean. What's more, just because it now lives in the Caymans does not mean the money isn't still being managed from Hong Kong. And therein lies one of the anomalies of the offshore world.

Money can be in one place, the management of it halfway around the world, the beneficial owner hidden somewhere else again. Money can be shifted through jurisdictions, manipulated around accounts, and brought out in other forms anywhere around the world without anyone ever having to physically be anywhere. In short, the entire offshore world is nothing more than the smoke-and-mirror figment of someone's imagination which manifests itself on the hard drive of a computer.

Welcome to Antigua, an island short on natural resources. The government doesn't spend a lot of time pretending that the banks chartered there are legitimate. Since 1993 they've licensed at least a dozen Russian banks, plus as many trust and insurance companies. In 1994, they licensed one called the European Union Bank (EUB). Paperwork filed at the time suggested it was an offshore subsidiary of Menatep, a Russian bank allegedly involved with organized crime. EUB's majority shareholder seems to have been Alexander Konanykhine, a man apparently wanted in Russia on charges of embezzlement – it is said he stole $8.1 million from the Exchange Bank in Moscow in 1992 – and who was, at the time that the charter was granted in Antigua, in prison in the States for having violated his visa conditions. Nevertheless, the government allowed EUB to open its doors. Or, better put, to open its website. In reality, the bank didn't exist in Antigua, or anywhere else for that matter, just cyberspace.

The bank was chartered to open accounts, take deposits, take orders for credit cards, and wire money anywhere in the world twenty-four hours a day. Its website pitch read, "Since there are no government withholding or reporting requirements on accounts, the burdensome and expensive accounting requirements are reduced for you and the bank." Naturally, EUB claimed to maintain the strictest standards of banking privacy, reinforced by the claim – somehow made with a straight face – that Antigua was a serious financial centre with serious penalties for anyone violating its serious banking secrecy laws.

Shortly after EUB went on line, the Bank of England warned the U.S. Federal Reserve Bank that while Menatep was denying any involvement in EUB, Konanykhine had asked the Antiguans to keep Menatep's involvement in EUB a secret.

It turns out that the computer server, which effectively was the bank, was in Washington, D.C., and that the man operating the computer server, who was effectively the banker, was in Canada. Just how much money was ultimately funnelled through the bank – washed by Russians for other Russians and for some of their Latin American drug-trafficking friends – is not known. Nor will it ever be. Because in mid-1997 – one day, just like that – someone unplugged the server, and that's been the last anyone has heard of the bank, or for that matter of the depositors' money. Upwards of $12 million disappeared.

The European Union Bank of Antigua illustrates only a few of the questions that need to be answered. If a bank only exists in cyberspace, who has the authority to investigate its operations? Whose job is it to police the international financial system? In the end, how will anyone ever bring the perpetrators to justice or recover the money?

The first hurdle is a huge one because, before anything else happens, it must be established where the crime was actually committed. The EUB operated on licence from the government of Antigua, but not in Antigua. Such a licence is, of course, meaningless. A company operating offshore of the offshore jurisdiction is, by definition, beyond the control of the licensing authority. In this case, offshore meant the Internet.

Where is it? And in whose jurisdiction is it? Under Antiguan law the theft of the bank's assets was not illegal. So again, where was the crime committed?

If anyone ever comes up with an answer to that question, the next two are: who committed the crime and who's going to investigate it?

The *Washington Post* reported that between 1994 and 1996, the government of Antigua authorized the formation of twenty-seven offshore banks on the island, four of them Russian-owned, one Ukrainian-owned. This on an island of sixty-three thousand people. This, too, on an island where the government has steadfastly denied that they encourage or otherwise tolerate money laundering.

Just as it is everywhere else, due diligence is required of Antiguan bankers who open accounts for foreign depositors. That's what it says on paper. It hardly comes as a surprise, however, that when pressed, bankers there admit that due diligence isn't always possible when the depositor is a foreigner. And it can be completely ignored when that same foreigner is talking about really large deposits.

Antigua and the Caymans are only two of about fifty countries around the world that effectively sell their sovereignty and offer protection to criminals from the laws of other countries. Another place where it happens is the half-Dutch, half-French island of St. Maarten/ St. Martin.

Both sides of the island are wall-to-wall duty-free zones. Neither side cares much about suspicious cash transactions. And the relatively lax customs formalities, at least on the Dutch side, mean that large amounts of cash are easily brought onto the island.

It is well known that Russian cruise ships come into port there every week, and that Russian "businessmen" sail off on those cruises with their Colombian and Italian associates. The Dutch police back in Amsterdam are concerned, but they can't do much about it. Nor can the Americans. So the Russians, Colombians, and Italians continue to meet openly in St. Maarten, knowing they can rely on the independence of the Netherlands Antilles to keep law enforcement from stopping them. The Russians, Colombians, traditional Italian groups, and the LCN are all actively investing in the islands, especially in casinos.

When Cuba finally reopens, it's a sure bet that the same groups will be there too. In fact, the only thing that is uncertain about Cuba is whether or not there will be any room left for the Italians and the LCN, because the Russians and the Colombians have had a huge head start. They're already there.

Not only are sovereignty, real estate, and businesses for sale everywhere in the islands, but many of them also flog citizenship.

Websites all over the Internet advertise passports for sale. Many will sell you a Costa Rican passport. Some offer Irish passports. The Miami *Herald* reported recently that as many as three hundred wealthy Russians have bought passports in three former British colonies. Between March

1995 and April 1997, the government of Belize sold 278 "economic citizenships," 50 of them to Russians. During that same period, Russians purchased 100 citizenships from St. Kitts and 200 from Dominica. At least in the case of the latter, new "citizens" are permitted to choose new names for their passports.

A passport usually takes fewer than three weeks to arrange and costs twenty-five thousand to fifty thousand dollars, depending on the quality of nationalization. Citizens then have the right to travel under whatever name they have decided to use for their passport. Individuals who carry these passports find there are sixty to seventy nations that do not require visas. Visas that would be required of anyone holding a Russian passport.

Some years ago the Seychelles advertised the ultimate in citizenship. For $10 million the government there was willing to provide an internationally recognized diplomatic passport, plus guaranteed immunity on the island from any sort of extradition requested by any other nation. It was no coincidence that the offer came at a time when the Sicilian Mafia was being ripped apart, limb by limb, at the hands of aggressive Italian prosecutors responding to the murders of Judges Falcone and Borsellino. It was only withdrawn when international condemnation directly threatened business interests in the Seychelles.

Attorney Jack Blum is one of the lone voices in the wilderness who warns ceaselessly about the offshore world in general, and the Caribbean in particular. "There are now $5 trillion in offshore tax havens. There are more than a million offshore, anonymous corporations, designed for the sole purpose of concealing the origin and destination of money. When you have dozens of countries around the world that offer their services and protect your privacy and your secrecy, it's just a question of where you'd like to have your privacy protected. And which flag. And which set of diplomats to argue that the records shouldn't be turned over."

The situation, he says, is serious now. But down the road he believes it will be critical. "You can't run the kind of integrated financial system, the kind of integrated trading on world markets that we have, where firms do business around the world twenty-four hours a day, trading every manner of commodity and currency, and still have large chunks of that kind of trading completely outside the realm of supervision. Where we can't be sure that the company's books are real. Where we can't be sure that the assets are really there. Where we can't be sure that there won't come a morning when somebody says, oh well, the money all fled and we have no idea where it went. The collapse of an institution that comes from non-supervision could very well alter the world financial markets. We've been here before. We've had unsupervised banking in some jurisdictions that destabilized world markets. In the United States we had the lesson of the Great Depression, which caused the imposition of regulation in the first place. The question is, are we going to go through the whole thing all over again, or do we have enough sense to know that it's time to reign it in?" He's not just speaking about the banking system, he adds, but about much of the world's economic system. He points out, for example, how much of the world's insurance business is now in jurisdictions that are substantially unregulated.

Such as the Caribbean.

"If you open an insurance company in the British Virgin Islands, no one will supervise whether there are any assets. Should a company like that be allowed to sell insurance? We've had dozens of cases of fraud in the United States where it turned out that the insurer, or the ultimate insurer, was in an offshore jurisdiction and the money was gone. In a major catastrophe, where that money is vitally needed to rebuild facilities, you could have a disaster."

Then, he suggests, look at banks. "Barings Bank had unregulated, unsupervised trading activity in Singapore, which is derivative of market activity somewhere in Japan, which collapses a bank that the Bank of England thinks it has under its thumb in London. That's the kind of problem we can confront and that's why we can't have holes, especially the size of the holes we now have, in the regulatory system."

He points to the tax ramifications. "You can't run modern government without revenue. In France, the government says to the people, we have to cut your social welfare benefit. In Germany, the government says, we can't afford to give you health care, we can't afford to give you retirement. Well, the question is, could they if all of the people paid their taxes? If they're not paying their taxes and the money isn't there to pay the social benefits, and the money isn't there to build the infrastructure to take care of the social problems, you have real political difficulty. In the Third World, it's catastrophic. How will the billion people or so in India take care of their needs for food, water, shelter, education, transportation, if the government of India can't raise tax money? Can Mexico straighten out the corruption in its government bureaucracy, can it build the kind of water and sewerage treatment that it needs to make Mexico City livable? Can it solve the air pollution problem in Mexico City? Without government revenue the answer is a flat no."

If current trends continue, he says, and the offshore world is democratized, then virtually anybody with a PC will be able to get out from under any and all government controls. "When that happens, the revenue base of both the United States and all of the major countries of Western Europe will begin to evaporate. Right now it's an issue that's not being addressed because of a combination of pressure from the bankers who are making money and the rich who are telling their own government, it's not us, we're doing it for other people." So the Caribbean is the financial equivalent of a colossal black hole sucking money into an oblivion we call banking and corporate secrecy. "Russian organized crime," Blum concludes, "has used the offshore system to great advantage."

So much so, the FBI reports, that they have now socked away enough money just in the Caribbean to self-finance their criminal activities, perhaps forever.

Every now and then, the U.S. State Department or the British Foreign Office sends a delegation down to the islands – oddly, it often happens in winter – to remind the politicians and bankers and businessmen there that they have a responsibility to the world community, that they need to get their act together, to self-regulate, to clean up what is termed, in diplomatic parlance, "an embarrassment." To placate their guests, the politicians and the bankers and the businessmen agree and for the next few days pay lip service to the problem. Sometimes they even institute changes. Evolution, not revolution, they say. They bring in reform slowly, as if to give the criminals the opportunity to find more sophisticated ways of doing the same thing.

The people who could solve the problem, Caribbean political leaders, have no incentive to do so. This is how their countries earn a living. In Britain, as in Holland and France – the other two nations with political investments in the islands – there is no will to act. There are no votes in it at home.

There are no substitute crop programs for banks that are shut, no alternative jobs for out-of-work company formation agents.

In many islands, the offshore wealth that has been generated does not necessarily filter down to the people. For all the billions sitting in banks and companies throughout the Caribbean – making some islanders very rich and many governments very corrupt – there is still extensive unemployment, underdevelopment, and poverty. A draconian crackdown on offshore criminality would not feed the poor or pave the roads. It would instead ruin the local economy, in turn destroy the tourist industry, and put everyone on the breadlines.

In the meantime, there is a direct correlation between the money sitting in those banks and the white powder being sold on the streets of North America, destroying our inner cities and killing our children.

When the car bomb went off that day in 1963, no one in the Sicilian village of Ciaculli imagined that this singular, ugly event which claimed the lives of seven policemen could possibly mark a turning point in the economic history of the Caribbean.

The intended victim of the bomb was Salvatore Greco, a local Mafioso. The men who wanted him dead worked for a rival clan. The death of the policemen was, as far as the bad guys were concerned, an unfortunate accident. But the Italian government didn't see it that way. Nor did the people of Italy. They wanted revenge. The government obliged with one of those final-straw, backlash reactions. It decided that it would punish the killers and all the other Mafiosi for that bomb.

Emulating Mussolini's purge of the Mafia, the government made up a list of everyone on the island believed to be involved with crime, and deported them. Most were sent to Northern Italy. Many eventually drifted back to Sicily. The ones who stayed merely carried organized crime with them to Milan and Turin, Bologna and Venice. But some left the country altogether.

Pasquale Cuntrera and his older brother Liborio were born in Siculiana, a tiny village on Sicily's southern coast. So was their friend and cohort Leonardo Caruana. The two families had dominated the village for generations, intermarrying and forming a clan that was held together by blood and tradition. Far enough away to be safe from the Mafia stronghold of Palermo, the families banded together to terrorize neighbouring villages and hold unrivalled power. But in 1951 or so, Pasquale and Leonardo were both indicted on double homicide charges, arson, and the theft of some cows. There was never any question but that they would be acquitted. But when they were, for some reason, the two men decided to leave Sicily and wound up in Montreal. Six years later they were granted Canadian nationality.

By the time the bomb exploded in Ciaculli, the families were well enough established that the ones who now left Sicily could come to Canada. But not all of them did. Some chose South America, where there had been an immigrant Italian population since World War II. The ones who settled in Venezuela found a neighbourhood in Caracas that might well have been anywhere in Italy. The language, the tradition, the food, and the cafés were all Italian. It was right next to the part of town that would become "Little Colombia."

The Mafia and the Colombians had been doing a *danse macabre* for years. It wasn't that they were looking for allies, exactly, it was that a seller's market in cocaine was developing in Colombia at the same time that the consumer's market for cocaine was developing in Europe and the United States. The Colombians were strictly suppliers. The Cuntrera-Caruana clan in Venezuela and Canada eased into the relationship as buyers.

Over the next thirty years they became almost inseparable partners in a global enterprise that grew to the point where the family controlled a significant portion of the estimated four-and-a-half to six tons of cocaine being shipped through Venezuela every month. The Colombians had a buyer they could trust. The Cuntrera-Caruanas had a source of supply they could depend on. Together, they all became fabulously rich.

The family exploited their Venezuela–Canada pipeline, and developed a new one between Venezuela and Miami, using the Florida metropolis as a gateway into the Caribbean. From there they opened new markets, moving family members around the world to assure corporate growth. They invested in shipping, a casino, hotels, a travel agency, real estate, oil, several produce companies, and Ganaderia Rio

Zapa, a cattle breeding ranch in the border region near Colombia that was big enough to have its own airstrip. They have since sold the ranch to the Gambino family.

The historical structure of the Cuntrera-Caruana as a crime gang is almost dynastic. The two families, with lots of brothers and sisters and cousins, started marrying each other back in Sicily and produced lots of children with lots more cousins for other cousins to marry. One reason they've survived, then, is because the cement of loyalty has been mixed with blood.

Another reason is that by moving to other countries, they evolved away from Sicilian organized crime. The Cuntrera-Caruanas weren't from Palermo anyway, and they didn't mix with the New York LCN families. They were, as a matter of policy, less prone to violence than, say, the Corleonesi under Tito Riina. They maintained a distance from the internal struggles of the other groups. They were patient, clever, low-key – they were operating in Britain for more than ten years before the police and Customs got onto them – and moved cautiously into new territories, only taking them over when the time was right.

It was Liborio who opened the branch office in England. From there he ran a heroin and money-laundering ring in Portugal and Austria, and expanded the family's interests to Hong Kong and Japan. Two Caruana brothers, Alfonso and Pasquale, also worked out of Britain for a time. They refined Liborio's money-laundering network, buying a hotel, a travel agency, and an import-export business through which to funnel the family's drug money.

But the main reason the family survived, almost intact, was that they'd found their niche early on and stuck with it. They didn't branch out into all sorts of other crimes. They dealt drugs and they washed money, and that was basically it. They were a business enterprise that devoted its energy to establishing new drug routes, setting up deals between their Sicilian and Colombian associates, and washing money for them, too. When their Italian heroin-processing plants were shut down, they took it in stride, wrote off the losses as the cost of doing business, and started refining in Thailand. At the height of their power, they were shipping fifty kilos of heroin a month.

In 1981, they set up a joint venture for heroin with other Mafiosi and Thai traffickers, marking the first time that the Italians and the

Asians had dealt together. Within a year, the FBI later estimated, the Cuntrera-Caruanas were responsible for more than half the heroin smuggled into the U.S. This was in addition to their core cocaine business plus a sideline in cannabis that couldn't be measured in pounds or kilos. One shipment known to have gone to Canada weighed six tons. Another bound for the U.S. weighed eleven tons.

They transported around $2 million in cash weekly into the States to keep the cocaine supply running smoothly into Canada. They masked all of their drug trafficking behind legitimate furniture companies, produce wholesalers, banks, and shipping firms.

In 1985, British and Canadian police seized a $300 million heroin shipment moving from London to Montreal. In 1987, the Canadians grabbed a six-ton hashish cargo in Newfoundland. By now, cases were being brought against the family, and they were clearly taking hits. But for some reason, whatever hits they were taking only had a minor effect on the way they did business, and almost no effect at all on the men running that business. Law enforcement couldn't understand why.

The first hint came in 1987 when a south Florida businessman, John Galatolo, was arrested on cocaine-smuggling charges. He admitted to the DEA that he'd personally brokered a deal for the Mafia to buy six hundred kilos of coke from the Cali cartel. That firmly established the family as cocaine franchisers for Italy. What the police still didn't know was how much further that relationship had developed.

At the start of their alliance, the Colombians tried to restrict the family to their home base. Cocaine could go to Italy, but North America and the rest of Europe were out of bounds. They reckoned they could distribute their own powder throughout the rest of the world. But Europe is a long way from Latin America, and although the Colombians could function easily in Spain, other parts of Europe proved to be more difficult. Little by little, they became more and more dependent on their Italian friends.

Finally, in February 1990, when the Dutch police found three tons of cocaine hidden inside a consignment of fruit juice, Pablo Escobar was willing to concede defeat. He understood that he needed Mafia distribution networks throughout Europe, and that no group was better placed to help them than the Cuntrera-Caruanas. The Cali cartel quickly followed suit.

Intelligent investing not only provided them with legitimate businesses as cover, but also gave them companies through which they could hide their drug trafficking while, at the same time, easily wash ever-increasing sums of money. Their assets were well diversified and spread out between Britain, Switzerland, Venezuela, Aruba, Italy, Thailand, Pakistan, the United States, and Canada.

It wasn't until 1992 that an Italian newspaper summed up, for the first time in public, just what the family was. "The Rothschilds of the Mafia," was the headline over a story contending that the sun never set on their narco-empire.

Just three decades after being thrown out of Sicily, the Cuntrera-Caruana family was a $1 billion multinational corporation worthy of a place in the Fortune 500.

The Caribbean consists of thirty-seven million people in twenty-eight political entities. Sixteen of these are independent states, the remaining twelve dependent territories. With little more than beaches to sell to tourists plus coffee and bananas to export, they've needed to find creative ways to survive. Cash crops such as marijuana are faster and easier than catering to tourists' demands. Shell companies and offshore banking are lucrative and don't pollute the beaches. Drugs and money are also two areas where smaller nations can compete globally against their Goliath neighbours to the north.

The seven island groups that make up the eastern Caribbean are key transshipment points for drugs being smuggled into North America. All seven – Antigua and Barbuda, Barbados, Dominica, Grenada, St. Kitts and Nevis, St. Lucia, and St. Vincent and the Grenadines – are independent members of the British Commonwealth. They are also key transshipment points for drugs heading the other way, to Europe. It is estimated that as much as one-third of the drugs being smuggled into Britain transship through these seven groups.

The presence of organized crime groups in the Caribbean is nothing new. Italian mobsters were holding hands with Meyer Lansky when he "invented" the place by showing them the benefits of dirty money. Since those days, all sorts of conferences, committees, task forces, action groups, associations, economic development boards, and other well-intentioned collections of high-minded people have been getting together to do something about the Caribbean. But in the end, they are out-gunned, out-financed, out-corrupted, and out-lawyered by the people who stand to lose the most if ever the status quo should change.

There is simply too much money at stake to let do-gooders do good.

Aruba is something of an odd man out. Not because they don't transship drugs or launder money there – they do that in huge quantities – but because it is not a Commonwealth nation. Like St. Maarten, it is Dutch.

Some sixty-eight thousand people live in the 193 square kilometres of land – an area about the same size as Washington, D.C. – that makes up a flat island, with few crops, no forests, no woodlands, in fact, no natural resources at all, except for white sand beaches. It is also one of the rare places in the Caribbean where unemployment is very low. That is thanks entirely to tourism, which is at the very centre of the economy, and to oil refining and storage, which also play a significant role. In between those two is the offshore banking industry.

Heroin and cocaine from Colombia, Venezuela, and Surinam are transshipped there on the way to North America and Europe. Money is laundered there through land investments, casinos, resorts, and the enormous Aruba Free Trade Zone.

Money laundering was criminalized in Aruba in 1993. The legislation gave the politicians the opportunity to tell those successive American governments, which are constantly trying to bully Caribbean nations into doing something about drugs and money laundering, hey, look, we're doing something. And there is no doubt that they are putting laws on the books that could have an effect. But they are not enforcing them.

The Dutch have taken a stand, too, hoping to change things in Aruba, which, as some Dutch police officers acknowledge, has always been an embarrassment. But there are plenty of laws on the books in Holland making drug trafficking and money laundering illegal there, and with their own unimpressive success rate at home, it's unfathomable how they expect to achieve much five thousand miles away.

It is a black market with a neon sign that says "corner store." From untaxed whisky and perfume to guns, whatever anybody in Venezuela wants, even today, they can find in Aruba. Like the moon pulling the ocean tides, so powerful is the island's pull on its nearest neighbour that in 1983, when the Arubans called in Venezuela's debt, the Venezuelan currency collapsed. The knock-on effect should have collapsed the Aruba economy as well. But the Cuntrera-Caruanas were there and they were in the drug business, and they helped to turn the corner store into a mall.

Among the local families who grew rich and powerful with them were the Mansurs. Arguably the most prominent family on the island, they are said to be the largest suppliers of Marlboro cigarettes in the entire Caribbean. They own hotels, the local newspaper, commercial real estate, a casino, stores, a huge import-export operation in the free-trade zone, a shipping company, retail stores, and Interbank.

Some of them have been publicly accused in the United States of being drug-money launderers. And while the Mansurs might not have been full partners with the Cuntrera-Caruanas, many of them mixed business with friendship. Interbank, for example, backed several Cuntrera-Caruana projects on the island. Together they turned the island into the playground of Caracas and created an infrastructure of offshore secret banking, casinos, and a flourishing tourist industry to assure Aruba's future as a prime Caribbean money-laundering sink.

When the Cuntrera-Caruanas arrived, the Mansurs owned just about everything. By the time the Cuntrera-Caruanas left, the Mansurs owned whatever the Italians didn't. In between, the Cuntrera-Caruanas owned enough and controlled enough of Aruba – including the politicians – to turn the island into the world's first Mafia state.

One of the original investments Paolo and Giuseppe Cuntrera made on the island, in 1987, was a nightclub called Visage. To do that, they needed a licence from the government. The only significance of the date is that it was four years after an international warrant had been issued on Paolo, and two years after his brother Gerlando had been arrested for heroin trafficking in Montreal. In both instances, their names and photos had appeared in the Venezuelan press. Despite their protracted insistence to the contrary, it is simply impossible that Aruban officials did not know with whom they were dealing.

If ever two men were destined to form a winning tag team in the battle against transnational organized crime, they are Alessandro Pansa and Ben Soave.

They are around the same age. Both were born in Italy, except that Pansa's family stayed while Soave's family migrated to Thunder Bay, Ontario, when he was ten. Both joined the police as young men. Both moved up through the ranks by being intelligent, hard-working, and very good at what they do.

By the mid-1990s, Pansa was busting organized crime groups as head of the Second Bureau in Rome. Soave was busting organized crime groups as head of the Combined Forces Special Enforcement Unit – a joint task force of the RCMP, the Ontario Provincial Police, York and Peel Regional Police forces, Revenue Canada, and the Canadian Immigration Service – from a large, secure office outside Toronto.

Both have the same easy charm. Both have the same look in their eye, one that warns these are not men to be messed with. Pansa's background is financial crime and the Mafia. Soave's background is undercover work. He was so good at it that the RCMP eventually made him coordinator of all undercover operations. And, for fifteen years, he was the force liaison officer at embassies around the world. Including Rome. Birds of a feather, Pansa and Soave are old mates.

Which makes it all the more fitting that these two should bring down the Cuntrera-Caruanas.

The seeds were planted back in the late 1960s, long before the two men knew each other. Buried deep in reports that came into various agencies during the French Connection days were the names Liborio Cuntrera, Giovanni Caruana, and Nick Rizzuto. But no one at the time realized their significance.

Most of the clan was living in Canada, sheltered there by the Cotroni family. After Paul Violi was killed and Nick Rizzuto had taken over, any Cuntrera-Caruanas connection to heroin in Marseilles was either forgotten or put on the back burner while the police went after bigger fish. And then it was forgotten.

Ironically, the dismantling of Lilo Galente's Pizza Connection left the Cuntrera-Caruanas with a corner on the North American heroin market. And the family's relationship with the Pizza Connection Sicilians only came to light when Alessandro Pansa accidentally stumbled across something odd.

In the early days of his career, one of his targets was Giuseppe Bono, a man the Italian police suspected of being a main link between the Sicilians and the Bonannos.

It was 1982. Pansa had been listening to endless hours of wiretaps, when he heard one that didn't sound like the others. It was a condolence call. Bono was telling a woman how sorry he was to hear about the death of her husband.

A transcript of the conversation probably wouldn't have meant much, even to Pansa, but listening to it was different. Bono was never talkative, at the best of times. Now he was blabbering. He'd always struck Pansa as arrogant. Now, he was suddenly a humble man. Pansa wanted to know why.

Bono's call was traced to a large villa at the beach just outside Rome. It belonged to Pasquale Cuntrera. It was his brother Liborio who'd passed away in London. Little did Pansa know how that one phone call would be the start of a ten-year preoccupation with bringing the family to justice.

Based on what Pansa found out about their drug trafficking, the Italians issued warrants in 1983 for the arrest of the three main brothers – Pasquale, Paolo, and Gaspare Cuntrera – and Alfonso Caruana. Two years later, on information supplied by Mafia turncoat Tommy Buscetta, Pansa was able to put together enough evidence for a second warrant issued against them. They were tried *in absentia* and convicted.

At the same time, in Canada, Gerlando Caruana – Alfonso's older brother – was arrested for conspiring to import heroin and sentenced to twenty years. He served eight.

In 1989, after two family members were arrested in Germany, a third warrant was brought by Giovanni Falcone against the three brothers. Falcone also issued a warrant for their cousin Alfonso. He'd arrived in Montreal in 1968 at the age of twenty-two, claiming to be an electrician. Family folklore has it that when Alfonso got off the boat, he had nothing more than the clothes on his back and a hundred dollars in his pocket. Family folklore neglects to mention that in 1968, ten members of the clan had been convicted of drug trafficking in England and Canada, that they had laundered more than $30 million that year through banks in Montreal, and that at the end of each week they had so many hockey bags stuffed with cash, they needed a pickup truck to deliver them all to the banks.

Family folklore also has difficulty explaining how, a decade later, the same Alfonso – the fellow with the hundred bucks in his pocket – was stopped by Swiss police at the Zurich airport carrying six hundred thousand dollars in his attaché case.

Like all members of the family – like many executives in large corporations – Alfonso moved around a lot. He lived for a time in Lugano – one of the world's major money-laundering centres – then in London. Police now say that from Lugano he oversaw the family's financial interests and from London he controlled the Thailand side of the drug-trafficking empire.

Just before British police could arrest him, he returned to Canada and opened a pizzeria and, oddly, for a man with as much money as he clearly had, worked behind the counter. Unable to indict him in Canada for suspected crimes in Europe, the Caribbean, and Asia, the RCMP "Caponed" him: they called in the tax inspectors.

Revenue Canada had already investigated him in 1985 about C$21 million that had gone through his bank account in 1981. He explained that he didn't know exactly how that happened, but maybe it happened because he'd allowed other people to deposit money into his account. They decided he lived too well for a fellow making pizzas, and seized C$827,962 from his account.

Now, in 1995, Revenue Canada decided they wanted his hide – all C$28.5 million worth. Alfonso claimed he never had that amount, didn't owe it and, anyway, couldn't pay it. He declared bankruptcy. Not long afterwards, he disappeared.

Speculation in the Canadian press was that he was beachcombing in Aruba. There was also, at one point, a rumour he'd been spotted in Brazil. Giuseppe Cuntrera, who was both his uncle and his father-in-law, was living in Brazil, shipping cocaine from there to Italy, and was known to own real estate in both Rio and São Paulo. So that sounded like as good a place as any. Some people around the RCMP, who'd been keeping track of Nick Rizzuto's son Vito, saw him travelling to Cuba and suggested that Alfonso might be there as well.

The Italians were no less anxious to find him – after all, he owed them twenty-one years' jail time. However, one press report mentioned that, having lost contact with Alfonso so long ago, Italian police no longer possessed a photograph of him to show what he looked like.

It turns out that the Italians knew exactly what he looked like, and the RCMP knew exactly where he was. Ben Soave not only had photographs, he had Alfonso's phones tapped.

If there ever was a Cuntrera-Caruana corporate headquarters, it had to be in Caracas. From huge, heavily guarded estates, the three Cuntrera brothers oversaw the entire family empire. The Italians had formally asked for their extradition three times since the first warrant that Pansa had helped to instigate. And each time Venezuela had refused, on the grounds that the law simply didn't provide for it. There was no extradition treaty between Venezuela and Canada or Italy. Nor was there one between Venezuela and the United States.

Then Giovanni Falcone made a personal plea. He met with Venezuela's minister of justice, who was on a visit to Italy, and tried to explain what monsters these men were. Chances are this fourth request would also have been rejected.

Three days later, Falcone was murdered.

Then his successor, Borsellino, was murdered.

And like the bombs that had killed those seven policemen and driven the family from Sicily in 1963, twenty-nine years later the murder of two prosecutors in Sicily would have a similar result for the brothers in Caracas.

The government of Aruba had already tried to sever its relationship with the family – maybe the Mansurs wanted their island back or maybe the politicians found religion – and now the Venezuelans decided to call time. It took several months to arrange, but in September 1992 they bundled Pasquale, Paolo, and Gaspare onto a flight for Rome.

Pansa later told an interviewer that he was at the airport to arrest them and that they looked like Hollywood-style godfathers with dyed black hair slicked-back, gold watches and white shoes. The three were tried on charges of drag trafficking and "Mafia Association." That law – which makes it a crime to belong to the Mafia – changed the way the Italian police could battle the mob and has been the single most effective weapon in dismantling so many clans in recent years. The trial, which brought guilty verdicts, sent Pasquale to jail for twenty years and Gaspare and Paolo both for thirteen years.

Now the Italians turned back to Alfonso. They had charged him in this case as well. They issued an extradition request to the Canadians and, for the second time, tried him *in absentia*. The extradition request was not granted and Alfonso was found not guilty.

Word then came to Soave that the Italians were going to ask for his extradition on the 1985 conviction. And they might well have got him had Soave and Pansa not had other ideas. The request was postponed.

Had it been granted, the Canadians would have been obliged to hand over Alfonso. He was in their backyard, alive and well in suburban Toronto. He'd given up pizzas for a car wash, working with his nephew in Woodbridge, Ontario. He was making five hundred dollars a week. At least, that's what he was admitting to.

They had located him in April 1995. While investigating Toronto mobster Enio Mora, they spotted him in Mora's company. Soave spent a year plotting Operation Omertà, to finish the job that Pansa had started all those years ago. He and his group followed money and drugs through Canada and the United States, through the Caribbean and into Europe. They charted money going into Switzerland and drugs coming out of Turkey. They identified heroin refineries in Thailand, and other family players living in Canada. Throughout it, Soave fought his way through all the complexities of collaboration with law enforcement in different countries.

"One of the biggest problems in law enforcement today," he notes, "is trying to coordinate agencies around the world for a common purpose. Even within one country you can have national agencies bickering among themselves, turf wars, petty jealousies. Now expand that to several. You also run up against a lack of funding. All too often, the financial crunch prohibits long-term investigations. Then there are different jurisdictions, legal and procedural differences, and cultural differences."

In this case, he needed to bring on board the FBI, the DEA, U.S. Customs, the Texas Department of Public Safety, the Italian police, and the Mexican police. While he was trying to juggle all of their agendas, his men were running nearly a hundred different wiretaps. In fact, they so successfully bugged the gang and had such accurate intelligence information about drugs coming into Canada – by spring 1998 they were picking off large shipments with great precision – that some of the family sussed it out. They were certain the cops were about to pounce and started talking about leaving the country.

Even though it had taken over thirty years to wear out their welcome in Canada, Venezuela, and most of Europe, there were still plenty of places they could go. There was always Brazil. They could always buy their way back into Aruba.

"The Cuntrera-Caruana organization has moved from jurisdiction to jurisdiction," Soave says, "specifically to hamper the efforts of law enforcement. Strategically speaking, how more effective can any organization be? They understand the problems we face in trying to apprehend them. They know about our lack of coordinating capabilities, about the lack of political will to provide the funding we need to take them on. They understand how all our problems play right into their hands. And so they thrive."

This time, however, they didn't move fast enough. The man in charge of transport for the family – fifty-year-old Nunzio Larosa, who worked for Gerlando Caruana in Montreal – had gotten sloppy. The authorities had been following him for eight months, watching him fetch drugs in Texas, then bring them back into the country. The border crossing Larosa used was at Sault Ste. Marie, on the Michigan-Ontario border, where Lake Huron flows into the North Channel to meet Lake Superior. It was always easy there. Most people just got waved through. When spot checks were made, officers asked a few routine questions, but kept traffic moving. That's why Larosa didn't worry in May 1998 that the secret compartment underneath the Ford pickup wasn't ready. Instead, $6 million worth of cocaine was picked up in Texas, stuffed into black garbage bags, and shoved behind the driver's seat for the ride back to Canada.

The first shot in the final battle came when Texas troopers grabbed the truck.

The reaction the RCMP investigators heard on the wiretaps came as something of a surprise to Soave. "It didn't even faze them. They just went ahead with plans for another $6 million shipment the following month."

There were more interruptions, and more disruptions to the family's business, and then on July 15, 1998, at just after 7 a.m., Soave took them down. By 7:15, fifty-two-year-old Alfonso Caruana was in handcuffs.

"If organized crime was the game of hockey," Soave said that morning, in one of those great sound-bite quotes that has been broadcast and printed countless times since, "then Alfonso Caruana would be Wayne Gretzky."

They got Alfonso's brothers, too. Pasquale and Gerlando Caruana were arrested in coordinated raids in Toronto and Montreal.

It took two hundred police officers to get five people in Toronto, five in Montreal, two in Mexico – police in Cancun captured Oreste Pagano, the Camorra member who served as the Cuntrera-Caruanas' ambassador to the Colombians – and two in the States. In follow-up raids, they collected drugs, jewellery, and money. Safe deposit boxes were located. Bank accounts, too. And in one house they found more than thirty kilos of cash.

With Alfonso in custody, the Italians have refiled for extradition and are appealing his earlier acquittal. Whenever the Canadians are done with him, they have plans for at least twenty-one years.

The family had been dealt a crushing blow. But anyone who has dealt with transnational organized crime for as long as Ben Soave knows that "hurt" doesn't mean "obliterated." He says that younger members are already stepping up to fill the void.

"The game may already be lost," he says, "but that's no reason to give up. Today's organized crime is global. Today's gangs are into everything. They move around the world and take advantage of laws which permit them to stay or reside or operate in other countries. They're like water, they flow to the point of least resistance. The world is no longer confined by borders. We'd been investigating the Cuntrera-Caruanas for years. Other international agencies have investigated the group. What took us so long to do something about them was not the lack of will. It was the difficulties of international co-operation and the lack of money."

Operation Omertà was budgeted at C$2 million. When his team ran out of money, Soave had to go, cap in hand, to the Criminal Intelligence Service of Ontario to finance the rest of it.

"On a one-to-one basis, co-operation with other law enforcement organizations in the U.S., in Britain, in fact throughout most of Europe, is excellent. Any two organizations will work together. But when you're talking transnational organized crime, you're talking about a lead agency trying to coordinate twenty international agencies with legal, jurisdictional, and procedural differences. You have real obstacles. That's where it becomes almost impossible. Just look at the problems we face when borders are imposed. But they're only imposed on us. The criminals don't have borders. They don't have to worry about jurisdiction."

The good guys have borders and no money, the bad guys have no borders and piles of money. The good guys get bogged down in jurisdiction, the bad guys do joint ventures. He shrugs: "It's not a fair fight."

And yet, there are men such as Soave and Pansa who are still willing to step into the ring. And transnational criminal organizations know it.

"Just think of them as dandelions," Soave says. "It starts with one weed in the middle of your garden. You rip it out by the stem and the next day there are two more. So now you rip those two out and then there are four of them. You keep ripping them out and they keep coming back, until your lawn is filled with them. So you get someone to dig up your lawn and take them out by the roots, but by then they've started showing up on your neighbour's lawn. He rips them up by the stems, until they cover his lawn. Then he gets someone to dig up the roots, except by then they're all over his neighbour's, and they've come back to your lawn too. That's transnational organized crime."

12

BANK IT AGAIN, SAM

Casablanca was a ninth inning, seventh game of the World Series, grand slam home run.

– Allan Doody, U.S. Customs

In 1989, police in California stumbled across twenty-one metric tons of cocaine warehoused in Sylmar, California, a sleepy town at the north end of the San Fernando Valley.

Along with the drugs, they seized $12 million in cash, accounting ledgers that outlined the movement of some fifty-five tons over the previous three months – more than $1 billion worth – and documentation suggesting that this group had previously tractor-trailered into California as much as two hundred tons.

In size alone, the Sylmar bust was a whopping success. But the most shocking thing about the haul, what really opened eyes, was that it established the magnitude of the joint venture the Colombians had now realized with the Mexican cartels.

Juan Ramon Matta Ballesteros's friendship with Alberto Sicilia Falcon and the Guadalajara cartel, and Juan Carlos "Chupeta" Ramirez Abadia's franchising to the Juarez cartel, had spearheaded a full-blown Mexican invasion of America's southern border. After Sylmar, law enforcement would never again routinely talk about seizures in grams or pounds. The jargon would become tons and multi-tons.

Today, the war along that two-thousand-mile border is being fought across it, under it, over it, and through it. American law enforcement has become overwhelmed by the quantity of drugs being smuggled into the country from Mexico. Unless they construct some kind of impenetrable fence to totally shut down trade between the two countries, the odds are monumentally in favour of the traffickers.

The border stop at Brownsville, Texas, is a huge, open-sided covered shed where tens of thousands of Mexicans arrive daily on foot, and tens of thousands of cars pull in to be given a quick once-over, and thousands of trucks arrive to be subjected to random searches. And while U.S. Customs and the U.S. Immigration and Naturalization Service do what they can, the small percentage of people or cars or trucks that are closely looked at reveals an even smaller percentage of the drugs coming across the border.

Further west, towards McAllen, there's a brand new bridge that crosses the border. There's a plaque in the middle indicating Mexico is on that side of the line which runs across the centre of the bridge, and the United States is on this side and every thirty seconds or so a huge cylinder truck, the kind you see with the word MILK painted on the side, comes roaring by carrying something from Mexico to the United States. The border guards stop as many as they can, and try to establish if there is a second, smaller cylinder hidden inside, but that isn't easy to do, and while they're looking at one, fifty more come into the country.

That's just two roads over the border fifty miles apart.

The Rio Grande River, which looks less like a river than it does a wide stream, stretches thirteen hundred miles from Brownsville to El Paso and from there to the Pacific Ocean. The border becomes a flat, arid stretch of land, some of which is fenced, most of which isn't. But then, neither the river nor the land – even where it is fenced – constitutes any real obstacle for large-scale organized smugglers who, regardless of whether their crop is drugs or aliens heading north or drug cash heading back south, operate with near-impunity on the Mexican side and near-invisibility in the teeming confusion on the American side.

It becomes a percentage game for both the bad guys and the good guys. Send a hundred shipments across the border and write off the one or two that will be stopped as the price of doing business. Stop a hundred trucks or cars or people and hope that you can find one or two shipments. Stopping the smuggling is impossible, but disrupting a little of it is a reasonable ambition.

The traffickers keep finding ways to improve their percentages. They fly drugs over the border in 727s that have been gutted and outfitted to transport multi-ton loads or they sail them around it in massive fishing fleets. They also sometimes dig under the border. In 1990 the Americans uncovered a tunnel connecting Mexico and Arizona. Three years later, they found a nearly completed tunnel running from Tijuana Airport up to and almost inside an unfinished warehouse on the California side.

One DEA estimate puts the amount of Colombian cocaine coming across the border each day at up to seven tons. The amount of Colombian cocaine stockpiled in Mexico, just waiting to be shipped to the United States – about one hundred tons of the stuff – is enough to provide one line of coke to every man, woman, and child on earth.

Mexico's cartels were born in the famine of the Depression, when families on each side of the border realized they could make a living moving people and contraband back and forth. By the 1970s, marijuana had become their major cash crop. Ten years later they added a little cocaine to the load, and whatever they got from the Colombians for the service represented pure profit because they were going that way anyway.

Being the mule made them rich. But it didn't give them real power. To manage that, they took a percentage of the coke to market as their own. Then, because business is business and loyalty has never been a strong suit among drug traffickers, they went in search of ways to cut the Colombians out of the picture. They started purchasing their supplies directly from the Bolivians and Peruvians, which was fine until the Colombians protected themselves by moving shipments through Puerto Rico – they caught American law enforcement looking the other way – then exerted enough muscle on the Bolivians and Peruvians to whittle the Mexicans back down to size.

The group Matta Ballesteros aligned himself with, the Guadalajara cartel as it was then called, had been put together by Miguel Angel Felix Gallardo, Ernesto Fonseca Carrillo, and Rafael Caro Quintero. They were on the ground floor of Mexican drug trafficking, controlled the high-level end, and were clearly onto a very good thing. At least, they were until 1985, when they got totally stupid and murdered DEA agent Enrique Camarena Salazar.

Under American pressure, the Mexicans cracked down. Even Matta

Ballesteros, then living in Colombia, couldn't escape America's wrath. Identified as one of the murderers, he hightailed it to Honduras, where nationals could not be extradited. Instead, the Americans kidnapped him. They carried him out of the country, bound and gagged, put him on trial, found him guilty, and stowed him away for the rest of his life in a federal penitentiary.

The alliance subsequently split into two factions.

One became the Sinaloa cartel, led by some former Guadalajara lieutenants who set up a joint venture with the Cali cartel and dug tunnels under the border to move their product. They also pioneered more circuitous routes from Mexico into the U.S., as discovered in 1993 when six tons of Cali-Sinaloa cocaine was seized in El Salvador. But the leaders were arrested that same year, and although the cartel still functions, they are no longer significant.

However, the other faction that emerged out of the Guadalajara group did become a major force.

The Tijuana cartel was established by the Arellano-Felix brothers – nephews of the Guadalajara group's founder – whose claim to infamy is the 1993 murder of Cardinal Juan José Posadas Ocampo. From their Baja California base, they maintain a violently guarded monopoly on smuggling across the border into California. To further secure their power base, they had the business sense in 1998 to join forces with central Mexico's dominant Sonora cartel. In partnership with the ruling Caro Quintero family – like the Tijuana group, the Sonora cartel was formed from remnants of the old Guadalajara crowd – they dubbed themselves "the Federation." Not only have they continued to smuggle Colombian cocaine into the U.S., but they've expanded their own interests in cultivation, processing, smuggling, and distribution of both heroin and marijuana.

For years, the most dangerous group of all was the Gulf cartel, run by an egomaniac named Juan Garcia Abrego, who saw himself as heir apparent to Pablo Escobar. Born in Texas and based mainly in Matamoros, just across the Rio Grande from Brownsville, he supposedly got into the trafficking business as a child, by floating bundles of marijuana across the river.

Like Escobar, he too courted the media to turn himself into a modern Robin Hood. Tales of his virility were legendary – it's said that he fathered several children by many different women – and he was apparently so superstitious that he had witch doctors on permanent call to protect him.

Yet it was Abrego who completed the metamorphosis of the Colombians, turning them into a full-blown international franchiser and himself into their primary franchisee. He left the other cartels in the dust when he told the Orejuelas that he would guarantee delivery of their product anywhere in the United States for 50 per cent of the load. It was a sure bet for the Orejuelas and a major break for Abrego. Before long, he was handling one-third of all the cocaine used in the United States and was said to be worth, personally, $15 billion.

Mimicking Escobar, he murdered dozens of people on both sides of the border, including his six closest rivals, which, by 1984, made him – by process of elimination – Mexico's principal cocaine trafficker. Yet he surpassed even his hero when the FBI honoured him as the very first international drug trafficker to make it onto their Ten Most Wanted list. Arrested in 1996, he was sent to Texas for trial – the Mexicans agreed with the Americans that because he was born in Texas he could not be protected by Mexico's law regarding non-extradition of nationals – found guilty, and sent to prison for life. The Gulf cartel still operates, but less boisterously than it did under Abrego. Much of its business has been taken away by the just-as-bizarre one-time head of the Juarez cartel.

The group, which was set up by Amado Carrillo Fuentes with the help of a former Mexican federal police commander, controlled the middle of the border. With Abrego in jail, Fuentes was smuggling four times as much cocaine as all the other cartels combined, running a global enterprise that is said to have grossed $200 million a week. He used Boeing 727s to bring drugs from Colombia to Mexico – and maintained a fleet of aircraft – then passed the drugs off to youth gangs, who would smuggle them into the States.

But once Abrego was out of the way, Fuentes found himself America's primary target. So he decided that, for the sake of his old age, he needed to become invisible. Which he nearly did in mid-1997 with the help of a team of plastic surgeons.

On the morning of July 4, 1997, the thirty-nine-year-old Amado Carrillo Fuentes lay down on the operating table and expected, later that same afternoon, to wake up as a younger looking, vigorous gentleman named Antonio Flores Montes. Instead, eight hours later, he was found expired in his Mexico City hospital bed, the victim of an apparent post-operative heart attack brought on by eight gruelling hours of plastic surgery to his face and liposuction to his belly.

The body was flown immediately north in a chartered plane to Culiacan for burial. Almost as quickly, rumours spread that Montes was Fuentes and that Fuentes was dead. Now the world divided into two groups: it is Fuentes, and he died; it isn't Fuentes, and he faked it.

It took the DEA to match Fuentes's fingerprints with those of the corpse, and the Mexican government to perform DNA tests to conclude: Fuentes is dead. Three months after the death, his surgeon was reported missing.

Jaime Godoy Singh and two doctor friends disappeared. They were found several weeks later, stuffed into oil drums that had been partially filled with cement and left on a main highway seventy miles southeast of Mexico City. All three had been handcuffed and blindfolded, strangled, and, for good measure, shot in the neck. Their fingernails had been pulled out and their bodies showed signs of burns.

That immediately reignited both camps: the DEA is right, it was Fuentes and his guys who killed the doctors as revenge; the government DNA tests are a cover-up, it wasn't Fuentes, and they killed the doctors to keep them quiet.

What no one knew at the time – at least no one in Mexico – was that a bunch of guys sitting in a secret office in Los Angeles were almost as shocked and saddened by the death as any close friend of Sr. Fuentes and/or Sr. Montes.

In Mexico, hand in hand with drug trafficking and money laundering, corruption is a fact of daily life. But at no time in recent history has corruption been more evident than during the six-year reign of Carlos Salinas de Gortari.

He was elected president of Mexico in 1988, amidst outcries that the vote had been rigged. Rumours began circulating almost immediately that the Institutional Revolutionary Party (PRI) in general – which had autocratically ruled Mexico since 1929 – and this president in particular, were utterly corrupt. But there was little to substantiate those rumours until 1992, when the president's cousin and an employee of the president's father were arrested and convicted of drug trafficking in the U.S. Word was that the two had been working for Juan Garcia Abrego.

It was hardly coincidence, then, that Salinas now limited the number and scope of American narcotics agents who were authorized to work on Mexican soil.

The depth of Salinas's venality manifested itself around the same time in the form of a very private, top-secret dinner party at a mansion in Mexico City's "millionaires' row" Polanco district. The president was the guest of honour. Thirty of the wealthiest men in the country were brought together to demonstrate their support for the PRI and the 1994 presidential campaign. Put more bluntly, this was payback time for the massive depravity that had allowed some of these men to grow mega-rich under a party that had turned drug trafficking and money laundering into vital ingredients of the nation's GDP. To no one's genuine surprise, before the night was over, the thirty men said thank you by pledging an average of $25 million each. It is said that Carlos Salinas viewed this moment as the birth of his family's dynasty.

Unfortunately for him, not everyone in the family was quite as adroit. And brother Raul proved especially clumsy. With illicit drugs quickly becoming the most dynamic sector of a feeble Mexican economy – after the peso crash of 1994, drugs surpassed oil as the prime source of much-needed hard currency – Raul recognized that the leaders of the main cartels were about to become the country's de facto power brokers. So, acting in consort with his brother or with the blessings of the PRI elders or both, he did what any worried but loyal member of a ruling family would do. He invited the drug barons to the banquet.

Within months of that $750 million dinner, newspapers in Mexico were printing stories about a meeting at the Salinas ranch, with Raul present, where envelopes with cash in them were handed over by known drug traffickers.

With hindsight, it shouldn't have been a surprise. From the day Carlos opted to run for president, *Newsweek* magazine had been claiming that the Salinas family was connected – especially Raul, who was linked to Abrego. Knowing, as we do now, that Abrego was paying as much as $50 million a month for his own protection, it's easy to understand why, when a police task force sought military help to arrest Abrego, the request was refused by the chief of staff of the president's office, who also happened to be in charge of the national drug and intelligence agencies.

Enter here Deputy Attorney General Mario Ruiz Massieu and his top aid, Jorge Stergios.

In December 1993, Stergios transported bales of cash to a branch of the Texas Commerce Bank in Houston. Two dozen cash deposits ranging from $120,000 to nearly $480,000 were made by Stergios over the next year with instructions to the bank not to invest any of it, but rather to leave the full amount in a chequing account. During that time, Raul not only loaned a relative $29 million but also fixed the bid for him to purchase a formerly state-owned television station.

With the 1994 elections about to take place, Luis Donaldo Colosio, tipped to succeed Salinas, was assassinated. This brought the PRI's second choice, Ernesto Zedillo Ponce de Léon, to office, and along with him came José Ruiz Massieu's brother, José Francisco, elevated to majority leader. That's when José Francisco was assassinated. The very next day, a PRI congressman who would eventually become a suspect in the Ruiz Massieu murder disappeared and was presumed dead. Two months later, Mario Ruiz Massieu mysteriously resigned from the investigation of his brother's assassination.

In late February 1995, Raul Salinas was arrested for his involvement in the murder of José Francisco Ruiz Massieu, who happened to have been married to his sister, Adriana Salinas. Rumours also surfaced that either Carlos or persons close to his former administration were somehow connected with the Colosio murder.

The same week that Raul was arrested, Mario Ruiz Massieu was questioned by police about his possible role in his own brother's assassination and a potential cover-up to protect Raul. Immediately after being released, Ruiz Massieu flew to Houston. He was arrested the next day at Newark Airport, in New Jersey, about to board a flight for Spain carrying forty thousand dollars in cash.

Some three thousand miles away, at almost the very same time that Ruiz Massieu was being arrested, Ernesto Zedillo was meeting secretly with Carlos Salinas in Mexico City. When that meeting ended, all allegations that the Salinas administration had somehow been involved in the Colosio murder were officially rescinded.

The next day, the U.S. government seized $9 million, supposedly belonging to Ruiz Massieu, from the Texas Commerce Bank. Which was the same day that Carlos Salinas left Mexico.

For the next six months, the so-called Salinas Affair continued to make front-page news around the world, at times pushing other stories to the inside pages. Among them: the arrest of nearly three dozen Mexican Federal Judicial Police officers who had been part of a $40 million a month racket to protect drug traffickers; and the seizure of a plane that had been flown from Colombia carrying seventeen tons of drugs, all of which had been off-loaded by Mexican state and federal police, resulting in the arrest of another twenty officers.

Like any good soap opera, this story took all sorts of twists and turns, but few as odd as the November 15, 1995, arrest in Switzerland of Raul's wife. Paulina Castanon de Salinas had reportedly tried to withdraw $84 million from a safe deposit box at a private bank that had been opened in the name of Juan Guillermo Gomez Gutierrez, a presumed alias used by her husband. When asked why she would take so much, why she didn't simply take a little at a time, her answer is said to have been, "I *was* taking a little at a time."

As if all this wasn't surreal enough, in October 1998 Swiss prosecutors – who'd gone on to discover accounts in six cantons that they believed to have been owned by Raul using false names – dropped their money-laundering charges against Raul for technical reasons. Proceedings were also dismissed against Paulina. Although the ever-canny Swiss insisted that $114.4 million in Raul's alleged accounts were indeed drug proceeds and seized them. Another $20 million was subsequently found in London.

While all this was going on, Carlos Salinas was setting up residence in Ireland.

In January 1996, Juan Garcia Abrego was arrested and deported to the United States. The inevitable void created by his sudden departure from the scene created a battle for succession. After much bloodletting, the thirty-seven-year-old Oscar Malherbe had successfully fought off both his own associates and members of the Juarez cartel who'd tried to take over. Like Abrego, Malherbe would also soon become a pawn in his government's game plan.

Throughout that year, just enough Mexican police and judicial authorities were arrested to make it seem as if the government was taking action. A body was found buried on Raul Salinas's ranch and a story found its way into the newspapers that it had been put there to frame Raul. It was only after a gunman was accused of actually pulling the trigger in the José Francisco Ruiz Massieu assassination and the body on his ranch turned out to be the missing PRI congressman that Raul was charged with killing the congressman whom he had allegedly paid to handle the contract on José Francisco. Abrego received eleven life sentences, Carlos Salinas was questioned yet again about the Colosio murder, Mexico City's chief prosecutor was fired for incompetently handling the Raul Salinas case, and Mexico's attorney general was fired, supposedly on similar grounds.

While prosecutors were now asking Carlos about the murder of Ruiz Massieu, the Mexican army was raiding a wedding, intending to arrest the bride's brother, Amado Carrillo Fuentes. But they arrived to find that the party was being guarded by federal police and that the drug baron was nowhere to be found.

As much as seven tons of illegal drugs – particularly cocaine, heroin, marijuana, and methamphetamines – were now being smuggled across the U.S.-Mexican border daily, but, strangely, Washington continued to praise Mexico's spirit of co-operation. Meanwhile, on the front line, U.S. agents talked of nothing but mutual suspicion, distrust, and resentment. Summing up U.S.-Mexican relations at this point was the photograph of American drug czar General Barry McCaffrey alongside General Jésus Gutierrez Rebollo, head of the National Institute to Combat Drugs, Mexico's equivalent of the Drug Enforcement Administration. McCaffrey called Gutierrez, "a guy of absolute unquestioned integrity."

Three weeks later, Gutierrez was in jail, accused of being a mole for the Juarez cartel. The agency Gutierrez once headed has since been disbanded for having been corrupt beyond mending. The general himself was convicted of working for Amado Carrillo Fuentes and was sentenced to thirteen years. An embarrassed McCaffrey was forced to admit, "Our intelligence was wrong." This on the heels of his March 1996 remark that Attorney General Antonio Lozano Gracia was "a man of tremendous courage and integrity." Nine months later, Lozano was fired for his incompetence and mishandling of the investigation into the Salinas family's affairs.

Around now, documents surfaced from prosecutors in Houston that suggested Raul Salinas, his father, and late brother-in-law José Francisco Ruiz Massieu were partners in drug trafficking.

In 1997, when it came time for President Clinton to decide whether or not he would certify Mexico – a bad report card on a country's efforts in the war on drugs carries with it economic penalties – there were plenty of reasons to suggest the Mexicans deserved to fail. However, the day before Clinton was scheduled to make his decision the Mexicans just happened to stumble across and arrest Oscar Malherbe de Léon. Then, just hours after Clinton agreed to Mexican certification, Humberto Garcia Abrego – who had been brother Juan's chief money launderer at the Gulf cartel – decided he didn't like prison life and simply walked out. He chose to escape despite the fact that his jail cell had apparently consisted of six rooms equipped with telephones and fax machines so that he could keep in touch with his business interests.

With Raul Salinas in jail, his brother Carlos out of the way in Ireland, their family in tatters, Ruiz Massieu and others either awaiting trials or already convicted, and Citibank helping police with inquiries into how they came to funnel more than $100 million into Swiss and other foreign accounts for Raul, the White House was forced to concede in a report to Congress, "Corruption is rife within the ranks of Mexico's police and members of the security forces."

As if that wasn't damning enough, a former Gulf cartel trafficker, Juan Antonio Ortiz, testified in one of several cases against Mario Ruiz Massieu, "Everybody could be bribed. From what I know, everybody was being paid all the way to the top."

The depth of the corruption and the havoc it created was best summed up by Special Agent Phil Jordan, former head of the DEA's Intelligence Center in El Paso. "If Saddam Hussein had done what Amado Carrillo Fuentes has done with the complicity of the government's corruption, we would have declared war."

In fact, we did.

Late in the autumn of 1995, U.S. Customs agents out of Los Angeles began a modest undercover operation with the help of a "CI." That's cop lingo for "confidential informant," a bad guy whom the good guys have convinced to work for them, usually in exchange for various "considerations": a reduced sentence if everything goes well; no sentence if all goes better; a free ride on the Witness Protection Program if things don't work out exactly as planned; flowers at the funeral if the bad guys the CI is double-crossing find out about it before the good guys can get his butt out of town.

In this case, the CI – who called himself Javier Ramirez – was hoping for a get-out-of-jail-free card because, before he switched sides, he'd been running the Emerald Empire Corporation, a one-stop shop for drug dealers with dirty money to launder based in a storefront warehouse in Santa Fe Springs, California, a rough-and-ready town east of where the Santa Anna Freeway meets the San Gabriel River Freeway. Ramirez brought the Customs agents in as his partners. He then connected them to high-level money launderers for the Cali cartel, and before long, the undercover agents were collecting drug money off the streets of half a dozen U.S. cities.

Through contacts developed with the Colombians, the opportunity arose to open an offshoot operation – more cash pickups, but this time for Mexican traffickers – which brought the undercover team inside the financial infrastructure of the Juarez cartel.

In turn, these two operations led to yet another opportunity. They were picking up huge amounts of cash, ranging from $500,000 to $2 million at a time, all of which needed to get into the banking system. The idea was to wire it out of the United States to the Cayman Islands, Venezuela, and Mexico, then bring it back to the U.S. as bank drafts or cashier's cheques made payable to third parties. But because there was so much money involved, to manage it, Emerald Empire needed help.

The CI put out the word and one of the people interested in his plight was Juan Carlos Alcala Navarro, a.k.a. Dr. Navarro, the main fixer for the Juarez group. He agreed that, for a fee of up to 4 per cent on each transaction, he would hook up Emerald Empire with some Mexican bankers. He would then pay them an under-the-table commission of 1 per cent for whatever amounts they could wash through their bank.

So now, on behalf of Emerald Empire, Navarro provided a collection of tame bankers who opened accounts in fictitious names in California, Mexico, and the Caymans. Before long, there would be more than two dozen of them, representing twelve of Mexico's nineteen largest banks, including Bancomer, Banco Serfin, and Confia. Getting inside the banking system was a major coup, because mid-1990s Mexico had become the single most important money-laundering centre in the western hemisphere.

As the three investigations meshed together almost seamlessly, they became known as Operation Casablanca. Overall responsibility for the operation lay on the shoulders of Bill Gately – then Assistant Special Agent in Charge of the Financial Investigation Division for Customs in Los Angeles – a superb financial investigator who'd tangled with the cocaine cartels throughout his career. But this was unlike any undercover operation he'd ever worked before. Then, too, it was unlike any undercover operation anyone had ever worked before. It was bigger, more complex, more wide ranging, and offered unbelievably huge prizes if they could pull it off.

Dr. Navarro was a prime target. But a notch higher on the list was José Alvarez Tostado, a.k.a. "Compadre," the man who apparently oversaw the Juarez cartel's U.S. interests. And just above him, number one on the list, was Tostado's boss, Amado Carrillo Fuentes, head of the Juarez cartel. For the first time in any drug money investigation, three of the most powerful traffickers/money launderers in the world were within reach.

To get those three, their flunkies in Mexico and the States, and to round up the bankers too, Gately needed to call on assistance from offices and agencies all over the country. But constructing such a monster operation was a nightmare. Gately needed constant input from hundreds of people and all sorts of other agencies, many of whom brought their own agendas with them. There were also more than enough petty jealousies to go around. Doubters and begrudgers came out of the woodwork. Later, of course, those same people would line up to take credit. But in the beginning they got in the way, as Gately fought for approval all the way up the chain of command through U.S. Customs to the Treasury and Justice departments.

As the operation expanded Gately established a command post in a secret location away from the Customs office. More and more agents were moved into the safe house to back up the agents in the field. By mid-1996, such huge amounts of cash were being picked up on the streets of Los Angeles, Chicago, Miami, Houston, and New York – much of it owed to the Colombians by the Mexicans for drug consignments – that a team of forensic accountants had to be given security clearance and moved into the office to keep track of it all.

At the same time, administrative support back at headquarters also became more complicated. Time-sensitive material poured in, much of it the kind that needed to be handled no later than yesterday. Agents would find out on a Tuesday afternoon that they needed to fly somewhere to meet a bad guy on Wednesday morning, which didn't give anyone in Washington a lot of time to obtain appropriate approvals. Before long, the U.S. Customs Service would have two hundred people working on Casablanca.

The operation was inherently dangerous. Lives were on the line. Gately and his team needed continually to reassess their strategy, develop new lines of intelligence, update the needs of Casablanca, decide who could do what to whom, look at what had already transpired, and commit the operation to what would follow. And always, at the forefront of their minds, was the knowledge that the price of even a minor failure was unacceptable.

To maintain security, everything was highly compartmentalized. Gately and a few others in Los Angeles knew the big picture. So did a chosen few senior managers at headquarters. But the other people involved – and this was especially important when they dealt with outside agencies – were only told what they needed to know to accomplish their part. State and local agencies had roles to play, particularly in gathering intelligence, but with Customs agents risking their own lives undercover, no one was willing to trust anyone else, even other law enforcement officers, more than they absolutely had to. Other agencies, especially, needed to be told who and what to stay away from. The last thing anyone in Los Angeles or Washington wanted was for some overambitious patrolman to stumble across a money pickup, try to be a hero by busting it up, and expose the entire operation.

There were contingency plans in case the CI got burned, or something happened during a pickup. And there were plans at the ready to arrest as many people and to seize as many bank accounts as they could if they had to fold up at a moment's notice. But drawing up contingency plans is one thing. Living with accidents is another. And none of them was emotionally prepared when that accident occurred.

On August 6, 1997, a money pickup was going down at a McDonald's in New York City when one of the bad guys tried to double-cross one of Gately's undercover guys. Emergency backup was in place, as it must be on any undercover transaction, but warfare in the streets occurs suddenly and violently, and when the bad guy tried it on, all hell broke loose. One of the undercover agents went down. The bad guy was killed and the good guys survived, but the shooting lifted Casablanca onto another plane.

Tony Mangione, who worked on the support team at Customs headquarters, happened to be in New York when the shooting occurred. "I heard about it the next morning. It's a pretty sickening feeling. At that point, I didn't care much about the operation. I don't think anybody did. The important thing was the agent who got shot and the officer who shot the bad guy. It was only after we found out that our guys would be okay that anyone began thinking of what to do next, of how to salvage the operation."

Gately immediately flew to New York to visit his undercover agent in the hospital and to help the agent who'd killed the bad guy get through his trauma as well. Then he began to deal with damage control, focusing on how to save Casablanca.

With the help of the CI, the team in Los Angeles concocted a cover story. Based on partial truths, it went like this: The bad guys who had tried to rip us off were rogues, they weren't the people who were supposed to drop off the money, it was an isolated incident, the police just happened to stumble across it and intervened because that's what cops do, the good guys escaped, law enforcement is no wiser about what was going on, it was one of those bad-luck things that sometimes happens, no one expects it to happen again, so the shooting should not change anything.

Of course, if it could happen once, it could happen again. And the next few pickups were tense. There was always the question, are they giving us a contract for the pickup because they knew we're cops or will they buy our cover story? Is this the end of it? Are they starting to have doubts?

It was nearly a month later before the Colombians seemed comfortable enough with the cover story that they could put the shooting behind them. "That was, undoubtedly, the closest we came to being compromised," notes Allan Doody, at the time a very senior manager for Customs' Criminal Enforcement back in Washington. "The shooting in New York was horrible. But because everything was so compartmentalized, I don't think it could have compromised the entire operation. Still, we were very lucky to get through it the way we did. We were able to make up a story that was plausible and they eventually bought it."

That said, he contends, it was clearly in the bad guys' interest to buy into the cover story. "They needed our service and were willing to accept that there'd been an interruption. Both the Mexicans and the Colombians needed us to continue as the middlemen. Before long, we began to get introductions to Venezuelan business people and bankers who were in the money-laundering end of the drug business. We also met relatives of some of the Mexican cartel folk who were living in Italy, and they introduced us to Italian nationals involved with distributing cocaine in Europe and subsequently laundering money."

The Italian connection began when Emerald Empire was asked if it could arrange pickups outside the U.S. Naturally, the answer was yes. But in order to get this phase off the ground, a lot of people in Los Angeles, Washington, and Rome had to move quickly. What's more, they had to bring in the Italian authorities.

Relationships between U.S. law enforcement and foreign law enforcement tends to hang on what FBI Director Louis Freeh terms "cop-to-cop bridges." The bridges to Italy have built up steadily over the years and are carefully maintained; it is one area where those bridges work best. The Italians were approached, they understood the problem, and, most of all, they trusted their American counterparts enough to sign up.

Now, at the invitation of Emerald Empire's Italian representative – Special Agent Matt Etre, who worked out of the Customs Attaché office at the U.S. embassy in Rome – Colombians flew to Italy. They met with Etre and his partners – Italian undercover agents – and once they were satisfied everyone was who they claimed to be, the deal was done.

"We worked the Milan area," explains Etre. "We provided the front, which was an investment company, and the Italians managed the money pickups. What I found so amazing was that once the traffickers decided we were all right, no further bona fides were necessary. It was, Hi, you must be Tony, here's the money. They'd hand half a million dollars in cash to someone they'd never met before and, just like that, turn around and walk away."

The six pickups in Italy totalled just under $5 million.

Through information acquired there, U.S. Customs and the Italian National Police were able to identify an important Italian-Colombian alliance, with Colombians stationed in Italy to oversee it. That led to five arrests, including that of Alberto Minnelli, a trafficker linked to the Canadian side of the Cuntrera-Caruana crime family. It also almost opened up yet another front.

The Colombians continued to put out contracts for pickups. They were willing to pay commissions ranging from 6 to 20 per cent, depending on the currencies involved and the difficulty in handling the money. But as commissions increased, so did competition to service them. Other criminal organizations were always waiting in the shadows to move in on the Emerald Empire business. Nothing more than the slightest hesitation by Emerald Empire was needed to hand the contract to a competitor. Which is what happened when the Colombians asked if Emerald Empire could work pickups for them in Great Britain. Unlike the Italians, the Brits took too long to grant permission authorizing American undercover work, and the contract went elsewhere.

By this time Emerald Empire was hooked into the Cali-Juarez alliance so deeply that the opportunity presented itself for another offshoot: taking down the Juarez cartel's substantial command and control centre in Chicago.

"We'd actually known about Chicago for quite some time," says Doody, "but didn't understand just how much money and how much drugs they had there. We decided to target them and try to disrupt what they were doing there. A lot of their key people got arrested. We seized two to three million dollars at a time, along with large quantities of cocaine. We were in a position of trust, so while we were busting them in Chicago, they were confiding in us in California that something was going wrong in Chicago, that they were in disarray there. They never suspected us."

Terry Neeley had been working as the Assistant Customs' Attaché at the U.S. embassy in Ottawa, Canada, when he first heard about Operation Casablanca. But he only got involved with it when he was transferred back to Washington in the summer of 1996, and assigned to Allan Doody's group as National Program Manager for Undercover Money Laundering Operations, of which Casablanca was merely one. He remained in that support role for a year until Gately, an old pal, called on Neeley to risk his life.

For more than a decade and possibly two, Chicago had been the narco-turf of the Herreras from Durango, Mexico. Not a cartel in the Juarez or Gulf sense, it was more a conglomerate of six blood-linked families – something akin to the Camorra branch of the Mafia in Italy – who quietly and effectively had gone about their business building a network of more than a thousand dealers for their Colombian cocaine and "Mexican mud" brown heroin. To service their key markets in New York, Boston, Philadelphia, Dallas, Louisville, and Oklahoma City, they took a lesson from the airlines and set up Chicago as their main hub.

Back home, they have traditionally controlled much of the state and local government, doing their Robin Hood act, replacing some municipal services by building sewer systems, hospitals, and public housing. They supported any number of poor farming families by subsidizing legal crops.

After the fall of the Medellín cartel and the imprisonment of the Orejuela brothers, the Herreras seemed to back off from cocaine, content to run what was effectively their heroin monopoly. It was one reason why other cartels tended to stay away from them: they weren't really in competition. However, the family did develop some sort of relationship with Amado Carrillo Fuentes. And when the Juarez cartel began looking for their own axis in the United States, the Herreras seemed willing to let them superimpose a cocaine structure over their own heroin hub.

Gately had originally seen the Chicago pickups as a chance to develop intelligence against the cartel. Now he concocted a plan to deploy a task force that would report directly back to him as a part of Operation Casablanca.

Neeley recalls that he was invited to head the task force on a Monday. On Tuesday, Gately arrived from Los Angeles to brief the Assistant Commissioner for Customs in Charge of Enforcement, Bonni Tischler, and to list the task force's real-time needs. They decided they would need up to forty people, all hand-picked, their own intelligence section, and some help from other agencies, such as the DEA and state and local police. They also needed somewhere to work, somewhere to live, funding, and all sorts of equipment.

Neeley arrived in Chicago on Wednesday. "There's an unbelievable adrenaline rush, a real high, when you go out into the field to conduct some very significant enforcement activity. At the same time there's the stress of going away and knowing you're going to be gone for an extended period of time. You worry about who's going to take care of your dogs and who's going to collect your mail and who's going to take the newspaper off the front porch. I sorted all that out, as best I could. Then, as soon as I arrived, I got into a car and started driving around looking for a place to operate from. Bill joined me on Thursday. On Friday, he and I spent the day purchasing some of the equipment we needed. Saturday and Sunday we were still looking for a location, and I think we found that by Sunday. We moved in on Monday as agents started coming in from all over the country. We went over information that we had obtained from previous activities in Chicago, made a determination on where we needed to exercise our authority immediately, briefed the troops, and were in business that same afternoon."

They worked out of a suburban motel, using the cover story that they were employees of a company trying to build up sales in the import-export field. Two rooms were turned into a command centre and extra phone lines were installed. Other rooms were set aside to house the troops. Gately returned to Los Angeles, but Neeley was on the phone to him at least a dozen times a day. "Right from the start the pressure was unbelievable. There was no such thing as a day off. Some of the guys would take a few hours to do their laundry or see a movie. But my front-line supervisors and I were always working, always talking strategy, always planning what we were going to do next."

The task force's motto became "We Rock Your World."

In the very first house they hit, they found what they were looking for, a *colleta* – a secret compartment, professionally built, in which drug traffickers hide cash and contraband. This one was in the garage. The whole floor had been tiled, but some of the tiles had been grouted above a very big trap door. Below that was a room, large enough to drop into, where they discovered half a dozen guns, some money counters, cellular phones, and a kilo-press, which is a homemade press to make up kilo packages of cocaine. But this *colleta* had flooded and was also filled with four inches of water, so there was no money.

They found money in a second house where there were two *colletas*, both under construction. One was in the garage – also tiled and grouted shut – the other in a laundry room where they'd also tiled the floor. That led them to a third house, where the *colleta* was in the basement. By this time they'd seized $3.7 million in cash.

Ever aware of the dangers that came along with an operation like this, Neeley and the others continued to identify targets, raid them, and use each raid to identify more targets.

"It's like a house of cards that starts falling. During those first few weeks, we pulled off maybe twenty raids. We didn't sleep. We couldn't sleep. We developed intelligence around the clock until we were just too tired to stay up any longer. We then got a few hours' nap and went right back to it. It was our intent to take back the city from the cartels, and the only way to do that was through very very aggressive investigations and by hitting them non-stop. This was not a nine-to-five job."

Nor was it a job where, for even a second, anyone could afford a lapse of concentration. "The shooting in New York hung over us. We were constantly worried about safety. And we were constantly revising contingency plans should something go wrong. We had our cover teams in place. We knew where the hospitals were. We had our code words established. We had good communications. But Chicago was a Juarez stronghold. We were in their neighbourhood, at their homes, where they'd established themselves, inside their *colletas*, inside their command and control centres. Because we were in their face, constantly, there was always a very real chance of someone getting hurt. Regardless of whether your gun is drawn or not, you never know who or what is behind a door."

On more than one occasion, information came back to Neeley at his motel room command post that the cartels believed they were being followed from undercover meetings. On more than one occasion they needed to drop back fast, to regroup and analyze the situation. On more than one occasion they had to rely on the skills of other agencies, and a lot of luck, that everything would work out whenever they had to surrender immediate control.

One night, a Cook County Sheriff's officer on patrol in the Chicago suburbs spotted a Jeep Cherokee making an illegal lane change. He pulled the driver over and, after writing a ticket, discovered two suitcases containing $1.6 million. Later, an additional fifty thousand dollars would be found at the driver's house in suburban Burbank.

Roberto Orozco Fernandez, a thirty-six-year-old suspected laundryman and assassin for the Juarez cartel, believed he'd succumbed to bad luck when the Sheriff's officer stopped him. But it wasn't just luck. He had been one of the team's targets, tailed by undercover agents who, according to plan and at just the right moment, brought in the Sheriff's deputy.

From what Gately's undercover agents were hearing in other cities, the Juarez cartel was, for the first time, feeling real pressure in Chicago. They didn't understand what was going on. And their first reaction was to look for someone low-level, on the bottom, who might be leaking information. They even dispatched Dr. Navarro to Chicago. His solution for minimizing the big hits they were taking was to rely more heavily on Emerald Empire to get money out as quickly as possible. He never suspected high-level involvement.

By this time, though, Dr. Navarro's fate was being seriously discussed. He and Tostado were each moved one notch higher on the target list, because right in the middle of Casablanca, Fuentes died.

A lot of people who knew that his face had been painted squarely over the bull's eye took the loss personally. They were not sad for him, but sad for themselves. He never knew just how close they'd gotten to him. And, in a grotesque way, he had the last laugh, although the price he paid for it was pretty heavy.

"We were so very close to Amado Fuentes," Neeley goes on. "We were in bed with him. We were there. If he hadn't died, we would have put the handcuffs on him. When he died, there was a power struggle. We had to identify who was now controlling the cartel, and we settled on Tostado."

Serious talk about taking the operation down began during the summer of 1997. It arose because some people way up the chain of command were getting cold feet. For many reasons, the decision was to keep going. And, in retrospect, that was the right decision because they were still developing fresh leads and accumulating better evidence.

Allan Doody admits that he was sitting on the fence about when to call it quits. "I kind of half did want to take it down, and half didn't. The argument to keep working it was that we hadn't yet implicated as many people as we could. We were going off in new directions. I think it could have continued for a very long time."

The argument for stopping it was more political. Pressure was mounting from the top to bring the operation to a conclusion. Some people worried that Casablanca, by laundering so much money, had become part of the problem. The State Department, Treasury, and Justice each had their own agenda, one of them being the certification of Mexico, which was coming up in the spring of 1998. A few very senior people felt it would be better to have Casablanca out of the way before the President took his decision.

But it was something a lot more sinister that worried Gately's team. His agents in the field were starting to bump into other investigations run by other agencies, and none of them meshed with Casablanca's.

Allan Doody again: "There are a lot of agencies out there working their own cases, like the DEA, the FBI, the IRS, plus state and local police. It's not uncommon when you run any major operation that you bump into a piece of a case where someone else might have a wiretap or a search warrant. The problem arises that when you've given them a piece of information they can use, because of the way our legal system works, that information might wind up on an affidavit they then file for a search warrant. Eventually someone gets arrested and the information on the affidavit gets released. Now, in and of itself, that one piece of information may not hurt you. But when you start to add up all those little pieces over the course of time, especially when you have people undercover, you can easily find yourself in a very dangerous situation. Lives are at risk. So you add all of these things up and make a decision."

It wasn't until Thanksgiving 1997 that everyone generally agreed it was time to focus on the end-game. That took four months of planning. Gately came up with a time frame for the takedown – he wanted to run it in March – and then he and the senior managers in Washington decided on an actual date. They chose May.

A strategy briefing was called in the final week of April 1998. It was attended by a small coterie of Customs supervisors and senior managers, plus a few people from Justice, Treasury, the DEA, and various U.S. Attorneys' offices – about twenty altogether – at Nellis Air Force Base near Las Vegas. It was a convenient location for everyone to get to, it would not attract attention, and it was close enough to the takedown site that they could scout it. Also, because the base was secure, their meeting would be secure. As it was, just in case, they met in a secure conference room with armed guards outside.

Gately briefed everyone about the takedown plan. He went through it hour by hour. Some bankers would arrive in San Diego. He mentioned who they were and told the group how many people he'd need there. Others would be flown to a casino in Nevada – by coincidence, it was called The Casablanca – and he outlined how many people he'd need there.

Plotting all this took two full days. They started at eight in the morning and were still in the conference room by six at night. They repeated the schedule the next day. When it was over, a few of them drove out to the casino which was in Mesquitte. It had been chosen because it was isolated – a good ninety-minute drive from Las Vegas – and had a private airstrip. No one at the casino knew what was about to happen.

The actual arrest plans, and all the legal coordination that needed to go along with them, were made in Los Angeles. The idea was to bring one group to San Diego – because many of those people were fearful of venturing any further inside United States territory – and invite the others to a jolly Saturday night celebration in Nevada.

The money going through the system was slowed down so that Customs could grab as much of it as they could before it slipped out of their control. Excuses were easy. They had worked with the traffickers and the bankers for nearly three years. They'd earned a level of confidence. So no one suspected anything when minor errors cropped up: a clerk forgot to sign something, there were typing errors on a form, one of the banks put the money in the wrong account. Pretexts were easy. With one week to go before the takedown, Emerald Empire had almost entirely turned off the money tap.

Those targets who showed up in San Diego believed they were going to win some contracts. The ones invited to Nevada believed they were going to celebrate past successes and discuss the laundering of mega-bucks in the future. Neither group knew about the other, because Gately had deliberately set it up that way.

The San Diego takedowns were designed to happen at four different sites and at four different times. It was a nightmare putting that together, because they had to make sure they had enough time between takedowns so that the CI could get from one meeting to the next. They also had to make sure that if someone was arrested downtown, the next group of bankers wouldn't be sitting in the hotel next door.

In Las Vegas, the bankers had a jovial dinner, and then were ushered into limos for a trip to "more entertainment." Privately, some of the bankers somehow got the impression that they were off for an evening at a house of prostitution. Like lemmings, three or four bankers at a time piled into each limo. Departing the casino at well-timed, staggered intervals, they were driven by chauffeurs who also happened to be armed undercover agents. The planned route took them into the desert, along a dark, isolated road, where Nevada Highway Patrol officers pulled them over on the pretext of speeding. The takedown team then showed up to formally announce that they were under arrest.

They were in the middle of nowhere, there was no place to run, no place to hide. And as soon as one limo was out of the way, word was sent back to the casino to dispatch the next one.

Needless to say, every one of them was more than just surprised. Especially Navarro. When the Highway Patrol stopped his limo, the driver announced, "I'm afraid I might have been speeding." But the moment that Navarro spotted a second car arriving at the scene, he knew there was something wrong. He reportedly mumbled, "This isn't just about speeding."

Additional arrests were made across the country, in Aruba, and in Italy throughout the weekend. Then, on Monday morning, teams of agents and assistant U.S. attorneys fanned out across the country to seize bank accounts.

When the dust of that weekend settled down, 160 people from six countries were in jail. Criminal indictments had been levied against Bancomer, Serfin, and Confia. And Customs agents had seized in excess of $150 million in assets from the Cali and Juarez cartels.

The one who got away was Tostado. But only just. Although Gately didn't put handcuffs on him, he seriously disrupted life as Tostado once knew it. Corruption often is the price of freedom in Mexico: the only way Tostado is going to be able to move around is by paying mega-bribes. Thanks to Casablanca, he may not have that luxury anymore.

News that three major banks had been busted, plus bankers, lawyers, and cartel members arrested, sent the Mexican stock and bond markets into a nose dive. Bank stocks plunged 8.5 per cent. The Mexican government tried to put a brave face on what was, undeniably, a major embarrassment. Finance Minister José Angel Gurria claimed, "This does not mean that the Mexican banking system itself is under scrutiny, only that some employees unfortunately committed illegal acts and were found out."

During the first couple of days after Casablanca, the Mexicans even seemed willing to help. They rounded up half a dozen fugitives, among them Enrique Mendez Urena, whom the Mexican police arrested based on the U.S. indictment. Urena was a Juarez cartel investment advisor who'd worked at the Union Capital Bank in Guadalajara. He had made very clear statements, which the Americans had on tape, indicating that he was laundering money for the Juarez cartel and that he also handled money for people within the Mexican government. He was obviously a man who knew a great deal. Which is why it didn't come as a major shock to anyone in the United States that, suddenly, he was dead.

Two conflicting stories were put out by the Mexicans. One was that the cartel had captured him and were torturing him as a traitor, and that the police had tried to rescue him. This version had Urena dying from cartel-inflicted injuries on the way to hospital. The second story was that when the police arrived at his home in a wealthy neighbourhood in Guadalajara, he wasn't there. Instead, they found residents complaining about a man running over rooftops. The police said they chased the man, who turned out to be Urena, who was trying to escape. They eventually convinced him to climb down and he was arrested, but, they added, at some point in his attempted escape, he'd fallen, was injured, and lost consciousness during questioning.

While neighbours did not witness a fall, the fact that he lost consciousness at some point, and that might very well have been during questioning, is reasonable because, somewhere between home and hospital, he suffered severe head wounds. He died from those head wounds just after dawn on Tuesday, May 26. For whatever reason, the Mexican authorities did not release his name for more than forty-eight hours. And then they categorically denied having any culpability in the death.

No one in Los Angeles or Washington knows for certain what happened. Nor is anyone ever likely to find out. It could have been an accident. It more likely was murder. Either way, the cause of his death soon ceased to be relevant. Almost as soon as it was announced, the Mexicans began accusing the Americans of having violated their sovereignty. The political landscape shifted significantly. The politicians moved in and co-operation ended.

The Mexicans argued that the undercover operation had severely damaged the trust and co-operation that they'd previously shared with the Americans. Attorney General Jorge Madrazo said that Mexico would fully investigate Operation Casablanca and that he could not rule out formal requests for the extradition of U.S. agents who had illegally operated on Mexican soil.

"I don't know what they [the Americans] will think," Madrazo warned, "but the obligation of the Federal Public Ministry is to carry out this investigation." He continued, "The lack of communication has severely strained co-operation between the two countries. In our joint efforts, we demand respect and reciprocity."

The Mexicans had every reason to be embarrassed, although no one was quite embarrassed enough to explain how or why Mexico's three largest banks had come to launder $157 million worth of drug money.

Nor could they admit either to their own people or to the world that the secret of Casablanca would never have been safe had the Americans shared it with them.

President Zedillo criticized the Americans. So did the Mexican foreign minister. So did all the opposition leaders. In fact, their rallying calls to Mexican pride – which, without question, had been wounded – made this the rarest of political events in that country. It brought together all factions spanning all side of the political spectrum. Natural enemies joined hands. And for the first time, perhaps ever, the country spoke with one political voice.

Secretary of State Madeleine Albright warned Mexico that prosecution and requests for extradition of U.S. drug agents would be counterproductive. Congress took a more blunt approach. "Any attempt by Mexico to extradite U.S. law enforcement agents," promised the then

House Banking Committee chairman, James Leach, "would risk irreparable damage to relations between our two countries."

"Sovereignty," added Senator Charles Grassley, "is not meant to be a shield for criminality."

With emotions raw and tempers flaring, the White House opted for diplomacy and apologized to the Mexicans.

Doing the President's bidding, Attorney General Janet Reno – albeit with carefully chosen words – insisted that Casablanca was neither an indictment of Mexico nor of its banking system. It was, she said, "Just an indictment of some corrupt banking employees and three banks."

For some of those undercover agents who risked their lives, and some of their managers who had helped pull off the most massive international drug-money-laundering sting ever, apologies were not merely inappropriate and unacceptable, they were the most heinous of all insults.

13

END RUNS

They're here, they're there, they're everywhere. When the first rocket ship lands on Mars, the spacemen will be greeted by Nigerians.

– Intelligence officer, British police

In the mid-1990s there was an international heroin conference held in Washington, D.C., co-sponsored by Interpol and the DEA, attended by representatives from about sixty countries. It was the first major conference on heroin in twenty-five or thirty years. Among the delegations attending was one from Nigeria. And from the very first day, they were on everyone's target list. They were verbally beaten up at every turn. Everybody at the conference took shots at them, deriding the country's abominable reputation for heroin trafficking and multiple varieties of fraud.

Throughout the conference, however, the woman who headed the delegation maintained a dignified silence. Finally, on the last day, she politely asked for the floor.

She told the delegates that there had been much talk over the past several days about Nigerians being involved in smuggling, about them being involved in advanced-fee schemes, about Nigerians with false documents, about Nigerians going all over the world to commit all sorts of frauds.

She said, "What I need to explain to this group is, this is what we do in Nigeria."

The British gentleman who responded to the official request for his help confessed afterwards that he should have known better.

Everyone says that afterwards.

It looked like an important business letter from an important company, but it was addressed by hand. It was too good to be true, the British gentleman later confessed, and yet he fell for it.

"Dear Sir: This letter comes to you on the advice of a mutual friend, who thought you might be able to help me. I am acting as an agent for Shell BP . . ."

At least it sort of sounds like a real company.

". . . because a particular problem has arisen with blocked funds. A large sum due the company is being held in a Swiss account and, as the result of a legal complication, the money cannot be released directly to the company. We are anxiously looking forward to securing a foreign partner who can offer us the benefit of having some money remitted into any company's or personal buoyant account. This money runs in millions of U.S. dollars."

The problem duly explained, the proposition was straightforward. If the gentleman would allow that money to pass through his bank account, he would be paid handsomely for the service.

"The third party will wire the money due, $20 million, into your account without you assuming any liability. All you have to do is wait for the money to clear, then forward $14 million to us. You are welcome to the $6 million difference as your share. You are not being asked to do anything illegal, just to step into the middle of a legitimate commercial transaction. I would be pleased to meet with you, to show you references and to discuss all of the background paperwork."

The only problem was that the money had to be paid by a fast-approaching deadline.

"However, to save valuable time, may I suggest you furnish to me your banking details, plus your personal authorization for the transfer, written on your own letterhead so that we may proceed."

The British gentleman was much too savvy to send anyone authorization to his bank account, so he phoned the man who had written the letter, some sort of Nigerian prince – they are usually royalty or lawyers or government officials or ministers in a church – and asked for more details.

His Highness was more than happy to oblige and even arranged a meeting. The British gentleman flew to Germany, where the prince was waiting for him with an entourage and plenty of supporting documents.

But now, the prince regretted to explain, there was an additional problem. Unfortunately, in order to make the transfer, the bank was demanding that a fee be paid. Shell BP couldn't pay it because the money was tied up. However, the prince would be willing to deduct the difference once the money came into the British gentleman's account, and sweeten the pot for his trouble by adding a few dollars to his share.

The British gentleman wanted to know how much the fee would be. The prince said 1 per cent. And just how much, the British gentleman wanted to know, would His Highness be willing to add to his share to sweeten the pot. The prince wondered if five hundred thousand would be all right.

When the British gentleman seemed to hesitate, the prince suggested that perhaps they should put the half million pot sweetener in writing. Which is what they did. The prince, acting for Shell BP, signed a contract guaranteeing that the two-hundred-thousand-dollar bank fee should be deducted from the $14 million the British gentleman was agreeing to forward to the company once the $20 million cleared his account. And that he had the right to withhold another half million dollars as an additional fee.

The British gentleman kept telling himself he'd just done a deal of a lifetime. And in one sense, he was right.

When the money did not arrive, the prince and his entourage asked the British gentleman to meet them immediately, again in Germany. In fact, the money had been paid, the prince told him, but not through the bank. It had been paid in cash and the British gentleman was, of course, more than welcome to his share as agreed. The British gentleman asked when he could have it. The prince told him right away.

Except, there was a new problem.

Because of currency controls and a strict tax regime in Nigeria, the money had to be smuggled out. The prince even took the British gentleman to see it. Piles of it. Twenty million dollars in hundred-dollar bills, packed in several huge cases.

Except, it was all black.

The prince explained that in order to get it out of the country, they had to coat it with a special chemical. That way Nigerian Customs couldn't seize it. Watch, he said, taking one of the bills and rubbing it with a liquid. And, sure enough, out of the black a hundred-dollar bill appeared.

The British gentleman was sceptical. The prince allowed him to pick up another piece of black paper and clean it. And again, right there in front of him, a second hundred-dollar bill appeared.

The problem was, the prince admitted, they were out of the special chemical. But because they'd already caused him so much inconvenience, when he was merely trying to do them a favour, instead of returning $13.3 million, they would be satisfied if he only returned $13 million.

So, just like that, he made an extra three hundred grand.

But to get it, he had to stake them the money to buy the special chemical. That set him back another seventy-five thousand dollars. And he's still waiting for His Highness to return from his chemical shopping trip.

A typical advance-fee fraud, this particular scam is referred to today as "a 4-1-9 scam," named after Nigerian Decree 419, which made it illegal in 1980.

It is also, today, one of Nigeria's major exports.

Nigeria represents one-fifth of Africa's population. It is the most urbanized nation on the continent, and among the most politically powerful. But it is not, nor has it ever been, what might be termed a "natural" country. It is, rather, a confederation of tribal states. Boundaries were imposed by the British – who granted it independence in 1960 – because those boundaries suited the colonial masters. Within six years of independence the country slipped into chaos when the first military coup took place. Since then, ethnic-based wars and *coups d'état* have been common. There are something like two hundred different tribes in Nigeria, and at least as many different dialects are spoken there.

Around 30 per cent of the population is Hausa-Fulani. They live in the northern half of the country and are largely Muslim. The Yoruba make up a little more than 20 per cent and populate the southwest corner, which includes Lagos. The Ibo are about one-sixth of the population and are found mainly in the southeast.

There was an old saying when the British ruled the country that the

Hausa were the military, the Ibo were the civil servants, and the Yoruba were the entrepreneurs. Nigerians as a group are historically recognized as the best traders in Africa, and were already doing business with the Arabs before the days of the slave trade. If nothing else, Nigeria has produced many of Africa's most talented, freewheeling con men. Their global reputation is based largely, but not exclusively, on 4-1-9 frauds.

While the letter the British gentleman received is typical, there are dozens of variations. Besides money due that is supposedly blocked, there are pleas for help with over-invoiced contracts, currency conversion problems, and the sale of a commodity at below market prices. Letters may come from an individual claiming to be the beneficiary of a will. Some come from what appears to be a church organization, and are usually aimed at churches and religious groups. Some letters involve the sale or purchase of real estate.

In one European case, Nigerian fraudsters offered to buy a huge property and secured the sale with a pile of "black money." The seller of the house was coerced into advancing the fraudsters $950,000 for the chemical to wash the money. One very odd feature of that case was the presence of another foreigner. There was so much "black money," the seller was told, that certain security arrangements were needed. The other foreigner was there to provide muscle. He happened to be Russian. It was the first time any police investigating a 4-1-9 fraud had seen Nigerians teaming up with Russians. It has not, however, been the last.

An FBI investigation in the New York–New Jersey area unravelled a Nigerian gang working a scam in partnership with a Russian organized crime group. But then, Nigerian criminals are perhaps the most relaxed of all the organized crime groups when it comes to forming strategic alliances with other criminals.

The 4-1-9 letters always come out of Lagos. They're thrown into post office sacks and loaded onto flights bound for international postal hubs in London, Frankfurt, or New York. There the letters are sorted by the British, German, or U.S. post office, which then forwards them.

Or not, as the case may be.

Post offices have gotten so good at spotting these letters that they now routinely take them out of the system. In average years, British postal inspectors remove twenty thousand a week. U.S. postal inspectors annually grab 3.2 million.

In fact, the Americans have the Brits to thank for spotting a useful legal loophole. By law, the U.S. post office believed they were obliged to let the letters go through the system. That was, until the British informed them that the stamps were counterfeit: lithographic reproductions.

The Secret Service then entered into the picture – because they deal with counterfeit instruments of every kind – and under their authorization, postal inspectors can now remove the letters from the system.

But still they keep coming. The Hong Kong post office, for instance, announced not long ago that 95 per cent of all the mail from Nigeria consists of 4-1-9 letters. Post offices all over the world are flooded on the principle that some will always get through. It is believed that 1 per cent of the people who receive the letters respond, and that the average loss per response is two hundred thousand dollars. If the four million letters the U.K. and U.S. postal services stop each year got through, that would represent losses of $80 million. As it is, worldwide, Nigerian 4-1-9 scams are believed to be worth nearly $1 billion.

The Nigerians have become successful, almost to the point of being blasé. So much so, in fact, that one of the prized possessions of the National Criminal Intelligence Service in Great Britain is a 4-1-9 letter addressed to "Sir Paul Condon, Commissioner, Metropolitan Police."

Nigerian criminals are wonderfully conscientious when they set up a scam. Before working in a country, they seed it, bringing people in to live there and to set up their infrastructure. They need addresses for the letters and bank accounts for the money. Police in Ireland, for example, witnessed a sudden, and otherwise unexplainable, growth in the Nigerian immigrant population in 1998. It was followed by a rash of 4-1-9 scams.

During the Atlanta Summer Olympic Games, no one could figure out why hotels were emptied of all their telephone directories, business directories, and Yellow Pages. It turns out that some athletes on the Nigerian national team and loads of fans were paid to bring them home. Within three months of the games, Atlanta was flooded with 4-1-9 letters.

The Germans have a massive problem with Nigerian crime. So do the Scandinavians. So do the Dutch. The British keep telling the French they have a problem but the French won't accept it.

Half a million Nigerians live in the U.K. – at least those are the ones that the Immigration Office knows about. There could be as many as half a million more they don't know about, not just illegals, but overstayers and people on false passports.

In Europe and North America, they never meet the victim in his own country. In Australia and New Zealand, advanced-fee frauds are a scourge. The only thing working against them there is that it's a lot more difficult to hide behind international borders.

There are Nigerians working scams throughout Asia. On average, in countries like Korea, one case of Nigerian fraud is reported to the authorities daily. In larger countries, like Japan, Nigerians have installed themselves, married local women – which prevents deportation – and worked their fraud schemes to such an extent that British law enforcement terms it "a plague." There is evidence to suggest that since they moved in on Japan, the yakuza have since moved in on them. The Nigerians are allowed to operate but under a yakuza umbrella. For a percentage of their earnings, the yakuza provide the Nigerians with banking facilities and backup.

Nigerians have also begun to establish themselves in Russia. How long that will last is a matter for conjecture. It's unlikely that groups such as Solntsevskaya are going to be any more receptive to foreigners working their turf than the yakuza were in Japan. But, given the Nigerian proclivity for doing joint ventures, if in the next few years the streets of Moscow aren't filled with dead Nigerian con men, then a deal has been done somewhere.

If not totally ruthless, these con artists are undeniably heartless. One couple who'd been running a company in Britain received a 4-1-9 letter from someone in Nigeria they had been doing business with for years. The man appealed to their friendship in asking for help to get money out of the country. The couple fell for it and lost their business.

Obviously, they play off greed. But their understanding of human nature runs deep. In many cases, when a victim has been hooked, he goes through a distinct personality change. Even when the scam is explained to him, he still somehow believes it's going to work out all right for him. In one case in Britain, an American turned up with half a million dollars in cash. The police intercepted him on his way to meet his Nigerian contact. They told him what was about to happen. The man refused to believe it. And soon the half million was gone.

A popular ploy is to let victims think that they'll get their money back by recruiting others into a separate conspiracy. In another case in Britain, one victim tried to recoup his losses by luring twenty others into the scam. The group's total losses added up to £4.5 million.

The kind of money that the scam generates was summed up recently by a Nigerian who, over a nine-month period, deposited $46 million in cheques plus $9 million in cash in a British bank. He told his bankers that the money was coming from outside the U.K., although the source of the funds was not disclosed. On one occasion, he handed over forty supermarket carrier bags and announced to the teller, "There's about $4 million in there. You count it. If it's not, tell me."

In addition to funnelling cash through normal high-street banks, they use Western Union to move a lot of their money. Intriguingly, they also have Lebanese banking connections. It seems that in the Muslim north of Nigeria, there is an old established Lebanese community. For some reason, Nigerian criminal enterprises have come to rely on these Lebanese to move money through their laundering system.

Every six months or so, the Central Bank of Nigeria advertises a warning in world newspapers about the 4-1-9 fraud. They take out full-page ads but, if they have any effect, it is hard to detect. It leads one to wonder why the Nigerians themselves can't do something about it.

The answer is, they need the money.

Besides Decree 419, there are laws that could be used to prosecute swindlers. There are money-laundering regulations on the books, and there is Decree 33. Banks and financial institutions are required to report transactions in excess of five hundred thousand naira (about C$9,600) and presumably some of them do. The Nigerian authorities have even conducted money-laundering investigations that have resulted in property seizures. The Nigerians don't trouble themselves by securing convictions, however, and so seized property is frequently returned. Decree 33 also makes it a criminal offence in Nigeria for any Nigerian to commit a criminal offence abroad. Double jeopardy in its purest form, it states that any citizen who is arrested, convicted, and sentenced to a jail term in another country will, when deported back to Nigeria, be imprisoned for an additional five years.

It's on the books. The government points to it every time anyone in the West chides them. They just don't bother enforcing it. Nor do they bother fulfilling their obligations to UN conventions, or to co-operate in any meaningful way in the fight against transnational organized crime. It is therefore down to Western law enforcement to act. But that's easier said than done.

"They're well organized and nothing flaps them," says one senior London Metropolitan Police fraud squad officer. "They shy away from violence in the U.K., although there has been violence reported in New York and we worry that violence might be coming to the U.K. They use various passports and work in little cells, we believe with a Mr. Big somewhere, at the top. They are intelligent and understand our jurisdictional problems. If there is a U.K. victim of a 4-1-9 letter fraud, then they work it out so that he won't be paying any money in cash to anyone in the U.K. He'll have to go to Canada or the States. They hide behind borders. They always put another jurisdiction between them and us."

Borders complicate the investigative process and seriously muddle the judicial process. "If we arrest someone in this country with a victim here, we invariably find that there are another twenty-three victims someplace. In America, the police can say to the court, there are another twenty-three victims, your Honour, and the judge can take that into account in sentencing. We can't do that in Great Britain. We have to travel to wherever those twenty-three victims are and take statements from them, and then prove in court that the person they're talking about is the same one we've got in custody. That usually means flying twenty-three people over to this country to go through an identity parade and identify the person. Otherwise the court won't accept that this is the same person. It's very costly and very difficult to arrange. And the Nigerian criminals know that."

Since 1992, the U.S. Secret Service has been collecting intelligence on these fraudsters and their scams. Not just the 4-1-9 letters, but all sorts of counterfeit identification documents – pay stubs, employee ID cards, benefit slips, income tax returns, passports – which the Nigerians use to obtain a post office box number. With a post office box in place, they redirect mail so that they can steal credit cards, redirect bank statements so they can empty accounts, form companies, bilk insurance companies, and apply for mortgages and even student loans. They also have a fondness for counterfeit birth certificates from the Virgin Islands. They use them inside the United States to obtain social security cards and driver's licences, with which they can open bank accounts.

The Secret Service has databased hundreds of thousands of 4-1-9 letters and documents, interviewed tens of thousands of people, and continues to log three hundred to five hundred documents received every day from victims and intended victims. Link analysis on a document can usually pinpoint which group sent the letter or forged the document and, at times, even point to the location of the group's leaders in Nigeria. The Secret Service is also feeding counterfeit credit card information into that database.

The Nigerians start with credit card blanks, stamp them themselves, and use them throughout North America until the cards get stopped. Then they get on a plane and fly to Europe because they know they've got another twenty-four hours to spend on the cards before they get stopped worldwide.

Police in Britain say it is not uncommon to go on a bust and find twenty to thirty West African counterfeit credit card blanks. They have even intercepted birthday cards sent from one Nigerian to another, with a counterfeit credit card stuck inside as a gift.

The U.S. embassy in Lagos says they are "inundated" with 4-1-9 cases and receive requests daily for help from defrauded Americans. Despite their warnings not to come to Lagos – echoed by all Western embassies there – some victims still insist on showing up. And that's where things can go tragically wrong. Hostages have been taken and held for ransom. Over the past few years, there have also been at least fifteen deaths recorded in Nigeria of foreign victims hoping to recover their losses.

"Violence attracts attention," notes the FBI's Tom Kneir. "So, if you think about it, violence is pretty stupid. The Nigerian problem in the U.K. is like locusts. They just eat away. We're talking about billions of pounds. It's the same in this country. Now ask yourself, why are they so successful? The answer is, because they go about their business without pissing off anybody. They do frauds, they don't do violence. They come in, do their deals, and get out. Most of us go on a two-week trip with multiple pairs of socks and underwear. These guys go on a two-week trip with multiple sets of identification. But that's changing because they also do heroin. And it's because of the heroin that they're showing up on the radar screens."

Inconceivable abuses, carried out in the name of apartheid, created an extensive breeding ground for crime in South Africa.

Among the scores of illegitimate acts committed under the old regime, police used drug syndicates and dealers to get to political opponents. The vestiges of that history are manifest today in the nearly eight hundred crime syndicates that are acknowledged to be operating there. Most are street gangs. But some are organized along traditional lines, and some have established direct partnerships with major transnational criminal organizations. Some serve as local franchisees for them.

Of course, the major gangs are present in South Africa as well. Chinese Triads, Russian *Maffiya*, traditional Italian Mafia, the Colombian cartels, and Nigerian criminal enterprises have had the experience and the wherewithal to make their mark. They have updated and modernized the old smuggling networks for drugs, arms, diamonds, and stolen cars – Bulgarian gangs move cars out of South Africa and into eastern Europe, often in conjunction with Russian organized gangs – and have used the nation's financial infrastructure to launder their money.

Especially attractive are South Africa's highly developed diamond and gold markets.

The new government inherited much of this criminal activity, but since 1994 it has failed miserably to come to grips with the problem. Besides the fact that legislation is insufficient to mount an effective fight against local crime – and absolutely incapable of doing anything about transnational crime – police are underfunded, undermanned, undertrained, outgunned, and overworked. Of those eight hundred acknowledged gangs, it is believed that fewer than two hundred are currently being investigated or otherwise actively pursued by the police.

Compounding the problem, the country is surrounded by neighbours whose interests are in direct opposition to South Africa's. Drug smuggling and weapons trafficking bring them much-needed hard cash at South Africa's expense. They moved in en masse the moment South Africa's international isolation ended in 1994, taking advantage of South Africa's modern transportation, communication, and financial sectors. The worst offender was Nigeria.

In Johannesburg, Nigerian criminal enterprises dominate the cocaine market, frequently in partnership with criminals from other West African states, especially Ghana. Exact figures are not available, but it is estimated that perhaps as many as a hundred thousand illegal immigrants from Nigeria and Ghana live in that city, many of them working in some facet of the illicit drug trade.

Johannesburg was the receiving end of a Brazil–South Africa air bridge, and a magnet for drug traffickers. As police and Customs at Johannesburg International Airport began to have some success in stopping drugs from entering the country there, the traffickers – in this case, Nigerian – simply diverted to Cape Town, or brought drugs in overland from Mozambique, Zambia, Zimbabwe, and Namibia. They also began to use courier services that transship through Britain and Germany. Customs inspectors in both countries have increasingly stopped shipments of cocaine sourced in South America and addressed to traffickers in Angola, Botswana, Swaziland, Lesotho, Mozambique, and Zimbabwe for eventual smuggling into South Africa.

The Nigerians have not made much headway in dealing synthetic drugs, because the users are mostly white South Africans and the market is dominated by Dutch and British expats. In 1997, South African police busted a drug laboratory and arrested the scientist, who'd once been in charge of the nation's chemical and bacteriological warfare program. The lab had been established under the old regime, supposedly to study the use of narcotics as a weapon for neutralizing an enemy, and was producing both Mandrax, which is a strong tranquillizer, and ecstasy. Both drugs have saturated schools all the way down to junior high.

But whether it be cocaine, marijuana, heroin, or synthetics, the violence that shadows these markets is inescapable. Pretoria and Durban have both been ravaged by drug-related criminal activity, while Cape Town has become the Wild West.

In a part of the world that could have as many as a hundred thousand gang members, the most visible and most violent of Cape Town's groups has been the Hard Livings. It was formed in 1971 by the identical Staggie twins. Rashaad was the brains behind the gang and Rashied was the enforcer, a psychopath who enjoyed his nickname, "Mad Dog." They flourished under the previous government, using much of their wealth and power to expand into Cape Town's prostitution business.

In response to their lawlessness, and the new government's inability to control such gangs, an equally visible and equally violent vigilante group was formed in the Cape Flats, east of Cape Town. Largely Muslim and known as People Against Gangsterism and Drugs (PAGAD), in 1996 they shot, killed, and then burned Rashaad Staggie. They also eventually shot and seriously wounded Rashied.

Until the gang's leadership was neutralized, one of the Hard Livings' rumoured alliances was with the Pizza Connection's laundryman.

Roberto Vito Palazzolo was one of the men who had escaped American justice. A jeweller by profession, he was in those days running Consult Fin SA, a private bank in Lugano, Switzerland. Both the Americans and Italians asked for his extradition. Instead, the Swiss charged him with money-laundering offences, and, rather than face life in jail in Italy, Palazzolo got three years in the more lenient Swiss court.

As a non-violent offender, about halfway into his sentence in 1988, he was given Christmas leave. He skipped. His destination of choice was South Africa, where legend has it that he arrived carrying 16 million rand – nearly C$4 million – in cash and a second fortune in diamonds. Within weeks he bought a vineyard and settled into his new life on a fabulous ranch in Fransehoek.

The Swiss found him there when his face appeared in the crowd of a televised report of a National Party fundraising event and requested his deportation. Despite his ties to the National Party, the South Africans sent him back to Switzerland, where he served out the remainder of his term, plus an additional two years. Finally released, he returned to South Africa.

But Palazzolo was declared an undesirable by Pretoria, and refused residence. He sidestepped officialdom by obtaining citizenship in the Ciskei homeland, using the name he had in an Austrian passport, Roberto von Palace Kolbatschenko. Someone in the Ciskei agreed to appoint him "ambassador plenipotentiary" to South Africa, which would have allowed him to live in Cape Town with diplomatic status, except Pretoria saw through that subterfuge and refused his dubious credentials. In 1995, however, the homelands were abolished and his Ciskei citizenship automatically became South African citizenship.

The following year, a colleague presented evidence to Deputy President Thabo Mbeki that the police organized crime unit in the Western Cape was run by a chap with criminal connections to the former government and therefore could not be trusted. André Lincoln also informed Mbeki that Palazzolo was now living in Cape Town. Mbeki's solution was to establish the Cape-based special undercover Presidential Investigations Task Unit. He decreed it would bypass all the usual law enforcement chain of command and report directly to him. And he named Lincoln as the Unit's head. With Mbeki's authority, Lincoln set off on a bizarre voyage of inquiry.

He contacted the Italians, who told him that Palazzolo was perhaps the most important Mafia financier since Roberto Calvi and Michele Sindona, late of the Banco Ambrosiano affair. They claimed that, immediately following Calvi and Sindona, the ruling Commission had taken a decision in Sicily that, rather than control bankers, it was wiser to own banks. As a result, a number of banks were acquired by the Sicilians, one of which was in Zimbabwe. Palazzolo, they said, had been a key part of this transaction, and the Italians wanted him back.

Shortly afterwards, Lincoln flew to Rome to meet with the Italians – he introduced himself as General Lincoln – and received further information about Palazzolo. He then invited them to South Africa to arrest a whole bunch of suspected Italian mobsters who were living there. A few weeks later, a team of Italian policemen arrived in Johannesburg. But all that happened was that they sat around for two weeks. When no arrests were imminent, they went home.

During the time Lincoln was supposedly investigating Palazzolo, he put in a funding request to travel to Angola. It was granted and he went – with Palazzolo.

A secret South African report had named Palazzolo as the mastermind behind a Western Cape Mafia-style organized crime group and had linked him to the Hard Livings. It also named his South African underboss as a former police intelligence officer and noted that their crew was made up of fugitives from Morocco, Russia, Germany, and France. Much of the information on Palazzolo is widely believed to have come from the Italians, who had been investigating him for several years. Yet, despite his direct association with the Pizza Connection case, Palazzolo has always denied having Mafia links. According to the Italians, Palazzolo is the Mafia's chief laundryman in southern Africa. According to the FBI, who have issued a warrant against him in the U.S., he is one of the top seven members of the Sicilian Mafia.

The Italians have failed at least twice to extradite him. On both occasions, Pretoria turned down the requests on grounds of double jeopardy. Italy wanted to try him for his role in the Pizza Connection case, but South Africa's Department of Justice believed Palazzolo's Swiss jail time had erased that charge. When Italy switched gears, using the Mafia-association law as the basis for extradition, South Africa answered that they could only extradite someone for crimes recognized in South Africa, and that Mafia association is not one of them. The Italians, having no alternative, decided to try him *in absentia*.

Almost without warning, Lincoln shut down his probe and announced that he was clearing Palazzolo of any wrongdoing. As head of the unit, he wrote on official stationery to Palazzolo's attorney, "None of these activities is the subject of any complaint of irregularity whatsoever. No past or current investigation carried out by myself or my office can implicate your client in the extortion of Italian businessmen in South Africa." These words were written despite the inclusion of Palazzolo's name on Interpol's wanted list. Since writing that letter, André Lincoln has been arrested for fraud and theft.

In the meantime, Palazzolo continues to be referred to as the godfather of South Africa, and the Italian Justice Ministry lists him as one of their "100 Most Wanted." There are stories that he has given sanctuary to several wanted men and that he oversees the activities of several émigré Italians who have established money-laundering and drug connections in South Africa. His business interests range from ostrich farming, mineral-water bottling, and toxic waste disposal to weapons trafficking and drug smuggling. He is known to own a game farm in Namibia and to have a stake in the Angolan diamond industry.

South African police confirm that investigations are continuing and that the most recent Italian extradition request is, in fact, being considered. Unofficially, they admit that two of the things they're looking at is the alleged Palazzolo–Hard Livings link, and the Hard Livings–Nigerian cocaine link.

Both allegations, if substantiated, would connect Palazzolo and the Mafia with Nigerian criminal enterprises. Making that connection might be the first step towards reclaiming a country that is being choked to death by criminal organizations.

After all, if the single most important asset of any democracy is its justice system, then it is reasonable to argue that a government unable to convince its citizens that justice will prevail undermines its own legitimacy.

Despite all the international optimism and goodwill that walked alongside Nelson Mandela when he left prison and made his way to political power, the failure of the governing African National Congress to come to grips with the difference between opposition and power has brought about the bankruptcy of law and order throughout much of the country.

It is only one short step from the prosperous future that should be South Africa's to the corruption and anarchy one sees in, say, Colombia.

In the very early 1980s, some Nigerian naval officers were sent to a training course in India. They saw how easy it was there to obtain Southeast Asian heroin and decided that if they could buy some, and get it into Europe or the United States – which they thought they could do by travelling in uniform – they could earn a fortune. That was Nigeria's leap into drug trafficking.

Shortly thereafter, the Nigerian economy collapsed. Poverty and political corruption led to substantial emigration. Unfortunately, the exodus coincided with the upsurge in international drug trafficking, which meant Nigerians found themselves living in centres where drugs suddenly became available. More and more Nigerians were not only willing to carry drugs for traffickers, because they needed the money, but were anxious to do so. At the same time, more and more Nigerian criminals realized that drugs would lead to riches.

The alarm went out to Customs officers around the world to be extra vigilant when dealing with anyone carrying a green Nigerian passport. So Nigerian criminals went in search of new passports.

The end of apartheid couldn't have come at a better time. The new government opened up the country and Nigerian criminals fraudulently proved they were South African. It wasn't difficult to manage, with their superior counterfeiting skills. And anyway, because so much of South Africa is without a register of births, marriages, or deaths, the country has for years been run on bogus documentation.

Four million Nigerians now live in South Africa. The retail value of drugs reportedly flowing through the country represents slightly more than half of South Africa's GDP. Some 60 to 65 per cent of those drugs are then exported to Europe and North America by Nigerian criminal enterprises. A vital ingredient in their South Africa success is that direct airlink to Brazil. It perfectly suited the Nigerians because there are half a million of them living in São Paulo. It also suited the Colombians. They'd spotted the possibilities in South Africa and were anxious to open the market. All the Nigerians had to do was flash their money. The Colombians based agents in Lagos and the two groups were in business.

The circuit remains the obvious one. Drugs are trucked down from Colombia to Brazil, then flown across to South Africa. Some of those drugs are sold on the spot, the rest are moved north into Europe. Or they're transshipped via West Africa or through Europe – there is heavy traffic in and out of Italy, giving rise to the suspicion that traditional Italian groups have joined hands with the Nigerians – to North America.

Savvy traders that they are, the Nigerians did not want to be dependent on the Colombians, so they moved their own buyers into Thailand to supplement their income with an assured supply of Golden Triangle heroin.

By 1996, Nigerian trafficking had become an international concern. A conference of the most senior law enforcement officers in the G-8 group of nations put together a subcommittee, chaired by Britain, on Nigerian criminal enterprises. It served to highlight the increasing demand for a coordinated response. Following that meeting, HM Customs and Excise formed a seventeen-man operational response group, with its own integrated intelligence unit. Tim Manhire is the British Customs officer who runs the West African Organized Crime Unit. "We've come to think of Nigerians as the world's middlemen. They don't usually source drugs and they don't generally sell them in the marketplace. But they do everything and anything in between." Their method of choice, he says, is "little and often."

When Customs officers intercept two kilos of heroin, the bust doesn't make headlines. It is still, however, worth a lot of money. The way the Nigerians stay off law enforcement's radarscopes is by sending two kilos today and two more kilos tomorrow. It quickly adds up to a great deal of money.

"It's very easy to underestimate a problem when each seizure you get is very small. We took out ten couriers from one organization going to the States with a kilo or less. But the Nigerians didn't start out working like this, which shows how dangerous they really are. They learned from their mistakes. They've always been willing to make changes along the way. As we've got better at finding them, they've evolved, and have found better ways to get around us."

Initially, Nigerian criminals smuggled large amounts in containers, much as the Colombians still do. As seizures mounted, they saw that they weren't fooling anyone, so they switched to strapping drugs on couriers. At first they used Nigerian women, often prostitutes. That didn't work for very long, so they shifted to "stuffers and swallowers."

They paid couriers to hide drugs in body cavities or to swallow condoms stuffed with drugs. The dangers of that became obvious when condoms broke and couriers died. Before long they were also getting caught, as various Customs agencies developed methods to spot them. U.S. Customs uses X-rays. U.K. Customs came up with a urine test. It reached the point where travellers carrying a Nigerian passport might as well have had "smuggler" stamped on their foreheads. So they side-stepped again, recruiting white European and North American couriers. They reduced the amount each courier carried and increased the number of couriers. It was now a percentage game. One courier with ten kilos might get stopped. Ten couriers with one kilo each means nine might get through. Put ten couriers on ten flights, and they've suddenly got a ninety-kilo bundle for sale.

They pay couriers as little as possible. Payment might start from about two thousand dollars per kilo, which is not a lot of money considering the value of the drugs and the punishment for getting caught. But they prey on people with no money. They've also been known to pay couriers with a counterfeit U.S. passport so that once they get into the States, they can stay.

Nigerian criminal enterprises have teams of talent spotters. In one recent case, the caretaker of an apartment block recruited two Dominican girls. One was flown to Bangkok to pick up heroin for New York. The other was flown to Rio to fetch coke destined for London. The caretaker was handed one thousand dollars for his help.

Recruiters cover every category of traveller, from college kids backpacking around Europe to middle-aged couples travelling with their children. In a well-publicized case, they recruited American sailors based in Italy to smuggle drugs for them, a reminder of their earlier faith that men and women in uniform are not frequently searched by Customs. They've even gone so far as to enlist athletes in wheelchairs on their way to the States for the Paralympics.

To hedge their bets, they then complicate routes. Couriers no longer travel directly from drug hot spots to drug markets. The first destination is almost never the country where the drugs will be sold. This means they're also relying on the weakness of international law enforcement co-operation.

They bring heroin from Bangkok into Africa – currently staging in Ethiopia, Kenya, Ghana, and South Africa, in addition to Nigeria – then send the drugs to North America via Amsterdam, Zurich, London, and Frankfurt. When a courier arrives from Africa at London's Gatwick Airport, for instance, someone is waiting there with another ticket from Heathrow to New York, making it look to authorities at JFK as if this person is just arriving from London. Or they bring heroin from Bangkok into Zurich, hand it off to another courier who brings it by train into Britain, where a third courier takes it to the States. They use a route for a while, then change it to keep the cops from detecting patterns.

A typically convoluted route was uncovered during a major West African organized crime bust in Chicago called Operation Global Sea. A single courier flew from Chicago to New York, then on to Amsterdam and Bangkok, where he picked up his heroin. From there he went to Malaysia, where he was handed a new passport and his old one was mailed back to him in the States. He returned to Amsterdam, picked up a flight to Guatemala, went from there to Mexico City, and then to McAllen, Texas, where he crossed the border as a tourist and caught a domestic airplane home to Chicago.

"That a courier took this routing," Manhire says, "is one thing. That someone actually thought of it shows how far these gangs are willing to go to meet their needs."

Their latest gimmick is the post office.

Packages stuffed with drugs are mailed anonymously, addressed to fictitious names at mail drops. The cost is considerably less than airline tickets, accommodations, and fees for smugglers, and because delivery dates can be reasonably accurately predicted, any delay is a signal that law enforcement has taken an interest in the package and it can then be abandoned.

Because of the volume of mail that modern post offices have to handle each day, only a very very small percentage of the smugglers' shipments could ever be stopped. Here, too, it's the little-and-often approach.

Their ingenuity is endless. Stopping them, Manhire explains, is made all the more difficult by their extraordinary ability to communicate. "We usually find when we do a job that there are common telephone numbers and addresses in everybody's address book. If I draw a flow chart I can keep on going because there are always links and connections. They talk to each other. They're not secretive when they have an operationally successful method. They'll share it with their friends and their friends will use it until it's no good."

He cites a case he worked in New York. The name of a housing project near JFK had been misspelled in the suspect's address book. Three months later, doing a job that had no connection at all with the first one, the same address appeared in this suspect's book, misspelled the same way. Even today, that misspelled address keeps popping up.

The gangs are loosely structured and constantly changing. It is widely accepted that there are several "Mr. Bigs" back in Nigeria. But the Nigerian criminals who work outside the country can be the boss for one job and a hired hand for another. When one hundred thousand dollars was needed to finance a recent drug run, the Nigerian in charge contacted four of his friends and they each put in twenty thousand dollars in exchange for 20 per cent of the profits. The next job the same fellow did was financed by a different group of friends.

As classic free-market entrepreneurs, they're willing to deal with any other organization as long as there is something in it for them. Over the years, they've developed strong alliances, not just with the cocaine cartels in South America, but separately with Dominican street gangs in New York and New Jersey, and Jamaican street gangs in London. These relationships form the basis of their coke-heroin swap business.

Although prices vary greatly, depending on market forces, a kilo of heroin in Bangkok will cost a Nigerian trader around eight thousand dollars. Bringing that into the U.K. will see him get a return of around fifty thousand dollars. But the U.K. market is for "brown heroin" – sometimes called "mud" – which comes from Turkey. And the market for Thai "white heroin" is North America. The price there is three to four times as much. So the Nigerians don't bother with the British market, they get their heroin into North America and now have product worth, say, $150,000.

Another anomaly of the market is that cocaine in North America is worth half as much as it is in Britain. So the Nigerians hand off their heroin to the Dominicans or the Jamaicans, or even to the Colombians themselves – whoever needs heroin and has coke to trade for it – and then bring the cocaine back to Britain, handed off to "Yardie" gangs who sell it on the streets of London. Their $150,000 gets turned into $300,000.

It's a good deal for everybody, including the Yardies. Until the Nigerians came along, Jamaican gangs were sourcing their own cocaine through the Caribbean. The Nigerians offered them a lower price with no smuggling risks.

"Some Nigerian somewhere had to go to some Jamaican somewhere and cut a deal," a senior British Customs officer notes. "We've never come across any other organized crime group willing to work with as many different groups as the Nigerians. But when you factor in the Jamaicans, it is not without some risk to them. The Jamaicans tend to stick to their own community and are not particularly structured, but they are notoriously violent. Nigerians are notoriously non-violent. Although in the States we're told they're starting to arm themselves. And that may be what happens in Britain as a result of their alliance with the Jamaicans. Yardies will rip off anyone. They'll take gear and never come up with the money."

All of this now comes full circle, starting and ending with a serious company in a serious industry that takes seriously its own security.

There are electronic security checks to get into the building, and electronic checkpoints throughout the building which only allow people who need to go to different floors to do that. Anyone who has not been given the proper clearances is stopped. The chairman himself worked it all out and as far as he's concerned, it's foolproof. What he never thought about, however, were the ladies with the mop.

Every night, crews of cleaners come into the building. The company hired them through an agency. And all of them can go to every floor. And some of those women are West African. And it only takes one to help herself to a few sheets of company stationery sitting in a desk drawer.

From that come forged letters of recommendation – to an embassy for travel visas or to a bank for a loan – and that leads to identity fraud, in which a Nigerian con man becomes an employee of the company with all sorts of privileges, including the right to empty out corporate bank accounts. Or he uses the letterhead to contact banks, alters addresses on accounts, waits a month, orders a statement to see how much is in the account, then orders a new chequebook and empties it.

It's not much more than a short step, once someone is inside a building, to illegally penetrating the computer system.

Nigerian criminal enterprises have regularly tapped into all sorts of official information: reports from banks and credit bureaus, files from Social Security offices, birth certificates, tax records, and voter registrations. These documents allow them to steal an identity and use it to commit myriad frauds. Those frauds, along with 4-1-9 scams, are the cash cows that supply the down payment for drug trafficking. The money comes round, full circle.

The chairman worked out the corporate security, all by himself.

14

CHASING GHOSTS

It's like chasing ghosts. Once you think you've identified it, it disappears, changes its form.

– Sgt. Jim Fisher, Criminal Intelligence Service Canada

It took a strategic alliance of the RCMP, the Vancouver police, and the U.S. Secret Service in 1998 to bust a major international counterfeit and credit card ring, which turned out to be something none of them had ever seen before – a strategic alliance of a Vietnamese gang, the Italians, and the Russians. One officer called it "a whole new ballgame."

An Italian organized crime gang came up with a good method for counterfeiting Canadian banknotes. And that alone might have been enough to make the case unusual, because the currency of choice had always been U.S. dollars. Counterfeiting Canadian fifty- and hundred-dollar bills was a relatively new phenomenon.

The banknotes were fed into scanners, the images loaded into computers, and perfect copies were reproduced on ink-jet printers. Experienced officers commented that the reproductions were among the most sophisticated they'd ever seen. The quality was also reflected in the price – thirty cents on the dollar – which apparently is a huge premium to pay for counterfeit money.

Along with counterfeit money, the gang was also making counterfeit credit cards. They used thermal silk-screen printers to produce and stamp the cards with the logos of half a dozen major banks. The numbers assigned to the cards were purchased from a Russian gang who ran petrol stations from which they were doing gas-tax fraud. The Russians were double-swiping high-value cards – platinum and gold – handed over by unsuspecting clients to pay for gasoline. The money and the credit cards were being marketed around North America by the Vietnamese gang.

Taking out all three groups was the object of a ten-month operation that had an undercover agent dealing directly with one of the Vietnamese gang. But just as the police were about to pounce, things went awry.

The undercover agent had negotiated a deal to buy C$3 million worth of counterfeit money from the Asians. Two days before that was to go down, one of the surveillance units got burned. Someone spotted them. By total coincidence, someone also broke into a car used by another surveillance team that was unrelated to the unit that got spotted. The team's target sheets were stolen. The officers had no way of knowing whether the break-in was committed by a common thief or whether those target sheets were the reason for the theft and wound up in the hands of the gang. But it was a definite security breach that prompted an immediate rethink.

As a result, instead of taking the gang down when they'd originally planned, the officers extended the operation for two months.

The criminals also reacted to the surveillance burn. Suddenly they worried about getting caught in a big sting and refused to sell more than five hundred thousand Canadian dollars to any one customer. The agent's cover was still good – the gang hadn't sussed him – but there was no way they'd go for the original C$3 million.

When the operation was finally taken down, culminating in simultaneous raids on eighteen locations, including multiple manufacturing sites around Montreal, they only got the credit card end of it. The important people in the counterfeit money group got away. So did the computer, the printer, and the scanner, which means the gang is still capable of producing more Canadian fifty- and hundred-dollar bills.

Although the police were able to recover C$2 million in counterfeit bills, which is apparently the single largest seizure of cash in Canadian history, the police believe that another million is still out there. And if it isn't yet in circulation, there is some Vietnamese operator somewhere in North America who is stuck with a lot of pieces of paper, and it's destined to show up eventually.

The term that's most often used is "Asian organized crime."

And, as far as catch-all phrases go, it pretty well labels criminal groups with links to Hong Kong, Macau, mainland China, Japan, Korea, Singapore, Malaysia, and the rest of Southeast Asia. But it doesn't describe the problem any more than the word *car* tells you what a Rolls-Royce is. Nor do all the sound-bites on the evening news describe the problem when law enforcement officers talk about "a giant spider spreading its web across the world" and "the invisible empire," and organizations that are "more flexible than the Mafia and more savvy than Colombia's drug cartels." The problem is that there are various types of Asian organized crime groups, with major structural and philosophical differences, but most of all, cultural differences.

Start with the Japanese yakuza.

Most experts agree that it is Japan's biggest corporation, turning over $75 to $85 billion a year, which is more than four times the combined revenues of Sony and Toyota. What's more, nearly one-third of its worldwide income is derived from legitimate business.

Descendants of a band of samurai who turned criminal in 1612 and were known as "the crazy ones," it wasn't until 150 years later that the group became an amalgamation of four groups – traditional gamblers, street peddlers, members of the political right, and hoodlums – and assumed a form that is recognizable today.

The name derives from a card game in which the worst hand is eight (the Japanese word is *ya*), nine (*ku*), and three (*za*), although the police in Japan insist on calling them *Boryokudan* – "Violent Ones" – which is not a name the yakuza themselves like.

Organized into families, with a father overseeing his children and the children always showing respect to the father, they are also said to be the largest organized criminal group in the world, boasting around eighty thousand members.

The relationship the yakuza have with traditional Japanese society is best illustrated by a story from 1960. Prime Minister Nobusuke Kishi had invited President Eisenhower to make a farewell visit to Japan before leaving the White House. It was a gesture intended to assure ratification of a mutual security pact. But because the treaty was so openly opposed by the left wing in Japanese politics, Kishi worried that demonstrators might try to disrupt Eisenhower's visit. He mentioned his concern to one of his party's major backers – a yakuza godfather – who simply took it upon himself to organize an army of his followers to head off any demonstrations. As it turned out, the visit was cancelled. But the relationship between the yakuza and the political life of Japan remains strong.

The yakuza has also been used to lobby on behalf of Western corporations. Some years ago, the group worked themselves into a deal as Lockheed's silent partner in securing sales to the Japanese airline industry.

At other times, they are blatant corporate extortionists, demanding payment to stay away from a company. Every few years, for instance, the yakuza approach publicly held corporations, threatening that, unless the company comes up with protection money, they'll disrupt the shareholders' next annual general meeting. One year, the harassment was so blatant and widespread that two thousand Japanese corporations conspired to hold their AGMs on the same day, for no other reason than to nullify the yakuza's threats.

As early as the 1970s, and with the help of Malaysian Chinese gangs, they opened stock brokerages in Malaysia and Singapore, and quickly expanded into Hong Kong, Australia, New Zealand, Indonesia, and the Philippines. When a yakuza stock market ring was shut down by the authorities in Malaysia, without charges ever being lodged against anyone, the gang showed up intact in London. Some people are convinced that they are also operating on Wall Street. They certainly play the markets, trying to manipulate prices however they can. That's known. But doing it on Wall Street, right under the nose of the Security and Exchange Commission, demonstrates a whole lot of self-assurance.

One of their favourite scams is buying from, and selling to, themselves the same Tokyo real estate. They artificially run up the price, apply for a loan against the building, and never pay back the loan.

Actually, their loan scams show the gigantic scope of their criminal prowess. In 1991, the presidents of Japan's two largest stockbrokers – Nomura Securities and Nikko Securities – resigned in disgrace when they learned that each had lent 2 billion yen, then around C$19 million, to a large yakuza group. It then emerged that another seventeen financial houses had each also lent the group around 2 billion yen. In 1994, when a bank manager in Nagoya tried to force a yakuza group to repay their loans, they sent a loud and clear message to other bank managers by murdering him.

When bad debt provoked the financial crises that rocked Japan in the late 1990s, conservative estimates put down 30 per cent of those bad debts to the yakuza.

Policing them is particularly difficult in a country where banking secrecy is absolute. Japanese law enforcement does not readily share financial intelligence about them for fear of violating the draconian banking laws and being sued by the yakuza.

The group runs prostitution, blackmailing, and gambling. They do not usually get involved with theft or robbery, which they consider to be shameful. They murder people – even though that is strictly prohibited by their code – and they deal drugs. They seem to have cornered the "ice" market in Hawaii – crystal methamphetamine is a staple of drug users in the islands – where they have distinct cultural advantages. At least fifty major properties in Hawaii are said to be owned by Japanese criminals.

Their major strategic alliance is with the Colombians for the importation of cocaine. They sanction Nigerian criminal enterprises by taxing them for the privilege of operating on Japanese soil. And they have connected with Russian organized crime groups in eastern Siberia, where they deal together in weapons, metals, and prostitution.

Faced with a recent law that makes it a crime to profit from monies earned by criminal organizations, and staring at the same economic downturns as the rest of Japanese industry, the group has actively sought overseas investment opportunities. They have moved in a significant way into the U.S., Australia, the Philippines, and Southeast Asia. There are yakuza connections with the LCN in gambling on the East Coast of the United States, and interests in oil leases, nightclubs, and travel agencies on the West Coast.

They have a very public face. Some of them have seen far too many American gangster movies: they dress like Hollywood bad guys in dark suits and sunglasses, and they even have crewcuts. They actively mix in nationalist Japanese politics – several twentieth-century Japanese leaders have had ties to the group. Affiliated gangs have been known to publish newsletters and members sometimes even print their yakuza association on business cards. After the Kobe earthquake in the mid-1990s, the first group on the scene offering assistance wasn't the government, it was Yamaguchi-gumi, the largest yakuza organization in the world. It is based in Kobe, and has 26,000 members in more than 944 affiliated gangs. There are many people in Japan who do not look on them as a criminal group, but rather, simply, as an alternative business.

After the yakuza come the Vietnamese gangs.

When Saigon finally fell to the North Vietnamese army, waves of South Vietnamese refugees were forced to look beyond their own land for sanctuary. There was a large exodus in 1975 that saw Vietnamese communities spring up on the West Coast of North America from San Diego to Vancouver, and in Europe, too, notably in France.

Five years later, a second, more powerful wave of Vietnamese left home, accounting for nearly 40 per cent of today's total Vietnamese population in North America. The largest concentrations of them settled in California, Washington, and Texas. Hidden inside this second wave, as it spread through the Pacific, North America, and Europe, were small groups of criminals and profiteers, who quickly took advantage of their own people in these emerging communities. Typically, extortion and robbery were their entry-level crimes.

Family and village alliances are an important part of Vietnamese culture, and foreign military intervention has been an important part of their recent history. Not surprisingly, gangs form along family and village lines, with organized military structures. In several cases, gang leaders were ex-military leaders.

The younger Vietnamese gang members tended to migrate to the bright lights of Chinatowns. Many of them were ethnic Chinese from Vietnam. Those who weren't were perhaps too young to harbour their parents' prejudice towards the Chinese. In other instances, they were from villages in the north where, even though Vietnam and China were at war, there was still a lot of trade going on. The presence of soldiers created black markets all along the border region: Vietnamese black marketeers traded with Chinese black marketeers, and they both traded with soldiers on both sides, too.

A symbiotic relationship developed out of the contacts these young gang members were making. The Chinese were the importers. The Vietnamese became their distributors and their muscle. That relationship is now changing as the dynamics of the Vietnamese groups change. They're becoming more sophisticated and beginning to exert themselves on an equal level with the Chinese groups. They're moving up. They're accumulating capital. They're getting the experience. And they're making connections.

Not long ago, a Vietnamese gang spotted a real opportunity – computer chips – and alighted on California's Silicon Valley exactly like a plague of locusts. Pound for pound the latest computing hardware is more valuable than heroin. The gang members forced their way into factories and warehouses at gunpoint and stole millions of dollars' worth of chips and motherboards, which they then sold into the so-called grey markets.

It took a joint task force of police from three states – California, Oregon, and Washington – to break up one operation. Although the raiding party itself was never more than twenty bad guys, there were at least fifty others involved in the trade. Most were Vietnamese gang members, but there were other Asian gang members involved as well, pointing up yet again their tendency to co-operate with anyone who can help get a job done. In this case, it's a $60 to $75 million-a-year job.

Where drug dealing is concerned, the Vietnamese come to the game with a real advantage in that they have direct access to the source. The size of Vietnam's opium crop has doubled in recent years. Its easy availability has allowed certain gangs to become independent and control a poppy-to-powder business without a Chinese connection.

Today, the FBI categorizes Vietnamese organized crime among the most serious threats to national security. The sentiment is repeated in Canada and Australia. The Australians gave shelter to thousands of Vietnamese refugees, many of whom are now second generation, with the third on its way. The gangs that developed followed a similar course to their American-based cousins, first working for the Chinese, then working with them. There is now evidence that they have become the country's major heroin importers and consequently taken control away from Chinese gangs in key markets such as Sydney and Brisbane. Yet, despite having moved in on the Chinese drug business, the two groups are doing widespread credit card fraud together, using cards manufactured in Hong Kong.

As Vietnamese gangs expand their influence, violence expands accordingly. But throughout the Western world, at least to date, much of the violence that typifies Vietnamese organized crime has largely been confined to the Vietnamese community.

Where many other gangs would wait for someone to leave their house before robbing them, the Vietnamese gangs often invade the home while the family is there. They know that many Asians don't trust banks and keep their money and jewellery at home, and they believe they need to terrorize their victims in order to get to the money.

Many law enforcement experts worry that it's only a matter of time before this sort of violence spreads outside the Vietnamese community. If and when that happens the stakes will have been raised for police and criminals alike because in the violent world of Asian organized crime, Vietnamese violence is notorious. Even other gangs that also are infamous for violence sit up and take notice. Even the Hells Angels motorcycle gang have made accommodations with Vietnamese gangs to head off confrontation.

British Columbia is the home turf of the richest Hells Angels club in the world. An organized criminal gang known to have manipulated shares on the stock market, run all sorts of lottery scams, prostitutes, and drugs, they are definitely not just a bunch of hairy guys who ride Harleys and drink beer for free because they can intimidate the bartender.

A few years ago, one of the chapter presidents in B.C. went missing. The story was quickly passed around that he was last seen entering the house of a Vietnamese drug dealer. The Vietnamese denied having any knowledge of his disappearance. It was later learned that the Hells Angel owed four hundred thousand dollars to some California bikers and they had simply grown tired of waiting for him to pay up.

But his disappearance spurred a meeting between a Chinese gang member and the Hells Angels. The Chinese fellow was trying to work his way into the middle of an alliance. He told the Hells Angels that he could control the local Vietnamese groups, but warned that there would be peace only if they made a deal. If not, there would be war. When the bikers didn't seem particularly intimidated by the prospect of a gang war, he reminded them that with the Vietnamese, war is eternal. He told the bikers: there are perhaps fifty of you in this whole province, and there are perhaps fifty of them in that apartment building down the block. If you start to kill them, then you must accept that, for the rest of your life, you will be at war with them.

He didn't get in the middle of the deal, but the Hells Angels did come to a "coexistence" accommodation with the Vietnamese.

The Dai Huen Jai are also known as the Big Circle Boys.

In the 1960s, in the China of the Cultural Revolution, the Red Guard was purged by Mao and many of its members were thrown into prison. As it happened, the prisons were laid out in a circle around Canton City. Some of the prisoners who survived starvation and torture eventually joined up again on the outside and organized themselves into small working cells. They named their criminal organization after the circular arrangement of those prisons.

Their common military background gave them discipline. Their criminal instincts drove them. They were accustomed to violence. One of the characteristics of Dai Huen Jai – and in many ways this is typical of most Chinese criminal groups – is that they are not organized along lines that could even remotely be called traditional. There is no one person sitting at the top. There is no Commission.

Today's Big Circle Boys have few or no ties with the Red Guard founders. Those men are all in their forties and fifties while most gang members are half that age. So the term Dai Huen Jai is used to describe ethnic gangs from southern China. Unlike many other Chinese criminal groups, Big Circle Boys do not have initiations and do not swear oaths.

There is a *dy-lo*, or elder brother, and there are *cy-lo*, or younger brothers. There is no set size to a cell. They fluctuate from half a dozen to whatever is needed. If the *dy-lo* is running a gambling operation, he will need loan sharks, collectors, prostitutes, dealers, and security people. If he's importing drugs, he will need fewer people. As requirements change, *cy-lo* move on. There is no required lifelong loyalty as there is in the Mafia. Some *cy-lo* stay with the *dy-lo* for their whole career. Others move all the time, depending on who's making the most money.

And therein lies the group's motivation. Money is power. There's no mystique about whom the gods have blessed and all the other legends that go along with Triad societies. The Dai Huen Jai is about making money. They market heroin and do massive credit card frauds, and everything is done with a corporate strategy. They don't think of themselves as organized criminals, they think of themselves as organized businessmen. They will co-operate with any other group. It doesn't matter to them whether they're Vietnamese, Laotian, Fukienese, Taiwanese Hells Angels, or even the LCN – it's the deal that matters, not the dealers.

They possess a special mentality, well summed up in a letter written from jail by a Dai Huen Jai to his girlfriend. He told her, "I got to know a lot of Dai Huen Jai guys here. They are mostly twenty-eight to thirty-two years. Their golden years are over. Once in middle age, with half your life over, nothing much to do except to be a criminal. It's difficult to find a job. Why work till fifty or sixty years. They want to earn lots of money then quit. Operate business. Then safely spend the other half of life."

One of the primary keys to business, the Dai Huen Jai believe – as do the other Chinese gangs, for that matter – is *guanxi*. It means "connections."

The power of the cell comes from the cell leader's networking. Cells are like fraternal organizations, where one member can always find a club house in another town. If a Dai Huen Jai cell leader in Amsterdam needs heroin, he may pick up the phone and call someone he knows in London, who will call someone he knows in Toronto, who will call someone he knows in San Francisco, who will call someone he knows in Sydney, who will call someone he knows in Hong Kong, and once the connection is made, the heroin will wind its way back to Amsterdam.

Cell leaders are always networking, calling in favours from other members who pass the request down the line until someone can fill it. Which was why, when a cell leader in New Zealand needed some muscle, the Dai Huen Jai crew that showed up to help him came from England.

Sometime in the 1980s the group went international. They established themselves first in Holland, as a beachhead for the rest of Europe, and have since taken over the Dutch heroin market. From there they moved on to Britain. Their first appearance in North America was in Vancouver. Once they had established their credentials in that city, they emigrated east across Canada and south along the West Coast, all the way down to Los Angeles. The Boys of the Circle can go wherever they like. Their reputation is their calling card: they will be accepted into another group, hidden from the police, and permitted to do business in the new territory. And so their businesses have spread.

In Quebec, for example, more than 350 hardcore Asian criminals are divided among thirty-five loosely structured gangs, two-thirds of which are national or international in scope. These gangs regularly share personnel and expertise. They don't restrict themselves to any one variety of crime: they're pure opportunists. While wiretaps on, say, an LCN family might reveal that they are into heroin, wiretaps on Asian organized groups pick up talk of gambling, extortion, loan sharking, prostitution, gun running, and drug dealing all at the same time. Theirs is a "whatever makes a buck" mentality.

Although, sometimes, the signals received by the people listening to those wiretaps can be deceiving. As part of a heroin investigation, police in Toronto were monitoring the telephones of a Dai Huen Jai group when the leader placed several calls to a Dai Huen Jai group in Montreal. The police didn't know about this second group and were pleased that such a lead had been opened. The two *dy-lo* agreed to a meeting, but kept referring to how they would look for the best dim sum. It was obviously a code of some sort. The police decided, after considering the possibilities, that dim sum stood for heroin.

Because they knew about the meeting, they could cover it, and they did. It was in a restaurant. But dim sum turned out to mean dim sum. And all the *dy-lo* did was eat lunch.

The most famous of the ethnic Chinese gangs fall under the umbrella of the Triad. The name, coined by the British in Hong Kong, refers to the triangular shape of the Chinese character for "secret society." The three points represent the relationship between heaven, earth, and man. Dating back to the seventeenth century, the Triad were resistance groups determined to overthrow the non-Chinese Manchu Qing dynasty.

Today, the Triad is not a gang but rather a society of member gangs. The league, if you will, in which teams play.

Those member gangs are organized hierarchically, although commands do not always come from the top down, nor do members send a percentage of their profits up the ladder. There are, however, initiation ceremonies and oaths that are enforced through retribution and death. But the oaths are sworn to the Triad. Loyalty is to the secret society. Membership at the gang level is fluid and easily transferred. In fact, members of one group often become members of other groups, including non-Triad gangs such as Dai Huen Jai.

What the Triad does is provide bona fides for access to all the gangs and all the gang members, like a brotherhood where the secret handshake means you've been vetted. Members of one gang can trust members of another and ask for favours. More often than not, those favours are assistance with some criminal scheme. "The best description I ever heard," says Jim Fisher, Asian crime coordinator for the Canadian Security Intelligence Service, "came from a fellow in Hong Kong who told me, Triad is the water that allows the fish to survive. His advice was, always focus on the fish."

There could be as many as fifty groups united under the Triad umbrella. Not all are active. Some are subgroups of a main group and most main groups have many subgroups. There are four major groups: 14K, based in Hong Kong with branches in Holland, the U.K. – this is the largest Triad group in Britain – New York, California, Chicago, Boston, Houston, Taiwan, Vancouver, Toronto, Australia, and New Zealand; the Wo group, consisting of several elaborately intertwined subgroups with branches in England and Scotland, and fast becoming the most powerful gang in San Francisco; United Bamboo, who are out of Taiwan and based in California, Honolulu, Phoenix, Houston, Miami, and Chicago; and San Yee On, the largest single group in the Triad, with branches in North America, Asia, and Australia, and whose membership has been estimated as high as sixty thousand.

While gangs within the Triad compete at the local level, they co-operate with each other internationally. No matter where they are, they always act within the context of their own culture. Law enforcement officers who have not been raised in that culture are severely handicapped: assessments of the Triad threat are all too often based on an inaccurate understanding of the people involved. Triad culture is reflected, for instance, in its members' approach to violence. And all too often, talk of their business skills and prowess hides the fact that they are eminently violent.

Unlike certain groups that will not hesitate to kill a law enforcement officer – the Russians are a good example – Asian gangs in general, and Chinese gangs in particular, understand that killing a cop is dumb. Instead, they might attack an officer's reputation. They will make allegations about his honesty that will tie him up in investigations for years.

However, when it comes to dealing with their own, they are extremely brutal. Instead of putting a single shot to a rival's head, they may punish him by killing his eldest son. And therein lies a defining difference between what the public thinks of as organized crime – Russian and Italian – and Asian groups.

Case in point: A gang member in Vancouver named How was trafficking heroin for a man in China. A fifty-kilo shipment was late in arriving. How complained to his boss that he was being severely pressured by his own investors. The boss didn't seem to respond. How told the man that he was losing face with his own investors and that they would exact revenge. And still the man did not respond. How threatened that if the heroin didn't get to him soon, something might happen to the man's family.

The drugs never arrived.

How invited the boss's mistress out to lunch. She arrived with her two children – both fathered by the man in China – including their five-month-old son. He told the woman that he'd been drinking and asked her to drive. He suggested a restaurant, let her four-year-old daughter sit in the front seat, and climbed into the back seat, where her son was strapped into a car seat, facing backwards.

On the way, How kept repeating what a lovely baby she had. And as he did, he took revenge on the man in China by wrapping the strings of the baby's bonnet around its throat and strangling the child.

Alien smuggling is an increasingly attractive alternative to drug trafficking. It offers multi-billion dollar profits without the same severe penalties for getting caught.

At the end of the 1990s, it was believed that the international traffic in human beings was a $7 billion industry. It is expected to double by 2005, and perhaps even double again by 2010. The International Organization for Migration reports that four million people are trafficked around the world each year. The U.S. Immigration and Naturalization Service estimates that 90 per cent of all illegal aliens are being transported by professional smugglers and transnational criminal organizations.

There is a regular influx of illegal immigrants from China into European Union states, especially those with an indigenous Chinese population, such as Britain. The United States is, however, the first choice of most Asian illegal immigrants, with Canada second. Traffic worldwide has become so huge that the INS believes there are up to a million illegal aliens warehoused around the world at any given time, waiting to make the next stage of their journey.

There are possibly as many as three hundred thousand in Moscow alone, staged there by Chinese organized crime groups with the full compliance of Russian organized crime groups. The Chinese gangs pay "rent" to the Russians for the right to use the staging post. At the same time, Russian gangs cater to the huge market demand in fake passports and visas and other counterfeit travel documents stemming from Afghanistan, Turkey, Iran, Iraq, and China. Russian and old Soviet passports sell for around five hundred dollars; with visas stamped in them to Sweden, Denmark, or Belgium, the value increases to about eight hundred dollars. American and Canadian visas are said to cost five thousand to seven thousand dollars. A visa to Britain can be had for three thousand to five thousand dollars. It is believed that several hundred thousand people leave Russia every year for the West with counterfeit passports and visas and other forged travel documents.

Up to twenty thousand illegal immigrants are estimated to be warehoused in Prague, thirty thousand in Austria, and possibly as many as one hundred thousand in France. It is known that several Asian organized crime gangs have members to coordinate their operations living permanently in California, Guatemala, Belize, and Surinam.

That's the latest smuggling hot spot. The tiny country on the northeastern corner of South America was originally a Dutch colony. Today, the fifty thousand ethnic Chinese living there make up 10 per cent of the population. Surinam is the second-poorest country in the western hemisphere – first prize goes to Haiti – which made it ripe for organized crime gangs to buy their way in and create a logistics hub for traffickers.

Cocaine passes through from Colombia to Holland, illegal immigrants pass through from China to North America. The travel routes are usually anything but straightforward. From Fujian Province, there is one well-worn route to Bangkok, then to the subcontinent – either New Delhi or Karachi – and from there to Nairobi, Lagos, or Johannesburg. Now the route splits. One branch heads for Britain via North Africa and Spain. Another crosses the Atlantic to Buenos Aires or Rio de Janeiro, then comes north either to Mexico for the border crossing into Texas, Arizona, and California, or to one of the islands, such as Cuba, which is then an easy hop to Florida or Puerto Rico, and from there to New York.

Other routes pass through Russia. From there, one goes through Poland to Germany. Another goes through the Baltic states to Scandinavia. The destination in either case might be Britain, or the United States by way of the Caribbean.

A Chinese organized criminal gang is based in São Paulo, to facilitate the movement of illegal aliens who come across on the southern route. Those who have been staged in West Africa have been aided by Nigerian criminal enterprises, also based in São Paulo. There are as many as fifty United Bamboo members based in Guatemala City who provide a similar service for illegal aliens moved through there and then into Mexico. There are instances of Vietnamese organized criminals working alongside the Chinese groups, ferrying illegal aliens in fishing vessels across the Pacific where they are dangerously off-loaded at sea onto smaller boats for the trip to Mexico and north into the States.

Occasionally, perhaps rarely, the trip has been comfortable and the route direct. In one case in 1995, eighty illegal aliens from China posed as rich businessmen to get into Canada.

A businessman in Toronto was duped by an organized Chinese criminal gang leader into setting up a tour for "investors." For a fee of C$3,600 per visitor, the Canadian businessman arranged flights, visas, and a week-long program to show the Chinese what Canada and Toronto had to offer. But shortly after the "investors" arrived, they disappeared. Only two were found by the RCMP and returned to China.

The others are believed to have made their way into the United States through Akwesasne, with the help of certain St. Regis Mohawk Natives and the Toronto-based members of the Chinese gang. The "investors" paid C$70,000 for the passage to North America.

On those rare occasions when air travel is used, flights are usually arranged through travel agencies in China actually owned by Triad society gangs.

The trip from Fujian to North America can take up to two years. It is not always a lot shorter coming into Britain. During that time the illegal aliens are subjected to appalling treatment, squalid living conditions, unsafe travel – they are herded onto often-unseaworthy ships like cattle – and in the case of women, there is always the possibility of serious sexual abuse.

The severity of the conditions first came to light in the early morning hours of June 6, 1993, when a decrepit, 150-foot, rusted-hull freighter called *The Golden Venture* ran aground off the Rockaways, near Fort Tilden, on Long Island. There were 286 illegal Chinese immigrants on board. Many of them jumped twenty-five feet into the water and tried to swim ashore. Ten died.

Their voyage began in Fujian nearly a year before, after each agreed to pay thirty thousand dollars to the traffickers. They were taken on a ten-day journey to Bangkok, mostly on foot, where they were forced to wait three months for a freighter called *Nadj II*. They were crammed on that ship for a month until it broke down off Kenya. It was six months before *The Golden Venture* arrived. When it did, they were stuffed into the hull, held there without adequate food, sanitary conditions, or even ventilation for the Atlantic crossing, during which most of them were seriously ill most of the time.

The traffickers' original plan was to rendezvous off the New England coast with a smaller vessel operated by Vietnamese organized criminals who had subcontracted with the Chinese gang to off-load the illegal immigrants at sea, warehouse them in the Boston area, then drive them to what would be virtual servitude in New York. They had all agreed to work off the monies they still owed, which in every case was a considerable sum. The fate awaiting them was slave labour in a sweatshop or forced prostitution.

That *The Golden Venture* never made the rendezvous with the

Vietnamese gang might have been the most fortunate thing that ever happened to the 276 people who lived through the trip. The crew, under orders of one of the traffickers, who had taken control of the vessel from the captain during a high-seas mutiny, sailed directly for New York instead.

Of the survivors, almost all were subsequently deported. Only forty-two were granted asylum, although additional cases are pending. The crew and the traffickers were arrested and sent to jail. Ironically, almost five years to the day after *The Golden Venture* ran aground, a boatload of Chinese illegal aliens – each of whom had paid forty thousand dollars for the trip – ran aground on the other side of New York harbour, along the New Jersey coast. One illegal alien caught in that incident had already been caught and deported as a result of *The Golden Venture* disaster.

Generally speaking, organized criminal gangs in China use two methods to ship people to North America: by sea, a treacherous voyage of forty days to four months, to the North American West Coast; and by air to Vancouver. The price of the sea voyage is now around thirty-five thousand dollars. By air it is forty-five thousand dollars. But no guarantees are given and many of these illegal aliens are caught and returned to China.

Smuggling ships have been bringing four hundred to six hundred illegal aliens from China across the Pacific every month throughout the 1990s. Most of the Chinese immigrants have come from Fujian province but smugglers are opening new "gateways," now recruiting from the next province up the coast, Zhejiang. The smugglers are anything but humane as British police discovered in June 1998 while investigating what, at first, looked to them like illegal alien smuggling. They called their investigation Operation Kronos.

A Triad gang was bringing Chinese nationals from Fujian into Britain. The route took them across various staging points in Thailand and Burma, into the Czech Republic, then to Holland, and into the U.K. At each staging point, the gang phoned back to China to demand further payment from the aliens' families. But once the gang smuggled the people into Britain, the case took an even more brutal turn: the illegal aliens were held for ransom.

Six hostages in one house were told that if their families didn't pay yet again, they would be killed. And the method the gang intended to use was horrible. The six would draw lots, and the one with the short straw would be allowed to live as long as he murdered the other five. The gang explained that the sixth man could never testify against them because by doing so he would have to confess to five murders. If the chosen hostage refused to kill the others, his hand would be cut off. And just to make certain the gang could do that effectively, they tied tourniquets around their victims' arms for a couple of days so that when a hand was cut off, the person wouldn't bleed to death. Tourniquets were still in place when the police arrived to save the hostages.

That the gang in Operation Kronos chose to transit through the Czech Republic is hardly a surprise, because Prague is the European base for several organized Asian groups. It is also proof positive that, despite history, Asian groups can work together.

If the past was the only criterion, it would be fair to say that no two Asian gangs would ever work together, that joint ventures and strategic alliances naturally go against the grain. For centuries, there's been no love lost between the Chinese and the Japanese, or between the Chinese and the Vietnamese. But then, anyone who thinks history matters to criminals has never been to Prague.

North Vietnamese immigrants first arrived in 1975 when Czechoslovakia, as it then was, agreed to take one hundred thousand "volunteer labourers" as partial payment for Czech assistance during North Vietnam's war with the United States. The first group was made up of solid, hard-working youths. But by the time Hanoi got to the second and third instalments, they'd run out of solid, hard-working youths and used the program to get rid of juvenile delinquents. By this point, too, the Czechs had grown weary of this workforce and started withholding monies due them. They promised that the Vietnamese would get the rest of their pay once they returned home. To supplement their incomes, the Vietnamese youth responded by orchestrating smuggling networks, bringing Asian goods into Eastern Europe.

By 1990, after the Iron Curtain had come down, many of those young men had firmly implanted themselves. To avoid going home, they married locals or went underground as illegal aliens. Smuggling networks matured, and the gangs running those networks matured too.

They branched out to form international alliances with other Vietnamese gangs – such as the Flying Dragons, which is made up of ethnic Chinese born in Vietnam and aligned to a similar gang in New York – or with established Chinese Triad gangs in Germany.

From smuggling Asian goods they graduated to smuggling cigarettes, and from there to smuggling drugs. Today, Vietnamese gangs in the Czech Republic control the marijuana and hashish markets, supplied by Arab and Balkan state distributors, and are the main client of Kosovar traffickers. They also deal in small amounts of heroin, supplied by two Triad groups – Red Sun and 14K – who likewise see Prague as a revolving door into Western Europe. Triad money is being laundered in Prague through local real estate deals and restaurants.

It is a certainty that any alien smuggling ring staging in the Czech Republic does so with the knowledge of the Triads already there. The Triads may even have used the Vietnamese for protection.

There is a similar Asian presence in Italy. Alien smuggling rings are based in Rome, Turin, and Florence. The gangs also traffic drugs, run extortion rackets, and oversee some prostitution. Needless to say, respect is always paid to their traditional Italian criminal hosts. In Spain, the government has always been concerned about allowing the resident Chinese population to expand. Staging illegal aliens there would therefore be too noticeable. So the gangs keep the local Asian population level, just topping it up with illegal aliens on their way to somewhere else by reusing the identification papers of local residents who pass away.

"To understand Asian crime," explains Jim Fisher, "it is essential to understand the culture. That's the basis of how they operate. That's the basis of how they choose a restaurant. That's the basis of how they make a connection for kidnapping. It's ingrained in everything they do, and if you can understand their cultural connections, you're halfway there." Unfortunately, he adds, at least for law enforcement, the other half is getting somebody to talk about it in court, finding a victim who isn't too terrified to testify.

There had been a street war in Vancouver between Gum Wa, known as the Golden Boys, and the Lotus Family, two fairly historical groups from the late 1960s and the early 1970s. Their combat peaked when a boy was beaten to death with a steel bar on the main street of Chinatown at four o'clock in the afternoon. At that hour of the day, and in that one block, there were probably eight hundred to one thousand people, most of whom saw what happened. But when the police asked for co-operation, nobody would say anything. Nobody would come forward.

Within seven months, the two group leaders were working together, robbing jewellery stores under the control of a Dai Huen Jai group. In fact, the two were arrested together in the same house. The police later learned that someone from the Dai Huen Jai group told them that there was enough money to be made here, they didn't need to fight, when they fought the police gained more information, which made it difficult for all of them. So they simply stopped fighting and started making money together.

15

MILLENNIUM BUGS

Transnational organized crime will proliferate in the next century because crime groups are among the major beneficiaries of globalization.

– Professor Louise Shelley

It has taken mankind until the earliest hours of the twenty-first century, until the dawn of the third millennium, to arrive at a point where, finally, it is possible to stuff a million dollars' worth of cash into an attaché case. The European Union in Brussels is to thank for this.

For the first two thousand years since Christ, the only time anyone has been able to manage such a feat was in spy movies when some James-Bond-or-other held up an attaché case and bragged that he had the readies right there. The problem has always been that a million in cash represents far too much bulk for one attaché case. Five would be more suitable. No longer.

The bureaucrats in Brussels have come up with the brilliant idea of issuing a note worth five hundred euros. Roughly the equivalent of $950, it drastically reduces the bulk of a million. This is a development any cash-rich, transnational organized criminal would welcome. Especially a drug trafficker, who will have considerably less trouble transporting his money around the world.

The euro also resolves a second niggling problem for transnational organized criminals. It automatically separates their money from the origin of the crime, an essential by-product of the money-laundering process.

Take, as an example, Turkish heroin sold in France. Before the appearance of the euro, traffickers were paid in francs. No matter where they went in the world with their cash – whether they pwashed it in Switzerland, or carted it off to St. Maarten and dumped it in a bank there – the francs were a dead giveaway, pointing straight back to France.

So traffickers used to worry about getting rid of their francs. Say they pre-washed into German marks, then moved into dollars. Once they'd accomplished that, they could begin to feed their cash into the banking system. Now as blips on computer screens, the money moved around the world and no one could associate the money with drugs sold in France. The Eurocrats have saved the traffickers that annoying preliminary step. Drugs sold in Spain will be paid for in euros and drugs sold in Denmark will be paid for in euros, and when the day comes that Britain surrenders the pound, drugs sold in Britain will also be paid for in euros. Traffickers will no longer have to worry that an attaché case or two of five-hundred-euro notes will lead the cops to the crime scene.

On top of that, because euros will eventually earn a place in the world's money markets and may someday even challenge the dollar for global supremacy, there will be little need for traffickers to move from euros into the traditional currency of choice, U.S. dollars. They will be able to stay in euros, which shortens the laundering process further. Better still, now that Europe's borders are gone, euros earned through crime can be transported anywhere inside the EU without anyone asking to look inside that attaché case.

It will take no more than one crooked banker somewhere inside the European Union – or one small bank owned by a criminal – to null-and-void every single money-laundering regulation in every single member state.

If a transnational organized criminal group were to be given a magic wand and granted just one wish, it would be a borderless Europe with a single currency that printed five-hundred-euro notes.

The new century will, thanks entirely to globalization, see smaller gangs join the major league of the big transnational organized groups, who will themselves form and reform alliances to create a super-league. A prime candidate for promotion are the Hells Angels.

The most famous motorcycle club in the world was born in San Bernardino, California, in 1948 when a bunch of World War II veterans decided they wanted to ride big bikes together. In those days they were just a bunch of big, hairy guys with tattoos. Nine years later, a Hells Angel named Sonny Barger opened the Oakland branch of the club, quickly turned it into the "mother chapter," and out of that came a criminal organization.

He nurtured their rebel image with sound PR techniques, trademarked their logo and their name, incorporated much of their business interests, kicked out dissenting members, brought in drug dealing as a means of paying their legal bills – and eventually of becoming very, very rich – orchestrated takeovers of smaller groups, and nudged the Hells Angels onto the international stage by opening chapters abroad.

It wasn't until nearly thirty years after Barger first came onto the scene that the Feds were able to prosecute the Hells Angels big time.

They had gone up against the gang throughout the 1960s and 1970s, prosecuting members for firearms offences, bringing them up on murder charges – a murder case against Barger was eventually dismissed – and even going after clubs as businesses under the Racketeer Influenced Criminal Organizations Act.

But in the late 1980s they took aim at the Oakland chapter and came out with dozens of convictions. They subsequently turned their attention to several chapters on the East Coast, which they were able to shut down. They also started forfeiture proceedings against various chapters, seizing property, including real estate, by claiming it had been used for drug dealing.

Of course, the Hells Angels are not the only biker-criminals. Counted among their nearest rivals are the Outlaws in Florida, the Midwest, Canada, and Australia; the Bandidos in Texas, Washington State, the South, Australia, and Marseilles, France; and the Pagans, who operate along the U.S. East Coast.

But Hells Angels have the best PR machine – their "toys for tots" program has been skilfully designed to make them look as if they care about society – and they are, without any doubt, the most violent. They are also the richest, and the only outlaw motorcycle gang with the firepower to rival the LCN or the Russians.

The structure of this transnational criminal organization is a model of Harvard Business School efficiency. The Angels are decentralized. Each club is given autonomy to operate within the overall corporate philosophy. The United States is divided into sectors, with regional officers coordinating activities and settling disputes, while the international chapters – found throughout Europe, Canada, Australia, and New Zealand, and in some South American countries – operate as separate entities. Although there is no international governing body, all the clubs are linked by a communications network that is technically superior to anything found in all but the richest police forces. Each chapter also has a designated intelligence officer whose job is to gather information about rival gang members and also police officers who might pose a threat to the gang.

Membership is strictly controlled, initiation sometimes entails killing a rival gang member, and dues are paid. All chapters are violent but some are more violent than others, and a French-Canadian chapter in Quebec is according to legend the most violent of all. One of their most celebrated members, Yves "Apache" Trudeau, admitted to killing forty-three people between 1970 and 1985. It was in 1985 that one chapter in Quebec decided to wipe out another by killing everyone in the gang. Three bikers were eventually convicted of six murders.

Because drug money is divided up among the members and not kept by the club, many Hells Angels today bother with ponytails and leather gear only for ceremonial purposes. They drive Mercedes, live in big houses, sail yachts, and wear expensive suits with white shirts and ties.

It was methamphetamine – a white powder version of speed – that made them rich. The original connection was made through Mexico. The gangs did a distribution deal with the cartels there, which gave them exclusive rights to North America. But that deal soon lapsed. The Mexicans got greedy, decided they didn't really need the Hells Angels because they could distribute meth themselves or, as a last resort, cut a more favourable deal with the drug-anxious Vietnamese gangs. Around the same time, the Hells Angels started figuring they didn't need the Mexicans and the worries about smuggling drugs across the southern border with Mexico, because they could cook the drugs themselves and get a lot less hassle moving them back and forth across the completely porous northern border between Canada and the United States.

One infamous Hells Angels meth trafficker, Kenneth Jay Owen, was arrested in 1987 with $1 million in cash hidden around his house. He was reportedly moving $230 million worth of meth at the time. He was convicted and sentenced to forty-one years, fined $2.1 million, and had an additional $2.4 million in property seized.

The gang has since expanded to traffic in hydroponic marijuana, a market they thoroughly own, growing in Canada and distributing throughout North America. The RCMP reports that there are huge tracts of land in Alberta, Saskatchewan, and Manitoba where they have constructed elephantine underground hothouses. It has been such a success that almost all the international clubs, including those in Britain, are studying the possibilities of adopting those hydroponic methods.

Hells Angels all over the world operate exactly along the same lines as their American brothers. But independent of any other groups, British chapters forged their own alliances with the Colombian cartels, held bank accounts in Switzerland, and had investments in property throughout Europe. The brains behind the Colombian connection is said to have been William "English Bill" Anderson, a man with eight convictions for possessing weapons, and who escaped from a prison in Sudbury while serving a five-year sentence for stabbing someone.

Demonstrating, again, that these are not scruffy guys in leather jackets, two of Anderson's associates were Canadian Hells Angels whom British police arrested in their suite at the London Hilton on Park Lane.

The gang bought a fleet of merchant ships to smuggle cocaine into the country. On one that was eventually seized, Customs officers found three tons of drugs. The off-loading method the gang used was to sink drugs nine thousand feet to the ocean floor and patiently wait until law enforcement was nowhere to be seen before retrieving them with a mini-submarine.

Another group of British Hells Angels had a tanker running drugs from Australia to the U.K., where watertight containers were attached to electronically activated buoys, then sunk. When the mother ship was in place to retrieve the drugs, the buoys would be activated and the containers would rise to the surface.

It wasn't until 1992 that British police even realized they had a problem with biker gangs. That was the year when a Hells Angel from the Midlands was arrested in France driving his Porsche packed with twenty kilos of marijuana.

Like the North American clubs, the British gangs have also shown a keen interest in intelligence and are known to have penetrated the Driver and Vehicle Licensing Agency, giving them the ability to track licence plates, telephone numbers, and home addresses.

In the mid-1990s, war broke out between the Hells Angels and a gang based in London called the Outcasts. The rumour is that instructions came from Hells Angels in the States that gang supremacy must be maintained at all costs. One attack on the Outcasts occurred at a public concert. Hells Angels showed up wearing headsets with microphones so they could communicate during the battle, which they fought with axes, knives, and baseball bats. There have been several deaths as a result of this war, and one Hells Angels member has been sent away to prison for fifteen years. In related cases, murder charges against other gang members were dropped when witnesses refused to testify.

But British biker gangs seem almost tame by comparison to the gangs in Scandinavia. The wars there have raged for years, with ruthless killings and shootouts in airports and on crowded streets.

Hells Angels in Switzerland have been convicted for murder, rape, procuring explosives, and trafficking $5 million worth of cocaine. Hells Angels in Holland have gone down for drug trafficking and murder. And Hells Angels in New Zealand have quietly gone about franchising local motorcycle gangs to expand their empire into the Pacific.

The new century will also be one in which old crimes are brought up to date.

Start with counterfeiting, not of negotiable instruments, such as money – there will always be that – but counterfeit software, luxury designer goods, pharmaceuticals, and airplane parts. The world market for phony goods is huge, the chances of getting caught are minimal, and even when counterfeiters do get caught, convictions and sentencing are considerably less than for drug trafficking. What's more, much of the business requires little more than the capacity to print cardboard boxes.

Filling plastic vials with some concocted chemical and putting them in boxes that have all the right markings and all the right colours and all the right minuscule disclaimers along the edge, and then shipping them in volume to South America as Viagara – or, even more reprehensible, as counterfeit baby formula – is worth tens of millions of dollars to Italian and Russian organized crime groups. Printing other perfect-copy cardboard boxes and stuffing them with reconstructed automobile brake pads or oil filters is a $12-billion-a-year business.

Even worse is the business of taking parts off airplanes made surplus by the Russian air force and selling them in counterfeit boxes to distributors of genuine airplane parts. The potential hazard to the public is staggering.

The bogus airplane part industry is still in its infancy and, for obvious reasons – not least of which is the possible provocation of widespread panic – government bodies like the Federal Aviation Agency play down the problem. They remind anyone inquiring about this subject that there are all sorts of controls in place among the world's major airlines to limit the horrendous possibility of a wing falling off in mid-air. But not every airline is a major one. It would take only one company cutting costs on something like a combustion liner, which is a critical component of a jet engine, to create a monumental disaster.

Counterfeit luxury designer goods used to be the exclusive domain of the Mafia. They had factories all over Italy producing knock-offs of every conceivable item labelled Gucci, Saint Laurent, Hermès, Vuitton, Chanel, Armani, Dior, Rolex, Piaget, Breitling, Cartier, and so on. From perfume to clothes to handbags, watches, and jewellery, they were into everything.

Successive crackdowns – first by the Italian police, because this stuff caused a nuisance, then at the insistence of the French government, because millions were being lost by French companies – prompted the Italian counterfeiters to find a better way. They started selling the goods and the labels separately. Street markets all over Europe had what appeared to be knock-off Chanel handbags, Ray-Ban sunglasses, or Hermès ties, but because they didn't say Chanel or Ray-Ban or Hermès anywhere on them, the police couldn't do much about it. After the sale, someone would slip the buyer a counterfeit label that said Chanel or Ray-Ban or Hermès. That worked for quite a while, until the Asian gangs got involved.

Chinese gangs manufactured, and Vietnamese gangs worked the street markets, and together, they pretty much took over the market. They expanded it, as well. They didn't concentrate only on high-end European designer goods; they also went into Nike, Reebok, Adidas, LaCoste, Hilfiger, Tiffany, Levi's, Swatch, Versace, Prada, and others.

Watches have always been a popular item with these gangs, even more so than they were with the Mafia, because they can be made so competitively in the Orient. A cheap quartz imitation of a designer watch can be manufactured for three to four dollars in Hong Kong. The logo, made separately, costs under a dollar. Shipping adds another dollar, tops, bringing the maximum investment to six dollars. The watch then carries a seventy-five- to one-hundred-dollar price tag on a street corner and goes for a knock-down, well-haggled price of around thirty-five dollars. It is such a big-profit, small-risk business that the former head of the Vietnamese street gang Born to Kill testified that he personally was earning $13 million a year just on Rolex and Cartier counterfeits.

With that kind of money in the pot, these gangs have approached the business like a business. They have been manufacturing their product throughout the Pacific basin precisely where the designers themselves make the real thing, and using the smuggling routes established for drugs to bring the counterfeit goods into the country. They soon realized that as long as they were counterfeiting the goods, they might as well counterfeit bills of lading, so they set up shell companies that looked like wholesalers – especially grey market and surplus wholesalers, because they would have access to product outside normal designer marketers – and started bringing goods into the country, even paying duties on them. That has the added benefit of being a way to launder drug money. Various watchdog agencies around the world tend to agree that counterfeit goods cost legitimate businesses around $200 billion in revenue each year. If the gangs are working on an average price ratio of, say, thirty cents on the dollar, that makes their counterfeiting industry worth at least $60 billion, and probably more. These gangs don't pay tax on their profits, either.

Then add counterfeit videos and CDs – usually called piracy instead of counterfeiting – into the mix. A raid some years ago at a video store in the Detroit area resulted in the seizure of twenty thousand counterfeit cassettes. Expand that across North America and into Europe and the numbers become gigantic.

Music and video counterfeiting goes on all over Eastern Europe and throughout the Middle East, notably Kuwait and Israel. It's a big money spinner for Russian organized gangs too.

But it is the software industry where the numbers are mind-bogglingly big. Not everybody wants or is even willing to pay thirty-five dollars for a phony Rolex. Not everybody wants a two-dollar copy of *Casablanca* that risks running out of tape before Rick can tell Ilsa how they'll always have Paris. But as software prices climb and official technical help lines keep you waiting for half an hour, or charge you for advice that used to be free, the idea of paying $30 for a $250 program has its obvious attractions.

They even counterfeit the manual.

The software industry complains that it loses around $12 to $13 billion a year through counterfeiting, which is nearly as much as Microsoft's 1998 sales figure. Customs in Europe and North America have gotten good at spotting these fakes – with the help of Microsoft, which makes teams available to police agencies around the world – but the border controls in Asia aren't as good, and counterfeit software there is used in staggering numbers. In Malaysia, for example, 99 per cent of all the software in the country is counterfeit. Only one out of every hundred CD-ROMs in the entire country is real. In Russia the figure is 97 per cent counterfeit. In China it's 95 per cent. In Thailand, where many of the CD-ROMs are counterfeited, the figure is 93 per cent. Singapore is 73 per cent. Hong Kong is 72 per cent.

Managing this end of the industry is only slightly more complicated than printing cardboard boxes. Here, the gangs need to copy CD-ROMs. But once they've managed that, often using the same industry-standard copiers that the major software houses use for their legitimate product, all that's left are the holograms. And they can be made by the same gangs that make counterfeit credit cards.

U.S. Customs reports seizures by the truckful of holograms. They stopped one shipment coming into San Francisco of twenty-nine thousand counterfeit Microsoft holograms. That was less than one month after they raided a factory in California and seized another batch of forty-seven thousand.

In early 1999, the FBI made what is said to be their largest ever counterfeit software bust. They raided a site in California and confiscated stacks of CD-ROMs with Microsoft logos destined for the Microsoft

Office 97 and Windows 98 markets as well as a $1.5-million commercial CD duplicator. The cache in this record bust was valued at $30 million. Given the nature of this business, the amounts of money involved, and the ease with which it happens, the betting line is that the record may not stand for long.

There will always be smuggling, but in the new century there are some high-profit products that will challenge drugs as the contraband of choice.

By international agreement, the 1987 "Montreal Protocol on Substances that Deplete the Ozone Layer" set a timetable for phasing out and ultimately banning the use of chlorofluorocarbons (CFCs). Generally used as refrigerants in home fridges, commercial refrigeration units, and car air conditioners, the most common CFC is called Freon. Among Freon's industrial and commercial uses, for example, are cooling supermarket display cases and, interestingly enough, cleaning computer chips.

A single sixteen-ounce can of CFCs, the kind that used to be sold at auto supply shops for people to pour into their car air-conditioning systems, can destroy seventy thousand pounds of the ozone layer.

With other, less harmful substitutes readily available, 130 nations agreed that getting rid of CFCs was the right thing to do. Except that not everybody who agreed to do it, did it. Today the hole in the ozone layer is much larger than it was then – it's now bigger than all of Europe – and Freon is high on the list of highly profitable illicit materials, alongside drugs. In some cases, there is reason to believe that it is trafficked by people with interests in both. The main source is Russia.

Although Russia – it was the Soviet Union then – originally signed the Montreal Protocol, they have since opted out on the grounds of being "a developing country." Russia is a major producer of CFCs, and production at seven former state-owned factories is now at levels far exceeding local demand. A European chemical publication estimated that Russian organized crime groups have been flooding Europe with a thousand tons of CFCs every month. A standard forty-foot container holds around a thousand thirty-pound cylinders of Freon, or fifteen tons. At around half a million dollars per container – and sixty-five to seventy containers per month – the *Maffiya*'s European turnover in CFCs is around $35 million.

The North American market is half again as important, with an estimated eighteen thousand tons being shipped annually. An estimated eighty million pre-1994 cars are on the road in North America and they are expected to still be on the road in some numbers until 2006. Their air conditioners support the smugglers.

It is also said that smugglers, over a three-year period in the middle of the 1990s, brought sixty million pounds of CFCs into the U.S.

In many cases, traffickers take advantage of a loophole in the law, which permits some movement of recycled CFCs. They simply label their shipments "recycled materials." It works because telling the difference between recycled and non-recycled Freon is very difficult. And anyway, once it slips past Customs and is mixed with the available supply, it's impossible to prove it was non-recycled Freon.

Even if it gets stopped by Customs, detection is not much easier. The fastest way for inspectors to distinguish between Freon and legal refrigerants is to check the pressure in the containers. Freon is kept at a lower pressure than legal refrigerants. So traffickers add inert nitrogen to Freon to raise it to admissible levels. Customs has had to resort to special devices that can identify gasses through wavelengths of infrared light. It's a lengthy procedure, meaning that only spot checks are possible. By one estimate, 15 to 20 per cent of all the CFCs currently in use around the world is contraband Freon.

Knowing that U.S. Customs were on the lookout for CFCs coming in from China, Russia, and India, some smugglers started transshipping through Mexico and Canada. Others found supplies in Britain and Australia and moved those into the United States. And just like drugs, when Customs cracked down on CFCs coming into the port of Miami, the traffickers shifted to the southern border and brought them across from Mexico.

In Tijuana, a town where you can buy just about anything – shops and storefronts sell sex, drugs, counterfeit software, pirated CDs, pirated videos, and kiddie porn – there are now signs hanging out in front of stores saying, "We Have Freon." A two-hundred-dollar canister purchased there is worth four times as much to a wholesaler in California and ten times as much when parcelled out to the retail market.

Tijuana is the world's busiest border crossing – probably the noisiest, too – averaging thirty-seven thousand cars a day. Customs inspectors do what they can to stop Freon smuggling but it isn't much because looking for drugs takes up most of their resources. They still get an average of one Freon smuggler per day. These are people smuggling 200 thirty-pound cylinders per trip. At commercial points of entry, the seizures are bigger. And there, the Russians are not the only traffickers in the business. A woman in Ft. Lauderdale, Florida, got caught smuggling three thousand tons of Indian-manufactured CFCs into the U.S. with a street value of $52 million. She wound up serving almost five years in prison.

Another shipment of eighty-four hundred tons was seized en route from India to Mexico when smugglers attempted to divert it to the U.K.

In Philadelphia, one firm was charged with conspiring to smuggle more than fifty-two thousand cylinders of CFCs into the country. It would have made them a $10 million profit. A company in Maine got caught importing 246 tons from Canada. The U.S. Justice Department even extradited a Freon offender from Costa Rica on charges of conspiring to import three hundred tons of Freon. He was accused of using shell companies to cover the smuggling, then to launder the profits into offshore accounts. He eventually pleaded guilty.

One smuggler was arrested for shipping forty-six tons from Britain and Australia into the U.S.

In Europe, a small German company imported eighty containers, with twelve tons of CFCs in each, from China, bringing them into Rotterdam with false paperwork. Once inside the European Union, the accompanying documents were changed to read "recycled CFCs."

In Hong Kong, dozens of companies have been charged with illegally importing CFCs from China, where production is still taking place, for use there and markets in Australia and the West Coast of America and Canada. CFCs bought in China, for instance, sell for one dollar a pound. They can be resold in North America for fifteen to twenty-five dollars a pound.

For several years after signing the Montreal Protocol, one of the worst offenders was Britain. Even though it was clearly illegal, CFCs were still being imported into the U.K. as late as 1995. That year, nearly four thousand tons entered the country.

According to the United Nations, in the eight years that followed the Montreal Protocol, after everyone had agreed to phase out CFCs, production increased by nearly 90 per cent. Exports increased seventeen-fold. India flooded the Middle East with CFCs. The Chinese flooded Asia with CFCs. Despite the supply curve heading sharply upwards, the price curve did too. Prices in some countries trebled. In the U.S. and Canada, they increased as much as ten-fold. When Britain finally complied with the 1987 agreement, nearly ten years later, the Russians moved in big time to fill the gap.

In Brownsville, Texas, Ernesto and Antonio Medina ran an export business called Medina Forwarding Corp. They'd contracted to ship 1,200 thirty-pound cylinders of CFCs from Russia through their warehouse to Mexico. This was a perfectly legal transaction, because Mexico also enjoys Third World exemptions from the Montreal Protocol. The goods arrived on schedule at the port of Houston and were trucked in bond down to Brownsville. Six weeks later, the cylinders were driven out of the warehouse en route to Mexico.

U.S. Customs inspectors at the Brownsville-Matamoros bridge did a routine check of the tractor-trailer and the accompanying paperwork. The listed value of the shipment, ten thousand dollars, didn't seem right, so they made a thorough search of the tractor-trailer. They found an eight-thousand-dollar invoice from an Ohio company for empty cylinders. That turned their attention to the cylinders being exported. And they were empty.

The Medinas were arrested, and eventually pled guilty. But not before their connection was traced. The CFCs had been dispatched from Brownsville to two men in New York who moved them into the retail market. And those two were connected back in Russia.

Production in the Third World won't be stopped, at least officially, until 2010. As that deadline draws closer, supplies will dwindle. A pack-rat stockpiling mentality will, by then, have driven demand and prices – and profits for transnational organized crime groups – right through the very ozone layer the Montreal Protocol was designed to protect.

Another high-ticket item for smugglers will always be people. As U.S. and Canadian authorities have cracked down, illegal alien traffickers have moved their operations to Mexico. Organized criminals there act as brokers – the remnants of the Amado Carrillo Fuentes drug cartel is said to be one of the main gangs involved – receiving the aliens and moving them north into the U.S. An astonishing 1.75 million people are apprehended every year just along the U.S.-Mexican border. No one knows exactly how many get through.

Other active human smuggling networks are found in countries with certain ethnic populations – Korean, Thai, Indian, Pakistani, and Bangladeshi – and, increasingly, in Europe, where people from the former Yugoslavia have settled.

Kosovar and Albanian gangsters exploited the Balkan refugee crisis, as did the Italian Camorra. Gang members patrolled the refugee camps, looking for anyone willing to buy their way out of there and into Western Europe, especially Britain. Because there is no inherent difference between smuggling people and smuggling drugs, the gangs take people across the established drug routes. And for the Albanians and Kosovars, the routes are well established. Interpol reports that one out of every eight drug traffickers arrested in Europe is either Kosovar or Albanian. The price for the one-way, no-guarantees trip from the Balkans to Britain has been reported to be three thousand pounds.

It is considerably less than Chinese illegals have to pay. The best deal for them appears to be a C$2,400 one-way trip which includes a Russian-made counterfeit passport and, Interpol believes, access to a lawyer in Britain if the authorities get involved.

Aliens have been found hidden in trucks, in buses, under trucks, under buses, inside freight, and in luggage compartments of trains. According to those authorities, seven hundred to eight hundred illegals are caught annually trying to come into Britain, although the figure is rising sharply every year. At the beginning of the 1990s, it was only one-tenth as many. How many get through is another matter.

Those women who don't get caught often wind up forced into prostitution to pay back their smuggling fees. This is in addition to the women and children who are trafficked around the world specifically to supply the sex trade.

Well-organized traffickers using sophisticated international networks, often with the compliance of corrupt government officials in the countries supplying women, bring women into industrialized countries, especially the European Union, from the former Soviet Union and Eastern European bloc, and from Ghana, Nigeria, Morocco, Brazil, Colombia, the Dominican Republic, the Philippines, and Thailand.

Exact figures are impossible to come by, but the International

Organization for Migration believes that more than five hundred thousand women are illegally trafficked each year – that figure could be doubled by 2010 – while the International Campaign to End Child Prostitution in Asian Tourism says that criminal organizations operating in Russia, the Ukraine, and Belarus are behind much of the trafficking.

A Brazilian man was sent to prison in 1998 for his role in smuggling women into Britain over an eight-year period beginning ten years previously. Over that same period, he reportedly earned C$12 million for his services.

In 1998, Operation Seek and Keep broke up an alien smuggling cartel, said to be the largest in U.S. history, responsible for bringing nearly twelve thousand people, mostly South Asians, through Russia, Cuba, and the Bahamas. They were delivered into the United States at the behest of South Asian businessmen already established in the country who were looking for sweatshop labour.

The investigation was led by the Immigration and Naturalization Service with the help of law enforcement in Canada, Ecuador, the Dominican Republic, the Bahamas, and India. Its complexity was underlined by the fact that during the year it lasted, law enforcement agencies monitored more than thirty-five thousand telephone calls. Among those identified as ringleaders were two men carrying British passports with addresses in London. Nitin Shettie used the alias Nick Diaz. He was arrested in the Bahamas. Navtej Pall Singh Sandhu was arrested in Puerto Rico. They stand accused of bringing illegal aliens into North America over a three-year period to supply low-cost businesses with cheap labour. The price for the journey was twenty thousand to twenty-eight thousand dollars, making this venture worth $240 million. In a few reported cases, instalments were demanded at different points along the smuggling route. If the aliens couldn't pay, the owners of the businesses being supplied were required to put up the money. They then held the illegal aliens in servitude until they paid back the fees, with all the usual interest charges added on. The gang's money was laundered in Canada and the United Arab Emirates, before being wired on to India.

There are some people in Britain who believe a similar network brings South Asians into the U.K. by contract with low-cost businesses, often in the fast-food industry.

Another circuit, used by another group, has South Asians being moved through Russia to Nicaragua, then through Guatemala and Mexico. The illegal aliens are then escorted to the Rio Grande, where they are given inner tubes to float across the river.

As long as cash is king, money laundering will be a major preoccupation for transnational organized criminal gangs, who will, more and more, form joint ventures to make their cash disappear. But it won't go on for very much longer, because technology is offering better solutions.

The magnetic strip on the back of every credit card tells a computer somewhere that this is your card, that you control a certain amount of money, and that, as long as the PIN number used with this card is correct, a transaction can be completed. The magnetic stripe can be read by ATM machines in Oslo and Singapore and Ecuador, allowing you to have access to your money globally. But buying something with a credit card or getting a cash advance through an ATM machine involves a third party – a store, a bank, a credit servicing agency – and therefore leaves a record of the transaction. Which is why bad guys don't use credit cards. They don't want a trail that can lead back to them.

The future is theirs.

Over the next few years, credit cards will be implanted with microchips that will, effectively, turn the card into a bank. It is already commonplace in its crudest form – phone cards. When a person purchases a five-dollar phone card from a newsagent in Winnipeg she can make calls in Halifax without anyone being able to connect the purchase of the card to the call she made on it. The caller and the card are completely anonymous. Whoever owns the five-dollar microchip, controls the money implanted in it.

Now consider the next two stages. Because the microchip is the money, the difference between five dollars and fifty thousand dollars is simply a matter of programming. Similarly, the difference between a card that allows only withdrawals and one that permits deposits, too, is also simply a matter of programming. Banking corporations all over the world are rushing to develop and market this particular new product. The demand for it is certain to be substantial. It is no longer a question of *if* it happens – it will happen soon – and when it does, the world we know will change, yet again.

For all intents and purposes, we will have our bank in our pocket. The card with the sophisticated microchip will come along with what's called a "wallet" – something about the size of a pocket calculator – into which two cards will fit. The wallet will read the value implanted on both microchips and transfer some of it between cards.

It will no longer be that John Doe has a thousand dollars in his bank account, and every time he writes a cheque there is a paper trail of the transaction. John Doe will now have a thousand dollars implanted in a microchip, which he can spend simply by validating a PIN number, without any record whatsoever of the transaction. Or, John Doe will be able to receive a thousand dollars from another card through the exact same procedure, without any record whatsoever of the transaction.

We will buy our newspapers this way, or our drugs this way, or be paid our salary this way, or be paid for a shipment of heroin this way.

There will be no account because there's no need to have an account. The value goes from one chip to another chip. And it won't even have to be done face to face. It will be done long distance for the price of a local phone call thanks to the Internet. By slipping the microchip into a special reader attached to a computer with a modem, value can be transferred from the chip you've been carrying in your pocket to a chip in Cali, Colombia, or in Ottawa, Ontario, or in the Cayman Islands. There won't be an account relationship because the value is going directly from one chip to another without the intermediary bank involved.

It is a legitimate product with unlimited advantages. An obvious one is that cash and cheques, both of which are expensive methods for making payments, will become things of the past. That will save many businesses enormous amounts of money. It will also save governments great sums because they will no longer have to mint currency, store it, or pay it out.

The United States government, for example, sends out one million cheques a week, to cover everything from salaries, social security, and retirement to welfare and Medicare payments. To cut down on those costs, a law has been proposed that all payments should be made electronically, that money should be transferred directly into bank accounts. It would be fast, there would be no risk of loss in the mail, it would be convenient for everyone, and it would be cost-efficient.

Fifteen per cent of the American people don't have bank accounts. And the government can't make someone have a bank account if they don't want one. Smart cards with two-way withdrawal-and-deposit microchips solve that problem.

As long as people trust the value implanted on their microchip, the system will work. And there is no reason why we won't come to trust microchips as money. After all, we've learned to put out trust in pieces of paper. There was a time when you could take a dollar bill to the government and they would give you several pieces of silver for it. But quarters aren't silver anymore. The piece of paper is backed only by the government's word. Microchips similarly will be acts of faith: it's called trusted value. What's more, they will be multi-currencied. You may have one thousand dollars on your chip and need to spend five hundred pounds. The card will automatically handle the currency conversion.

Until now, cash has been one of the major hurdles that transnational criminal organizations have had to deal with. That problem is being solved. Suddenly, a million or ten million will fit into your back pocket.

The future is theirs.

Microchip technology will make even five-hundred-euro notes look like the bad old days.

In the meantime, credit card fraud and cybercrime form a new, and very dangerous, category, called "Identification Theft."

At the end of the 1980s, sophisticated credit card frauds were negligible because the technology wasn't there to support them. By the end of the 1990s, as gross bank card volume hits $10 trillion, cumulative credit card fraud losses are fast approaching $15 billion. It is a major growth industry.

Credit card fraud investigators singled out six specific problem areas in the world. They are California, where nearly one-fifth of all U.S. credit card fraud losses occur, Florida, Texas, New York, Asia, and Great Britain.

Regardless of what the credit card companies do to stop it, whatever security measures they put in place, it's almost as if the transnational criminal organizations behind these frauds are one step ahead.

Magnetic stripes were supposed to solve the problem because they contained sophisticated algorithms that were "impossible" to break. So the bad guys learned to copy magstripes and break algorithms. Then someone decided holograms were the answer. So the bad guys learned to make holograms. There has been talk of voice prints and photos, but that won't solve much because the bad guys can easily put their own voice prints and photos on the cards, and set up the magstripes to match. PIN numbers haven't been a cure-all either.

The Dai Huen Jai were among the first to crack PINs, by installing video cameras near ATM machines so they could watch people punching in their codes.

Some credit card companies are betting that smart cards will be the future, offering them the protection they need. Some law enforcement officers who deal daily with professional credit card fraud are betting that smart card chips won't last two months before they're compromised.

In those rare instances when an international effort to combat identification crime has been mounted, there have been successes. One recent case began with the arrest of some Malaysians in Britain who were using counterfeit credit cards to buy diamonds and gold. When that was followed by arrests of more Malaysians using comparable cards in Denmark, Sweden, and South Africa, the authorities in Kuala Lumpur were notified. They then spent a year to hunt down and break up the ring behind the cards. Similar successes are few and far between.

"Dai Huen Jai absolutely dominate this market in Canada," says Jim Fisher. "Just under $70 million is currently being lost every year by Canadian institutions through counterfeit credit cards. That's not phony applications or subscription fraud or stolen cards, that's just counterfeit cards. Some Tamils and Iranians are moving into the business but the Dai Huen Jai are 99 per cent of it. They're the counterfeiters in Canada."

The Russians have also discovered credit cards. Their act is to create non-existent shops, use them to charge large sums to stolen cards, take the money, and leave the banks wondering how both the customer and the store disappeared.

More sinister is the idea that credit cards are just one facet of identity theft. Access to someone's individuality – which in the age of computers is often represented by a PIN number, date of birth, and mother's maiden name – provides access to that person's bank balance. It also gives access to a wide range of credit, cash, goods, and services.

In 1997 the FBI arrested Carlos Salgado in San Francisco. He was attempting to sell a CD-ROM that he'd made which contained information about a hundred thousand people. The information had been obtained from credit card accounts held by a company doing business on the Internet. He bought the data from them. Considering the damage that could have been inflicted with this information, his asking price seemed cheap at a mere $2.60 per account.

The Internet is, arguably, the most powerful force on the planet since Christ.

The possibilities offered by the Net for both good and evil are unlimited. The extent of criminality already present is staggering, and the future is beyond comprehension.

In 1994, twenty-year-old Vladimir Leonidovich Levin pleaded guilty to having gained access to a computer system inside Citibank's Cash Management System in New York and to having transferred $3.7 million into accounts that he and his partners controlled in Finland, the Netherlands, Germany, Israel, and the United States. He managed it all while sitting in front of a laptop in an office in St. Petersburg, Russia.

Since cyberbanking opened a hornet's nest of potential financial fraud, the FBI has had their hands full. They monitored Levin's intrusion into Citibank, not knowing who or where he was, from July until October 1994. They recorded forty transactions as he wired money from Argentina and Indonesia to San Francisco, Finland, Russia, Switzerland, Germany, and Israel. In the end, they arrested six foreign nationals and recouped all but four hundred thousand dollars.

Levin himself was arrested at Heathrow Airport in February 1995 by Scotland Yard and extradited to the U.S. in September 1997. He pled guilty the following January, was sentenced to three years and a fine covering the losses that Citibank hadn't been able to recoup. He is now out.

Until his deportation, he'd never set foot in New York. And therein lies the very nature of cybercrime. Anybody can be anywhere because cyberspace is nowhere. It's almost as if it was another dimension. And, as such, it is almost always beyond the reach of law enforcement.

Like so many of the hackers who have come before him, Levin was an amateur working a makeshift scheme, leaving a money trail to be followed. It will not be the same when transnational organized crime groups use their economic power to buy the kinds of skills and set up the kinds of scams that don't leave a money trail.

Not long ago, the Boeing Corporation in Seattle had to change the PIN numbers used by employees to access certain retirement accounts because someone, somewhere, cracked the code.

The *Times* of London reported that a number of banks in the City have paid fees to hackers who successfully invaded their computer systems. While the banking industry denies making any payoffs, police officers insist that at least some of the reported stories are true.

Stories abound pointing up the vulnerability of organizations that believed they were secure. Hackers, meanwhile, hold publicly advertised conventions in Las Vegas. In 1996, one group got to the New York City police department. They infiltrated a telephone switchboard so that people dialling a precinct would hear this message: "You have reached the New York City police department. For any real emergencies, dial 9-1-1. Anyone else – we're a little busy right now eating some doughnuts and having coffee."

The Center for Strategic and International Studies claims that cybertheft from banks averages $250,000, while bank stickups only average around $6,000. Nearly 80 per cent of the balaclava variety get caught. Fewer than 1 per cent of the computerized bank robbers are ever found.

Another huge area of concern is cargo theft. It is said to be a $10 billion business. Organized thieves somewhere in the world gain access to freight-forwarding companies and airlines, seek out shipments of goods, and digitally reroute them to their own warehouses. It is fast, efficient, and highly profitable. By the time someone realizes the goods are missing, they have disappeared into some untraceable black market. Even if the goods are somehow found, the cyberthieves are usually thousands of miles away.

In a very real sense, the Net is being turned into the digital equivalent, or smart-fraud medium, of what might be called dumb frauds, such as telephone canvassing and sweepstakes gimmicks. For instance, a company that went on the Net under the website name Netware International is said, by the FBI, to have been nothing but a pyramid selling scheme. Their website suggested they were forming a private bank with deposits insured by the National Union Fire Insurance Company of Pittsburgh. They then claimed that the bank would declare profits of around 25 per cent a year, and that those monies would be divided up among those members – apparently they had already solicited funds from twenty-five hundred people – who sold at least two more memberships. National Union Fire Insurance Company immediately and vehemently denied any affiliation with Netware. The FBI has since seized $1 million from Netware.

Clearly the old rules no longer apply.

Cybercrimes affect a wide variety of industries, businesses, and citizens. The 1999 Melissa virus, which disrupted e-mail, illustrates how vulnerable computers have become. Cybertheft of trade secrets illustrates one way in which such vulnerability can cost industry, businesses, and citizens billions of dollars.

The Web is a sewer of fraud, scams, and piracy. It is unpoliced and unpoliceable. The argument is made that freedom of speech and freedom of the press demand it stay unpoliced. Proponents argue that it represents the ultimate inalienable right of citizens to speak freely, think freely, and congregate freely, even if some of those citizens are speaking, thinking, and congregating for criminal reasons. But that does not mean industry, businesses, and citizens should not be protected. It simply suggests that such protection should serve industry, businesses, and citizens, not governments with their own agendas.

In a white paper titled "Criminal Threats to Business on the Internet," published by Global Technology Research Inc. of Portland, Oregon, the author, Kent Anderson, outlines seven levels of Internet intruders:

- Low level threats, being stereotypical hackers such as the ones who accessed a computer system in the Czech Republic and walked away with $1.9 million.
- For-profit fraudsters, who are often the digital equivalent of the old telephone canvassers, sweepstakes fraudsters, and the people behind the Freedom Star National Bank of Arizona who went on the Net offering high interest rates to depositors, and only got stopped when the Office of Controller of Currency in Washington happened to notice that no one had ever granted this bank a charter.
- Organized criminals, such as the gang that successfully penetrated the security systems of the Bank of Russia in Moscow and walked away with $4.7 million.
- Political, religious, and anarchists' fringe groups, such as the German Chaos Computer Club that tried to extort money from the French

telecommunications industry in protest against nuclear testing in the Pacific.

- Industrial espionage and sabotage, which according to an FBI study of five hundred companies suggests that nearly two-thirds of them had suffered computer security breaches during a twelve-month period.
- International espionage and information warfare, which is the ability to intercept phone calls, fax transmissions, and e-mail, a feat well within the grasp of an experienced crypto-technician and made all the more real by the fact that experienced crypto-technicians are available for hire to transnational criminal organizations around the world.
- Terrorists, an obvious threat to national stability, especially in a situation where they team up with transnational organized crime groups first to empty the coffers of a national health-care or social security network, then to digitally dismantle it.

All of these threats will, however, pale by comparison in the new millennium.

The main targets will be global banks and those multinational corporations using "electronic data interchange." That's where companies farm out many of their billing, invoicing, and other data services to specialist companies overseas.

It is only a matter of time before a transnational organized crime group sets up such a company, runs it successfully for several years to gain a reputation and trust, then empties out their clients' bank accounts, wreaking unimaginable devastation on multinational business and possibly even crippling certain sectors of the Western economy.

When it happens, with the bad guys being light years ahead of the good guys, there may not be a law enforcement agency anywhere on the planet who will know where to look.

EPILOGUE

As good advances by the foot, evil leaps by the yard.

– Chinese proverb

The criminal justice system is on the verge of collapse.

Petty cases clog the courts. Complex frauds bemuse juries who vote to acquit because it's easier than trying to understand them. Loopholes are often illogical and large enough to drive a Mack truck through. Prosecutors have neither the time nor the budget to take on an otherwise important case if it doesn't have better than a fifty-fifty chance of ending in a conviction. Transnational organized criminals hide behind governments they've bought, lawyers with the skills, know-how, and funds to impede the system, bankers and accountants and company formation agents who are not held responsible for the obstructions they deliberately create, and international borders that keep law enforcement at bay as a rule rather than the exception.

In Britain, when it comes dishing out justice to major criminals, the Crown Prosecution Service has a thoroughly dismal track record.

In Canada, the police are so stretched for funds that it is now impossible to mount a long-term undercover investigation targeting transnational criminals.

In the United States, a proposed law that would have required banks to be much more vigilant about money laundering was soundly defeated by a lobby entirely financed by the U.S. banking industry.

With drug trafficking now accounting for 2 per cent of the world's economy, Louise Shelley, director of the American University's Center for Transnational Organized Crime and Corruption in Washington, sees this as a defining issue of the twenty-first century, just as the Cold War was for the twentieth and colonialism was for the nineteenth. "No area of international affairs will remain untouched, as political and economic systems and the social fabric of many countries will deteriorate under the increasing financial power of international organized crime groups."

She sees national security threatened by continuing trade in nuclear materials; large-scale arms smuggling fuelling regional conflicts; the human costs of international drug trafficking and illegal alien smuggling observable in both source and destination countries; and the massive profits of these transnational organized crime groups, laundered in international financial markets, undermining the security of the world financial system.

The key word is sovereignty.

What chance is there of anything happening if it means turning over protected rights to some international authority? Justice throughout the English-speaking world is a direct descendant of the infrastructure of colonial Britain. The French and Belgians built their system on the Napoleonic Code. The two traditions vary greatly. It is common practice in the United States and Canada, for example, for law enforcement to mount sting operations. As long as they function within set guidelines, the results are admissible in court. The Napoleonic Code prohibits acts of *agents provocateur*. (Interestingly enough, there is no handy French expression for "undercover cop.") German law has come from other roots, yet again. Until recently, wiretaps were totally illegal in Germany. They are now legal, but only under certain, very restricted conditions.

The United States Constitution guarantees, as an inalienable right, Fifth Amendment protection. No defendant can be forced to testify against himself. But the right of the accused to remain silent is not the same under British law. So where do the twain meet? If some super-jurisprudence is drawn up, will it include Fifth Amendment rights? There is no way Americans would subscribe if it doesn't. What then of undercover operations in France and wiretaps in Germany? How ready would those two systems be to sacrifice their long-established legal principles?

When the European Union established Europol, a police structure specifically designed to investigate drug trafficking and terrorism within the EU, a furious debate raged over what powers it would have. In the end, the politicians in Brussels did what politicians everywhere always do whenever faced with difficult questions. They fudged an answer that protects their own interests rather than solving the problem.

Europol's powers were so whittled down in the name of national sovereignty that it functions today as little more than a repository of whatever information the member states are willing to share. Europol does not have an operational role. It is not a Europe-wide police force with powers of arrest. It is just another level of bureaucracy. The politicians merely built a superstructure on top of the already top-heavy white elephant that is called international law enforcement co-operation. "Europol must become an operational force," says Michael Sika in Vienna. "It should be a European version of the FBI. It is necessary, and vitally important, but it will be very difficult to do because it will require member states to give up some sovereignty. That will take a very long time."

Europol still doesn't talk to everyone in Europe. Switzerland, which is not a European Union member, is one of Europe's biggest transit centres for drugs, one of the world's most important money-laundering centres and outside Europol.

North America is the world's largest market for illicit drugs and the prime target of transnational criminal organizations, so one might expect that there would be full co-operation between Europol and the United States and Canada. But why should Europol succeed where Interpol has failed?

For public consumption, everything is hunky-dory. Privately, American law enforcement deeply distrusts these sorts of organizations. They worry enough already about sharing information among themselves. Trying to get U.S. agencies to share intelligence can be like pulling teeth. Bring in Interpol and they're outright phobic.

At Interpol Headquarters in Lyon, France, officials remind the Americans that they only keep post-arrest information. That they don't maintain an intelligence database which might otherwise be accessed by any law enforcement anywhere in the world. That while they do handle intelligence material, they always return it to the agency it's come from. That any agency can classify anything they send to Interpol as they see fit, and specify who can and cannot see it.

When they're being diplomatic and quoted, American law enforcement officers insist that everything works perfectly well, that Interpol serves a much-needed purpose, that they have full confidence and co-operate at every turn. When they're being frank, and not credited as a source, they admit it's a load of bureaucratic crap.

Britain offers a perfect illustration of why everybody really needs to start again, of why new rules might be the only answer.

Besides being a drug market, the U.K. is also a major transshipment point. Couriers come through on their way to and from North America. Arresting a courier at Heathrow with a few kilos of cocaine is a short-term measure that keeps that much off the streets. But getting the guy in the middle doesn't put even a minor dent into the much larger, global scope of drug trafficking. To manage that, the Brits need to get to the people on both ends of the deal. That means arresting the people who control the business. They may or may not be in Britain. And in most cases, they aren't.

In order to act, someone has to turn the courier, get him or her to co-operate, which can only be done if they can also secure all the authorizations required, locally and internationally, to bring about the controlled delivery. As it happens, controlled deliveries are managed all the time from the U.K. to the States, Canada, Switzerland, Germany, France, and Italy. They are a very important law enforcement tool. But each one requires all the relevant authorities to agree.

If a law enforcement officer in Birmingham, England, makes a request for assistance that has to go up his force's chain of command, then to the Home Office, then to the Foreign Office, then across the Atlantic to the State Department, then to the Justice Department, then to the FBI, then to some state authority and then down the chain of command to the police in Birmingham, Alabama, just to get someone there to look after a courier and a controlled delivery, it's not going to happen.

The answer comes back to Louis Freeh's "cop-to-cop bridges" – street-level planks of wood that ordinary cops can use to step over the bureaucratic puddles. Some sort of system that would allow the investigator in one Birmingham to telephone an investigator in the other Birmingham and, in effect, to hand over some sort of deputized authority to act in this case.

International law enforcement meetings and conventions are great networking opportunities – a way to establish bridges – but, invariably, sovereignty and jurisdiction get in the way.

Law enforcement around the world must be able to form joint ventures and strategic alliances with one another – easily, fluidly, and without bureaucrats or politicians in the middle to screw it up – exactly the same way transnational criminal gangs form their mergers.

Given that radical problems merit radical solutions, there are many people now proposing that the intelligence services – which are, by nature, extra-jurisdictional – be given a role in law enforcement, much along the lines of the British experiment.

Both MI-5 and MI-6 have been recruited into the war on organized crime. Funds have been committed and personnel assigned. All that's missing are answers to questions such as, will intelligence officers with material information in a case be called to testify? If not, if they are shielded by national security considerations, what then of the defendant's right to face his accusers?

There are strict laws in Britain that the police must adhere to in the gathering of evidence, especially where wiretaps are concerned. MI-5 and MI-6 and the folks at GCHQ – the government's secret listening post – are not bound by those same restrictions. How then does the information obtained by them get called into evidence?

Even if laws were passed in Britain that permitted secret agents to use code names and to testify behind screens, or for GCHQ wiretaps to be considered de facto proof without technicians being subjected to cross examination, if information is obtained by means that are otherwise beyond police authority, how would any of that hold up in the pursuit of criminals outside British borders? Would evidence presented in such a trial be sufficient to demand someone's extradition from Canada that doesn't recognize the use of GCHQ's eavesdropping or the untested documentation of a James Bond?

Putting aside the fact that, over the years, most intelligence services have shown very poor judgement – witness the CIA's record on Vietnam and Iran-Contra, and their total failure to predict the disintegration of the Soviet Union – there are just too many serious legal hurdles that would have to be jumped in order for the spy services to be effective law enforcement agencies. And even if the changes were made, it isn't certain the agencies would be effective.

By definition, crime is a violation of some law. By definition, law enforcement is about mechanisms, organizations, and policies charged with bringing about compliance of the existing laws. Implied is that law enforcement will always operate within the rule of law. But the intelligence agencies are not mandated to operate within the rule of law. Their job is to do whatever they have to, with very few limitations, in order to accomplish their mission. Although political assassination was ruled out by U.S. law after the death of President Salvador Allende in Chile, other nations do not observe similar limits. Would that mean a Pablo Escobar who stayed beyond jurisdictional reach could be assassinated?

It seems fair to wonder, for instance, where at CIA headquarters they keep their copy of the Constitution. Is it on the same shelf as their operating manuals?

Matty Maher, a former director of international operations for the DEA, has studied this particular point in detail. "The intelligence services are the first to tell you, we don't operate inside the country, we operate outside. So then explain to me, how can you declare transnational crime, or drug trafficking, as threats to national security and then say that the intelligence community will only operate outside the three-mile limit on these issues? Because if you're operating outside the three-mile limit and you develop intelligence or evidence about criminal activities that are also threats to national security, then what exactly have you gathered? Is it top-secret national security information, or is it evidence of a crime that needs to be shared in a law enforcement context and used in criminal proceedings? It's that dichotomy which causes the problem."

He says that using the term "threat to national security" is like using the term "pregnant." Either you are or you aren't. It is or it isn't.

"Is transnational crime up there with Korean missiles and nuclear generators? Is drug trafficking up there with warheads in the Ukraine? If it's not, then why are we calling it this? Because once you call it a threat to national security, you have put this thing in a whole new package and the rules should change substantially."

Regardless of the product – weapons, drugs, counterfeit credit cards – the suppliers are outside the country. But the distribution organizations, the profit-making mechanisms, the money-laundering machines are inside the country. The two ends meet in the middle and form a conspiracy. It can be vertical, horizontal, a hubbed wheel, whatever, but it's a conspiracy under the definition of conspiracy: two or more people having a common goal of committing a criminal offence.

Maher can't see how the intelligence services and law enforcement can come together in such a situation. "You've got the intelligence community on the supply end. At the same time, it's going to be very hard to segregate any information you get on the distribution end or the money-laundering end because it's all one conspiracy. Under a principle of law, all of the co-conspirators are joined. They don't have to know one another. At least in U.S. law, all there has to be is a common understanding and two or more people agreeing on it. So you've got your CIA working outside the country. Inside the country you've got your Secret Service, FBI, Customs, DEA, ATF, and everybody else working on the domestic end of this. But it's still all one conspiracy. Does the CIA neutralize their end of this? And then, do the domestic enforcement agencies arrest and prosecute the domestic end of this? If you compartmentalize it, how do you compartmentalize the evidence to prosecute it? What about the judicial process? What about discovery, witnesses, sources, and the methods that need to be examined to see if they comply with the law? They're never going to do that."

One of the lessons that law enforcement in the United States learned from the cocaine wars of the 1970s and 1980s was that turf battles between agencies were counterproductive. When the FBI insisted that an operation was theirs alone and locked horns over it with the DEA and Customs, the energy they expended only served to make life easier for the bad guys. So co-operation became the operative word in the 1990s. Of course, not everyone heard.

When you ask other law enforcement agencies, including the RCMP, about the FBI, they seem unanimous in the opinion that if the FBI doesn't own the bat, the ball, the gloves, and the umpires, the FBI doesn't play. The DEA have always shared a culture and kinship with the CIA – in fact, the DEA was born out of the CIA's rib – and they understand the foreign intelligence mission. But the DEA also plays an important role domestically. That sometimes means stepping on toes at U.S. Customs. The borders are, by law, secured by Customs, but they lay claim to an anti-money-laundering mission as well, which sometimes means stepping on toes of the CID branch at the Internal Revenue Service. Because the two are both Treasury agencies, sibling rivalry is compounded.

The point is, all the best speeches urging co-operation are doomed to fail because egos get involved.

So do budgets. It is a fact of life that when governments dole out money, whoever has caught the biggest fish will wind up with the biggest dinner.

Some nations do what they can within the confines of sovereignty. There are Canadian, British, French, and German law enforcement investigators stationed in Miami. These are not people doing liaison duty – there are already plenty of those in Washington – these are foreign law enforcement officers working operationally inside the United States. That suggests there are American investigators operationally active inside Canada, Britain, France, and Germany.

Jack Blum believes co-operation can go further, that nations can harmonize legal systems and also reach common definitions of crime. He would like to see a common international understanding that no nation-state may use its sovereignty to harbour criminals. "We urgently need a global convention on the gathering of evidence in criminal cases. Police must have an easy, uncomplicated way to get the evidence they need in admissible form from foreign jurisdictions without extensive red tape."

Getting such agreements signed and ratified should not be beyond the scope of possibility. Still, experience is not encouraging. The United Nations once proposed that money laundering be made an internationally extraditable offence. Some eighty nations, fewer than half the UN membership, agreed to ratify a pact. Even that many would have been great, but five years later, only four had bothered to actually sign it.

Addressing the UN on transnational crime in 1998, President Clinton argued that we must create a world in which criminals have no place to run, no place to hide. The member states readily agreed. And yet, nearly a quarter of those same member states continue to provide secret banking, much of it aimed specifically at aiding and abetting the concealment of dirty money. Even more of those same member states continue to offer shell companies that can be bought for minimal fees in jurisdictions halfway around the globe, whose specific purpose is to obscure a money trail that might otherwise aid law enforcement in connecting criminals to their ill-gotten gains.

Sure, there is wide agreement in the international community that nations must get together to combat transnational organized crime, that individual efforts are no longer sufficient when faced with this global threat, and that by denying criminals their profits, transnational crime can be reduced. But such rhetoric is little more than the equivalent of approving of motherhood, apple pie, and the flag.

Transnational criminal organizations are businesses that rely on cash flow and reinvestment in order to grow. Denying them either, or better still, denying them both, could bankrupt them. That means going after the people who handle their money. But the people who handle their money are often the same people behind those who make our laws.

Significantly, not one single nation on the face of the planet has ever proposed legislation that would require lawyers, bankers, accountants, and company formation agents – who, knowingly or unknowingly, service transnational criminal organizations by laundering their money – to verify, under threat of criminal penalty, the beneficial owner of the money they are handling before they handle it.

If lawyers, bankers, accountants, and company formation agents could be taken out of the equation, if companies and secret bank accounts based in tax havens were denied the right to function in the rest of the world, if the Caymans and the Antiguas and the Arubas and the Colombias and the Nigerias and the Switzerlands and the Liechtensteins and even the Niues of this planet were outright ostracized for their role in transnational criminality, that's when something might begin to change.

ACKNOWLEDGEMENTS

I owe a great debt of gratitude to the many men and women on active law enforcement duty who spoke to me on the record, and to those who, for various reasons, could only speak to me off the record. In the United States, among those I can name, including retired agents, my thanks to: Billy Ahern, Peter Grinenko, and Ron Rose of the New York Police Department; Hardrick Crawford, Jr., Tom Fuentes, Tom Kneir, Robert Levinson, and Jim Moody of the Federal Bureau of Investigation; Allan Doody, Terry Neeley, Fred McGreevy, Tony Mangione, Mark Robinson, Jerry Sullivan, Roger Urbanski, and Dick Weart at U.S. Customs; and Brent Eaton, Tom Clifford, John Costanzo, Brian Crowell, and Matty Maher of the Drug Enforcement Administration.

In Washington, I am grateful to: John McDowell of the U.S. Department of State's Bureau for International Narcotics and Law Enforcement Affairs; Tanya Meekins of the Environmental Protection Agency; John Sopko at the U.S. Department of Commerce; Frank Cilluffo at the Center for Strategic and International Studies; George Malbois at the embassy of Switzerland; attorney Jack Blum; Rogene Waite at the DEA; Michael Bopp and Mary Roberts at the United States Senate's Permanent Subcommittee on Investigations; Professor Louise Shelley at American University; Joyce McDonald at Financial Crimes Enforcement Network (FINCEN); George

Abbott at the International Anti-Counterfeiting Coalition; and General Heze Leder at the embassy of Israel.

Thanks as well to John Moscow, Assistant District Attorney for the City of New York; Lee Seglum and the New Jersey State Commission of Investigations; Pam Brown at the DEA in Miami; Tom Cash at the Kroll Agency in Miami; Alexis Johnson in Arizona, and others.

In Britain, my thanks to the following law enforcement officers: Chris Pope at the Dyfed Powys Constabulary; Dave Cooper, Simon Goddard, John Leek, and Jim Morrison at National Criminal Intelligence Service; Paul Cook, Ranald Macdonald, and Tim Manhire at HM Customs and Excise; Lindsay Anderson and Graham Saltmarsh at the National Crime Squad; Allan Jones at the Merseyside Constabulary; and Bob Denmark at the Royal Lancashire Constabulary. Also, my thanks to Norbert Garrett and Andre Pienaar at the Kroll Agency and Rowan Bosworth-Davies.

There are a number of officers at the Metropolitan Police in London to whom I would very much like to say thank you. Their co-operation was outstanding and well in keeping with the high level of professionalism for which officers of the force are rightfully respected. But I dare not mention their names for fear of reprisals from a shameful, petty, and, I would claim, dangerous cult of secrecy that has pervaded the force over the past few years through the "Palace Guard" mentality of the Press and Public Relations Office. Their attitude stupefies and angers me, because the men and women who serve that force deserve so much better.

My thanks to many people throughout the rest of Europe go to: Alessandro Pansa at the Servicio Centrale Operativo of the Italian National Police and his staff of Marcella Montaina, Aquilino Dortona, Andrea Il Grande, Massimo Mazzarella, Vittorio Rizzi, and Amalia Bonagura. Also in Italy, my thanks to Special Agents Armando Ramirez and Matt Etre, U.S. Customs officers stationed at the American embassy in Rome. In Holland, among others, my thanks to Hank Zwam. In Austria, I am grateful to three officers from the Vienna Police: Chief of Police Peter Stiedl, Chief of Detectives Dr. Walter Schubert, and Chief of Major Crime Bureau Max Edelbacher; Michael Sika, Director General of the Ministry of Interior; Jean François Thony, Director of the Money Laundering Program, Office of the Control of Drugs and the Prevention of Crime, United Nations; Bernard LeRoy, Senior Legal Advisor to the United Nations; David Kyd of the International Atomic Energy Agency; and various people at the Austrian intelligence agency, EDOK.

My thanks as well to Rick McDonnell of the Financial Action Task Force Asia/Pacific and others in Australia; Bernard Delias and others in France; Don Shruhan, Stuart McDonald, and others in Singapore; plus several people who assured me they were not officially permitted to talk, and yet did, at the Hong Kong Organized Crime and Triad Bureau and the Australian Federal Police.

In Canada, my appreciation goes to: Pietro Poletti and Brian Scharf at the Criminal Intelligence Service Canada; Bruce Tuck and Rob MacCallum of the Toronto Metropolitan Police; Ben Soave and Reg King of the Royal Canadian Mounted Police.

I am equally grateful to many journalists, including those friends at *Newsday*, the *New York Times*, *Wall Street Journal*, *Washington Post*, Miami *Herald*, Los Angeles *Times*, *International Herald Tribune*, London *Times*, *Telegraph*, *Guardian*, and *Independent*.

Finally, a special note of thanks to several people: John Forbes and John Hurley in Washington, Bill Malarney in Atlanta, Jim Fisher in Ottawa, and Yvon Gagnon in Montreal. I add my sincerest thanks as well to Jonathan Webb at McClelland and Stewart for his wisdom, patience, and world-class editing; to my Canadian agent Linda McKnight; to my American agent Milly Marmur, and, of course, to La Benayoun.

A WORD ON ETHNICITY

In referring to certain types of organized criminal groups, I have used a kind of shorthand. I know very well that Italian is not synonymous with the Mafia, that Asian is not synonymous with the Triad, that Nigerian is not synonymous with criminal enterprises that originate in Nigeria. And I never meant to imply otherwise. I know very well that the overwhelming majority of immigrants in Brighton Beach in Brooklyn are hard-working, family-loving people simply trying to get ahead in the New World, and that they abhor the criminality that originates from such a tiny sector of their community. To speak then of Italian organized crime or Asian organized crime or Russian organized crime – even when some of the latter is, more correctly, Chechen or Ukrainian – is nothing more than a convenience. In my interview with Ben Soave, I promised him I would make these distinctions. As he is an Italian-born Canadian, I understand and appreciate his sensitivity on this issue. I include this proviso, not only because it's important to keep one's promises, but because I feel it is also important to stress the point on which my promise was made. To anyone who might still be offended and finds my shorthand politically incorrect, I sincerely apologize.

SOURCES

The problem with printed sources is that mistakes get repeated. It is often the case that one sloppy inclusion, early on, can take on the air of truth as that inclusion is recited, with each new version of the story merely referencing the previous one. Unless an author checks back to the original source, the risk is great that such misinformation will, eventually, simply be accepted as fact. I have, therefore, always considered printed sources with the greatest of scepticism. I look on them as no better than secondary or, in most cases, tertiary sources and have tried to limit their use. Previously printed sources do serve as a great help, but as a road map to primary sources. In cases where individuals have been quoted, wherever possible, I have endeavoured to find them. In instances where circumstances have been described and primary sources are no longer available, I have endeavoured to find at least two versions of the story from separate and distinct sources, in order to corroborate the accuracy of those circumstances. And, except where propriety dictates otherwise, sources are quoted.

BOOKS

Abadinsky, Howard: *Organized Crime*; Nelson Hall, Chicago, 1990

Abadinsky, Howard: *The Mafia in America – An Oral History*; Praegar, New York, 1987

Albanese, Jay: *Organized Crime in America*; Anderson Publishing, Cincinnati, 1996

Anastasia, George: *The Goodfella Tapes*; Avon Books, New York, 1998

Appleton, Peter and Clark, Doug: *Billion $$$ High – The Drug Invasion of Canada*; McGraw-Hill Ryerson, Montreal, 1990

Balsamo, William and Carpozi, George: *Crime Incorporated, or Under the Clock – The Inside Story of the Mafia's First Hundred Years*; New Horizon Press, New Jersey, 1991

Baum, Dan: *Smoke and Mirrors – The War on Drugs and the Politics of Failure*; Little, Brown, Boston, 1996

Beare, Margaret E.: *Criminal Conspiracies – Organized Crime in Canada*; Nelson, Scarborough, 1996

Black, David: *Triad Takeover – A Terrifying Account of the Spread of Triad Crime in the West*; Sidgwick and Jackson, London, 1991

Blum, Howard: *Gangland – How the FBI Broke the Mob*; Simon and Schuster, New York, 1993

Blumenthal, Ralph: *Last Days of the Sicilians – At War With the Mafia, The FBI Assault on the Pizza Connection*; Times Books, New York, 1988

Bonanno, Joseph and Lalli, Sergio: *A Man of Honor*; Simon and Schuster, New York, 1983

Bonavolonta, Jules and Duffy, Brian: *The Good Guys*; Pocket Books, New York, 1996

Booth, Martin: *The Triads – The Growing Global Threat from the Chinese Criminal Societies*; St. Martin's Press, New York, 1991

Brashler, William: *The Don – The Life and Death of Sam Giancana*; Harper and Row, New York, 1977

Bresler, Fenton S.: *The Trail of the Triads – An Investigation into International Crime*; Weidenfeld and Nicolson, London, 1980

Carrigan, D. Owen: *Crime and Punishment in Canada – A History*; McClelland and Stewart, Toronto, 1991

Chin, Ko-Lin: *Chinatown Gangs*; Oxford University Press, New York, 1996

Cook, Fred: *Mafia*; Fawcett, New York, 1973

Cummings, John and Volkman, Ernest: *Mobster – The Astonishing Rise and Fall of John Gotti and His Gang*; Warner Books, London, 1996

Davis, John H.: *Mafia Dynasty – The Rise and Fall of the Gambino Crime Family*; Harper Collins, New York, 1993

Du, Phuc Long and Ricard, Laura: *The Dream Shattered – Vietnamese Gangs in America*; Northeastern University Press, Boston, 1996

Dubro, James: *Dragons of Crime – Inside the Asian Underworld*; Octopus, Toronto, 1992

English, T.J.: *Born to Kill – America's Most Notorious Vietnamese Gang, and the Changing Face of Organized Crime*; William Morrow, New York, 1995

Fiorentini, G. and Peltzman S.: *The Economics of Organized Crime*; Cambridge University Press, Cambridge, 1995

Fogel, Jean-François: *Le Testament de Pablo Escobar*; Grasset, Paris, 1994

Fox, Stephen R.: *Blood and Power – Organized Crime in Twentieth Century America*; Morrow, New York, 1989

Franzese, Michael and Matera, Dary: *Quitting the Mob – How the Yuppie Don Left the Mafia and Lived to Tell His Story*; Harper Collins, New York, 1992

Friman, H. Richard: *Narco Diplomacy – Exporting the U.S. War on Drugs*; Cornell University Press, Ithaca, 1996

Gage, Nicholas: *Mafia, U.S.A.;* Playboy Press, Chicago, 1972

Gambetta, Diego: *The Sicilian Mafia – The Business of Private Protection*; Harvard University Press, Cambridge, 1993

Gately, William and Fernandez, Yvette: *Dead Ringer – An Insider's Account of the Mob's Colombian Connection*; DI Fine, New York, 1994

Gentry, Curt: *J. Edgar Hoover – The Man and the Secrets*; New American Library, New York, 1992

Giancana, Sam and Giancana, Chuck: *Double Cross*; Warner Books, New York, 1992

Goldfarb, Ronald L.: *Perfect Villains, Imperfect Heroes – Robert F. Kennedy's War Against Organized Crime*; Random House, New York, 1995

Goode, James: *Wiretap – Listening in on America's Mafia*; Simon and Schuster, New York, 1988

Gosch, M.A.: *Last Testament of Lucky Luciano*; Little, Brown, Boston, 1975

Gotti, John and Gravano, Salvatore: *The Gotti Tapes – Including the Testimony of Salvatore "Sammy the Bull" Gravano*; Times Books, New York, 1992

Gugliotta, Guy and Leen, Jeff: *Kings of Cocaine – Inside the Medellín Cartel: An Astonishing True Story of Murder, Money, and International Corruption*; Simon and Schuster, New York, 1989

Gunst, Laurie: *Born Fi' Dead – A Journey Through the Jamaican Posse Underworld*; H. Holt, New York, 1995

Handelman, Stephen: *Comrade Criminal*; Yale University Press, New Haven, 1995

Jacobs, James B.: *Busting the Mob*; New York University Press, New York, 1994

Kaplan, David and Dubro, Alec: *Yakuza*; Addison-Wesley, Massachusetts, 1986

Kefauver, Estes and United States Senate: *Crime in America – Special Committee to Investigate Organized Crime in Interstate Commerce*; Doubleday and Co., Garden City, 1951

Kelly, Robert J.: *Handbook of Organized Crime in the United States*; Greenwood Press, Westport, 1994

Kenney, Dennis Jay and Finckenauer, James: *Organized Crime in America*; Wadsworth Publishing, California, 1995

Kerry, John: *A New Kind of War – National Security and the Globalization of Crime*; Simon and Schuster, New York, 1997

Kessler, Ronald: *The FBI*; Pocket Books, New York, 1993

Kirby, Cecil and Renner, Thomas C.: *Mafia Assassin*; Methuen, Toronto, 1986

Kirkpatrick, Sidney and Abrahams, Peter: *Turning the Tide – One Man Against the Medellín Cartel*; Dutton, New York, 1991

Kleinknecht, William: *The New Ethnic Mobs – The Changing Face of Organized Crime in America*; Free Press, New York, 1996

Lacey, Robert: *Little Man – Meyer Lansky and the Gangster Life*; Little, Brown, Boston, 1991

Lallemand, Alain: *L'Organizatsiya – La Mafia russe à L'Assaut du Monde*; Calmann-Lévy, Paris, 1996

Lamothe, Lee and Nicaso, Antonio: *Global Mafia – The New World Order of Organized Crime*; Macmillan, Toronto, 1995

Lavigne, Yves: *Hells Angels – Into the Abyss*; Harper Collins, Toronto, 1996

———: *Good Guy, Bad Guy – Drugs and the Changing Face of Organized Crime*; Random House, Toronto, 1991

Lyman, Michael: *Gangland – Drug Trafficking by Organized Criminals*; Charles Thomas, Illinois, 1989

Lyman, Michael D. and Potter, Gary W.: *Organized Crime*; Prentice Hall, New Jersey, 1997

Maas, Peter: *The Valachi Papers*; Putnam, New York, 1968

Macdonald, Scott: *Dancing on a Volcano – The Latin American Drug Trade*; Praeger, New York, 1988

Martin, John M. and Romano, Anne T.: *Multinational Crime – Terrorism, Espionage, Drug and Arms Trafficking*; Sage, California, 1992

Mermelstein, Max: *The Man Who Made It Snow*; Simon and Schuster, New York, 1990

Mustain, Gene and Capeci, Jerry: *Mob Star – The Story of John Gotti, the Most Powerful Man in America*; Penguin, New York, 1989

Nadelmann, Ethan: *Cops Across Borders – The Internationalization of U.S. Criminal Law Enforcement*; Pennsylvania State University Press, University Park, 1993

Nash, Jay Robert: *World Encyclopedia of Organized Crime*; De Capo Press, New York, 1993

Naylor, R.T.: *Hot Money and the Politics of Debt*; Black Rose Books, Montreal, 1994

Nicaso, Antonio and Lamothe, Lee: *Global Mafia – The New World Order of Organized Crime*; Macmillan, Toronto, 1995

O'Brien, Joseph and Kurins, Andris: *Boss of Bosses*; Simon and Schuster, New York, 1991

O'Kane, James M.: *The Crooked Ladder – Gangsters, Ethnicity, and the American Dream*; Transaction Books, New Jersey, 1992

O'Neill, Gerard and Lehr, Dick: *The Underboss – The Rise and Fall of a Mafia Family*; St. Martin's Press, New York, 1989

Padilla, Felix M.: *The Gang as an American Enterprise*; Rutgers University Press, New Jersey, 1992

Peterson, Virgil W.: *The Mob*; Green Hill Publishers, Illinois, 1983

Petrakis, Gregory J.: *The New Face of Organized Crime*; Kendall/Hunt Publishing, Iowa, 1992

Pileggi, Nicholas: *Wise Guy – Life in a Mafia Family*; Pocket Books, New York, 1985

Pistone, Joseph D. and Woodley, Richard: *Donnie Brasco – My Undercover Life in the Mafia*; New American Library, New York, 1988

Poppa, Terrence E.: *Druglord – The Life and Death of a Mexican Kingpin*; Pharos Books, New York, 1990

Posner, Gerald L.: *Warlords of Crime – Chinese Secret Societies, the New Mafia*; McGraw-Hill, New York, 1988

Possamai, Mario: *Money on the Run*; Viking, Toronto, 1992

Raufer, Xavier: *Les Superpuissances du Crime*; Plon, Paris, 1993

Robinson, Jeffrey: *The Laundrymen* (revised and updated edition); Simon and Schuster, London, 1998

Ryan, Patrick J. and Rush, George E.: *Understanding Organized Crime*; Sage, California, 1997

Seymour, Christopher: *Yakuza Diary – Doing Time in the Japanese Underworld*; Atlantic Monthly Press, New York, 1996

Shana, Alexander: *The Pizza Connection – Lawyers, Money, Drugs and the Mafia*; Weidenfeld, New York, 1988

Sterling, Claire: *Thieves' World – The Threat of the New Global Network of Organized Crime*; Simon and Shuster, New York, 1994

Sterling, Claire: *Octopus – The Long Reach of the International Sicilian Mafia*; Norton, New York, 1990

Strong, Simon: *Whitewash – Pablo Escobar and the Cocaine Wars*; Macmillan, London, 1995

Theoharis, Athan and Cox, John Stewart: *The Boss*; Temple University Press, Philadelphia, 1988

Tyler, Gus: *Organized Crime in America*; University of Michigan Press, Ann Arbor, 1962

Vaksberg, Arkady: *The Soviet Mafia*; Weidenfeld, London, 1991

NEWSPAPERS AND WIRE SERVICES

Associated Press:

November 29, 1998: Koppel, Naomi – "Swiss Trial Highlights Russian Mob Influx"

December 20, 1994: "Seized Uranium – Weapons Grade"

December 19, 1994: "Czech Police Seize Uranium"

November 23, 1994: "Soviet Nuclear Complex at Risk"

June 7, 1994: "Yeltsin – Russia a Superpower of Crime"

Boston *Globe*:

June 29, 1994: Neuffer, Elizabeth – "FBI Director Presses World Effort on Crime"

January 23, 1994: Constable, Pamela – "U.S.-Colombian Drug War Shifts Its Focus to Cali"

Chicago *Tribune*:

November 24, 1996: Witt, Howard – "Gangsters Squeezing Russia"

July 21, 1996: Hundley, Tom – "Red Hot Deals Draw Russians to Poland"

May 14, 1993: Hanley, Charles J. – "Drug Bust May Signal Colombia-Russia Link"

Christian Science Monitor:

May 15, 1998: Kiefer, Francine – "Waging War on Global Crime"

October 8, 1997: Prusher, Ilene R. – "Worldwide Webs – Mafia's Reach Grows"

September 17, 1997: "Mexico's Growing Drug Cartels Seep Across American Border"

January 11, 1995: Tanner, Adam and others – "Russian Mafia Expands into New Areas, Using the U.S. to Launder Dirty Money"

July 5, 1994: Sloane, Wendy – "FBI's Moscow Mission: The Mob, Nuclear Theft"

June 29, 1994: "Russian Mob Holds Summit in Austria"
May 4, 1994: Burke, Justin – "Russian Mafia Thrives in Berlin"

Dallas *Morning News*:
September 10, 1995: Katz, Gregory – "Russian Mafia Sets off Growing Wave of Crime, Fall of Communism Opened Gates to Europe, Corruption"
September 10, 1995: Katz, Gregory – "Russia's Underworld Finds Fertile Ground in America; Profits, Legal System Are Irresistible Lure"
December 17, 1992: Rodrigue, George – "Smugglers of Nuclear Materials Proliferating; Officials Fear Dealers Will Get More Sophisticated"

Detroit *News*:
April 9, 1998: Girard, Fred – "Fetisov Denies Links to Mob"

Financial Post:
January 9, 1999: Rubin, Sandra – "RCMP Investigated YBM in Early 1995, Informant Says Mounties Warned Him of 'Something Foul' in Company"

Fort Lauderdale Sun-Sentinel:
March 6, 1993: Caribbean News Agency – "Sicilian Mafia Attempts to Buy Caribbean Island"

Guardian:
January 4, 1997: Thomas, Richard; Hooper, John; Hearst, David – "The Godfather, Part IV"

Independent:
June 17, 1997: Cockburn, Patrick – "Ministers Quizzed on Links to Russian Mafia"
December 9, 1993: Doyle, Leonard – "Russian Mafias Carve Up Drugs Trade; The Bosnian War Has Forced Crime Clans to Find New Balkan Routes for Smuggling Heroin into Europe"

International Herald Tribune:
April 15, 1994: Erlanger, Steven – "In Moscow, the High Life Flowers at Gangland Funeral"

Jerusalem Post:
March 27, 1998: Derfner, Larry – "The Lerner Legend"
September 19, 1997: Ben-David, Calev – "Crime Time"

June 26, 1997: Harris, David – "Police – Israel Is a Global Money-Laundering Center"

May 23, 1997: Rabinovich, Abraham – "A Man of Means"

March 8, 1996: Hutman, Bill – "Police Concerned Russian 'Mafia' Infiltrating Government"

January 4, 1996: Dan, Uri and Eisenberg, Dennis – "The Real Mafia"

July 8, 1995: Rodan, Steve – "In Harm's Way"

June 29, 1995: Hutman, Bill – "Hefetz Warns of Infiltration by Russian Mafia"

June 2, 1995: Marcus, Raine – "New Police Unit to Lead War on Int'l Crime"

April 23, 1991: Rotem, Michael – "Soviets Want Oleh Arrested by Swiss"

Los Angeles Times:

December 12, 1998: "Swiss Court Clears Russian Businessman Linked to Gangs"

December 11, 1998: Alonso-Zaldivar, Ricardo – "Immigrant Ring at U.S.-Canada Border Cracked"

September 23, 1998: Paddock, Richard C. – "A New Breed of Gangster Is Globalizing Russian Crime"

November 17, 1997: Darling, Juanita – "Colombian Cartels Find New Drug Paths to U.S. Narcotics – In Effort to Cut Out Mexican Traffickers, South Americans Have Forged Ties with Smugglers in Caribbean and Guatemala, Sources Say. Russian Mafia Is Reportedly a Partner in Europe"

January 10, 1997: Gerstenzang, James and Jackson, Robert L. – "U.S. Authorities Try to Put Freon Black Market on Ice; Probe: Fifteen People Are Charged with Smuggling Illegal Air-Conditioning Chemical Linked to Depletion of Ozone Layer"

October 9, 1994: Hood, Marlowe – "The Taiwan Connection"

July 17, 1994: Cole, Richard – "Asian Gangs Could Be the Future of U.S. Organized Crime, Experts Warn Law Enforcement"

Montreal *Gazette*:

September 20, 1998: Schwarcz, Joe – "The Rise and Fall of a Gas: Freon Saved One Generation from Food Poisoning, but Left Gaping Holes in the Ozone Layer"

June 27, 1998: Marotte, Bertrand – "Another Blow For Troubled YBM: Auditor Resigns, Refuses to Certify '97 Statements Because Of Possible 'Error or Fraud'"

May 28, 1998: Van Hasselt, Caroline – "TSE Suspends Trading in YBM: Police Probe of Bicycle Firm Hurts Exchange's Reputation"

May 22, 1998: Marotte, Bertrand – "TSE's Listing of YBM Draws Barbs"

October 16, 1994: Marsden, William and Baker, Geoff – "RCMP Traces Cash in Huge Money-Laundering Case"

September 1, 1994: Baker, Geoff – "Many Fish Caught in Mounties' Net; But Biggest Got Away, They Say"

Moscow *Times*:

October 23, 1994: Gubarev, Vladimir – "The Car Theft Industry"

Newsday:

August 24, 1996: Fallon, Scott – "Suspected Mobster Extradited/Italy Hands Over Russian Accused in B'klyn Killings"

March 10, 1995: Gelman, Mitch – "Glittering Palace of Smoke, Mirrors"

March 10, 1995: DeStefano, Anthony M. – "Russian Thugs Defy U.S. Screen Weakness in Refugee System"

March 9, 1995: Buettner, Russ – "Marble Foyer and a Bullet-Proof John"

March 9, 1995: Kocieniewski, David – "Russian Godfather Collar, Italy Cops Grab Him for U.S."

March 1, 1995: Gelman, Mitch – "Brooklyn Mystery Led to Russia, Italy"

July 28, 1993: Gambardello, Joseph and Tyre, Peg – "Russian Mob Boss Survives Hit"

New York *Daily News*:

April 22, 1997: Mustain, Gene and Capeci, Jerry – "2 Dance Bullet Ballet"

April 21, 1997: Mustain, Gene and Capeci, Jerry – "Infamous from Moscow to N.Y."

April 20, 1997: Mustain, Gene and Capeci, Jerry with Gorin, Julia – "Mob Russian in for Crime Time"

March 10, 1996: Gordy, Molly – "A Russian Goodfella? He'd Ice Agents"

New York Times:

December 20, 1998: Olson, Elizabeth – "Ex-Soviets Are Focus of Inquiry by the Swiss"

July 22, 1998: Landler, Mark – "Macao Journal; A Reputed Mr. Big Upholds Colony's Reputation"

January 10, 1997: Cushman Jr., John H. – "U.S. Prosecutors in 6 Cities File Charges of Smuggling Refrigeration Gas"

December 8, 1996: Myers, Steven Lee – "Fighting International Crime"

July 9, 1996: Richardson, Lynda – "Russian Émigré Convicted of Extortion"

May 3, 1996: Wren, Christopher – "Mexican Role in Cocaine Is Exposed in U.S. Seizure"

April 28 1995: Dunn, Ashley – "Golden Venture Passengers Opting for China"

November 2, 1994: Erlanger, Steven – "Scandals Put Russian Defense Chief on the Defensive"

August 23, 1994: Raab, Selwyn – "Influx of Russian Gangsters Troubles FBI in Brooklyn"

April 1, 1994: Fyodorov, Boris – "Moscow Without Mirrors"

August 29, 1993: Faison, Seth – "Gang Leader Is Arrested in Hong Kong"

April 9, 1993: Kristof, Nicholas D. – "China Police Have Gang Link in Hong Kong"

June 21, 1992: Cowell, Alan – "Inquiry into Sicilian Slaying Looks for Mafia Link to Colombia Drug Cartel"

Observer:

December 15, 1996: Sweeny, John and others – "Global Gangsters – Russian Mafiya Invades Britain"

Ottawa Citizen:

July 9, 1998: McDermott, Jeremy – "Colombian Drug Cartels Hook Up with Russian Mob"

June 29, 1998: McIntosh, Andrew – "Mafia Boss Bribed His Way Back to Canada: RCMP: Internal Mountie Report Says Mob Paid $800,000 to Free Ailing Kingpin"

June 15, 1998: McIntosh, Andrew – "RCMP Sting Broke U.S. Laws: Mounties Changed U.S. Criminals' Cash for Months Without U.S. Authorization"

June 15, 1998: McIntosh, Andrew – "National Bank Executives Worried About Role in Sting"

June 14, 1998: McIntosh, Andrew – "Mounties Didn't Have Government's OK for Covert Drug Sting: RCMP Laundered Cash for Five Months Before Getting Cabinet Approval"

June 13, 1998: McIntosh, Andrew – "RCMP Feared Mob's Mole Might Foil Probe"

June 12, 1998: McIntosh, Andrew – "Agents 'Reinvested' Profit in Drug-Money Business: Cash-Strapped RCMP also Put $400,000 into Failed Dutch Sting"

June 11, 1998: McIntosh, Andrew – "How the RCMP Helped 'Push' $2 Billion Worth of Cocaine: For Four Years, the Mounties Laundered Drug Money for the Mob, for Bikers, for the Colombian Drug Cartels, and for Transient Dealers on Montreal's Streets. Few of the Deals Were Ever Investigated"

May 22, 1998: Marotte, Bertrand – "YBM Stock Listing Shames TSE"

May 20, 1998: Marotte, Bertrand – "CEO Attempts to Restore YBM 's Flagging Credibility"

March 5, 1993: Clough, Patricia – "Mafia Family Reported Buying Own Caribbean Island"

Philadelphia *Inquirer*:

January 15, 1999: McCrary, Lacy – "Stock Sensation's Trappings of Success Shape Up as Sham"

February 20, 1994: Hanley, Charles J. – "As Russian Crime Grows, so Do the U.S.-Russian Police Links"

January 30, 1994: Seplow, Stephen – "In the New Russia, Blood Trails Billions"

Reuters:

January 28, 1999: Edmonds, Sarah – "Canadian Regulators Assailed for Laxity on Suspect Firm"

December 10, 1998: Vicini, James – "U.S. Says Chinese Smuggling Ring Used Tribal Land"

December 9, 1998: Anderson, Scott – "Canada, U.S. Break Up China Immigrant Smuggling Ring"

August 23, 1996: Szekely, Peter – "Italy Extradites Alleged Russian Crime Boss to U.S."

November 24, 1994: "138 Countries Seek to Combat Global Crime"

April 15, 1993: Roche, Andrew – "Hong Kong's Triads Find Odd Bedfellows in Beijing"

Rocky Mountain News:

March 28, 1995: Jensen, Holger – "Russia Must Break Crime's Stranglehold"

San Diego Union-Tribune:

October 4, 1992: Lavelle, Philip J. – "Sting Put Cocaine's Global Web into Focus"

September 29, 1992: Lavelle, Philip J. – "Drug Sting Here Is Massive, International Ruse Nets 260 Suspects"

San Francisco Chronicle:

December 1, 1997: Wallace, Bill – "Chinese Crime Ring Muscles In. Violent Gang Moving into State from Canada"

March 19, 1995: Wallace, Bill – "The Next Red Menace. Organized Crime Syndicates from the Former Soviet Union Have Arrived in Cali"

January 22, 1995: Geiger, Eric – "Austria Feels Chill of Booming Russian Mafia"

December 30, 1993: Burdman, Pamela – "Human Smuggling Ships Linked to One Huge Ring Bases in California, Guatemala"

Scotland on Sunday:

November 26, 1995: Ronay, Gabriel – "Western Businesses Bought as Front for Russian Mafia"

South China Morning Post:

July 13, 1998: Fraser, Niall – "Infighting Breaks Out for Control of Macau Syndicate"

March 27, 1994: "Spain – Chinese Illegal Immigrants on the Increase"

April 25, 1993: Dobson, Chris – "Police Report – China Initiated Triad Contacts"

April 12, 1993: Torode, Greg – "Triad-PSB Links Threatening Crime Fighting"

April 11, 1993: Dobson, Chris – "PRC Minister Reportedly Met Triad Members"

December 8, 1991: Marsh, Jon and Dobson, Chris – "U.S.A. – Government Sets Up Taskforce to Stop Triads"

St. Petersburg Times:

February 19, 1999: Testerman, Jeff – "Prosecutors–Crime Ring Eyed Casinos. Edward Halloran Is Accused of Bilking Investors by Claiming He Was Connected with the Seminole Casinos"

Sunday Telegraph:

November 20, 1994: Davies, Hugh – "Russian Mobs Have American Dream in Sight"

Toronto Star:

February 2, 1999: Van Rijn, Nicolaas and Brazao, Dale – "The Long, Rugged Road to Gold Mountain"

December 12, 1998: MacCharles, Tonda – "Huge Smuggling Ring Not Unique"

May 30, 1998: Daw, James – "Never Put Your All in One Stock It's Still Buyer Beware on the TSE, YBM Proves Spot on TSE 300 No Guarantee"

May 22, 1998: "Canada-U.S. Hold Summit on Crime"

Toronto *Sun*:

July 18, 1998: Lamberti, Rob And Magnish, Scot – "Cops Seize High-Priced Assets, 30 Kilos of Money Snapped Up After Arrest of Reputed Mafia Boss, Associates"

July 16, 1998: Lamberti, Rob And Magnish, Scot – "Cops Topple Mob's Drug Empire Police, Crime Tentacles Circle the Globe"

July 16, 1998: Lamberti, Rob And Magnish, Scot – "Drug Empire Crushed 'Wayne Gretzky' of Underworld, 11 Others Arrested"

United Press International:

December 12, 1998: "Alleged Mafioso Returns to Moscow"

December 10, 1998: "Alien Smuggling Ring Broken"

March 15, 1994: Hail, John – "New York–based Gang Smuggling Thousands of Chinese to U.S."

September 1, 1993: Richardson, Paul – "Bail Rejected for Reputed Gang Kingpin in Human Smuggling Case"

Wall Street Journal:

December 5, 1994: "Global Gangs"

March 22, 1990: Penn, Stanley – "Asian Connection – Chinese Gangsters Fill a Narcotics Gap Left by U.S. Drive on Mafia"

September 15, 1987: Morgenthaler, Eric – "Smuggling Aliens – A Shadowy Operation Shows How Hard It Is to Keep Out Illegals"

February 6, 1987: Pasztor, Andy and Gutfeld, Rose: "Fuel Fraud – Gasoline Tax Evasion Ignites a Crackdown by U.S. and the States; FBI Cites Organized Crime; Treasury May Be Losing as Much as $800 Million"

Washington Post:

February 17, 1998: Kovaleski, Serge F. and Farah, Douglas – "Organized Crime Exercises Clout in Island Nations"

March 30, 1997: Farah, Douglas and Moore, Molly – "Mexican Drug Traffickers Eclipse Colombian Cartels"

October 7, 1996: Farah, Douglas – "Russian Crime Finds Haven in Caribbean"

August 18, 1996: Constable, Pamela – "From Russia with Chutzpah"

August 12, 1996: Anderson, John W. and Moore, Molly – "Mexican Cartels Diversify"

September 17, 1995: Reding, Andrew – "The Fall and Rise of the Drug Cartels"

August 2, 1994: Drozdiak, William – "European Unity for Organized Crime"

May 26, 1994: Smith, Jeffrey – "Freeh Warns of a New Russian Threat"

April 2, 1994: Coll, Steve – "Russian Crime Syndicates Moving West"

December 28, 1993: Weymouth, Lally – "Organized Crime – The New Russian Menace"

October 5, 1992: Drozdiak, William – "World Crime Groups Expand Cooperation, Spheres of Influence"

October 21, 1989: Parmelee, Jennifer – "Cocaine Trail Forks, Leads Into Europe; Colombian Cartels, Mafia in Italy Working Together"

Washington *Times*:

December 30, 1998: Alden, Edward – "Canadian Star YBM Turns Out to Be Sham"

October 26, 1998: Gertz, Bill – "Mafia Runs Half of Banks in Russia"

September 28, 1998: De Borchgrave, Arnaud – "Subsidizing the Kleptocracy"

December 13, 1997: Seper, Jerry – "Russian Mob Figure Met with Clinton"

December 12, 1997: Seper, Jerry – "Man Tied to Russian Mob Met with Clinton, Gore"

September 20, 1996: Hacket, James – "Missile Disaster Wake-up Call"

November 3, 1995: de Borchgrave, Arnaud – "Clinton Targets Global Organized Crime as Security Threat"

December 17, 1994: Hedges, Michael – "DEA-IRS 'Bank' Hits Cocaine Cartel in Pocketbook"

December 5, 1994: Gertz, Bill – "Most of Russia's Biggest Banks Linked to Mob, CIA Report Says"

October 19, 1994: Copeland, Peter – "Traffickers Planning a Deal, Ex-Agent Says"

PERIODICALS

American Criminal Law Review:

Winter 1995: "Money Laundering"

American Spectator:

January 1996: Bernstein, Jonas – "A Fistful of Rubles"

December 1991: Adams, James Ring – "Medellín's New Generation"

September 1988: Adams, James Ring – "Losing the Drug War – Drugs, Banks, and Florida Politics"

Anthropological Quarterly:

April 1996: McDonogh, Gary – "The Sicilian Mafia"

Arms Control Today:
March 14, 1996: Holdren, John P. – "Reducing the Threat of Nuclear Theft in the Former Soviet Union"
October 1995: Potter, William – "Before the Deluge? Assessing the Threat of Nuclear Leakage From the Post Soviet States"
December 1994: Mueller, Harald – "Fissile Material Smuggling – German Politics, Hype and Reality"
January 1993: Potter, William – "Nuclear Exports From the Former Soviet Union"

Asian Affairs:
September 1, 1995: Bolz, Jennifer – "Chinese Organized Crime and Illegal Alien Trafficking – Humans as a Commodity"

Atlantic Monthly:
June 1994: Hersh, Seymour – "The Wild East"

Australian and New Zealand Journal of Sociology:
November 1987: Trahair, Richard – "Organized Crime, A Global Perspective"

Banking World:
February 1984: Lonsborough, Richard – "Dirty Money in the Caribbean"

British Journal of Criminology:
Spring 1992: Ruggiero, Vincenzo – "Crime Inc. The Story of Organized Crime"

Brookings Review:
Winter 1995: Leitzel, Jim and others – "Mafiosi and Matrioshki, Organized Crime and Russian Reform"
Winter 1993: Flynn, Stephen – "World Wide Drug Scourge, the Expanding Trade in Illicit Drugs"

Business and Finance:
October 6 1994: Dunne, Mark – "Cleaning Dirty Money"
December 9, 1993: Fitzgerald, Kyran – "Laundering the Loot"

Business Today:
April 1994: Sakurada, Keiji – "Yakuza Storming the Corporate Ship"

Business Week:

June 8, 1998: Weber, Joseph – "Red Flags? What Red Flags?"

January 29, 1996: Bremner, Brian – "How the Mob Burned the Banks – The Yakuza Is at the Center of the $350 Billion Bad Loan Scandal"

April 6, 1992: Reichlin, Igor – Germany's Brash New Import – Dirty Money, Its Banks Can Legally Launder Cash and Do So, by the Suitcase"

Canadian Banker:

September/October 1994: Ballard, Michael – "Money Laundering and the Canadian Banks: An Industry Position"

Canadian Lawyer:

January 1997: Lundy, Derek – "It's a Law Firm, Not a Laundry"

Canadian Police News:

Summer 1989: Desjardins, Fred – "The Mob in Canada"

Winter 1987: "Bikers – A New Kind of Organized Crime"

Comparative Economic Studies:

Winter 1995: Minniti, Maria – "Membership Has Its Privileges – Old and New Mafia Organizations"

Conservative Review:

September 1996: Douglass, Joseph Jr. – "Narcotics Trafficking, Organized Crime, and Terrorism"

May 1995: Douglass, Joseph Jr. – "Organized Crime in Russia – Who's Taking Whom to the Cleaners?"

Contemporary Crises:

March 23, 1990: Gaylord, Mark – "The Chinese Laundry – International Drug Trafficking and Hong Kong's Banking Industry"

Crime and Delinquency:

July 1993: Kersten, Joachim – "Street Youths, Bosozoku, and Yakuza – Subculture Formation and Societal Reactions in Japan"

Crime, Law and Social Change:

Fall 1995: Paoli, Letizia – "The Banco Ambrosiano Case"

Summer 1995: Myers, Willard H. III – "The Emerging Threat of Transnational Organized Crime From the East"

Spring 1994: Friman, H. Richard – "International Pressure and Domestic Bargains: Regulating Money Laundering in Japan"

Spring 1994: Van Duyne, Petrus and Block, Alan – "Organized Cross Atlantic Crime"

Summer 1993: Kelly, Robert and others – "The Dragon Breathes Fire"

Summer 1993: Passas, Nikos and Nelken, David – "The Thin Line Between Legitimate and Criminal Enterprises"

Winter 1993: Maguire, Keith – "Fraud, Extortion and Racketeering – The Black Economy in Northern Ireland"

Winter 1992: Jenkins, Philip – "Narcotics Trafficking and the American Mafia – the Myth of Internal Prohibition"

Fall 1992: Brodeur, Jean-Paul – "Undercover Policing in Canada – Wanting What Is Wrong"

Spring 1992: Lee, Rensselaer W. III – "Dynamics of the Soviet Illicit Drug Market"

Criminal Organizations:

Spring 1997: Builta, Jeff – "Mexico Faces Corruption, Crime, Drug Trafficking and Political Intrigue"

Current Digest of the Post Soviet Press:

December 1995: Levchuk, Sergei – "Ukrainian Mafia Has Found Its Niche Doing Shady Business in Europe"

October 1995: Kryshtanovskaya, Olga – "Russia's Mafia Landscape"

Current History:

May 1995: Lee, Rensselaer – "Global Reach – The Threat of International Drug Trafficking"

Défense nationale:

December 1992: Sola, Richard – "L'Internationalisation de la Mafia chinoise"

The Economist:

February 12, 1994: "The Covert Arms Trade"

Equity:

June 1992: Dubro, James – "The Big Circle Boys"

Euromoney:

February 1996: Celarier, Michelle – "Stealing the Family Silver – From Mafia Ties and Drug Trafficking to Bribery and Insider Dealing, Allegations of Corruption Have Tainted Numerous Privatizations Around the World"

European Journal of International Affairs:

Summer 1990: Naylor, Thomas – "Criminal Empires"

European Sociological Review:

December 1985: Gambetta, Diego – "The Entrepreneurial Mafia"

Europe-Asia Studies:

July 1996: Kryshtanovskaya, O., and White, S. – "From Soviet Nomenklatura to Russian Elite"

L'Express:

December 8, 1994: Raufer, Xavier and Coste, Philippe – "Les Multinationales du Crime"

October 1994: Raufer, Xavier – "Du Rififi dans les Triades"

March 1993: Lecomte, Bernard – "L'Empire du Milieu"

Far Eastern Economic Review:

November 23, 1995: Chen, Shu Ching Jean – "Pungent Prices – Taiwan's Triads Have Taken Over the Garlic Trade"

November 23, 1995: Thayer, Nate – "Cambodia – Asia's New Narco State?"

February 2, 1995: Aniskiewicz, Rick – "Taiwan – Organized Crime Pushes into Politics; Pingtung Just Like Sicily"

February 9, 1995: Smith, Charles – "Out of Gangland – A Glut of Illegal Guns Worries the Authorities"

January 20, 1994: Lintner, Bertil – "Khun Sa – Asia's Drug King on the Run"

August 5, 1993: Baum, Julian – "Human Wave – Rise in Illegal Immigrants From China Alarms Taipei"

April 8, 1993: Mooney, Paul and Zyla, Melana: "Braving the Seas and More"

FBI Law Enforcement Bulletin:

April 22, 1990: Florez, Carl and Boyce, Bernadette – "Laundering Drug Money"

Financial Post Magazine:
February 10, 1992: Capeci, Jerry – "Why the Mob Loves Canada"

Financial World:
February 1, 1994: Cordtz, Dan – "Dirty Dollars – Uncle Sam Looks for New Ways to Stymie Crooks and Their Smurfs, Who Launder $300 Billion a Year"

Forbes:
December 15, 1989: Stern, Richard – "How the Mafia Manipulates Stocks"

Foreign Affairs:
March 1994: Handelman, Stephen – "The Russian Mafiya"

Foreign Policy:
Spring 1993: Lee, Rensselaer W. III and MacDonald, Scott B. – "Drugs in the East"

Fortune:
November 30, 1992: Serwer, Andrew – "Hells Angels' Devilish Business"
June 22, 1987: Rowan, Roy – "How the Mafia Loots JFK Airport"

Futures Research Quarterly:
Spring 1995: Moore, Richter – "Twenty First Century Law to Meet the Challenge of Twenty First Century Organized Crime"

Futurist:
September 1994: Moore, Richter – "Wiseguys – Smarter Criminals and Smarter Crime in the 21st Century"

Global Finance:
October 1996: Leander, Ellen – "Finance's Top Cops"
January 1996: Shibata, Yoko – "Quaking Lenders, How Gangsters Complicate Japan's Banking Crisis"
January 1994: Celarier, Michelle – "Laundering Dirty Money in Russia"

IASOC Magazine:
Summer 1997: Williams, Phil – "Drugs & Democracy"

International Criminal Justice Review:

Summer 1992: Huang, Frank and Vaughn, Michael – "A Descriptive Analysis of Japanese Organized Crime – The Boryokudan From 1945 to 1988"

Summer 1992: Song, J., Long, H., and Dombrink, J. – "Asian Emerging Crime Groups – Examining the Definition of Organized Crime"

International Currency Review:

October 1993: MacDonald, Scott – "Asia Pacific Money Laundering"

International Journal of Comparative and Applied Criminal Justice:

Spring 1991: Martens, Frederick – "Transnational Enterprise Crime and the Elimination of Frontiers"

International Journal of Intelligence and Counterintelligence:

Winter 1990: Bacon, John – "The French Connection Revisited"

International Journal of Offender Therapy and Comparative Criminology:

Spring 1993: Jones, Mark – "Nigerian Crime Networks in the United States"

International Quarterly:

May 1993: Rothacher, Albrecht – "Yakuza, The Socioeconomic Roles of Organized Crime in Japan"

International Relations:

August 1995: Clutterbuck, Richard – "Peru – Cocaine, Terrorism and Corruption"

May 1990: Jamieson, Alison – "Mafia and Political Power 1943–1989"

International Spectator:

January 1997: Rutland, Peter – "Business Lobbies in Contemporary Russia"

International Tax Journal:

Spring 1997: Barrett, Richard W. – "Confronting Tax Havens, the Offshore Phenomenon, and Money Laundering"

Jane's Intelligence Review:

January 1993: Galeotti, Mark – "Red Mafias and National Security"

Jeune Afrique Économie:
September 2, 1996: Ndir, Mansour – "Blanchissement d'Argent"

Journal of Contemporary Criminal Justice:
March 1995: Albanese, Jay – "Contemporary Issues in Organized Crime"
December 1994: Carter, David – "International Organized Crime – Emerging Trends in Entrepreneurial Crime"
September 1993: Ryan, P. J., ed. – "Organized Crime II"
March 1992: Vito, Gennaro, ed. – "Organized Crime"

Journal of Crime and Justice:
Spring 1993: Gay, Bruce and Marquart, James W. – "Jamaican Posses – A New Form of Organized Crime"

Journal of Economic Issues:
June 1, 1998: Tomass, Mark – "Mafianomics – How Did Mob Entrepreneurs Infiltrate and Dominate the Russian Economy?"

Journal of Modern Italian Studies:
Spring 1996: Chubb, Judith – "The Mafia, the Market and the State in Italy and Russia"

Journal of Research in Crime and Delinquency:
November 1994: Joe, Karen A. – "The New Criminal Conspiracy? Asian Gangs and Organized Crime in San Francisco"

Justice Report:
March 1996: Laplante, Laurent – "Counteracting Criminal Biker Gangs"

Maclean's:
December 21, 1998: "Nabbing Smugglers"
October 12, 1998: Noble, Kimberley – "Battling the Mob – An Unlikely Group Tackles a Russian Gangster"
February 17, 1997: Sheridan, Maureen – "A Trade in Criminals – Canada's Policy of Deporting Lawbreakers Helps Fuel Jamaica's Soaring Crime Rate"
April 29, 1996: Kaihla, Paul – "The People Smugglers – Canada Is a Top Destination in the Global Trade in Humans; How Criminals Victimize the Innocent"
July 10, 1995: Kaihla, Paul – "The Cocaine King – How a Poor Colombian Became Canada's Biggest Drug Baron and Got Away"

October 2, 1995: Kaihla, Paul – "Inside an Immigration Scam: More than 80 Chinese Posed as Investors to Be Smuggled into Canada"
December 6, 1993: Fennell, Tom – "Up in Smoke"
October 7, 1991: Bruning, Fred – "Taking Money From Gangsters – Political Leaders Have Permitted the Mafia to Flourish and Infiltrate Extensively What Is Laughingly Called Legitimate Business"
October 23, 1989: Jensen, Holger – "Hiding the Drug Money – Criminals Are Using Canada to Launder Billions of Dollars in Drug Profits"

Medicine, Conflict and Survival:
January 1996: Walker, William – "International Responses to the Threat of Nuclear Smuggling From Russia"

Narcotics Control Digest:
July 22, 1992: "26 Biker Gang Members Indicted on Drug Charges"
October 24, 1990: "Authorities Strike a Blow Against Hell's Angels"

The Nation:
December 1994: Kwong, Peter – "China's Human Traffickers – Wave of the Golden Venture"

National Forum:
Summer 1992: McKeown, Patrick – "Computer Crimes and Criminals"

National Security Studies Quarterly:
Summer 1996: Richard, Daniel – "Overseas Tasking of the CIA for Domestic Law Enforcement"

New African:
June 16, 1995: Rake, Alan – "Drugged to the Eyeballs"

The New Republic:
April 11, 1994: Sterling, Claire – "Redfellas, Inside the Russian Mafia"

Newsweek:
March 10, 1997: Brant, Martha – "Most Wanted Kingpin?"

New York Times Magazine:
January 24, 1993: Handelman, Stephen – "Why Capitalism and the Mafiya Mean Business"

Organized Crime Digest:
May 11, 1990: "Bandidos Outlaw Biker Gang Survived Nationwide 1985 Crackdown by Feds"

Parade Magazine:
February 25, 1996: Maas, Peter – "Who Is the Mob Today?"

Police Chief:
June 1995: Noble, Ronald – "Russian Organized Crime a Worldwide Problem"
June 1994: Chu, Jeannette L. – "Alien Smuggling Syndicates Are Increasingly Involved in Other Criminal Activities, Infiltrating Legitimate Businesses and Deriving Millions of Dollars in Illicit Proceeds"
October 1993: Mosquera, Richard – "Asian Organized Crime"
January 1989: Schramm, R. R. – "Organized Crime"
January 1988: "Special Issue on Organized Crime"

Police Studies:
Winter 1990: Burke, Tod and O'Rear, Charles – "Home Invaders – Asian Gangs in America"
Winter 1990: Florez, Carl and Boyce, Bernadette – "Colombian Organized Crime"
Autumn 1989: "Corruption as a Fundamental Element of Organised Crime"

RCMP Gazette:
September 1998: Nyhuus, Kim – "Chasing Ghosts"
September 1998: "Motorcycle Gangs"
September 1987: Hamilton, R. B. – "Triad and Crime Gangs of Vietnamese Origin"
October 1980: Martin, W. G. – "Motorcycle Gangs"

Reader's Digest:
November 1997: Wilkens, Russell – "Biker Gangs, Getting Away With Murder"

Revue de Canadien Criminologie:
October 1993: Alain, Marc – "Les Bandes de Motards au Québec"

Saturday Night:
December 1993: Elliott, Patricia – "A Life in the Drug Trade"

Scientific American:

January 1996: Williams, Phil and Woessner, Paul – "The Real Threat of Nuclear Smuggling – Although Many Widely Publicized Incidents Have Been Staged or Overblown, the Dangers of Even a Single Successful Diversion Are Too Great to Ignore"

Social and Legal Studies:

March 1996: Ruggiero, Vincenzo – "War Markets, Corporate and Organized Criminals in Europe"

Society:

March 1995: Godson, Roy and William, Olson – "International Organized Crime"

January 1990: Lee, Rensselaer – "Cocaine Mafia"

The Spectator:

May 27, 1995: Clark, Ross – "Do We Really Want Opium Dens?"

Studies in Conflict and Terrorism:

October 1994: Filippone, Robert – "The Medellín Cartel – Why We Can't Win the Drug War"

January 1992: Jamieson, Alison – "Recent Narcotics and Mafia Research"

Time:

July 14, 1997: Drummond, Tammerlin – "Enter the Redfellas – Are Russian Mobsters Dallying with Drug Lords?"

February 8, 1993: Walsh, James – "Triads Go Global"

November 4, 1991: Richard Behar – "Offer They Can't Refuse, Mob Families in the U.S. Are Considering a Merger"

Transnational Organized Crime:

Summer 1997: Blickman, Tom – "The Rothschilds of the Mafia on Aruba"

Spring 1995: Lupsha, Peter – "Transnational Narco-Corruption and Narco Investment: a Focus on Mexico"

U.S. Naval Institute Proceedings:

July 1996: Tomney, Christopher and DiRenzo, Joseph – "Countering High Tech Drug Smugglers"

U.S. News and World Report:

August 3, 1998: Kaplan, David E. and Caryl, Christian – "The Looting of Russia"

April 14, 1997: Witkin, Gordon – "One Way, $28,000 – Why Smuggling Aliens into America Is a Boom Business"

September 30, 1996: Kleinknecht, William – "The Hottest Import – Crime"

October 23, 1995: Cooperman, Alan and Zimmermann, Tim – "The Russian Connection"

June 19, 1995: Parshall, Gerald – "The FBI Nabs a Russian Gotti"

March 7, 1994: "The Mobsters Who Now Rule Russia"

June 21, 1993: "The New Slave Trade – A Shocking Story of Human Smuggling; The Growing Backlash Against Immigrants"

October 19, 1992: "Cocaine Kings and Mafia Dons"

January 18, 1988: "Ethnic Gangs and Organized Crime"

February 3, 1986: Powell, Stewart – "Busting the Mob"

Washington Quarterly:

Winter 1995: Williams, Phil – "Transnational Criminal Organizations – Strategic Alliances"

Fall 1985: Nadelmann, Ethan – "International Drug Trafficking and U.S. Foreign Policy"

World and I:

December 1997: de Borchgrave, Arnaud – "Organized Crime's Global Shadow"

June 1989: Seper, Jerry – "Dirty Money Finds New Laundries"

World Policy Journal:

Spring 1995: Paternostro, Silvana – "Mexico as a Narco-Democracy"

The World Today:

January 1995: Dunn, Guy – "The Russian Mafia"

MONOGRAPHS, PAPERS, DISSERTATIONS, SPEECHES, AND REPORTS

Anderson, Kent: *Criminal Threats to Business on the Internet – A White Paper*; Global Technology Research, Portland, Oregon, 1997

Brandt, Daniel: *As Criminal Capitalism Replaces Communism – Organized Crime Threatens the New World Order*; NameBase NewsLine, January–March 1995

Center for Strategic and International Studies: *Wild Atom – Nuclear Terrorism*, Webster, William, project chairman; Washington, D.C., 1998

———: *Russian Organized Crime*, Webster, William, project chairman; Washington, D.C., 1997

———: *The Nuclear Black Market*, Webster, William, project chairman; Washington, D.C., 1996

———: *Global Organized Crime: the New Empire of Evil*, Raine, Linnea and Cilluffo, Frank, editors; Washington, D.C., 1994

———: *Report of the Project on the Global Drug Trade in the Post Cold War Era – The Transnational Drug Challenge and the New World Order*, Flynn, Stephen and Grant, Gregory, editors; Washington, D.C., 1993

Council of Europe: *Convention on Laundering, Search, Seizure and Confiscation of the Proceeds from Crime and Explanatory Report*; Council of Europe Publishing, Strasbourg, France, 1995

Criminal Intelligence Service Canada: *Annual Report on Organized Crime in Canada*; Ottawa, 1998

———: *Annual Report on Organized Crime in Canada*; Ottawa, 1997

———: *East European-based Organized Crime*; Ottawa, 1997

———: *Hell's Angels and Other Outlaw Motorcycle Gangs*; Ottawa, 1997

———: *Aboriginal Organized Crime in Canada and the United States*; Ottawa, 1997

———: *Italian Organized Crime in Canada*; Ottawa, 1997

———: *Colombian Drug Cartels in Canada*; Ottawa, 1997

———: *Asian Organized Crime in Canada*; Ottawa, 1997

———: *Annual Report on Organized Crime in Canada*; Ottawa, 1996

———: *Asian Organized Crime Workshop Papers*; Ottawa, 1996

Canadian Security Intelligence Services: *Smuggling Special Nuclear Materials*; Ottawa, 1995

Financial Action Task Force: *Report on Money Laundering Typologies*; Paris, 1997

Grassley, Charles: *The Emerging International Mafia*; speech made before The Heritage Foundation, Washington, D.C., February 23, 1996

Observatoire Géopolitique des Drogues: *Annual Reports*; Paris, 1997, 1998

———: *Atlas Mondial des Drogues*; Presses Universitaires de France, Paris, 1997

Province of British Columbia, Ministry of Attorney General – Interministry Committee on Criminal Gangs and British Columbia: *Action Plan Summary*, Victoria, B.C., 1994, 1995

Royal Canadian Mounted Police: *Aboriginal Organized Crime and Tobacco, Weapons and Gaming*; Ottawa, 1992

State of New York, Organized Crime Task Force: *An Analysis of Russian Emigre Crime in the Tri State Region*; Albany, N.Y., 1996

United Nations: *Report on the Conference for the Adoption of a Convention Against Illicit Traffic in Narcotic Drugs and Psychotropic Substances*; New York, 1994

United States Department of Justice, Bureau of Justice Assistance: *Urban Street Gang Enforcement*; Washington, D.C., 1997

United States Department of State: *International Narcotics Control Strategy Report*; Bureau for International Narcotics and Law Enforcement Affairs, Washington, D.C., 1998

———: *Report on Ethnic Chinese Organized Crime – Triad Structures and Capabilities*; Washington, D.C., 1994

United States Federal Bureau of Investigation: *Vietnamese Activity in the United States – A National Perspective*; Washington, D.C., 1993

———: *An Introduction to Organized Crime in the United States*; Washington, D.C., 1993

———: *An Analysis of the Threat of Japanese Criminal Organizations to the United States and Its Territories*; Washington, D.C., 1992

———: *Wanted by the FBI the Mob – FBI Organized Crime Report 25 Years After Valachi*; Washington, D.C., 1988

United States House of Representatives – Committee on Banking and Financial Services, *The Money Laundering Deterrence Act of 1998*; and *Money Laundering and Financial Crime Strategy Act of 1997*; Washington, D.C., June 11, 1998

———: *Money Laundering by Drug Trafficking Organizations*; Washington, D.C., February 28, 1996

———: *Organized Crime and Banking*; Washington, D.C., February 28, 1996

United States House of Representatives – Committee on Banking and Financial Services, Subcommittee on General Oversight and Investigations: *Use by the Department of the Treasury of the Geographic Targeting Order as a Method to Combat Money Laundering*; Washington, D.C., March 11, 1997

———: *U.S. Law Enforcement Response to Money Laundering Activities in Mexico*; Washington, D.C., September 5, 1996

———: *Money Laundering Activity Associated With the Mexican Narco Crime Syndicate*; Washington, D.C., September 5, 1996

———: *The Counterfeiting of U.S. Currency Abroad*; Washington, D.C., February 27, 1996

United States House of Representatives – Committee on Government Reform and Oversight: *National Drug Policy – A Review of the Status of the Drug War*; Washington, D.C., March 19, 1996

United States House of Representatives – Committee on Foreign Affairs, Subcommittees on International Security, International Organizations, and Human Rights and the Western Hemisphere: *U.S. Relations With Colombia*; Washington, D.C., August 3, 1994

United States House of Representatives – Committee on Foreign Affairs, Subcommittees on International Security, International Organizations, and Human Rights: *The Threat of International Organized Crime*; Washington, D.C., November 4, 1993

United States House of Representatives – Committee on International Relations: *The Threat from International Organized Crime and Terrorism*; testimony of Louise Shelley, Center for Transnational Organized Crime and Corruption, American University, Washington, D.C., October 1, 1997

———: *The Threat From Russian Organized Crime*; Washington, D.C., April 30, 1996

———: *Global Organized Crime*; Washington, D.C., January 31, 1996

———: *International Organized Crime*; Washington, D.C., June 27, 1994

United States House of Representatives – Committee on International Relations, Subcommittee on Asia and the Pacific: *Drugs in Asia – The Heroin Connection*; Washington, D.C., June 21, 1995

United States House of Representatives – Committee on the Judiciary, Subcommittee on Crime: *The Growing Threat of International Organized Crime*; Washington, D.C., January 25, 1996

United States House of Representatives – Committee on the Judiciary, Subcommittee on Immigration, Refugees and International Law: *Alien Smuggling*; Washington, D.C., June 30, 1993

United States House of Representatives – Permanent Select Committee on Intelligence: *Intelligence Community in the 21st Century*; Washington, D.C., April 9, 1996

United States House of Representatives – Select Committee on Narcotics Abuse and Control: *The Federal Strategy on the Southwest Border*; Washington, D.C., December 10, 1990

United States Senate – Committee on Appropriations, Subcommittee on Foreign Relations: *International Crime*; Washington, D.C., March 12, 1996

United States Senate – Committee on Armed Services: *Intelligence Briefing on Smuggling of Nuclear Material and the Role of International Crime Organizations*; Washington, D.C., January 31, 1995

United States Senate – Committee on Finance, Subcommittee on International Trade and United States Senate: *Threat to U.S. Trade and Finance From Drug Trafficking and International Organized Crime*; Washington, D.C., July 23 and 30, 1996

United States Senate – Committee on Foreign Relations, Subcommittee on European Affairs: *Loose Nukes, Nuclear Smuggling, and the Fissile Material Problem in Russia and the NIS*; Washington, D.C., August 22–23, 1995

United States Senate – Committee on Foreign Relations: *International Drug Trafficking Organizations in Mexico*; Washington, D.C., August 8, 1995

———: *Terrorism, Narcotics and International Operations*; testimony of Willard H. Myers III, director, Center for the Study of Asian Organized Crime, Washington, D.C., April 21, 1994

United States Senate – Committee on Governmental Affairs, Permanent Subcommittee on Investigations: *Fraud on the Internet – Scams Affecting Consumers*; Washington, D.C., February 10, 1998

———: *Global Proliferation of Weapons of Mass Destruction*; Washington, D.C., October 31, November 1, 1995, March 13, 20 and 22, 1996, March 27, 1997

———: *Russian Organized Crime, Security in Cyberspace*; Washington, D.C., May 15 and 22, June 5 and 25, July 16, 1996

———: *Russian Organized Crime in the United States*; Washington, D.C., May 15, 1996

———: *Criminal Aliens in the United States*; Washington, D.C., April 7, 1995

———: *International Organized Crime and Its Impact on the United States*; Washington, D.C., May 25, 1994

———: *The New International Criminal and Asian Organized Crime*; Washington, D.C., Report published December 1992.

———: *Current Trends in Money Laundering*; Washington, D.C., Report published December 1992

———: *Asian Organized Crime*; Washington, D.C., October 3, 1991, November 5–6, 1991, June 18, 1992 and August 4, 1992

———: *Arms Trafficking, Mercenaries and Drug Cartels*; Washington, D.C., February 27–28, 1991

———: *Nontraditional Organized Crime – Law Enforcement Officials' Perspectives on Five Criminal Groups*; Washington, D.C., 1989

United States Senate – Judiciary Committee: *Gangs – A National Crisis*; Washington, D.C., April 23, 1997

United States Senate – Judiciary Committee and Committee on Indian Affairs, joint hearings; *Criminal Gangs in Indian Country*; Washington, D.C., September 17, 1997

United States Senate – Judiciary Committee, Subcommittee on Technology, Terrorism and Government Information: *The Identity Theft and Assumption Deterrence Act*; Washington, D.C., May 20, 1998

———: *Methamphetamine – A Newly Deadly Neighbor*; Washington, D.C., April 6, 1998

———: *Internet Crimes Affecting Consumers*; Washington, D.C. March 18, 1997

Van der Heijden, Toon: *Policing In Central and Eastern Europe – Comparing*

Firsthand Knowledge with Experience from the West; College of Police and Security Studies, Slovenia, 1996

Williams, Phil, ed.: *Russian Organized Crime – The New Threat?*; Frank Cass, London, 1997

———: *Hysteria, Complacency And Russian Organized Crime*; Russia and Eurasia Programme, Post-Soviet Business Forum Briefing No.8, The Royal Institute of International Affairs, London, October 1996